ORGANIZATIONAL CHANGE MANAGEMENT

T0295493

Danielle A. Tucker, Stefano Cirella & Paul R. Kelly

ORGANIZATIONAL CHANGE MANAGEMENT

Inclusion, Collaboration and Digital Change in Practice

1 Oliver's Yard
55 City Road
London EC1Y 1SP

2455 Teller Road
Thousand Oaks
California 91320

Unit No 323-333, Third Floor, F-Block
International Trade Tower, Nehru Place
New Delhi 110 019

8 Marina View Suite 43-053
Asia Square Tower 1
Singapore 018960

Editor: Ruth Stitt
Editorial assistant: Charlotte Hegley
Production editor: Martin Fox
Marketing manager: Lucia Sweet
Cover design: Francis Kenney
Typeset by: C&M Digitals (P) Ltd, Chennai, India
Printed in the UK

Library of Congress Control Number: 2023939022

British Library Cataloguing in Publication data

A catalogue record for this book is available from the British Library

ISBN 978-1-5297-9225-6
ISBN 978-1-5297-9224-9 (pbk)

At Sage we take sustainability seriously. Most of our products are printed in the UK using responsibly sourced papers and boards. When we print overseas we ensure sustainable papers are used as measured by the Paper Chain Project grading system. We undertake an annual audit to monitor our sustainability.

To anyone who aspires to make a change and improve things

CONTENTS

DETAILED CONTENTS

LIST OF FIGURES

LIST OF TABLES

ONLINE RESOURCES

Organizational Change Management is accompanied by a range of online resources designed to support teaching, which can be accessed by Instructors at: **https://study.sagepub.com/ tucker.**

For Instructors

- **A Teaching Guide** including detailed case study teaching notes.
- **PowerPoint decks** that can be downloaded and adapted to suit individual teaching needs.

ABOUT THE AUTHORS

Dr Danielle A. Tucker is a Reader (Associate Professor) in Management at Essex Business School, University of Essex, UK. Her research interests focus on evaluating complex change management initiatives for public sector organizations (including police, local authority, local government, NHS Trusts, and health and social care providers). She has published in leading journals such as *Human Relations*, *Journal of Business Ethics* and *Journal of Business Research*, and is an Associate Editor at *Journal of Organizational Change Management*. Specifically, she is interested in the interpretation of communication during organizational change, and the use of organizational change agents and middle managers to facilitate change. She is particularly interested in the flow of information and ideas across boundaries, partnership working and collaboration arrangements, such as integrated care. Her teaching covers the areas of organizational change management, human resource management and research evaluation.

Dr Stefano Cirella is a Reader (Associate Professor) in Organization Studies and Human Resource Management at Essex Business School, University of Essex, UK, and Department of Industrial Engineering, University of Trento, Italy. He has been a visiting scholar at the Orfalea College of Business, California Polytechnic State University, USA. His main research interests focus on collective creativity, collaboration, organizational change and collaborative research methodologies. He has published in leading journals such as *European Management Review*, *British Journal of Management*, *Creativity and Innovation Management* and *Journal of Business Ethics*. Specifically, he is interested in collaborative and collective dynamics of creativity in organizations, doings and practices of university–industry collaboration, and transformational and distributed leadership in the context of change. He has collaborated in the context of various collaborative research initiatives. His teaching covers the areas of organizational behaviour, human resource management and organization development.

Dr Paul R. Kelly is a Lecturer (Assistant Professor) in Organization Studies and Human Resource Management at Essex Business School, University of Essex, UK. His research focuses on organizational power and practice, and socio-digital change, innovation and inequalities. He has published in leading journals and conferences, such as the *Information Systems Journal*, *Organization Studies* and the International Conference on Software Engineering. He is interested in impact evaluation and data/knowledge management in global development. He has worked with the United Nations Development Programme, British Council, and universities in the UK, Australia, Thailand and the UAE. He has collaborated with development organizations in Laos, Thailand, the UK, Myanmar and Papua New Guinea.

He is an Honorary Research Fellow at La Trobe University's Institute for Human Security and Social Change (IHSSC), and organizes the Developing Activity Theory in Information Studies workshop at the European Conference on Information Systems. His teaching covers the areas of leadership, corporate social responsibility and digital transformation.

FOREWORD

Oxford Dictionaries (2023) feature 'change' as among the most frequently used words in the English language. Change is certainly one of the most popular words in organizations, too. Organizations have to adapt to ever-changing contexts and thus are required to change. As I have found regularly in my own research, individual leaders see change as an opportunity to advance their careers. For instance, most CEOs will have a specific change agenda to mark their time as a leader of the organization. Often such change agendas are linked to the desire to leave a legacy where the change CEOs introduced is stabilized and becomes part of the organizational culture. However, change is also central for middle managers. Being able to lead a change project is in many organizations an important criterion for promotion and middle managers thus seek out opportunities to lead change processes.

The etymology of the word 'change' can be traced back to the late Latin *'cambiare'* which itself derives from *'cambire'* meaning barter and exchange (*Oxford Dictionaries*, 2023). In many ways bartering is a very apt description of how change in organizations happens. Change in organizations involves some form of trading between different actors. Those who might be resistant to change might have to be incentivized to engage in a change effort. They need to see what is in it for them to support the change. Such a bartering is not uncommon in organizations and shows how negotiation, power and influence are relevant for change processes.

That we use the word change today is the result of a twisting and turning journey that the word has taken. The word change has its likely origins in Celtic and it is presumed that the word was incorporated into Latin and from there found its way via Old French to English (*Oxford Dictionaries*, 2023). Likewise, change as a process in organizations is often not linear or straightforward. Many organizations report that change in fact resembles a maze where you get lost and have to turn around to find an alternative way. Change requires flexibility and adaptability. Even though change is often presented as neat and tidy, it is regularly experienced as a messy process.

It is also often presumed that change requires time. Many organizations have defined time frames for when they want to achieve a certain change such as being carbon neutral or having 50 per cent women and 50 per cent men in senior leadership positions. Such timelines are attractive because they are presumed to focus the minds of individuals to work towards these changes. Rather than achieving change sometime in the future, there is a timeline for the change to be accomplished. Yet whether individuals change their everyday decision-making, by travelling by train rather than plane or by promoting a woman rather than a man, is questionable. In many of those cases the timeline is perceived as far away which does not influence daily decision-making towards sustainability or inclusion. While it is evident that some change processes take a long time, in other cases change processes move swiftly. When the COVID-19 pandemic hit, organizations had to change their systems and processes overnight. Changes that would have taken five to ten years – for instance in relation to the digital transformation – were suddenly accomplished in a matter of mere weeks.

Change makers are central for change processes. Being a change maker can be exhausting or exhilarating. Many change makers are passionate about the change they want to see in the organization and for them it is a key challenge to maintain this passion as they encounter a multitude of obstacles. Others that might engage in change processes to further their own career might be in for a surprise when they realize that change might not be as straightforward as they had hoped. Regardless of why they engage in change, change makers have to manage their own expectations and their energy.

Although organizations are focused on change, the proverb *plus ça change, plus c'est la même chose*, which translates as the more things change the more they stay the same, encapsulates another strong force in organizations: that of continuity. Rather than changing something, many things continue in the same way as before. This is not surprising because although organizations might seek to change and adapt, this change happens in existing systems and structures that might change slowly or resist change altogether. I have often observed how radical change suggestions in organizations are watered down as they make their way through the organization leading to minimal or no change and thus maintaining the status quo. The interplay between change and continuity is therefore pivotal for understanding and shaping modern organizations.

This book offers you the tools to understand the interplay between change and continuity through a carefully laid out learning path encompassing pivotal theories in the field and practical insights through case studies and examples. Written by leading experts in the field, the book will undoubtedly become a go-to resource for anyone interested in learning about organizational change.

Elisabeth Kelan

Professor of Leadership and Organization

Essex Business School

University of Essex

Reference

Oxford Dictionaries (2023) 'Change'. Available at: https://www.oed.com/dictionary/change_n?tab=frequency#9803935 (Accessed 28 November 2023).

ACKNOWLEDGEMENTS

Our warmest thanks to Hadrian, Debora, Petra, Siri, Ben, Jee and Jem for their support and patience with us.

Thanks to Val, Neha and Stella whose contributions to the book were invaluable.

Thanks also to Ruth, Charlotte and Amy at Sage Publishing, the reviewers, and colleagues at Essex Business School and around the world who gave us inspiration and ideas.

INTRODUCTION

Why a Textbook on Organizational Change?

Organizational change is widely considered a specialism within business and management studies, often practised by management consultants and organizational leaders. It is also, however, an essential component of managing people in organizations effectively. Therefore, organizational change management is a regular feature in most business and management degrees at undergraduate and postgraduate level.

Research has highlighted the important role that different organizational members play in creating change in their organizations. For example, Balogun and Johnson (2004) highlight the importance of middle managers in making sense of change. Similarly, Alfes et al. (2010) highlight the need for proactive human resource managers in managing micro-level change processes. A people-centric view avoids the high project failure rate observed in much information technology (IT) or digitally driven, technology-inspired organizational change (e.g. Dwivedi et al., 2015).

This textbook offers a holistic introduction to organizational change management through a distinct and timely perspective of organizational change agency. It provides an overview of approaches and views which contribute to the perspectives of change makers about how they can enact change from within their organizations. Combining theory and practice, we suggest relevant managerial techniques to harness change emerging from a people-orientated perspective and a critical perspective on the implications of various strategies for change.

Throughout this book we use the term **change maker** to describe organizational members who become the architects and builders of change in organizations. Researchers have criticized change management research for the lack of conceptual clarity around agent roles (Chreim et al., 2012; Parry, 2003; Tucker et al., 2015) and we argue that part of the challenge of understanding the contribution of change makers is due to the use of different definitions and interpretations of change roles in different organizations, making it hard to gain a clear picture of how they add value. To *make change* is to construct, create or concoct something new from the resources available. Change makers are proactive and purposeful in promoting and enabling change (Dopson et al., 2010; Greenhalgh et al., 2004; Locock et al., 2001). Change makers imagine creative ideas and craft innovative solutions to problems and engage in collaborative work and processes of organizational re-design (Mohrman and Cummings, 1989). Taking this view, our book cover represents a nice metaphor of change. Flocks continuously involve collaboration and interaction between birds to fly together but changing shapes and orientations. This resonates with the idea of flocks as complex systems by Giorgio Parisi (see Parisi, 2023), winner of the Nobel Prize in Physics in 2021. For example, 'When the flock was turning, the impression that one has is that they are turning as a flock, but the reality is that some birds start to turn in advance and the others follow. We were able to get the acceleration of each bird and to see that some birds start to accelerate or turn in one direction and other birds follow and that this decision was propagating inside the flock' (Parisi in Fox, 2023). Out of metaphor, those are change makers.

Our approach places change experience as a starting point. It identifies and targets lessons for current or future professionals who become change makers. Such individuals play a pivotal role in change implementation but are bounded by the ultimate decision-making power of others, typically senior leaders, executives or business owners. This focus means we place relationships and people at the heart of organizational change and offer practical training to help develop skills of communicating change; learning about change; influencing key stakeholders; handling digital data and information; consulting, supporting and exploring. We discuss not simply how to 'do change', but how to understand the implications of organizational changes.

Acknowledging the important role of change makers and other organizational members at any level in implementing change leads us to another important implication. We show the need to advance traditional views of change management that place too much emphasis on the senior leaders who implement top-down change efforts via their power and hierarchical position. To achieve this, we approach change in a way that promotes inclusivity and collaborative practices by highlighting how change makers are the key to employee voice and action-based knowledge sharing. Another relevant challenge is to understand how both social and technological complexities shape change. We characterize this as socio-digital change. These themes are incorporated throughout the book.

Who is this book for?

This book is designed to help students manage change within their future organization, and to help current managers, practitioners and experts who want to deepen their understanding of theories and practices of change management to also improve efforts in their own organizations.

Today's business and management graduates face frequent and intensive periods of change in their working lives. The majority of employees do not experience change as a senior organizational leader; rather, they experience changes through involvement with projects in the organizations they work for. This book recognizes the crucial role that organizational employees play in organizational change and will prepare you to understand how innovation, creativity, digitalization processes and leadership interact with elements of organizing for change implementation and change evaluation.

The title is intended for business and management courses which feature organizational change management in their learning outcomes – a growing trend demanded by students and graduate employers. This could be a course which aims to offer students a specialism in organizational change or another people management focus (e.g. leadership, digital transformation, learning and development, or human resource management), where organizational change is a key challenge, in order to prepare students for a range of management scenarios. As a specialist textbook, this book is suited to both undergraduate and postgraduate students with a particular interest in the area.

How This Book Is Structured

This book is divided into three main parts, each representing a layer of knowledge that is useful for change makers' own understanding of change.

Layer 1 (Part I) covers general background and contextual aspects of change. This provides a knowledge baseline for readers and covers the language and concepts that change makers encountering their first change experience might need to understand.

Layer 2 (Part II) more deeply outlines the three pillars of change from the perspective of change makers. These pillars comprise: (a) the important role of organizational members in implementing change; (b) appreciating the prevalence and complexities of socio-digital change; and c) how change can be achieved in a way that is inclusive and collaborative. This section brings into focus the major influences on the change maker's perspective.

Layer 3 (Part III) takes a deeper dive into themes which may feature in many change experiences to a greater or lesser degree. Some of these topics are covered in other texts but here we curate aspects of these themes through the lens of change makers as they experience them.

Part I: The strategic context of change

Part I provides the basics to a reader without great previous knowledge (therefore extending the potential use of the textbook to a wider range of modules). In **Chapter 1** we explore 'what change is and why we do it'. This chapter acts as a starting point for readers who have little or no prior knowledge of organizational change management. We introduce the language of change and key terminology used by researchers and practitioners when talking about organizational change and examine how change implementation fits into the overall change process.

Chapter 2 examines various approaches to the study and understanding of organizational change (planned change, emergent change, systems approaches and process approaches). Rather than focusing on the detail of specific models the emphasis here is on ways of viewing change and how these approaches relate to modern-day strategies we see in organizations (e.g. organizational development, business process re-engineering). Finally in this section, **Chapter 3** explores a wider narrative about external drivers and influences on change (including current global challenges). Specifically, we examine the role of change makers in creating and implementing organizational strategy and the limitations that they have in doing this.

Part II: An approach based on change makers

In Part II we present the philosophy which drives the book. It is underpinned by three pillars of change: (a) the important role of organizational members in implementing change; (b) appreciating the prevalence and complexities of socio-digital change; and c) how change can be achieved in a way that is inclusive and collaborative.

In **Chapter 4** we consider the role of key individuals in the change management project. We focus specifically on those who are often thought of as the supporting cast in a change project, but in our research we have found them to be some of the most powerful 'leaders' of change: change agents, project management teams, middle managers, front-line champions, HR and digital teams. Based on our own research and previous academic writings (e.g. Tucker and Cirella, 2018; Tucker et al., 2015) we outline a framework for understanding the roles which change makers can play in organizational change. We also introduce some of the key challenges which change makers face in implementing change, drawing from literature on role ambiguity, power dynamics, shared meaning and language, and relationship and conflict management.

Chapter 5 explores perspectives on digital transformation. Firstly, we explore the history of models of 'how to do' digital transformation. Secondly, we look at the perspectives that underpin much digital transformation talk. This includes views of technological change as evolutionary, adaptation oriented or projects to be managed. We then describe broader views, such as the technological versus sociological determinism debate, socio-technical systems, technology-as-practice, sociomateriality and socio-digital change.

Finally, in **Chapter 6** we discuss the importance of including and representing a diverse range of voices in implementing change. Starting from the perspective that activities which might be traditionally viewed by change management practitioners as 'resistance' may also be viewed as constructive input into the change implementation process (Ford and Ford, 2010), we explore mechanisms for encouraging employee voice throughout the change process. We take a deeper critical dive into the challenges that change makers may themselves face in representing diverse voices within their organization.

Part III: Current issues on change

Part III is structured around current issues on change management. Having gained an overview of the pillars of change, we provide a more focused view on the implications for these thematic areas viewed through the eyes of change makers.

Chapter 7 explores leadership in organizations by reviewing traditional leadership concepts such as traits, skills, styles and personality, as well as more recent transformational and authentic leadership approaches that have been prevalent in organizational change research, plus more alternative or critical views of leadership. We follow this with **Chapter 8** which focuses on more traditional and more contemporary views of power, and their relevance to leading and supporting change. We discuss resistance to change and how resistance can be seen as a beneficial part of more expansive views of change. In this chapter, power is not always hierarchical, destructive or to be avoided, but instead it can be productive, negotiable, creative, and can contribute positively to changes.

Chapters 9 and 10 consider the perspective that creativity and innovation are key engines for generating ideas and changes in organizations. In **Chapter 9**, we discuss the increasing importance of creativity and we examine comprehensively capturing and sustaining creativity at a collective level. In **Chapter 10**, we explore the complexity of inter-organizational innovation efforts based on networks of agents by adopting open and collaborative innovation, design-driven innovation and user innovation.

Finally, in Chapters 11 and 12 we discuss the ability of organizations to harness learning from their own and others' experiences which is essential to successful organizational change. In **Chapter 11** we review perspectives and practical aspects of change evaluation, such as the use of indicators and metrics, and models which stress formative evaluations of change or innovation, plus network-oriented or stakeholder-sensitive approaches that support both formative and summative evaluations. And in **Chapter 12** we examine the relationship between learning, knowledge sharing and change in organizations. In both of these chapters we acknowledge the dilemmas involved in learning, revisiting key themes such as power, resistance and the problem of trying to distribute knowledge to diverse audiences as part of change initiatives.

Part IV: Integrated case studies

In the final section (Part IV), we offer a selection of longer **integrated case studies** which can be used to explore multiple chapter topics and understand how these are integrated in real life examples of change.

Of course, change will always appear to be dominated by senior leaders, powerful managers, strategic decisions and top-down processes that affect the whole organization. However, we hope that this book will contribute to a more nuanced view of change as a complex set of processes driven by people, challenges and opportunities that come in all shapes and sizes.

PART I
THE STRATEGIC CONTEXT OF CHANGE

1

AN INTRODUCTION TO CHANGE

WHAT IS CHANGE AND WHY DO WE DO IT?

Chapter Objectives

- To introduce the language of change and key terminology used by researchers and practitioners when talking about organizational change
- To explore different definitions of organizational change and understand what is meant by transformational change
- To explain how change implementation fits into the overall change process

1.1 Introduction

The last two decades have seen a huge increase in the place (increased cross-location changes), magnitude (scale of change), frequency (how often) and necessity (need for change) for organizational change. Despite this increased volume, failure rates are frequently cited as being as high as 70 per cent (CIPD, 2015). Most recently, the Boston Consulting Group annual survey found that 57 per cent of all transformations failed to hit their targets in terms of value envisioned, timeline, or both (Boston Consulting Group, 2021); and, even more dramatically, McKinsey & Company (2021) found that less than one-third reported that transformations taking place in the previous five years had been successful at both improving organizational performance and sustaining those improvements over time.

We should of course acknowledge that in recent years, since the COVID-19 pandemic, the ways we work in terms of location, focus on workplace wellbeing, flexible working and how we engage with workers have changed, and this has sparked significant change in many organizations (CMI, 2020). Yet, it has also increased the interconnectedness and accompanying complexity of changes meaning that transformations take longer and yield less value than they did previously (Boston Consulting Group, 2021). Even before the pandemic, companies were facing different challenges than they did five years ago, with digital solutions requiring focus on different capabilities and posing new obstacles and challenges to effective implementation (McKinsey & Company, 2018).

The aim of this chapter is to act as a starting point for readers who have little or no prior knowledge of organizational change management. We provide an overview of what we mean by change in organizations to help us understand how change makers can influence change from within. We begin by exploring change at different contextual levels and the interconnections between these. We will also discuss different definitions of change such as transformational or sense-breaking change as opposed to continuous improvement or more incremental forms of change (e.g. Cummings, et al., 2016; Greenwood and Hinings, 1993).

In the second half, we will discuss the process of change. The definition of organizational change success can be different for different actors. We will explore these differences, explaining how the implementation phase, which is the primary focus of this text, fits into the wider change process, and pose some questions for understanding any given change situation that might be helpful throughout this book.

1.2 What Is Organizational Change?

To understand how and why organizations change we must first examine what change is and what it means in the context of organizations. In this section, we will discuss different modes of change such as transformational or sense-breaking change as well as incremental continuous improvement (e.g. Cummings et al., 2016; Greenwood and Hinings, 1993; Mantere et al., 2012; Nadler and Tushman, 1989).

At the most basic level, organizational change refers to the process by which an organization intentionally changes its current condition. For example, organizational change occurs when business strategies or major sections of the business are altered in a way that impacts the activities of organizational members and other stakeholders. Organizational change is sometimes referred to as 'transformation', 'transition', 'reorganization', 'restructuring', 'turnaround' or 'strategic change'. All of these terms refer to change at the organizational level, although some terms (e.g. restructuring/reorganization) refer more specifically to changes in organizational structure, whereas others (e.g. strategic change) may refer more to changes in objectives and the way the organization is perceived by stakeholders – see more on this in Chapter 3.

Contextual levels of change

In this book we are primarily focused on organizational change; that is, change that happens *within* organizations and *to* organizations rather than individual change. To help situate this, we might consider what change looks like at the following levels of context:

- **Individual-level change:** where an individual agent changes their circumstances at work, day-to-day activities or environment; for example, a job change, a change in work location or work team. Here, change is experienced by one person (or several people but each experience of change is independent and unique). Key things to consider will be contextual factors at the individual level that impact on that change, such as the individual's personality traits, previous experiences, life and socioeconomic circumstances, and future goals and ambitions.
- **Group-level change:** where a small group of employees experience a change in their immediate work setting; for example, a departmental policy change, relocation or the closure of a regional branch. Here, change is experienced by a close social group who have had a shared experience of history and values related to the sub-culture of their group. Group dynamics play a key role in group-level change such as group cohesiveness and power dynamics within the group. Depending on the size of the group, change at the group level may require other aspects of the organization to adjust to accommodate the group-level change; however, more often a group change has minimal impact on the organization as a whole, even if it can be significant for those involved.
- **Organizational-level change:** where change happens at an organizational level it affects multiple sub-groups/departments collectively but also differently. For example, the adoption of a new digital system may affect the sales team differently from the finance team but they will all be affected by the same change and are interconnected – i.e. a change in one part of the organization will create further change elsewhere and these interconnections must be considered holistically. Change will often have multiple layers (strategic, operational, cultural) which are interrelated and experienced collectively by all organizational members. See Box 1.1 for some examples of organizational-level changes that you might come across.

- **Larger system change (industry/policy):** where changes in the political economy or market occur, these often have a significant impact for change at the organizational level but are also usefully studied as system-level changes in their own right (Ferlie and Shortell, 2001). These changes will affect multiple institutions who, themselves, will all react to change and respond in varied ways. Dynamics of change that occur at this level include: changes to the language and shared understanding of industry players; structural changes to regulation and power dynamics within the environment; and system changes that affect inter-organizational relationships.

─Box 1.1─

Examples of organizational changes

- **Merger or acquisition** – where two or more previously independent organizations come together and become one entity. Where both organizations are equal, this is called a merger; where one company (usually larger) buys another (usually smaller), this is called an acquisition.
- **Shift in product market or customer base** – when an organization changes its strategy within the external market, this could include moving into different countries or different economic markets (e.g. a different pricing strategy).
- **Decentralization or delayering** – restructuring an organization's hierarchy to remove bureaucratic layers and delegate decision-making throughout the organization.
- **Restructuring/reorganization of hierarchy** – changing the way that divisions and areas of responsibilities relate to one another within the organization.
- **Major new innovation or technology** – the implementation of a new system that changes the way that work is done by employees within the organization.
- **Change in culture or workplace values** – when the principles that govern the behaviour of organizational members are altered. This may result from a change of leadership or shift in mission and strategy where new ideals are taken up and embedded in work practice.
- **New place of work or relocation** – work activity is moved to a new facility (with different infrastructure) or a new/additional place. This could be a new country or regional subsidiary.

This is not an exhaustive list and organizational change may encompass more than one of these examples.

Although in this book we focus on change at the organizational level, it is important to understand how change at different contextual levels is interconnected and how changes at one level are often interdependent on change at other levels. For example, change restructuring at the organizational level will likely require individuals to move into different roles.

Similarly, we regularly see examples of national policy leading to significant change for individual organizations (e.g. Ferlie and Shortell, 2001; Tucker et al., 2022).

Furthermore, organizational change has to be viewed as context-specific; every change will be different and decisions about how to manage change in one case will likely not be effective in another. All change requires trade-offs and adaptations to the specific situation that occurs. This is why we explore so many case studies in organizational change, both as learning and teaching tools – such as those included in this text – and also in research. Detailed case study analysis allows us to explore the nuances of the complex connections and contextual details of organizational change. In practice, individuals often do not have a clear understanding of how the actions of other organizational members are constrained by broader social processes at the group, industry or individual level (Dopson et al., 2008). For example, a particular branch or department of an organization may be more resistant to a merger where they know that the merger partner has a larger branch located very close to them. These contexts are grounded in historical social experiences (Dopson et al., 2008); for example, where an industry has adopted certain historical norms about job security, an organization may find a change which jeopardizes this more challenging than in an industry where employees tend to be more transient.

Change comes in many different, sometimes overlapping, forms. But we can still recognize two essential paradigmatic groups of change. Some authors talk about large-scale, radical transformational change. Other authors describe more incremental, continuous improvements or micro-changes in organizations. Here, we will explore some of the key features of these different forms under the headings **continuous improvement** and **transformational change**.

Continuous improvement

Change may occur in organizations in one discrete block or may be based on a series of more limited improvements, for example in products, structures or processes. Bessant et al. (2001) define continuous improvement (CI) as a 'particular bundle of routines which can help an organization improve what it currently does' (p. 68). This approach usually involves the whole organization and consists of the adoption of small, frequent, continuous improvements over time towards a specific direction, in order to obtain significant results thanks to their cumulative effect.

A forerunner of continuous improvement was developed in the United States at the time of the Second World War. In the early 1940s, to support the increase in productivity required of manufacturing, a programme titled 'Training within industry' was launched which envisaged training initiatives for workers and managers aimed at developing their critical analysis skills and soliciting their contributions to quality improvements and productivity increase. After the war, this approach was also applied in Japan by experts from the American administration to support the recovery of Japan. But, while this approach was declining in the United States and other Western countries, it was further and successfully developed in Japan (known as Kaizen) between the 1960s and 1980s thanks to key experts, such as Imai and Shingo. It was successfully integrated into the industrial culture and, for example, Toyota represented the paradigmatic case of its application. Thanks to this success, and since the mid-1980s, the focus on quality and continuous improvement resumed in Western countries as well.

Bessant et al. (1994) argue that for continuous improvement to be successful it is key that management offers the direction of the change process to ensure that the different efforts of improvement are consistent. From the organization perspective, it is key that all employees are involved in terms of suggesting possible improvements, confirming their effectiveness and implementing the changes. Key organizational conditions are summarized in Table 1.1.

Table 1.1 A summary of key conditions for continuous improvement (adapted from Bessant et al., 1994)

	Conditions for continuous improvement
Clear strategic direction	• Identification of objectives • Sharing of objectives • Widespread, constant communication
Management of the process	• Long-term plan along with midway milestones • Involvement of management • Training intiative(s)
Organizational culture and values	• Giving importance to small steps • Potential contribution of all individuals • Mistake acceptance
Consistent organizational model	• Delegation and empowerment • Teamworking • Consistent incentives
Management of change	• Improvement as a long process • Continuing with different, multiple actions • Capturing cumulative effect
Use of support tools	• Focus on measuring performance • Statistical tools • Problem-solving tools

This approach strongly relies on creativity, collaboration, and the competence and experience of all organizational members. Unlike organizational change plans that are focused on a large one-time wholesale change, continuous improvement typically has a low set-up cost and offers solutions that are usually relatively quick and easy to implement. Of course, it may require more time to reach significant results overall, as improvements develop over a series of small steps.

Continuous improvement is usually supported by simple, visual tools. The most popular are the so-called **seven basic tools of quality** (e.g. Ishikawa, 1976). The seven tools are:

1   Check sheet: an important approach to collect data systematically and in a structured way using simple data sheets
2   Histogram: a representation of the distribution of the occurrences of different events/ issues
3   Stratification: a way to group data collected in subgroups
4   Pareto chart: a visual way to represent, using bars and a line graph, that a small group of causes generates most of the effects (Pareto, an Italian economist, suggested that about 20 per cent of causes are often associated with about 80 per cent of effects) – see Figure 1.1
5   Cause-and-effect diagram, also known as the fishbone diagram or Ishikawa diagram: a visual diagram with a fishbone shape to associate different groups of causes and sub-causes to the effect under study
6   Scatter diagram: a plot to investigate possible correlation between two variables
7   Control chart: a graph used in manufacturing to identify possible quality-related problems

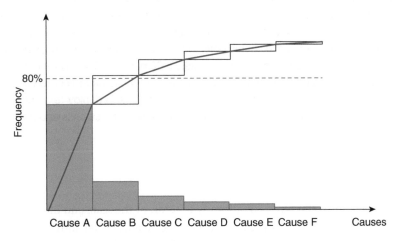

Figure 1.1   An example of the Pareto chart

The continuous improvement approach is often coupled with a specific management model, such as Total Quality Management (focusing on quality), Just in Time and Lean Production (matching production to demand, to reduce time and waste), Total Productive Maintenance (maintaining and improving manufacturing machinery) and Six Sigma (see Box 1.2).

—Box 1.2—

Six Sigma

Six Sigma is an example of a structured approach to improving the quality of the processes, whether manufacturing or service. It is aimed at customer satisfaction (either internal or external customer), achieving high-level performance and minimizing the costs of non-quality and therefore improving economic results. The key point is to implement a rigorous measurement system for the most important aspect(s) determining the quality of the outcome (product or service) and so creating value. Mikel Harry, quality expert and credited for developing Six Sigma, emphasized that 'we don't measure what we don't value'. In practice, it is important to identify the so-called critical-to-quality characteristics (CTQs) that are key to customer satisfaction and that should be considered to measure the performance of the process. When designing the outcome, a tolerance specification is defined – it refers to the target value for CTQs and its range that is acceptable in terms of customer satisfaction. Then, the actual process delivering the outcomes will be associated with an actual level of variability in relation to the target value (for the CTQs); the variability can be measured using its standard deviation (sigma).

The variability of the process should be placed in relation to the tolerance specification: a lower variability of the process means that it is more likely to meet the tolerance specification, resulting in a better process capability (process capability is the ratio between tolerance specification and variability). Six Sigma adopts the sigma level to measure the process capability and suggests that an excellent process should be at the six-sigma level. In short, the six-sigma level refers to an expected defectiveness of 3.4 parts per million, which means that acceptable outcomes of the process are 99.99966 per cent. The Six Sigma approach also suggests steps to develop in order to implement a Six Sigma project (DMAIC model, i.e. define, measure, analyse, improve and control) and roles to deploy (e.g. the so-called deployment champion, project champion, master black belts, black belts and green belts).

Transformational change

Organizational changes can range significantly in terms of the scale and impact that change will have on stakeholders (including those who work there). Several authors have sought to differentiate between different types of changes to help us understand the nature and implications that they might have on organizations. For example, Nadler and Tushman (1989) categorize four types of organizational change:

- **Tuning** – incremental change in anticipation of future events
- **Adaptation** – incremental change made in response to external events
- **Reorientation** – strategic change made in order to take advantage of perceived future opportunities
- **Re-creation** – changing when external events threaten the existence of an organization in its current form

Where Nadler and Tushman's typology focuses on the driver and scale of change, another way to distinguish changes is to compare how they evolve. Greenwood and Hinings (1988) describes four different 'tracks' by which movement from one organizational archetype to another might progress, i.e. possible change journeys. This theory distinguishes how the ultimate status of change relates to the organization's starting point. Here, they refer to changes in 'interpretive schemes' – a frame of reference based on shared assumptions that all organizational members have of the everyday workings of an organization – where, when changing, an organization seeks to replace one interpretive scheme with a different one.

1   **Inertia** – where, despite the efforts of organizational members, the organization sustains an attachment to one interpretive scheme. No change is achieved. This may be because change is resisted or innovation fails. Even in a case where small or surface-level changes in structure or processes have occurred, inertia may remain in reference to the way members think about the organization.

2   **Absorbed excursion** – where selective parts of an organization's structure or systems become decoupled from the organizational archetype but do not change the organizational system substantially enough for a new interpretive scheme to be adopted. For example, a change is made on a local level which might be characterized as experimentation with new ideas or processes. Whether intended or not, over time this change does not lead to significant disruption of organizational values and the new activity is assimilated within the existing schemes of the organization. Such changes are easily understood by organizational members and therefore resistance may be minimal. Similar examples have been referred to as incremental change or first-order change (Levy, 1986) – the change does not affect the system's ideology, goal or overall structure.

3   **Unresolved excursion** – where a change in one part of the organizational system results in split or silo-based practices which are maintained for a long period of time. Maybe one part of the system adopts a significant new change but others do not, which can lead to divisions within the organization and is often a source of conflict. When this happens, more than one set of values compete for organizational prevalence. Greenwood and Hinings (1988) refer to this as 'schizoid incoherence' where an organization may become stuck between processes of interpretive un-coupling and re-coupling around a new archetype interpretive scheme for the organization. It is often not possible to re-establish interpretive schemes from before the change due to sense-breaking activities which hinder the reversal of change (Mantere et al., 2012). Essentially, this is an example of failed change and can have negative consequences for the organization.

4   **Reorientation/transformation** – where an organization leaves behind one archetype design and wholly moves to another. Greenwood and Hinings (1988: 306) describe transformation as 'where prevailing ideas and values lose legitimacy and an alternative interpretive schema emerges carrying with it a new structure'. The new values and strategies of the new interpretive scheme will infiltrate all aspects of the organization, from its mission statement to interactions between

organizational members. This may not be a straightforward, linear process of decoupling from the old archetype, through a period of incoherence, to embryonic emergence of a new coherent archetype, but the new interpretive scheme eventually stabilizes. Instead, oscillations between old and new values, or delays followed by abrupt breakthroughs may contribute to the journey. Other authors have referred to similar processes as 'radical' change; 'second order change' (Levy, 1986) or 'frame-bending change' (Nadler and Tushman, 1989). All refer to an irreversible, all-encompassing change involving all organizational members, basic governing rules and systems.

Building on this work, other researchers have more deeply reflected on the characteristics of what is now commonly referred to as 'organizational transformation'. Ashburner, Ferlie and FitzGerald (1996) describe five criteria to judge whether transformational change is happening in an organization – see Table 1.2.

Table 1.2 Criteria for organizational transformation (adapted from Ashburner et al., 1996)

Criteria for Organizational Transformation	Examples of what this might look like:
Multiple and interrelated changes across the system as a whole	• Using structural changes in infrastructure to support/drive changes in work processes • New structures and systems supported by new technology/shift to digital provision • Where organizational spending in one area needs to be offset by cost saving in another • Multiple sequential changes – perpetual reorganization
New organizational forms	• Change in the degree of central control – more/less delegation of decision making • Increasing use of sub-contracting, networks or partnerships to deliver organizational products or services • Breaking up of longstanding rules, conventions and relationships; to be replaced by new ones
Creation of/change in individual roles	• Traditional patterns of work disturbed and recrafted • Revised responsibilities for decision making or resources • Different combinations of departments and teams working together • Requirement for new skills or training within individual roles
Reconfiguration of power relations	• New leadership groups emerge • Increase in managerialism within professional organizations • Increasing or decreasing 'real' influence of certain offices (e.g. office becomes 'a rubber-stamping' function) • Change in weight given to certain experience or prior relationships in reward, promotion or succession

Criteria for Organizational Transformation	Examples of what this might look like:
New culture, ideology and organizational meaning	• Changes in interpretive schemes – holistic view of how the organization behaves • Underlying values of the organization are altered • New role models or benchmarking referents • Change in the image of the organization, as presented to the outside • Adjustment of language, terminology, or stories used to express ideas within the organization

1.3 Urgency and Crisis in Driving Change

An interesting debate asks whether a crisis in current organizational functioning is needed to drive real transformational change (Pettigrew et al., 1992). In his famous book *Leading Change*, John Kotter highlights how complacency, or a failure to establish a **sense of urgency**, is one of the biggest mistakes that organizations make in managing organizational change. Convincing people (employees) to operate outside of their comfort zones is always considerably more difficult than anticipated – people tend to cling to the status quo. Complacency is reinforced by the visibility of resources, the focus of organizational structures, distraction of busyness or other stress and a need for security (Kotter, 2012).

Popular theories also suggest that it is imperative that the old system needs to be disregarded, thrown out or become no longer valid in order to convince people/organizations to change (e.g. Lewin's three-step model). Without this sense of urgency, there will be no incentive for change to happen. In Chapter 2 we will explore further Kurt Lewin's notion of 'unfreezing' – breaking down old ways of working in more detail. However, it should also be noted that other authors have warned of the danger of criticizing existing ways of working. Mantere et al. (2012) present a longitudinal single case study of a public sector organization where a merger was cancelled after significant attempts to transform organizational strategy. They found that when managers engaged in attempts to break down long-standing organizational understandings to unfreeze existing organizational strategies, this had a negative effect on future attempts to craft success if the organization wished to return to these strategies when change fails. This could result in the 'schizoid incoherence' described in the previous section by Greenwood and Hinings (1988).

Transformational change may be facilitated when a sense of urgency is established; however, breaking down existing strategies is difficult to reverse if plans change.

1.4 Change Implementation

So far in this chapter, we have explored different conceptualizations and definitions of organizational change and explored what makes change truly transformational for an organization. In this second half we will explore *how* the process of transitioning an organization from point A to point B might be achieved. Pettigrew and Whipp (1991) explain that to understand an organizational change fully, we need to understand the content, context and process of change. Table 1.3 summarizes some of the key information that we need to gain this understanding based on their writing:

Table 1.3 Understanding organizational change implementation (adapted from Pettigrew and Whipp, 1991)

	Definition	Consider...
Content	What changes between point A and point B	• area(s) of transformation within the organization • targets to be achieved by the change • assumptions and connections between areas of transformation
Context	The inner and outer context that causes and constrains change	• Inner context includes ongoing strategy, structure, culture, management and political processes of the organization. These will shape change and organizational strategy • External or outer context includes the national, economic, social and political context in which the organization operates
Process	How the shift from A to B is accomplished, by whom, and through which actions	• Actions, reactions and interactions of various parties in making decisions during the change journey • Models of change to be used (see Chapter 2) • Patterns of change behaviour during change • Responses and reactions to change by stakeholders

Many change authors have highlighted the importance of the change process (we will explore these theories further in Chapter 2). Change involves many activities, including studying organizational patterns in diagnosing what needs to be changed; planning and preparing for change; setting targets for success; harnessing stakeholder engagement; capturing learning by regularly reviewing change; and implementing and sustaining change (Hayes, 2022). Whilst we recognize the importance of all these change activities, here we focus on aspects of change related to implementation specifically.

The McKinsey Global Survey of organizational transformations (McKinsey & Company, 2021) found that 35 per cent of value loss to a company in organizational transformation comes from the implementation phase of a change. They argue that change implementation that takes shortcuts, loses track of timelines and fails to facilitate learning can lead to a loss of value from the transformation. In this book we focus on change makers who create change from within organizations. We argue that these individuals add most value to a change during the implementation phase of change, where they manage stakeholders, ensure that the organization's actions are enacted fairly, provide social and emotional support during uncertainty, and manage knowledge and learning to enhance success (Hayes, 2022). Change makers face challenges in the implementation of change as they experience pressure to deliver quick wins (Hayes, 2022) with limited resources and power at their disposal. To set the scene for the remainder of this book, here we will examine two contrasting ways of thinking about change implementation, and then consider how we might judge whether change implementation has been successful, and some of the common challenges that change makers need to navigate in implementing change.

Theory E and Theory O

Beer and Nohria (2000) propose a useful framework on organizational change known as Theory E and Theory O. These two theories represent distinct ways of thinking about change implementation. These different logics determine approaches to change leadership, how decisions are made and what matters for change success.

Theory E represents a model of change focused on creating economic value for the organization – where shareholder value is the main objective. It focuses on the so-called 'hard' aspects of the organization, such as financial performance, formal structure and management systems. From a Theory E perspective, organizational change means to implement hard actions (e.g. economic incentives, restructuring, downsizing) that are result-oriented and decided in a top-down manner, where behaviour change is motivated by economic incentives (e.g. bonuses, profit sharing) to align employee interests with those of shareholders.

Theory O represents a model of change focused on organizational capability, believing that the effectiveness of the organization relies on its culture and people. The assumption of this orientation is that change is not only for shareholders, but should aim to benefit all members of the organization and all stakeholders (e.g. suppliers, customers, communities). The focus is on developing everyone's commitment towards a new direction to achieve performance.

In order to pursue a sustainable perspective, Nohria and Beer (2000) believe that a combination of both orientations is necessary. A combined approach would have a goal to explicitly embrace the paradox between economic values and organizational capability, focusing simultaneously on the hard (structure and systems) and the soft (corporate culture) elements of change. A combined approach would be led from the top, but also engaging the people below and use incentives to reinforce change but not drive it. It would allow for a change process that embraces spontaneity, allowing plans and programmes to evolve as needed in order to achieve change in a sustainable way. In this time (e.g. post-pandemic, cost of living crisis, global supply chain crisis), organizations are facing greater challenges and this requires creative ways to integrate and achieve a balance between the two orientations and potentially develop sustainable changes that build on the strengths of both.

Measuring change success

It is regularly observed that organizational stakeholders are often dissatisfied with the outcomes of change. In 2015 a CIPD survey (CIPD, 2015) found that less than 60 per cent of reorganizations met their stated objectives; the McKinsey survey (McKinsey & Company, 2014) also found that only 38 per cent of the global executives reported that their most recent transformation had a 'completely' or 'mostly' successful impact on performance. Ten per cent claimed it was 'completely' unsuccessful (McKinsey & Company, 2014) and managing change scholar Bernard Burnes (2011) is regularly quoted as stating that as much as 90 per cent of change fails to meet objectives.

Measuring change success is tricky. As we saw with Theory E and Theory O above, different perspectives will place value on different outcomes of change (Theory E would deem change to be a success if stakeholder value has been increased; Theory O would deem change to be a success if there has been learning and growth). When we ask the question 'what does successful organizational change look like' we must also ask 'for who?' and 'after how much time?'. In other words, it is important to clarify from whose perspective we wish to examine success and how long we expect it to take for change value to be realized for those parties. A change may be successful in reaching financial cost savings which were the target of company shareholders, yet the impact of changes on front-line employees may have devastated morale and led to a loss of talented employees and reputational damage that will compromise the organization's long-term success.

Regardless of success in terms of organizational performance, there are many costs associated with organizational change (Burnes, 2011). Research on organizational change has consistently found that it increases stress, job insecurity and uncertainty, and results in longer working hours for employees involved in change. Whilst we know increasingly more about how to strategically achieve change, the question 'at what cost?' often remains in organizational practice.

We will explore in more detail in Chapter 11 how we might measure and evaluate change success in a variety of ways. But, for now, it is important to think about the link between change and organizational outcomes (Pettigrew et al., 2001). Some questions we might ask when considering how to measure change success include:

- What changes in organizational outcomes might you expect to see after the change?
- What do you need to measure to understand the performance of an organizational change?
- How do you know when change has been successful?
- How do you know when change is finished?
- What will be the legacy of this change for the organization?

Key questions for implementing organizational change

Organizational change can be complex and range from well to poorly engineered. Every change in every organization will be unique. There is no ideal diagnosis strategy, no ideal way to implement change, no ideal leadership style, no ideal communication strategy that can be applied to all circumstances. A central tenet of this book is to ask, 'How can we manage organizational change well?' The answer to this question depends on a lot of different factors (Pettigrew et al., 2001). To answer this question, we need to understand the complexity and uniqueness of each organizational change – this is something we will explore in each case study throughout this book. Pettigrew et al. (2001) provide us with five key categories as a good place to start. We begin to understand what change might look like in any given case by seeking the answer to a lot more questions.

1 Multiple contexts and levels of analysis

We need to think about the internal and external context of change. Pettigrew and Whipp (1991) distinguish between internal context – structures, culture, objectives, employee make-up, skills and abilities, and external context – industry, technology and innovation, markets. Both of these will impact on the way the organization operates within a dynamic environment. The relationship between contextual factors is not a one-way process; organizations are influenced by the internal and external context but also are part of this context themselves and their actions may lead to shifts in the external environment. For example, a major organizational merger within an industry may shift the nature of the competitive environment significantly whilst also impacting on the labour and product market opportunities.

We need to think about how change will affect different levels of analysis:

- How will the change affect, and be affected by, individual employees?
- How will it affect, and be affected by, groups, teams, sections, departments?
- How will it affect, and be affected by, the organization?
- How will it affect, and be affected by, the industry?
- How will it affect, and be affected by, society?

2 Impact of time, history and agency

People who will be affected by change have a history with the organization – they are not blank slates, and they have memory of what has happened before. Whether positive or negative experiences, these will influence their expectations of the current and future changes. Individuals within organizations may also bring experiences of change from other organizations or from interactions with others outside of the organization. For example, they may have a family member who had a negative experience of a similar restructuring in another organization. The actions of individuals and groups will impact on the change – you can't make people change, and their willingness and ability to solve problems, engage in consultation and adopt behaviours that will support change can have a significant impact on change success.

- How long is change going to take?
- Is this one change, or one in a series of changes?
- What is the sequence of stages in the change process?
- Will it be done all in one go, or broken down into phases?
- Has the organization been through similar changes before? How long ago? How did it go?
- What has the organization learned from recent change experiences? What will they do differently this time?
- What are the current levels of trust and commitment within the organization? Are employees likely to be supportive and engaged in change?

3 International and cross-cultural comparisons

Organizational change processes will reflect the norms and values of the national culture within which the recipients of change are situated. This is especially complex when organizational change occurs in multinational organizations. What seems like a perfectly reasonable behaviour change request in one cultural context may go against the cultural norms of employees working in different parts of the world. Similarly, we must be cautious in taking lessons learnt from an organization's experience in one national context, when applying those learnings in another context. Some questions we might ask are:

- What are the norms in terms of power and hierarchy for organizational members?
- What voice mechanisms do employees have (e.g. trade union)?
- To what extent can you change contracts or working conditions?
- Is the organization global, and if so what are the implications for parts of the organization in different countries?
- How do planned changes relate to organizational culture and, if relevant, local cultural values and norms?

4 Type of change – sequencing and pace of change

Earlier in this chapter, we identified a list of types of change; however, the process for achieving each of these changes will be different. We should also consider what resources for change are available – this will determine the extent and pace of change which you can feasibly achieve and how this might be managed.

In Chapter 2 we will explore in more detail different approaches to change such as planned change versus emergent change approaches, but some general questions that we might ask about sequencing and pace of change, determining a specific choreography of change, might be:

- Does the organization change often?
- Does it try to constantly change and adapt – continuous change – or is this a single, one-time change?
- If other changes are planned, what is the sequence of change (for example, an organization might decide to change IT systems before or after moving to new offices)?
- What resources can we draw on for change management?
- How much capacity for change does the organization have?

5 Translation of research to practice

As we have explored, here, each organizational change is unique. This means it is very hard to take a theory and apply it (unaltered) in any given context – in other words, there is no one best way to manage change. Making comparisons between organizations is virtually impossible – this is why we use many case studies in change research and to educate students of change. Translating research findings into practice requires a critical lens; often there may be a need to blend or draw from many change models to find the best fit between research and practice. Some questions which might help to begin this critical inquiry comprise:

- How is the change the organization is attempting similar to and different from changes it has experienced before?
- How is the change the organization is attempting similar to and different from changes experienced by other similar organizations?
- What worked elsewhere – and *why* did it work?
- What had unexpected consequences elsewhere – and *why* did those consequences arise?

Chapter Summary

- Organizational change occurs when business strategies or major sections of the business are altered. Change will often have multiple layers (strategic, operational, cultural) which are interrelated and experienced collectively by all organizational members.
- Continuous improvement is a type of change that is enacted by a series of small steps, mostly focused on quality improvement, following a specific direction. The impact comes from the accumulation of those improvements.
- Organizational transformation is where an organization leaves behind one archetype design and wholly moves to another. It will include multiple and interrelated changes; new organizational forms; change of individual roles; reconfiguration of power relations; and will result in a new culture, ideology and organizational meaning.
- Transformational change may be facilitated when a sense of urgency is established; however, breaking down existing strategies is difficult to reverse if plans change.
- Measuring change success is tricky. It is important to clarify from whose perspective we wish to examine success and how long we expect it to take for change value to be realised for those parties.

Activity

As we have seen in this chapter, organizational changes come in many different shapes and sizes. Understanding the context and drivers for change is important to developing a holistic understanding of change management. Boxes 1.3 and 1.4 are two examples of organizational changes. Considering each example individually, discuss the following questions:

1   What is the organization trying to achieve and how clear is this at the outset of the change?

2   Would you describe these changes as:

  i   continuous improvement or transformational change?
  ii   Theory E and/or Theory O?

3   Using Pettigrew and Whipp's (1991) categories, how well do you understand the content, context and process of these changes? (You may also use some of the key questions for implementing change in the last section of this chapter to explore more deeply.)

Note that you can apply these same questions to all other examples of change and case studies in this book as a starting point to understand the organization and its change context.

Box 1.3

Advanced Motion Technologies (AMT)

Advanced Motion Technologies (AMT) is a global engineering manufacturing organization. It has been in business for more than 50 years, operating in a number of industries, including construction, defence, aerospace, marine and medical technology. It specializes in the design and manufacture of motion control products. AMT became a leader in the surgical simulation market by capitalizing on rapid growth and being a frontrunner in developing new technologies in this field. This strategy had worked in the past but the medical technology market had become much more competitive. As a result, it was now difficult to earn profits from innovating and commercializing products faster than competitors, especially in the medical technology area. A new CEO who joined the organization in 2018 is keen that the medical technology division shifts its focus to concentrate on consolidating market segments where it already has a large share of the market and a loyal customer base.

There were a number of external and historical factors that influenced these decisions. The use of simulation in medical and surgical research, teaching and practice has a long history. High-fidelity, virtual reality visual and robotic technologies began to be incorporated into surgical simulation products in the second part of the twentieth century. The introduction of 3D prototyping and advanced haptics, in particular, led to major advances in surgical education meaning that surgical techniques could be practised repeatedly, reducing the risk to patients. AMT partnered with new innovative educational programmes across the healthcare sector, enabling surgeons and medical students to acquire skills prior to entering the operating room. AMT became a part of a wider medical technology ecosystem developing technologies collaboratively by offering subject matter expertise in motion control surgical simulation engineering.

However, over time, it has become clear that now that educational programmes using simulation are mainstream, only manufacturers that can develop simulators that reduce cost over time, enable experimentation or adaptation, and provide other support services, such as documentation or a help desk, are likely to do well. AMT is in this category. Despite initially having an edge in this now mature market, it was becoming more difficult to find ways to attract and retain surgical simulation customers. Moving to a focus on consolidating and support, this strategic change would discontinue the medical technology division's rehabilitation products line, which was performing less well, to allow research and development teams to focus on continuing to be a leader in the surgical simulation technology market. There will be particular focus on developing and incorporating AMT proprietary technologies into the products of other manufacturers, including other manufacturers making medical centrifuges, CT scanners and robotic surgical instruments.

This change in strategy requires a significant mindset shift for members of the medical technology division who are no longer trying to discover or develop breakthrough technologies with the view to be first to market – finding the 'next big thing' technology was no longer an important goal. There is concern from change makers that subject-matter experts may find it more difficult to understand how their expert knowledge and problem-solving skills will add value to the organization in the future. Likewise, the support for continuous education and the ability for individuals to learn within the organization may also be impeded and lead to higher turnover of young innovative engineers.

—Box 1.4—

Howe campus

Howe campus was an academic institution on a small rural campus about 40 miles from London. Originally offering vocational qualifications in agricultural studies and veterinary sciences, in 1992 it was awarded university status to provide specialist undergraduate and postgraduate degree programmes in these two areas. The campus was made up of older historical buildings converted from a former manor house and private estate. The upkeep of these facilities was costly, but they gave the campus an intimate and unique feeling that created real community between students and staff. The culture among employees at the rural campus was one of loyalty, according to the manager of the department, many of the employees having been in employment since the early 1990s or previously. Many of the employees had personal ties to the area (e.g. children at school). Following consistent funding and management problems throughout the 1990s and 2000s it became apparent that a merger with a larger academic institution would be necessary for the campus to survive.

Merging with a research-intensive partner

A London university was selected as a merger partner on the basis of a good match on specialities. The London university already had an established distance learning programme at other satellite campuses. The institution had a very strong reputation

(Continued)

and expected that academic staff who delivered distance programmes under its branding must meet its institutional expectations. The merger process was completed in 2010.

Employees at Howe campus were initially taken aback by the new institution's approach to performance management and the new merger partner impressed their rigorous research standards on the employees at the campus. Having not had previous experience of working in a research-intensive environment, academic employees at Howe campus struggled to reach these research objectives whilst also continuing to deliver high-quality teaching on their specialist programmes which were growing due to the reputational boost of the new merger partner's brand. Following a series of restructurings from 2010–2018 that aimed to streamline programmes and create more research activity, the London partner decided that it no longer wished to continue supporting the cost of the rural campus facilities and announced that all programmes and academic activity at the rural campus would be terminated. Veterinary science, the more lucrative of the specialities, was transferred to the main campus of the London institution in 2019. Of the ten members of staff at Howe who were offered alternative positions at the London campus, only two took up this offer; seven chose instead to leave the institution, and one took on an administrative position at the Howe campus for considerably less pay.

However, the historic relevance of the Howe campus and the embeddedness of the institution in the local rural community created political pressure from external bodies to keep the campus open. In 2020 the decision to close down the campus was re-evaluated and eventually the London university partner agreed that it would keep the campus open for a further 12 months (later extended to 18 months), giving the remaining department at Howe campus the chance to find an alternative merger partner, thus avoiding the redundancy of the academics and undergraduate degree course which they offered.

A new home?

The one remaining department underwent a second merger with another non-London based university in January 2022. The new partner institution, established in the 1960s and based in a nearby city in the same county, offers a broad range of university programmes and also expects its academic employees to produce research outputs. However, it has expressed that it is sympathetic to the background and specialism of Howe campus, and has offered employees access to additional research development at the city-based campus and intends to invest in a PhD programme at the Howe campus to develop a pipeline of research. Employees at the Howe campus are anxious about the prospect of the new partnership. Employees describe themselves as still undergoing a process of mourning the loss of their colleagues from the veterinary science department and recovering from the threat of closure. The prospect of merger with another research-focused institution provides opportunities but they are also wary of the experiences of the past.

Further Recommended Reading

To understand more about different organizational change trajectories and how this helps us understand the differences between organizations, see Greenwood, R. and Hinings, C. R. (1993) 'Understanding strategic change: The contribution of archetypes', *Academy of Management Journal*, 36(5): 1052–1081. DOI:10.2307/256645.

For insights from change management consultants on why organizational changes fail, see McKinsey & Company (2021) 'Losing from day one: Why even successful transformations fall short', 7 December 2021. Available at: www.mckinsey.com/business-functions/people-and-organizational-performance/our-insights/successful-transformations (accessed 28 November 2023).

For an overview of some of the key questions to think about organizational change, see Pettigrew, A.M., Woodman, R.W. and Cameron, K.S. (2001) 'Studying organizational change and development: Challenges for future research', *Academy of Management Journal*, 44(4): 697–713.

2

TRADITIONAL THEORIES OF CHANGE

AN OVERVIEW

Chapter Objectives

- To examine key theoretical approaches to change in organizations and various proposed frameworks for understanding the stages of change
- To compare planned versus emergent approaches to change management in organizations
- To discuss how systems theories that view organizations as complex adaptive systems conceptualize organizational change
- To explain the role of context and agency in the change process

2.1 Introduction

As we have seen in the previous chapter, organizational change is a complex and nuanced phenomenon in organizations, driven by a range of factors and experienced by a range of stakeholders. As a result, organizations use different orientations for organizational change and development. These orientations are guided by specific assumptions concerning human nature, the nature of organizations, the nature of work, as well as the purpose and meaning of change itself. To help us understand change, it is helpful to have a framework to organize these various assumptions and aspects of how and why change occurs. Thus, in this chapter, we will adopt a framework underpinning four key theoretical approaches to change in organizations, i.e. planned change, emergent change, system-related change and process-based change.[1]

In doing so, this chapter will bring together the change management contents that constitute the traditional pillars of any course or text on organizational change management. Many of the assumptions of these approaches will be further explored throughout this book as they relate to the experience of change makers; however, here we provide an overview of the different perspectives and ways that groups of scholars and practitioners view change.

Different approaches highlight different change experiences. The approach you use will help the observer explore some things but may also prevent them from seeing others. Rather than focusing on the detail of specific models the emphasis here will be on the overarching 'approaches' to viewing change and how these approaches relate to popular strategies we see in organizations (e.g. organizational development). We aim to create awareness of how change is experienced by organizations and how it happens.

In the first part of the chapter, we will explore the planned approach to change that views organizational change as a one-off defined event for an organization. In a planned approach to organizational change, although sometimes triggered by an unpredictable external event or a context-related threat, the process of change is managed through planned phases of intervention. Generally considered the most traditional perspective on change, we will introduce the key work of Kurt Lewin and his contributions to the planned change approach as well as other phase-based models that build on his work.

We then move on to compare the planned change approach to alternative perspectives, commonly known as emergent approaches change, where change is understood as more continuous and led by front-line stakeholders. Here, the emergent change is ongoing, continuous, influenced by daily evolving work events and sometimes even incredibly rapid and unpredictable (Cummings and Cummings, 2014).

---

[1] Each approach presented in this chapter can encompass continuous improvement or transformational change (discussed in Chapter 1). For example, an organizational transformation or continuous improvement project could equally be purposefully planned. For this reason, you will find references to both literatures in many parts of this chapter.

Related to this, we will also discuss the concept of an organization as a system and the view of change as a process. In doing so we will draw from complexity and systems theories as well as process theory perspectives (e.g. Langley, 1999). For each of the approaches discussed, we highlight the contributions and the criticisms of these approaches to help us understand what is gained and what is missing from each perspective.

2.2 Planned Change Approach

The most traditional and popular approach to theorizing organizational change is to see organizational change as an intentional, premeditated and planned endeavour that the organization undertakes. A majority of the thinking akin to the planned approach to change can be traced back to the work of Kurt Lewin, which serves as an appropriate starting point for this section. We will review Lewin's key theories and then discuss how the concepts of his work have been developed by other authors.

Lewin's three-step model

Kurt Lewin was a theorist on social change and social mobility whose work stretches across many disciplines (psychology, sociology, organizational behaviour, management theory, economics, behavioural science). As a theorist of social change, he was interested in the interconnection between individual experiences and group and institutional influences on their behaviour.

Lewin noted that when change was instigated it was often short lived – it did not stick, the group's behaviour soon reverted back to its previous pattern and any improvement in the group's performance was lost (Lewin, 1947a). He concluded therefore that improving productivity could not be the only objective behind a change project. The three-step model is the model most synonymous with the planned change approach and usually considered the first planned model of change. In this theory, Lewin argues that the change process is bigger than just the action taken to make it happen.

Figure 2.1 Lewin's three-step model

The three-step model (Figure 2.1) argues that a successful change project would include three stages:

1 Unfreezing the present level

Before new behaviour can be adopted successfully the old behaviour needs to be discarded otherwise the new behaviours may not be accepted. This can be achieved by creating dissatisfaction with the existing situation of work which, in turn, will create a willingness to change. Individuals will be motivated to explore new behaviours if their comfort levels with old behaviours are reduced. They also need to be empowered to make change and to do so proactively.

Lewin argued that explaining and understanding the rationale of the change is an important motivator for unfreezing the change and moving to the new system. Understanding the nature of the present situation and, where relevant, how this will play out into the future in an unsustainable way drives innovation and problem-solving, and empowers individuals to attempt to make improvements.

Unfreezing involves the identification and reduction of the restraining forces (see field theory below) which maintain present levels of behaviour. This might involve confrontation meetings or re-education of those involved about the methods they currently use. The idea is to convince those involved of the need for the change.

2 Moving to the new level

Having analysed the present situation and identified the most appropriate options, action is necessary to move to the more desirable system you want to adopt. This involves changing the behaviour of members of the organization, developing new behaviours, new values and attitudes with new organizational structures and processes of involving people and encouraging their involvement.

Exactly how this can be achieved will depend on the nature of the change and the organizational environment. Having invested in creating dissatisfaction with the old organizational form, emphasizing the permanency of the change actions at the moving stage is especially important. Individuals need to realize that they do not, after a short period, revert to the old ways of doing things. If adjustments need to be made, these will continue to move in a forward direction.

3 Refreezing the new level

Refreezing seeks to stabilize the organization at this new stage to ensure that the new behaviours are relatively safe from regression. This involves taking steps to stabilize and reinforce the changes that happened at the moving phase.

Supporting mechanisms are used to positively reinforce the new ways of working. This could include adjusting organizational structures, performance or productivity management criteria and socializing new organizational members as they join the organization. Included in this stage are the acceptance of culture changes, norms for new work groups and new policies and practices that demonstrate what is valued. Culture change can take a long time and, therefore, the need to maintain momentum at this stage through joint goal setting, responding to feedback and rewarding progress is also important.

In this three-step model, Lewin's aim was to put into perspective the moving phase, which he argues is often over emphasized, in relation to the unfreezing and refreezing stages, which are equally important.

Underpinning assumptions

The three-step model is often presented as Lewin's original theory of planned change; nevertheless, it is important to view this in conjunction with his other theories to understand how Lewin viewed behaviour and behaviour change as a social process. Only by doing this can we see the interconnection between individual experiences and the group and institutional influences on change behaviour.

Field theory (Lewin, 1952) helps us to understand some of the underpinning assumptions about how social groupings are motivated to change or remain the same. The core argument is that the behaviour of individuals is a function of the group environment – represented as a 'field'. The field is made up of driving and restraining forces. Driving forces (such as the desire to resolve a problem or to receive recognition from another person) put pressure on the individual to behave in a particular way; restraining forces (such as personal defences or group norms) prevent movement and create stability, encouraging individuals to behave in ways that have produced positive results before, and avoiding unpredictable new behaviours.

Understanding these forces helps us to conceptualize what the unfreezing and refreezing stages of Lewin's model represent and why they are important. Restraining forces support the status quo, encouraging resistance to change. Unfreezing can be facilitated by decreasing these restraining forces. An example of this might be to shake up group dynamics that produce norms of traditional behaviour by introducing change champions who will role-model alternative ways of working. Change can also be facilitated by increasing driving forces, an example of which might be helping employees to understand the context of change and why it matters to act as a set of guiding principles for what they are working towards.

Lewin's theory of change is one of intentional action on behalf of the organization. His ideas about action research (Lewin, 1946) shed more light on what this means. Before embarking on change, an organization should carry out research to look at both the external and internal factors which affect the organization's change decision, including: competitors' actions; environmental and current affairs; motivation and commitment of employees; group relations and the strategy and culture of the organization. Plans for change should be based on this research and action will be taken based on these decisions.

The two main assumptions of action research comprise:

1   It emphasizes that **change requires action** and provides direction to achieve this. It acknowledges that if left alone change will not be successful, and problems will develop.
2   It also emphasizes that **successful action is based on a process of learning** that allows those involved to analyse the situation correctly. It encourages those involved to identify all the possible alternative solutions and choose the one most appropriate to the situation at hand. Change is most successful when individuals can reflect on and gain new insights into the situation through learning and understanding.

Action research also introduces us to the cyclical orientation of planned change, whereby multiple cycles of activity are needed to address an organizational problem. There is no expectation that the first cycle of change will provide a perfect solution; indeed, several iterations may be needed to address unintended consequences and unexpected challenges. Whilst the planned approach to change does view change as having a defined start and end point, action research demonstrates that the end point and the journey to get there cannot be as statically defined as one might wish it to be.

The same cyclical interpretation in the context of continuous improvement is offered by the PDCA cycle (Box 2.1).

─Box 2.1─

PDCA cycle

The PDCA cycle is a popular model (Deming, 1986; Shewhart, 1986) used in continuous improvement in business settings. At the most basic level, the activities related to each improvement initiative refer to cycles of problem-setting and problem-solving. PDCA is the acronym of the four phases: plan, do, check, act (Figure 2.2).

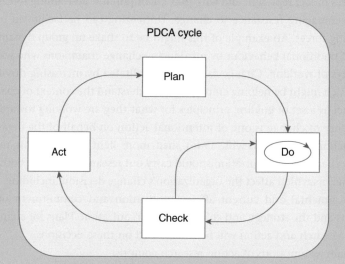

Figure 2.2 PDCA cycle

In fact, each initiative of improvement is developed throughout these phases, based on the scientific method:

- Plan: this is about analysing the situation and the problem(s), collecting data, and identifying possible actions of improvement to test and how;
- Do: this is focused on testing the actions of improvement; it is appropriate to experiment each change/action at a time;

- Check: this allows evaluation of the change/action, check if it had the expected improvement and re-do if necessary;
- Act: this is focused on stabilizing the improvement(s) and making them part of the normal process (resonating the *refreezing* phase of Lewin).

Other models of planned change

Kurt Lewin was the first to introduce the concept of planned change but his model has been criticized as being too simplistic and many other authors have produced revised or new models of planned change, some of which are considerably longer and more complex models with seven to eight phases. These variations are too numerous and the developments too incremental to examine in this chapter; however, it is useful to consider the commonalities that they have and to explore what this offers to change management as a discipline. We have grouped theories that have adopted a shared approach to our study of organization change and here refer to these as the planned change approach. In considering a range of models, we find that they all have the same underpinning assumptions about change:

1   They all view change as something which is **premeditated and consciously embarked upon** as opposed to types of change which might come about by accident, on impulse or which might be in some way forced onto the organization.

2   Beyond change, **organizations have a stable state** – therefore, these theories assume relative stability between changes. Change is something which organizations experience rarely and, once completed, the organization will return to a (new) stable state. In this way, change should be **self-sustaining** – once the desired state has been reached, the organization will seek to stabilize itself. Because change requires additional energy expenditure (going against restraining forces, innovating and problem-solving, convincing others, etc.), organizational members seek routine and habit over constant flux and uncertainty.

3   Planned changes have **clear finite objectives** and an end goal – the aim is movement between A and B, where both A and B are known. Some planned change models allow for scoping these objectives in early phases of change, and/or refinement in later phases; however, there is general agreement that these should be known before action is taken to try to achieve them.

4   Planned change is usually thought of as rare, intentional and significant. It is viewed as a **collaborative process.** It is most commonly thought of as a **top-down** approach, where high-level strategic decisions are then implemented with increasing levels of granularity as they progress down the organizational structure. It involves all levels and employees within the organization. Planned change approaches are the most common to achieve organizational transformation (as defined in Chapter 1).

5   Change is a **cyclical process** where an organization must complete one cycle of change before beginning another. There are many different planned-change theories but they all involve a sequence of stages. It is assumed that these progress in a forward motion. Whilst some planned change theorists acknowledge that sometimes multiple changes may happen simultaneously within organizations, they generally agree that this is not desirable and only realistically possible if each change follows its own distinct change cycle. There is an assumption that where multiple changes occur these are enacted largely independently of one another, or otherwise they should be considered all part of the same large-scale change and follow the same sequence collectively.

One notable development in the planned change approach is the work of Bullock and Batten (1985) – see Table 2.1. They conducted a review of over 30 planned change models produced by others since Lewin's original theory, which they then summarized into a model of four phases. From their review they examined research into which methods of change have been found to be successful in moving from one phase to another and were able to consolidate these into their four phases. This is helpful in advancing the planned approach because it provides a more detailed overview of practical steps that can be used to achieve change. The benefits of Bullock and Batten's theory include its broad applicability across a variety of industries and types of change and its clear distinction between the phases and the processes at each stage.

Table 2.1   Summary of Bullock and Batten's (1985) review of planned change models

Phases of Planned Change	Processes at this phase:
Exploration phase: awareness, establishing contracts This is an investigative and decision-making phase. The organization will research and decide whether it wants to make specific changes	• becoming aware of the need for change • searching for any outside assistance • establishing any contracts with outside consultants
Planning phase: diagnosis, goals, gaining support This stage is about understanding the organization's problem	• establishing a correct diagnosis of the problem • establishing goals • designing appropriate actions • getting support from key decision-makers
Action phase: gaining support, evaluating, feedback At this stage the organization implements the changes which were planned at the planning phase	• establishing appropriate arrangements • gaining support for actions • evaluating the activities • feeding back results so adjustments can be made

Phases of Planned Change	Processes at this phase:
Integration phase: reinforcement, monitoring Once the change has been successfully implemented the organization enters the integration phase This phase is concerned with consolidating and stabilising the changes so that they become part of an organization's normal operations	• reinforcement of new behaviours • giving feedback • rewarding behaviours compliant with the new system • decreasing the reliance on any consultant • All training and monitoring of managers and employees to seek improvement within the new systems

As an example of the planned approach to business process innovation, Box 2.2 offers an overview on Business Process Reengineering (BPR).

─Box 2.2─

Business Process Reengineering

The more recent influences of the planned change approach can be observed in the Business Process Reengineering (BPR) movement. BPR was introduced and became popular in the 1990s (Davenport and Short, 1990; Hammer, 1990) as a structured approach to organizational and managerial innovation aimed at achieving radical improvements in performance through the redesign of business processes (Bartezzaghi, 2002).

The overall process of BPR follows the same key activities of planned change in general, but with a heavy focus on design of organizational processes:

1   **Mapping business processes** can be developed in different ways (e.g. considering all processes, or only some key processes) and with different mapping tools, such as process flowcharts. The focus is on 'as is' processes; that is, the current set of interrelated activities and decisions as they exist before change. It can be more or less detailed but, in any case, represents an important starting point of the analysis and, in particular, to explain the current level of performance.

2   **Analysing the performance** is key to identify the gaps between the target level of performance and the current level of performance. This helps to focus redesign toward the improvements that are most needed. A comprehensive approach to analyse performance includes identifying a dashboard of dimensions of performance. First, it requires identification of the *critical success factors* – areas of the process that have an impact on the strategy and its objectives. Based on

(Continued)

these, it is then possible to identify specific *dimensions of performance* for the process, which fall into three categories:

a   general performance – volumes/quantities of input, output and resources of the process;

b   internal performance – from the perspective of the process owner; and,

c   external performance – from the perspective of the client of the process, either internal or external client.

The identification of dimensions of performance should cover different aspects about efficiency (costs, times), effectiveness (quality), flexibility and other specific elements. Other models suggest simplified ways to identify dimensions of performance. For example, the balanced scorecard model identifies four specific perspectives about performance; that is, financial, customer, internal processes, and learning and growth (Kaplan and Norton, 1992).

3   **Diagnosing the issues** focuses on determining the causes for the gaps. To support identification and analysis, it is popular to use tools or checklists. For example, Bartezzaghi (2010) suggests five key determining factor areas, based on the most important principles of business process management: workflow of the activities of the process, including its logics and procedures; organization of the process, including micro-organization (roles), macro-organization (structures) and coordination; competences and resources involved in the process; strategy for planning and controlling the process; and, technologies supporting the process.

4   **Redesigning the processes** involves developing possible new alternatives to the way the processes work (**'to be' processes**). The redesign should focus on overcoming the key issues identified and aiming at filling the performance gaps. Principles of business process management should be taken into account, for example focusing the redesign within all the five key determining factor areas. Some tools, for example industry-based best practices, can offer an important support to redesign the process but, at the same time, it is important to rely on creativity and innovative efforts by the team working on the project of change (see Chapter 9 on creativity).

BPR is a method that provides a deep dive into the process redesign and diagnosis stages that are highlighted by planned change theories. Following the popularity of lean production in manufacturing – a management philosophy focused on cutting waste and improving quality – BPR was seen as a similar approach for management innovation issues. It became so trendy that many specific organizational changes (e.g. introduction of new IT systems, downsizing) were sometimes branded as BPR, regardless of whether they followed the BPR methodology directly. Many BPR projects failed mainly due to lack of vision, weak alignment with the strategy and poor management in terms of commitment and planning (Grover, 1999). Yet, BPR is still often in use particularly relating to introducing new IT systems in the public sector and is the basis of new public management – a popular recent approach to public service management which seeks to focus on making public service organizations more efficient and performance based.

Criticisms of the planned change approach

Planned change models are designed for a traditional top-down decision-making organization with **rigid rules in a stable environment**, which is predictable and controlled. The idea of moving from one stable state to another assumes that each state is environmentally stable. However, many now believe that, given the turbulent world we live in today, organizations are no longer self-contained entities; their actions are both affected by and influence the wider environment which limits the applicability of planned change approaches in modern organizations. Others have noted its lack of applicability in situations where **rapid**, radical or transformational change are needed. The process of extensive research and planning are a luxury that is not always available when change is needed in response to a threat or environmental change.

Critiques of the planned change approach note that it ignores power and politics within an organization. It **assumes that everyone will agree on the best course of action** and that common agreement can be reached through collaboration and communication. There is always the possibility that not all parties will be willing or interested in doing so.

Planned change is a **'one best way' style approach**. It assumes that one type of approach to change is suitable for all organizations, all situations and all times managers would benefit more from a model which was adaptable to a variety of situational or contingency factors. In this sense, the unique context of organizations is underplayed in the planned change approach. Instead, it focuses on a set of phases and assumes that if all organizations progress through these effectively, then the desired change will be successful – success being defined at the outset by those who instigate and made the decision to begin the change.

Recent research has warned of some of the dangers of investing too heavily in the unfreezing stages of planned change. Mantere et al. (2012), for example, found in their study of a Nordic public sector organization that when a merger had to be cancelled, the attempts to create dissatisfaction with the 'old' organizational form to create motivation for change left a residual bad feeling about the organization. Therefore, it serves as a reminder that attempts at planned change can be very hard to reverse.

2.3 Emergent Change Approach

The emergent change approach is a different take on the nature of change, how it should be studied and managed within organizations. Within this approach, a wide range of theories are presented, most of which focus on different issues. What brings these theories together is their shared criticism of the use of plans to manage change (in direct contrast to the planned approach). They argue that organizations are too complex to be viewed in this way and influenced by external factors: 'Successful change is less dependent on detailed plans and projections than on reaching an understanding of the complexity of the issues concerned and identifying the range of available options' (Burnes, 1996: 13).

In considering a range of emergent change theories, we find that they all have the same underpinning assumptions about change:

1   **Change is a continuous process** – organizations always need to be constantly adjusting to an *uncertain* environment.
2   It involves experimentation and adaptation aimed at matching an organization's **capabilities** to the **environment** (both of which are viewed as *dynamic and unpredictable*).
3   Large-scale change is achieved through a multitude of small-scale incremental changes, often led from the **bottom up** or including **both** top-down and bottom-up momentum.
4   The role of managers is not to plan or manage change but instead to **create or foster an organizational structure and climate** that encourages and sustains experimentation and risk-taking and to develop a workforce that will take responsibility for identifying the need for change and implementing it.
5   Developing a **collective vision or common purpose** gives direction to the organization and guides the appropriateness of any proposed change.

Therefore, unlike planned change, emergent change focuses on activities rather than stages of change. The key organizational activities that allow these elements to operate successfully are culture, structure, organizational learning, managerial behaviour and power and politics, each of which we will discuss in turn.

Culture

For emergent change theorists, strategic management of change is viewed as a cultural phenomenon. Cultural change is a slow and incremental process. Culture is a culmination of the habits, attitudes and patterns of behaviour that are typical of the organization (Schein, 2010). An organization at its heart is a social group of individuals who come together to deliver a mission; therefore, these individuals have shared experiences which develop into norms of behaviour and prioritize certain values over others.

Schein's (2010) theory identifies **three layers of culture** (Figure 2.3). Firstly the 'visible artefacts' layer which is the most visible and accessible aspects of culture. Artefacts include patterns of behaviour, structures, corporate logos and branding, organizational rituals, stories and symbols, control and reward systems and HRM practices (Melin et al., 2007). The second layer is the shared values that members of the organization have. Although less visible, these can be understood by studying group behaviour norms and beliefs about what is acceptable and unacceptable behaviour. These values are learned by new members through interaction with existing members over time. Finally, the third layer comprises the 'assumptions' that underpin organizational culture. These assumptions represent the understanding of the world and the way things work within the organization by organizational members. It is how they perceive their identity and place in the world. This is the least accessible layer of culture; it is difficult to see, yet is the most powerful and difficult to change. To change an organizational culture, you cannot simply change artefacts of the organization; real change will result in a change of values and assumptions that guide the future behaviour of organizational members.

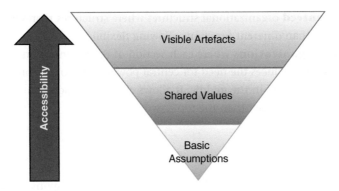

Figure 2.3 Schein's three layers of culture in organizations

Emergent change theorists tend to fall into two camps in their writings about organizational culture. Some focus on the challenge of culture change, arguing that it is unpredictable and difficult to achieve. Wilson (1992), for example, points out the non-linear relationship between culture and performance, warning that incremental changes that reinforce new values and assumptions are not guaranteed to reinforce a culture that is aligned with improved performance for the organization. Because culture change is slow and difficult to see, these changes can become quite advanced before the organization realizes that it has changed its culture in the wrong direction.

Another school of emergent change theorists has focused on how to create an organizational culture that facilitates change. This is sometimes referred to as creating a **'culture of change'** (Fullan, 2007), so that change, experimentation and innovation become norms that are valued within the organization. It becomes the norm for an organization to continuously change, update its methods, analyse its environment and evaluate its situation.

Structures

Emergent change theorists emphasize the **informal aspects** of the structure as much as the formal structure. Organizational structures represent the capabilities of an organization, and the relationship between different organizational sections and streams of work is an area where local-level innovation and change can develop. Instead of hierarchical decision-making, emergent change focuses on relationship building and collaboration.

These theorists support the general move towards flatter structures. A structure which devolves authority and responsibility will be more responsive to changing external factors. This might include:

- **customer-centred** organizational structures where structures represent different markets rather than different functions allowing flexibility;
- **networked organizations** where each section of the organization is semi-autonomous. This reduces the need for central power and avoids a big change-resistant 'lump' in the middle. It allows change and adaptation to be driven from the bottom up rather than the top down.

Organizational learning

Learning is the ability to develop new skills, identify appropriate responses and draw knowledge from their own and others' past and present actions. Proponents of emergent change argue that by allowing employees to learn about the organization, the external environment and factors which affect the running of the organization, they will develop a **shared ownership** of the organization's vision, actions and decisions and therefore work to improve it. There is a strong focus on **information-gathering**; that is, learning about the external environment and internal objectives and capabilities of the organization so that organizational members can better identify and recognize opportunities.

When people understand the challenges which the organization faces they will challenge existing norms and question established practices creating an opportunity for innovation and radical change. Rather than managers putting pressure on the employees to change, it becomes the opposite with the people within the organization pressurizing managers to change ineffective systems and asking fundamental questions.

Managerial behaviour

Managers need to operate as **facilitators** who bring together and motivate teams and groups who themselves identify the need for and carry out the change. They would take a more transactional role rather than the transformational role that the consultant would have with the planned change approach.

Managers must be prepared to challenge their own assumptions, attitudes and mindsets, and must be able to tolerate risk and cope with ambiguity through open and active communications. A key managerial skill will be to facilitate communication – the transmission of analysis and discussion of information to facilitate the learning of all organizational members.

Power and politics

Emergent change theorists criticize planned change for assuming that, given the right information, everyone will get on board with the change. All emergent change theorists deem power and politics to be essential in the success of change and believe that resistance to change is a normal and helpful response to change (e.g. Ford et al., 2008).

They advocate that change makers need to be politically astute within the organization. They will need to identify power sources and utilize them to bring about change through **engagement or influence**. We discuss these ideas much more in Chapter 8, which is on power and resistance.

Within the emergent change approach, change is not viewed as a linear process but instead is often messy and occurs with ebbs and flows, sometimes moving quickly and other times consolidating and appearing stagnant – possibly taking wrong turns or exploring avenues that turn out not to hold potential.

Criticisms of the emergent change approach

The emergent change theories are more often grouped together because of their scepticism of the planned approach rather than their agreement on a particular set of ideas or strategies. For example, where some theorists talk of continuous small incremental change, others differentiate between so-called '10 per cent' changes and fine tuning (Nadler and Tushman, 1989). Some believe change to be a cyclical process and others on a long continuum. This **lack of consistency** can make it difficult to determine concrete and practical actions that organizations should take if they wish to direct and manage change.

All of the theories assume that all organizations operate in a turbulent, dynamic, unpredictable environment. In practice, not all organizations face the **same levels of turbulence** and instability; while some operate in a closed or contained environment others may be constantly subjected to unpredictable surprises (Burnes, 1996). In some cases it is possible to manipulate the external environment; after all, not only are organizations affected by the external factors, they also have an influence on them.

There is a lot of emphasis on developing a culture of change which has proven to be extremely difficult to achieve. In addition a culture of learning may eventually result in an abundance of experience and knowledge in particular areas, leading to a bias towards certain strategies which have been previously successful, and a **lack of innovation** – there will be little incentive to use new methods when we have already perfected what works.

Managers are expected to challenge their own beliefs and values based on years of experience to allow for new and innovative ideas to be brought forward from the bottom up. Not only might they find this extremely difficult but **managerial resistance** might be a positive thing. Managers often have superior knowledge and experience which is valuable to the change process.

Planned versus emergent change

Both planned and emergent change have benefits in certain circumstances and, in choosing between approaches, organizations must make trade-offs and be aware of the possible consequences of their choice. Table 2.2 presents a summary of the advantages and disadvantages of each approach.

Table 2.2 Comparing planned and emergent change

Planned Change	Emergent Change
Advantages	
• Planning and budgeting opportunities • Engagement opportunities • Get it right first time (build confidence) • Well researched	• More responsive to environment/competitors • Often bottom-up change based on front-line innovations • Less intensive impact for recipients of change
Disadvantages	
• Assumes environmental stability • Ignores power and politics • Not applicable to situations that need rapid change • It is a 'one best way' approach • Limited flexibility	• More difficult to develop strategy • Over-focused on power and politics (often driven by them) • Organizational culture is treated as malleable • Ignores managerial resistance • Ignores choice • Change fatigue • Impact of failure (mistrust)

A popular, holistic approach to change is organizational development (OD). As we describe in Box 2.3, OD often combines both planned and emergent change factors.

─Box 2.3─

Organizational development

Organizational development is an integrated framework of theories and practices used to solve important problems within the human side of organizations – through planned organizational change, OD seeks to get individuals, teams and organizations to function better (French and Bell, 1995).

In organizational development, particular attention is devoted to the ways the changes are implemented and on the social factors of the organization, with the aim to improve the ability of the organization itself to adapt and be effective. Worley and Feyerherm (2003) suggest three criteria to identify organizational development: (1) it must focus on or result in the change of some aspect of the organizational system; (2) there must be learning or the transfer of knowledge or skill to the client system; and (3) there must be evidence of improvement in or an intention to improve the effectiveness of the client system.

OD is based on five values which should be prescribed to by practitioners (Hurley et al., 1992):

- **Empower employees to act** – to make them feel that they have the chance and power to influence the outcomes of the change.

- **Create openness in communications** – so everybody knows the purpose and status of the change process.
- **Facilitate ownership** of the change process and its outcomes – thereby making each employee feel that they have an important role to play in the change and that an achievement for the organization is an achievement for them too.
- **Promote a culture of collaboration** – bringing employees together on tasks to benefit the organization.
- **Promote continuous learning** of skills – which will benefit both the organization and the individual in the future. In order for the organization to change and grow, members of the organization will have to adapt and change as well, learning new skills as they go.

Throughout its 70-plus-year history, OD as a framework for organizational change has evolved in various ways. OD has gone in and out of fashion within organizations as a focus for managing organizational change. Initially, throughout the 1960–70s OD was considered a practical enactment of the core planned change movement, building on Lewin's work and adapting it for organizational practice. However, in the 1980–90s the emergent change movement had brought to the fore challenges for dynamic and unstable organizations.

Bernard Burnes (2004a) has been influential in studying and critiquing the history and evolution of the OD movement throughout its various iterations and has identified some notable changes.

Firstly, OD has developed a more results-focused approach. One of the reasons for OD's success has been its use in translating change theory into practical and action orientated frameworks, popular with entrepreneurial and pragmatic practitioners. These practitioners have needed to demonstrate its appeal to companies whose primary interest is commercial gain. This has led to more focus on hard data and evidence being needed and a more results-focused approach.

Secondly, whilst OD originally focused on workgroups in an organizational setting, the rise in the job design movement (1960s) made OD practitioners recognize that looking at individuals and groups was insufficient and that it was necessary to look at organizations in their totality within their environments. The popularity of the approach – especially in the US – has led to application on organizational problems of increasing size; it now focuses on transforming the whole organization rather than the organization as a series of workgroups. Responding to increasing turbulence in the external environment has refocused the attention of OD to transform organizations in their totality rather than focusing on changes of their parts. With this, original recognition of the importance of group norms and values grew into increasing concern for organizational culture, including cultural transformations. Recent iterations of OD have adopted some of the ideas of the systems approach to change which allows it to look at organizations in their totality and within their environments. However,

(Continued)

Burnes (2004a) and other writers have claimed that the more OD focuses on these macro issues, the less able it is to offer real individual choice which was at the core of its humanist and democratic origins.

Finally, and somewhat in conjunction with the increasing concern for organizational culture, this organization-wide perspective caused OD practitioners to develop an interest in organizational learning. Learning through action research is a feature taken from Lewin and many of its principles still apply in OD; however, by combining this with rising human resource management (HRM) and human resource development (HRD) movements, the scope of research and learning within the planned change model has been widened to include learning and knowledge exchange from one change project to another. Individuals with skills and abilities in implementing change are now especially valuable to organizations and there is more focus on developing these skills through education and training than ever before.

2.4 Systems Approach

Systems thinking refers to a range of systems theories across many disciplines. Here, we consider its impact for organizational systems. A systems-thinking approach looks at how things influence one another (Wang, 2004). Components of a system are best understood in the context of their relationships with other components, rather than in isolation. Therefore, this approach views organizations as complex dynamic systems that follow a set of goal-orientated processes.

A central consideration in systems thinking is acknowledging and understanding how components of the system are related to each other; in other words, what is the knock-on effect of changing one thing? Most change theories study the best way to change one component in a system in the best way; some consider more than one but treat multiple components either in blocks where everything changes together in one 'lump' (e.g. planned change), or focus on individual incremental changes as small stepping-stones (e.g. emergent change). In systems theory the focus is on the **relationships between components** rather than the components themselves. This means considering the potential magnifying, minimizing or cumulative effect of changes to other aspects of the organization. For example, changing an information technology software may be an intense but relatively planned and straightforward change for the technology team, but the work process-related changes that are needed by other organizational departments that now need to retrieve and manage data for the new system in a different way may be much larger, create longer-term disruption, and even challenge logistical work patterns and the power relationships within teams. It is only by understanding the magnifying relationship between IT systems and work practice that we can really understand and manage this change in organizations.

A system is made up of a set of habits or common practices that govern its actions – a 'common code' by which the system works (Katz and Kahn, 1978). Relationships between components can be viewed through interactions of organizational members. Of particular importance are the use of information, group dynamics and norms, and how the motives of different stakeholders align. Systems theorists are often associated with organizational communications or organizational learning theories (Kotter, 2012; Senge, 1990). Change management encourages communication between different departments of the organization, between different professional groups and between different organizational levels.

Equally important is to encourage communication with external stakeholders and the environment. Systems approaches focus on encouraging organizational members to gain knowledge of the environment and learn and adapt, to find innovative ways to adapt to the organizational environment. Systems theories focus on how different elements of the system contribute towards equilibrium in the wider system by focusing on interdependencies (Martinelli, 2001). A systems approach will consider how the change will be enacted for each of the organization's functions (e.g. finances, operations, sales, service delivery, etc.) and then consider the implications of this for other functions. The process of change is to continue to circulate through functions and consider the interrelationship between them until post-change alignment is found. This is to avoid the silo-effect created by most change, when the implications of changes are considered only within the group of organizational members who are directly affected by them.

Complexity theory

Drawing from the systems perspective complexity theory is an example of the theorization for explaining organizational growth and behaviour and therefore a version of this perspective most related to organizational change management. Complexity theory views the organization as a dynamic system. To grow and develop it must shift away from its status quo or equilibrium to take advantage of opportunities. Therefore, complexity theory encourages a certain amount of disequilibrium.

Disequilibrium is an important factor in organizational growth and development. We have discussed this idea previously; for example, Lewin's field theory describes a field of influence on individual behaviour made up of driving and restraining forces that are in constant flux. Similarly, in Chapter 1 we talked about organizations transitioning through a period of incoherence and instability in order to transform (Greenwood and Hinings, 1988). Complexity theory explores this more deeply at an organizational level and explores ways that this can be managed. All the systems within the internal structure of the organization interact with their environment (e.g. cultures, communities, individuals and groups) and through this they import energy from these surroundings which influence the system within (Yeow and Jackson, 2006). Therefore, change is continuous and incremental, driven by forces in the environment rather than within.

Organizations are **complex, non-linear** systems in which change emerges through a process of spontaneous self-organization. Complexity theory acknowledges that systems are also unpredictable and there is a fine line between growth and chaos. On the one hand, no change equals no growth but, on the other, too much change equals chaos. In other words, to achieve organizational change, the organization must step outside of its comfort zone and take risks in order to make opportunities happen, but 'the key to survival is to develop rules which are capable of keeping an organization operating "**on the edge of chaos**"' (Burnes, 2004b). The question, then, is how can this be achieved?

Lissack (1999) argues that no matter how dynamic and unpredictable outcomes might seem there is always some **underlying logic** or simplicity which can be found under large quantities of analysis. When you collect enough data, patterns and trends will emerge – once viewed with sufficient detachment, large volumes of data can reveal very simple patterns. These patterns are often buried under many layers of complexity and are not subject to time periods. In principle this means that a pattern may take years or even decades to emerge; however, in most cases, as long as the behaviour of a sufficient number and range of organizational actors within a system is observed, patterns are revealed more quickly.

Therefore, organizations that aim for innovation and novelty are often successful but risk falling over the edge of chaos (Frederick, 1998) – the challenge is to survive the chaos period!

Complexity theory suggests two key aspects of the organization are necessary in order for change to be successful.

1 Opportunity for self-organization

Dynamic systems are constantly changing – these transformations are like evolutionary growth. Change is necessary – as the environment changes, those who survive are the ones who adapt best to the new environment (Stacey, 1996). This process will involve trial and error, and constant adjustment, but is characterized by constantly moving forward (change is irreversible). Emergence is the process by which patterns of behaviour arise from the interaction of local-level processes and agents interacting according to their own local order-generating rules.

When complex dynamic systems experience periods of instability, the system will eventually reach a critical point where it will self-organize. Over a longer period of time certain global rules will emerge and be applied. Self-organization is a process where previous patterns of behaviour transform into a new structure of behaviour which is more appropriate to the new conditions. 'Self organizing principles explicitly reject cause and effect, top-down, command and control styles of management' (Burnes, 2005: 82). In other words, organizations in flux need to be left alone, there needs to be trust in the process and organizational leaders need to have faith that it will self-organize.

2 Order-generating rules

Brown and Eisenhardt (1997) suggest that organizations need semi-structures. These allow change to be organized but innovation and experimentation is still encouraged. Change management 'requires constant vigilance to avoid slipping into pure chaos or pure structure' (Brown and Eisenhardt, 1997: 29). They suggest that this could be done by enforcing a few simple rules referred to as order-generating rules. In their study, Brown and Eisenhardt (1997) found that the most successful organizations were neither intentionally incremental nor transformational in their processes of change. Instead, managers talked of *constantly reinventing themselves*. This would support the ideas of complexity theory as reinvention allows the organization to adapt to the environmental factors around it.

Underlying order-generating rules keep the emergence of new ideas within set parameters and provide an opportunity for direction from within the organization; however, it is important not to plan or predict behaviours and structures – they must be left to evolve naturally.

Criticisms of the systems approach

The systems approach to change argues that organizations are complex adaptive systems, most impacted by the connections between components of the systems (e.g. patterns of behaviour, relationships between groups of actors and the cause–effect implications of changing processes). This approach is useful for highlighting aspects of change that have previously been overlooked and explain many of the previous ambiguity and 'unpredictable' outcomes of change management practitioners' experience in trying to manage change. However, as an approach to change management it is not without its limitations.

Similar to the emergent change approach, complexity theory also assumes that change is driven from the environment, which is viewed as being turbulent, dynamic and unpredictable. Therefore, the same criticisms that it may not be the case that organizations face the **same levels of turbulence** and instability can also be applied to systems approaches to change.

The biggest criticism levied at the complexity theory of change, however, is the uncertainty in identifying underlying logics that govern patterns of behaviour. The approach relies, on the one hand, on keen observation of the behaviour of organizational members to identify patterns (albeit without knowing when enough data will allow accurate patterns to emerge) and, on the other, a hands-off approach to allowing self-organization. From a change management perspective, it can be difficult to know when and how manipulation of the system is needed (Yoon and Kuchinke, 2005) and achieving this balance may feel frustrating and anxiety provoking – waiting for self-organization to happen whilst experiencing chaos. In this sense, it might be more helpful to view systems approaches as more appropriate for the study of change than the management of it.

2.5 Process Approach

The final approach to change that we consider in this chapter is the process approach. Process theories are concerned with what happens in practice when change plans are put into action. Process approaches position change and movement at the cornerstone of implementation. From this perspective, change success results from local interpretation that occurs during interactions between organizational members. We are therefore interested in how employees perceive, interpret and understand a change.

Authors who have focused on process approaches to policy and change implementation (e.g. Candel and Biesbroek, 2016; Tucker et al., 2022) draw on four core principles of processual assumptions:

1   Implementation is **asynchronous**, fraught with discrepancies and time lags as different individuals and groups within and beyond the organization take small steps and partial moves towards implementation.

2   The change implementation process is **non-linear** – therefore there may be movement away from the desired objectives as well as towards them as problems are encountered or objectives and priorities change. For example, changes in the external environment may mean that a decided course of action becomes less likely to succeed and an alternative way to achieve the desired goals needs to be found.

3   Different parties in the implementation process have **mutual dependencies** – their actions impact other parts of the system. Most likely, they will have multiple, conflicting objectives and responsibilities (for example, they may have a responsibility to look after the wellbeing of subordinates, yet still need to delegate stressful tasks to them to improve organizational metrics.

4   **Actors** play a crucial role in shaping institutional change. It is their behaviours that will develop new norms and set an example to others. It is the replication and reinforcement of these behaviours that drives culture change from the bottom up.

Agency

Process perspectives are often routed in social constructionism – a perspective that our conceptualization of the world is a product of human construction and interpretation – and pays particular attention to the construction of meaning within organizations (e.g. theories of discourse or sense-making). Change can be planned or emerge incrementally, but is always subject to constant adjustment, modifications and local adaptation, which has longer-term consequences. Process perspectives question the assumption that how a change is planned determines how it happens in practice and process theorists would argue that there is a limit to the extent that change can be designed. People in organizations, who have their own intentions and ability to make decisions about their behaviour (agency), influence change through their enactment of change behaviour. Their actions are powerful and cannot be dictated.

Any kind of change implementation requires discretion, where organizational actors must interpret strategy and determine the actions that they need to take. This applies to all organizational members but change makers, in particular, are powerful role models that others will look to for interpretation of what behaviours are valid and expected. In day-to-day practice, the behaviour of organizational members is influenced by their personal beliefs, values and norms, and these can override adherence to any rules, procedures or training; therefore, understanding change makers' processes of interpretation is important to understand change implementation (see Fotaki and Hyde, 2015). A study of organizational change in response to public policy over an eight-year period explored the role of organizational change makers in shaping the implementation of change in two local authorities (Tucker et al., 2022). It found that change makers interact with each other within a social system; they take cues from discussion with peers and the collective enactment of change as they interpret it. The consistency (or lack thereof) of their interactions will produce episodes of misalignment or cohesion that further shape behaviour. For example, in seeing a positive reaction of senior management to how one change maker is addressing a problem, other change makers are more likely to address subsequent problems in a similar way.

Context

The actions of people in organizations are influenced by context. Pettigrew and Whipp (1991) distinguish between two different levels of context. The inner context refers to the structural, cultural and political environment individuals experience within the organization. The outer context refers to the economic, social and political context in which the organization operates within a wider network. Any agency that is exhibited by organizational members takes place within a context, where these dynamics influence the decisions and actions that are available and desirable. For example, whilst an individual may wish to dedicate time to supporting organizational change activities within their organization, in a situation where workload and responsibility for day-to-day tasks is high, they may lack the resources (time and energy) to take that desired action.

Therefore, change is also a political process. No matter how much effort is given to top-down communication, the objectives of change are never obvious or unambiguous in terms of how people in organizations view them. Unlike other change approaches, process theories recognize and embrace pluralism of interests – different actors have different desires to push their own interests using various means of power. Power may be expressed via: (a) resource allocation; (b) status and position; and (c) opportunities, for example career progression. The actions of organizational members are shaped by context, and agency shapes context.

Time

Process theories also acknowledge that any organizational change has a history which may be represented by myths, stories and organizational dogma within an organization (Sveningsson and Sörgärde, 2019). In this way, process theories pay particular attention to the temporal aspects of change; for example, how change is viewed when looking back, in the moment and imagined in the future are likely to be different (Pettigrew, 1992). Studying change in a more longitudinal and process-orientated way can also reveal discrepancies in the timeline of different actors or time lags – for example, episodes where actors come together to create cohesion or divergence that results in misalignment of activities (Tucker et al., 2022).

An example of showing the role of time and processes comes from a study by Denis et al. (2011) where they present a case study of a hospital merger. Decision-making about the future of the merged hospital is subject to the decision-makers' ability to work together to agree a strategy for moving forward. Over time they identified two processes:

1 Reification: where members of the group engage in practices to create shared meaning or create symbolic value to what the group is trying to achieve. This process is helpful in achieving irreversibility to collective projects by focusing on binding the interests of different parties together; for example, the establishment of a protocol for how different interests should be represented.

2 Strategic ambiguity: aims to create space where individual decision-makers retain their own views whilst making collective decisions; for example, postponing the finer points of an implementation plan (such as allocation of resources, definitive numbers) to a later discussion.

Denis et al. (2011) found that indecision escalated over time when reification and strategic ambiguity interact. The consequences were that the partners were bound to the relationship even when it was no longer serving the organization and a new approach was needed (reification) and strategic ambiguity masked the reality of the divergence, leading to inconclusive decisions that, instead of providing a clear vision to move forward, created a need for further decision-making as the change progressed. What a process approach reveals here is the cumulative effect of these processes over time, where repetition of both practices created an untenable and irreversible position that led to stagnation.

Bringing together these three elements of context, time and agency (see Figure 2.4), process theories are particularly relevant when considering the role of change makers operating from within organizations. Process theories help to understand the mechanisms of implementation of change by focusing on the behaviour of individuals within organizations.

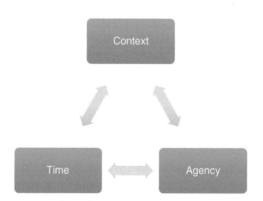

Figure 2.4 Three components of process approaches to change

Criticisms of a process approach

The process approach to studying organizational change is not without its limitations. As with all approaches, it brings certain aspects of organizational dynamics to the fore whilst focusing on other aspects less. The first criticism is that the plurality of views that process approaches acknowledge make it difficult to define and ascertain change success. We discussed in Chapter 1 how change success will be different for different stakeholder groups. Whilst some organizational leaders may be focused on the strategic and financial outcomes of change, those experiencing change may not feel that their experience reflects this success and outcomes may have become more negative.

Process approaches place a lot of emphasis on the observation that the end solution will be different from what was intended for the change or even needed by the organization. This is particularly problematic where a very specific change outcome is required. But, more broadly, it can be difficult to accept and embrace this uncertainty about how the journey may unfold and where it will lead. It requires organizational leaders to give autonomy to organizational members who will implement change, and trust that the direction of travel will be for the benefit of the organization. There will always be a temptation to try to guide implementation and, in doing so, there is a fine line between excessive managerial control and unifying organizational members to enact a shared vision.

Understanding organizational change from a process perspective requires a longitudinal approach to examining change. This makes it harder to compare and contrast experiences of different organizations to determine universal lessons learnt. The importance of context and situational agency means that no two change initiatives will be the same. The need to understand change from a range of experiences and perspectives (e.g. leadership intentions, front-line employee interpretation, external stakeholder influences) make it hard for those within the organization to gain a full and unbiased understanding of how change is progressing. Outside observers (e.g. from academic researcher or change management consultants) may be able to obtain a fuller picture of the change process and therefore opportunities to listen to this perspective will be crucial for good change management.

Chapter Summary

- Kurt Lewin developed the **three-step model** of change as a founding method of the **planned change approach**. Other authors have produced revised or new models of planned change with various phases. They all view change as something which is premeditated and consciously embarked upon, has clear finite objectives, an end goal and is a cyclical process where an organization must complete one cycle of change before beginning another.

- **Emergent change theories** argue that organizations are too complex to be viewed in this way and **influenced by external factors**. They view change as a continuous process, often led from the bottom up. Emergent change focuses on activities rather than stages of change such as culture, structures, organizational learning, managerial behaviour, and the influence of power and politics.

- In the **systems approach**, the importance of disequilibrium as a significant factor in organizational growth and development is highlighted by complexity theory. Organizations are non-linear systems, in which change emerges through a process of spontaneous self-organization. Opportunities to **self-organize** and **order-generating rules** can help an organization balance on the 'edge of chaos'.

- **Process approaches** argue that change success results from local interpretation that occurs during interactions between organizational members. Bringing together three elements of **context, time and agency**, process theories help to understand the mechanisms of implementation of change by focusing on the behaviour of individuals within organizations.

Activity

As we have seen in this chapter, different organizational changes may benefit from being approached in different ways. Consider the mini-case study (in Box 2.4 below) and discuss the following questions:

1   What approach to change has the organization taken in the past? To what extent has that worked for them?
2   What are the key challenges the organization, managers and change makers face now?
3   What approach(es) to change (planned, emergent, systems, process) might be helpful to think about this organization moving forward?

Note you can apply these discussion questions to the mini-cases from Chapter 1 (see Boxes 1.3 and 1.4) and to all other examples of change and case studies in this book as a starting point to understand the organization and its change context.

Box 2.4

GLC Logistics

GLC Logistics is a Canadian partner of a multinational wholesale logistics company (headquartered in the USA) employing approximately 300 employees, and is one of the leading distributors and service providers for IT and consumer electronics in Canada. The organization has worked with a number of high-profile brands such as HP, Lexmark, Samsung and Vodafone to offer purchasing, warehousing, packaging, project management and information services for consumers. Throughout 2015 and 2016 they had been leading the way in growth terms, expanding profit margins and premises across the country. To accommodate this growth, there had already been a series of incremental changes within the organization to cope with the growth over the previous three years. Senior leaders recognized that new, innovative ideas were needed to manage the growth within the organization but were happy to leave division leaders and middle-manager budget holders to implement change at the local level, allowing departments and individual employees to come up with solutions to the challenges that were most pressing for them.

These changes included:

- Individual employees developed and sold bespoke client packages to win new contracts.
- Two teams reorganized their work into shifts to extend the support office hours they could offer to consumers.
- One department invested significant resource in providing specialist training for all its team members in a new technology that they planned to offer services for.
- Another department had piloted and then moved to fully remote working for its members.
- The warehouse team tested and implemented a new stock rotation system that reduced waste and helped keep track of inventory.
- The sales team underwent major restructuring of their personnel, redistributing client relationship management relationships into industry specialist clusters.

Each of these initiatives was pitched and then given support by middle managers – as long as an identifiable problem and proposed solution was offered, managers were generally supportive and allowed small groups of employees to pilot these new initiatives and, if they worked, to keep them. The extent of the change experienced by employees varied greatly from employee to employee. For some employees they had new co-workers or working conditions, others had been promoted, others had new job roles or responsibilities.

However, with so many small changes happening simultaneously, problems were starting to emerge. There were grumblings from staff members who felt that they were being treated unfairly, and that other staff were being offered preferable work contracts and conditions (e.g. flexible working, development opportunities). Staff turnover was beginning to increase with exiting employees citing too much uncertainty and work intensification as reasons for leaving. Customers were beginning to express dissatisfaction that competitors were being offered 'special discounts', and relationship managers felt they were being pressured to offer services that they were unable to fulfil. This concern was shared by customer support who were dealing with increasing complaints.

Further Recommended Reading

For a contemporary appraisal of Lewin's theories of change, see Burnes, B. (2004b) 'Kurt Lewin and the planned approach to change: A re-appraisal', *Journal of Management Studies*, 41(6): 977–1002.

To further explore OD in recent times, see Worley, C. and Feyerherm, A. (2003) 'Reflections on the Future of OD', *Journal of Applied Behavioral Science*, 39: 97–115.

For a more in-depth exploration of concepts of complexity theory as these are enacted in organizations, see Brown, S.L. and Eisenhardt, K.M. (1997) 'The art of continuous change: Linking complexity theory and time-paced evolution in relentlessly shifting organizations', *Administrative Science Quarterly*, 42(1): 1–34.

For a case study example of how organizational and policy process evolution impacts change, see Tucker, D.A., Hendy, J. and Chrysanthaki, T. (2022) 'How does policy alienation develop? Exploring street-level bureaucrats' agency in policy context shift in UK telehealthcare', *Human Relations*, 75(9), 1679–706.

3

THE ROLE OF STRATEGY AND THE EXTERNAL ENVIRONMENT IN DRIVING CHANGE

Chapter Objectives

- To understand how strategy is created in organizations and how this informs change
- To examine the different drivers for organizational change and how these influence organizations
- To highlight some of the current central challenges in the external environment that are driving change in twenty-first-century organizations
- To explore the role of change makers in creating and implementing organizational strategy

3.1 Introduction

So far, in this opening part of the book, we have discussed what organizational change is and how it might transform an organization in many ways (Chapter 1); we have also explored a variety of different approaches to viewing and studying change in organizations (Chapter 2). It is also important to acknowledge factors such as the external environment, organizational strategy and the diagnosis of problems/drivers for change.

This chapter presents a wider narrative about external drivers and influences of change and how these might impact on change makers in their implementation of change. We will argue that these contextual factors are an indirect, yet important concern for change makers. In the first part of the chapter, we will explore the strategic context of change management. We will explore how business strategy is developed and different ways to approach strategy in organizations. We will especially discuss the balance between internal aspects of organizational strategy – balancing multiple aspects of strategy and internal stakeholder influences – and situating strategy within a dynamic external market.

In the second part of the chapter, we will explore the challenge of strategic change and how business strategy informs change management. In particular, we will discuss the process to manage change strategically. Finally, we will consider the influence that change makers can have on organizational strategy and how they can manage these whilst implementing change.

3.2 The Strategic Context of Change Management

Strategy is a concept long used in business management to understand and situate an organization purposefully within the external environment. Business strategy is made up of two key characteristics: (i) an environmental or situational analysis; and (ii) the goal-orientated use of resources (Bracker, 1980).

Corporate or business strategy is a representation of an organization's mission, objectives and values (Alegre et al., 2018). It outlines who the organization is, how it creates value and how it differentiates itself from other organizations. A strategy is then used as a guiding principle for decision-making. For example, how much of our resource do we allocate to certain activities, how do we price and market our products and services, and what are our priorities when it comes to our people and organizational structure?

External environment

One of the most popular frameworks for environmental scanning is the PEST analysis developed by Aguilar (1967). This method argues that organizations should examine four key macro-environmental factors to gather knowledge that may enhance or restrain how an organization operates within its external environment. Below we will discuss these four factors and discuss how they may be drivers for organizational change.

P – Political: Political factors relate to the interventions of government and other political players which intervene or interact with organizations. Organizations may be driven to make adjustments **following legislative, policy or regulatory changes** in their industry. For example, a need to comply with new regulatory standards or audit processes. A change in legislation or taxation may impact the ability of an organization to make profit and they may need to make changes to supply chains, raw materials, employment contracts or production as a result. For example, in April 2022 the UK introduced a Plastic Packaging Tax[1] to UK manufacturers, importers and business customers who use plastic packaging that does not contain at least 30 per cent recycled plastic. This policy change has led to behaviour change in businesses, encouraging the use of more recycled plastic. Businesses also had to introduce new administrative/financial processes to measure and declare the use of plastic resources and this has obvious cost for organizations.

E – Economic: Economic factors relate to ways the environment might impact on the organization's ability to grow and make profit. This may include **inflation rates and economic growth**. Different industries may be differently affected by economic conditions.

An organization may wish to reposition itself within a market, becoming more competitive by offering better value for money or a unique product. They may wish to move or enter a new market in another geographical location or a new product area. Similarly, shifts within the current market may require an organization to respond by making changes to retain an established position – for example, if two key competitors merge and are able to achieve better economies of scale and cheaper prices for consumers; or if a key competitor leaves the marketplace, an organization may wish to scale up their production to meet demand resulting from their exit.

S – Social: Social change in what the population deems to be valuable and important is an important factor of the external environment. For example, **changing social attitudes** to health or travel may lead to changes in how people wish to spend their money, resulting in an expansion of some markets and reduced demand in others. Social drivers can relate to changes in the places where people live and work. For example, the availability of resources to them. Different generations will have had different life experiences and their expectations will be shaped by these.

This affects the labour market in which an organization recruits its employees. The **attitudes of employees** (or potential employees who they seek to attract) may also drive change in an organization. Lumbreras and Campbell (2020) have found that different generations of employees have different personality characteristics and values. For example, millennials are found to seek more satisfaction from their work but also to value more work–life balance rewards such as leisure time. In the voluntary sector McGinnis Johnson and Ng (2016) found that despite being purported as being more materialistic, millennials were not more likely to switch sectors for money alone; instead, promotion and advancement opportunities are more important than pay for keeping millennial managers. They found that

---

[1]www.gov.uk/government/publications/introduction-of-plastic-packaging-tax-from-april-2022/introduction-of-plastic-packaging-tax-2021 (accessed 28 November 2023).

those who remain longer in the charity sector become more emotionally attached to the mission and values of the organization and the bigger picture of the impact of the work they have undertaken. Organizations need to respond to these changes in their workforce in order to make the workplace an appealing place to work, by adjusting the values that underpin the employment contract, the nature of work and roles within the company. A recent report from the Chartered Management Institute (CMI, 2020) found that 'Gen Z' individuals are especially concerned with job security. Managing and responding to changes in employee wants and needs can be especially challenging for organizations where multiple generations are employed as changes to suit one generation may disrupt the established psychological contract with other generations.

T – Technological: Organizations in all sectors are increasingly responding to drivers which implicate technology-related change, or what is coming to be understood as 'digital transformation'. This is true of SMEs selling products in online marketplaces, to public sector services, non-profits making digital data for funders (P.R. Kelly, 2018), or multinationals coordinating teams around the world. These changes are being implemented by technology and non-technology companies with different levels of success (Westerman et al., 2014), with some arguing that non-technology companies have to become technology companies to do digital transformation right (Saldanha, 2019).

Information technology-based change has been happening for decades (Avgerou, 2002; Castells and Cardoso, 1996; Zuboff, 1988), responding to needs such as automation, modernization, competitiveness, efficiency, effectiveness, and opportunities for innovation and disruption (Christensen et al., 2011). The need to become digital involves incremental processes, such as **developing digital capabilities**, **digitization and digitalization** (see Chapter 6). Full digital transformation is driven by many factors, including: streamlining operations; new business models and channels to capture new value; improving customer experiences and brand loyalty enhancement; integrating existing organizational IT systems; maximizing benefits from digital data (e.g. insights, analytics, big data, cloud computing, social media, mobile); and, altering customer behaviours and expectations (Vial, 2019). Critical drivers are becoming more evident in recent years, such as employee wellbeing, digital inclusion, social and sustainability reporting, although these are not prioritized in digital transformation literature to date.

Globalization is often cited as a key driver of major changes in organizations. To compete, businesses need to increase productivity, reach new markets and make use of different resources. Globalization itself is driven by economic and social forces such as technological change, international economic integration and the maturation of markets in developed countries (Kotter, 2012), meaning that all organizations, not simply those who seek multinational status, are impacted by globalization. Globalization creates more opportunities for organizations, fewer barriers to reaching new customers and bigger markets to expand into, yet also creates more obstacles to overcome, such as more competition, and a need for increased speed in product innovation, delivery and decision-making. Organizations may need to undertake restructuring or introduce a change culture. They may need to introduce new programmes of work or new strategic directions, or they may need to merge or acquire other organizations to become a stronger competitor, avoid such hazards or take advantage of these opportunities (Kotter, 1995a).

Boxes 3.1 and 3.2 present key examples of two contemporary external issues affecting organizations and driving change.

—Box 3.1—

Current external issues affecting organizations: climate emergency

Organizations and societies have been concerned about the effects of global warming on the Earth's population for some time amidst increasing scientific evidence of increases in greenhouse gases, expanding desert regions and heat waves, as well as melting permafrost in the Arctic. Recently, there has been increasing action by scientists, governments and organizations to declare a climate emergency. This action seeks to acknowledge their support of the existence of climate change and affirm a view that global actions, up until this point, have been insufficient. Through this declaration institutions articulate a commitment to taking actions to reduce climate change with urgency and above other organizational goals; by definition, this means changing the way they operate and behave. Inevitably, then, climate emergency is now a major driver of organizational change affecting sustainability strategies, energy use, remote working, diversity and inclusion, corporate social responsibility, talent sourcing and HR.

Even for organizations who themselves do not declare a climate emergency, the prevalence of this practice by government bodies means that they are unlikely to avoid pressures from the external environment to make changes. Environment policies may include restrictions on air or water pollution; waste management regulation; transportation, taxes or levies related to the use of certain materials (e.g. single use plastics) or the banning of toxic substances or their use (e.g. pesticides, petrol and diesel). This may mean that the most cost-effective way to use resources to create products or services may no longer be available to organizations (or they may cease being the most cost effective) and new methods will need to be developed. This requires considerable change and innovation from organizations to find the most suitable alternative for their individual goals.

As understanding of climate change issues grows amongst the wider population, demand for sustainable and climate conscious products and services is also growing. Many consumers are now conscious of their own carbon footprint and will take this into consideration when purchasing products. There is growing research that finds that company spending on socially responsible activities can lead to better financial performance, profitability and better brand image (e.g. Khojastehpour and Johns, 2014; Okafor et al., 2021). This too serves as a strong driver of change in organizations both in terms of their actual practices and in the way they present themselves in a market environment.

Box 3.2

Current external issues affecting organizations: COVID-19 global pandemic

The COVID-19 (also known as the coronavirus) pandemic was declared a public health emergency of international concern from January 2020 until May 2023. As of 14 May 2023, over 766 million confirmed cases and over 6.9 million deaths have been reported globally (WHO, 2023), making this pandemic one of the deadliest in history. It has triggered severe social and economic disruption around the world. During and since, organizations have had to rapidly rethink how work should be carried out across the globe.

Organizations and workers have been affected, and are still being affected, in a variety of different ways. For some organizations, the outbreak responses such as lockdowns/stay at home orders left them unable to trade for a period of time. At various stages alternative business models may have been rapidly introduced to allow work to be resumed in some capacity (for example, restaurants offering delivery services). Many employees may have been furloughed and, depending on the organization's ability to recover or adapt, there may have been redundancies or significant changes to work contracts. For many employees, the nature of employee support needed may have changed as a result of the pandemic; for example, family support when children or loved ones are out of school or unwell has become a key factor (Daniels et al., 2022).

For other organizations, the pandemic prompted rapid changes in the location and format of work (e.g. remote working). This resulted in significant changes in work relationships, use of digital systems and work–life dynamics. Research has found that perceived organizational support and supervisor accessibility during the pandemic had a significant effect on employees' commitment to the organization (Mihalache and Mihalache, 2022). For many employees this may have resulted in permanent adaptation of their work, for example continued hybrid or at-home working, that will have affected individuals in different ways. The pandemic has exposed many inequalities and inconsistencies within society and the way we work. School closures placed a heavier burden on parents; and those with physical or mental health conditions may have struggled more with isolation. Every employee will have experienced challenges during the pandemic, but these will be different for each person. Likewise, the coping strategies which employees have available to them will be varied. There is no one-size-fits-all approach to employee support (Daniels et al., 2022) but organizations who have supported employees well will find it easier to retain existing talent and attract the best employees to work for them in the aftermath of the pandemic.

Finally, for some organizations who employ key or essential workers, the pandemic led to a significant increase in demand for their products or services. This includes industries involved in the direct response to the pandemic (e.g. health workers), where the perceived responsibility and scrutiny increased. Essential workers also noticed an increase in the need to deal with ambiguity in regulations and 'red tape' that have increased stress and workload (van Zoonen and ter Hoeven, 2022).

When it comes to organizational change management, the pandemic may have acted as a catalyst for change, created a sense of urgency and enabled outdated processes to be altered with little opportunity for resistance. In the aftermath, it will be important for organizations to take some time to reflect on these changes; they will need to decide which changes should remain, which were temporary and then align these decisions with organizational values (Amis and Greenwood, 2020). Moreover, change in one area of an organization will often trigger a need for change in other areas – so now other parts of the system need to catch up. It may also be time to review and examine alignment between work practices and strategy. It may be that adjustments to organizational strategy will be needed as we emerge from these disruptive times; furthermore, these changes need to be reassessed in line with the HR practices which already existed, and those which have emerged or been adjusted during lockdown.

Stakeholder analysis

Whilst traditionally organizational strategic objectives are perceived to be geared towards maximizing the value for shareholders, it is now more commonly acknowledged that wider stakeholder mapping can help an organization determine if the values upheld by its corporate strategy are ethically and culturally appropriate. Stakeholders are those who may be affected by the organization's actions, often divided into: (i) primary stakeholders, who are ultimately most affected, either positively or negatively; and (ii) secondary stakeholders, who are indirectly affected either by association or through a primary stakeholder. Stakeholders come from both within and outside of the organization (Clarkson, 1995).

A stakeholder analysis is a process for mapping stakeholders, their influence, their expectations and the urgency of their claim on the organization (Mitchell et al., 1997). These dimensions are similarly represented in Mendelow's power–interest matrix (see Figure 3.1) along with suggestions for how these stakeholder views should be considered.

For example, stakeholders who have high power and high interest in the organization (such as company directors and high value investors) are sometimes called 'key players'. These stakeholders need to be managed closely. They should be kept informed of the organization's plans and challenges, and their feedback should be deeply considered and responded to with care. This does not mean that they dictate the movements of the organization; however, it is important that they have their voices heard and it must be understood that a decision to ignore their expectations could lead to a loss of support from this stakeholder and the consequences that come with this. In contrast, stakeholders who have low power but high interest (such as employees who work in a department peripheral to the proposed change, or organizations linked to the company via its supply chain) need to be kept informed of the changes in the organization so that they can understand how they will be affected by them and make their own adjustments. These stakeholders may raise questions or concerns about the organization's actions and these can be a good source of information about any unintended consequences that the change may have. It is up to the organizational

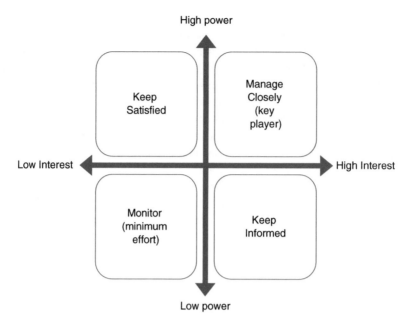

Figure 3.1 Stakeholder matrix (adapted from Mendelow, 1981)

change leaders to decide whether this knowledge changes anything about how they approach the change. Understanding the stakeholder matrix reveals how the organization's actions might be viewed and interpreted based on their impact on members of its network.

3.3 Developing a Business Strategy

Business strategy is traditionally taught in business courses as a stepwise process (Zubac et al., 2022), as shown in Figure 3.2, where an organization undertakes the following activities in the prescribed order:

1   Analyse external and internal environments.
2   Identify opportunities the organization can pursue.
3   Identify budget allocations and confirm top management accountability.
4   Develop a change management plan to achieve this strategy.

A popular feature of this analysis is the production of a SWOT analysis. SWOT stands for: Strengths and Weaknesses – which analyse the organization's resources and capabilities; and Opportunities and Threats – the external market situation. It is one of the most widely used devices for strategic decision-making in organizations due to its relative simplicity and easy to use structure (Panagiotou, 2003).

A problem with this approach in practice is that those responsible for leading and managing change are seldom the same as those who prepared the strategic plan. The strategic

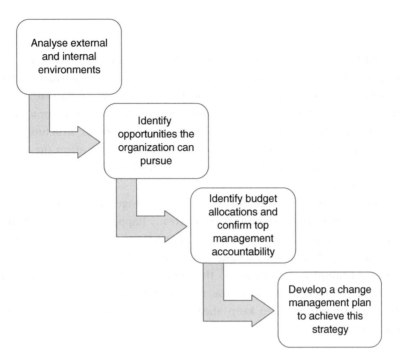

Figure 3.2 Traditional stepwise process of business strategy

process is often depicted as one of rational decision-making where options are systematically weighed against one another, whereas organizational change is commonly less rational, relying on the practices and relational dynamics within organizations which are diverse and multifaceted in their enactment, often involving power or resistance to different extents (see Chapter 8 for more on these issues).

In the 1990s a new strategic framework emerged which premised that an organization's core competencies can be used both to create short-term competitive positions and longer-term competitive advantage if 'capabilities' were managed in a way that could be easily integrated, grown or reconfigured in response to external environment changes. This approach is known as **dynamic capabilities** (Teece et al., 1997). It argues that organizations cannot grow and perform well sustainably in a constantly shifting external environment. When markets are dynamic, the ability of a strategy to consistently produce predictable performance is unsustainable. Focusing on dynamic capabilities that allow an organization to quickly orchestrate a response to a market shift is a possible means to address these strategy challenges.

For change makers, on the one hand, a dynamic capabilities approach can create a lack of security due to the need to manage ambiguous change with potentially open-ended outcomes and poorly defined expectations. Yet, on the other hand, it allows room for organizational members to inform and contribute to strategy and this may make them feel more empowered, and can strengthen the change process itself. Regardless, organizations that develop the skills of sensing, seizing and reorganizing in response to opportunities and threats find it easier to cope with organizational change (Zubac et al., 2022).

3.4 Managing Change Strategically

To understand the different nuances of strategic change, Nadler and Tushman (1989) have developed a popular typology to understand different types of change based on two dimensions to consider. The first dimension is the scope of the change comprising the extent to which the change will affect isolated sub-components of an organization or a whole organizational system. Incremental changes focus on changes in products, structures or processes (e.g. upgrading production equipment), whereas strategic changes affect the whole configuration of the organization, its purpose or position as a business in the market, its brand and how value is created.

The second dimension distinguishes between changes which are responding to events in the external environment that have already happened – relative changes – and changes which are made in anticipation of external events which may occur in the future – anticipatory changes (Nadler and Tushman, 1989). The former is a more reactive adaptation; for example, in response to the behaviour of a competitor; the latter is a more proactive interaction between the organization and its external environment where the organization seeks to keep ahead, or even influence the external context through its actions.

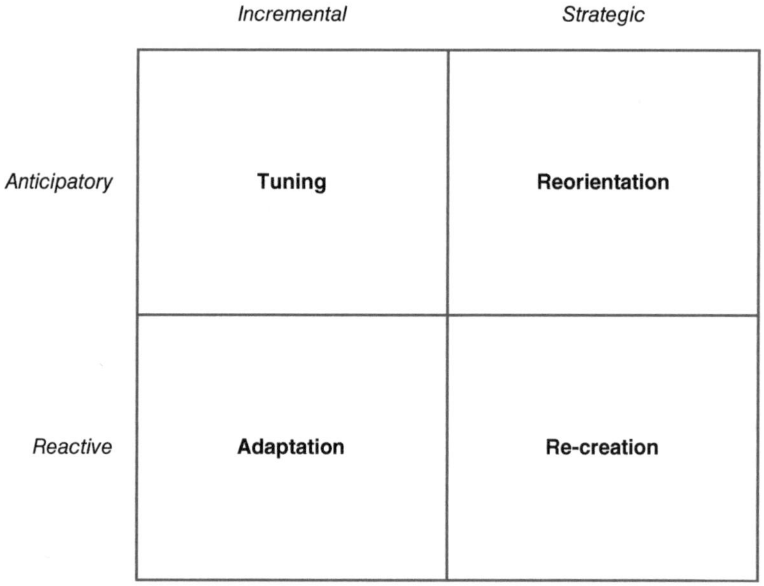

	Incremental	Strategic
Anticipatory	**Tuning**	**Reorientation**
Reactive	**Adaptation**	**Re-creation**

Figure 3.3 Types of organizational change

Source: Nadler, D.A. and Tushman, M.L. (1989) 'Organizational frame bending: Principles for managing reorientation', *Academy of Management Perspectives*, 3(3): 194–204.

The challenge for change makers implementing large-scale strategic change is to make sure to link the vision of the change with the overarching organization strategy, try to achieve the results that are expected and, at the same time, anticipate and get ready for possible difficulties during the change process.

Kotter (1995b) argues that change makers should follow a well-defined managerial process of change. This managerial process recognizes two key sequential parts (Bartezzaghi, 2010) illustrated in Figure 3.4 and described below:

1   Developing the strategic vision of change
2   Designing and implementing the interventions

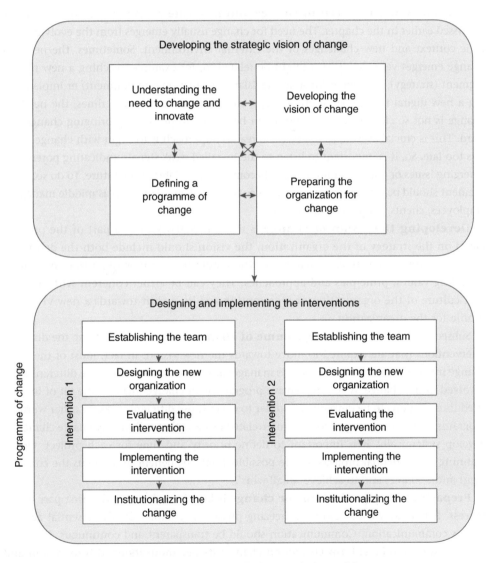

Figure 3.4 Process for managing planned change (adapted from Bartezzaghi, 2010)

Developing the strategic vision of change

Developing a strategic vision of change means envisioning how the new organization will be, its objectives, key values, along with principles and ways of working. Defining the vision is crucial to align the direction of change with the (new) overarching strategy of the organization. The vision of change also has an impact on how to frame the approach to the change activities themselves. So, the key activities for this part are understanding the need to change and innovate, developing the vision, defining a programme of change and preparing the organization for change (Bartezzaghi, 2010). They are not necessarily in sequence but can be beneficially developed in parallel.

Understanding the need to change and innovate refers to the drivers of change discussed earlier in the chapter. The need for change usually emerges from the evolving strategic context and new challenges of the external environment. Sometimes, the need for change emerges very clearly as it might be related to, for example, reaching a new market segment (strategy), implementing a new legislative regulation (environment) or implementing a new digital technology (both strategy and environment). Other times, the need for change is not so clear, or urgent, and it can be related to proactively bringing change forward. This is crucial as well, as the risk of a reactive approach is to begin with change when it is too late. So, it is important to listen to the so-called weak signals, indicating potentially emerging issues or opportunities that can become relevant later in the future. To do so, management should be actively *listening* to all agents and stakeholders, such as middle managers, employees, clients, suppliers and partners.

Developing the vision of change is the core activity of this part of the process. Based on the strategy of the organization, the vision should include both the definition of the long-term objectives to reach and the model for the new organization; that is, including values, principles and approaches. They can be either coherent with the current culture of the organization or representing a culture shift towards a new visionary profile for the organization.

Subsequently, **defining a programme of change** focuses on identifying the different interventions that are required to move towards the new vision. In fact, most of the time, change involves different aspects, so it is managerially important to define the different areas involved in the change. A comprehensive programme of change includes the set of interrelated interventions to be developed in order to cover those different areas. In other words, a programme of change is a portfolio of interrelated projects that collectively enable change to develop systemically. It is important to define priority and time for each project. Often, planning for sequential projects, where possible, might be beneficial, to focus the commitment and resources and to achieve 'small wins'.

Preparing the organization for change is key throughout all this first part of the process. It resonates with Lewin's unfreezing phase (see Chapter 2). The essential activity here is communication. Communication should be transparent and continuous. It should also involve the different aspects around change: its key motivations, drivers, vision and areas of intervention. It is also key to sustain a culture of change, in particular promoting creativity, risk taking and learning from mistakes.

Designing and implementing the interventions

The second part of the process of change involves specifically designing and implementing the interventions that are included in the programme of change. For each intervention (project), the key activities involve establishing the team, designing the new organization, evaluating the intervention, implementing the intervention and institutionalizing the change (Bartezzaghi, 2010).

Establishing the team for the project and defining the actors to involve is key. A change maker may take on the role of project manager and become a coordinator for the project. They may also bring in other change makers to support them. Team members forming the core work group should be also identified to cover all aspects involved with the change. A project manager and work group are in charge of the specific project and report to the steering committee of the overall process of change. At the same time, all stakeholders should be identified and potentially put together in a 'project reference group' to facilitate the dialogue about ideas and solutions between the work group and stakeholders. They can be internal (for example, managers of the units involved) and external (clients, suppliers). Finally, facilitators can be involved for example to bring in specific expertise on contents or methodologies. They can be internal (for example, from another area of the organization) or, quite commonly, external, such as consultants or researchers (see Chapter 12 about the involvement of *collaborative researchers*).

Designing the new organization is the detailed, comprehensive development of the new solutions to introduce. It usually represents the key responsibility for the work group; at the same time, the stakeholders should be actively involved. This activity begins with analysing the situation as it is ('as is' state). Based on that, it is possible to identify problems and opportunities. Then, the development of new solutions ('to be' model) represent designing the way(s) in which the new organization will work. For example, business process reengineering (BPR) is a relevant methodology to support the redesign of work processes (see Chapter 2). It is important to define, in parallel, the approach and the modality to implement such solutions, for example planning for training opportunities and support.

Evaluating the specific intervention is the next activity in the managerial process. Once the intervention is fully defined, an ad hoc evaluation should be developed to determine the economic impact, in particular costs and risks of the project (delivering an investment valuation, when appropriate), but also the organizational impact, in terms of communication, training, support that will be needed, in particular when some resistance to change is likely to emerge (see Chapter 8, on resistance; Chapter 11, on evaluation more broadly).

Then, **implementing the intervention** represents the execution of the solutions that were designed and positively evaluated. For example, it might include installing a new software (e.g. about customer relationship management or enterprise resource planning), or creating a new organizational unit (e.g. a new division), or adopting a new process or policy (e.g. a new approach to research and development). The modalities of this phase really depend on the contents of the intervention. In general, a gradual approach might be beneficial. For example, an initial pilot can help identify issues and refine the interventions, focus the energy on the trial, obtain some initial success and involve and motivate people.

Lastly, **institutionalizing the change** is the last managerial activity for each intervention. This resonates with Lewin's refreezing phase (see Chapter 2). It is still a crucial phase, where commitment should be kept high, people should be supported and initiatives to reinforce the new organization should be launched. In this way, the new solutions would gradually become part of the organizational culture. At the same time, it is critical to assess the results achieved thanks to the change, in particular developing a post-project review which is a vital organizational learning mechanism (OLM) to learn how to do better next time (see Chapter 12). This also helps to immediately identify further refinements and adjustments to the new solutions.

Once a planned strategic change is developed, the focus on change shifts to continuous, incremental change. In fact, the new solutions will incrementally need to be improved and updated in the near future. Specific managerial practices in relation to continuous improvement were discussed Chapter 1.

3.5 Change Makers Implementing Change From Within

In this chapter, we have focused on the external and strategic contexts of change management. For many books on managing organizational change, it is these aspects of diagnosis, strategy and environment that are the main focus of the text. Whilst these are really important influences of change for any change maker to understand, in our view they are often disconnected from many of the processes of change management. Often, change makers are brought in later, when change implementation is the main focus and they may have had limited or no previous involvement in the development of organizational strategy. In the final section of this chapter, we explore the role that change makers can play in the strategy process during implementation and also describe some of the frustrations that they can face, attempting to implement change to achieve objectives that are likely not determined by them. This sets the stage for the focus of Part II of this book, where we take a look at change management from the perspective of change makers themselves.

The role of change makers in strategy processes

Strategic consensus is believed to be beneficial for organizational performance but, more importantly, it has been consistently found that manager involvement in strategic processes enhances their support for strategy and for any organizational change associated with it (Balogun and Johnson, 2004; Lines, 2005; Wooldridge et al., 2008). In particular, referencing middle managers, Floyd and Wooldridge (1997) differentiate between convergent and divergent strategic behaviour as a core component of middle management work:

- **Convergent strategic behaviours** focus on the implementation of established organizational strategy (i.e. strategic objectives set by others – top/senior management). They do this by translating and synthesizing information and communicating with other organizational members.
- **Divergent strategic behaviours** involve middle managers enacting choice of which there are a multitude of strategic options to support and present to strategic decision-makers. They may also seek out strategic alternatives of their own and suggest these in place of pre-defined options already being considered. In this way, they help to inform strategy and contribute to the long-term goals of the organization (Tarakci et al., 2018).

Regardless of whether they are middle managers or more front-line leaders of change, change makers are often well positioned to understand what is required for the implementation of strategy in an organization. They may have varying degrees of influence in deciding what change is required but will have a front seat in making those changes happen whether they like the strategy or not.

Why do change makers feel frustrated?

As noted earlier, those responsible for coordinating and implementing change have often had limited influence and involvement in preparing the strategic plan, yet they are charged with selling change to other organizational members, convincing them that the change is needed and will impact on them positively, and with designing and implementing support systems to sustain the values of the strategic vision. This can be frustrating for change makers and they may need to operate within the parameters of a vision which may or may not make sense to them. Our aim in this chapter was to provide an overview of how strategic plans are developed by organizations. Regardless of the change maker's involvement in this process, understanding the influences and factors that contributed to this will help them to be effective in implementing change.

Change managers' sense-making of change has been found to be a crucial factor in determining the success of organizational change, because change makers play such a crucial role in interpreting change for front-line staff from many different groups (Balogun and Johnson, 2004). Change makers may find themselves in a position where they are implementing change initiatives that have become ideologically different from their own personal beliefs and experiences and this can lead to feeling inauthentic, surface acting, higher emotional labour and identity conflict (Tucker et al., 2022). We will discuss this in more detail in Chapter 4, namely the ambiguity of change-maker roles and potential conflicts in resources and power relations that are ever-present in change-maker roles.

In the remainder of this book, we explore change from the perspective of change makers. We will show examples and literature that help clarify the role limitations and opportunities. This is not to say that external factors are not covered at all, or that we do not consider them to be important aspects of change. Having established this, we can focus the rest of this book on what change makers can do to create real impact given the parameters that they have. We argue that diagnosis and strategy remain a peripheral concern for internal change makers and, therefore, we focus on issues that are closer to the experience of change makers and are within their sphere of influence. For example, we will explore how change makers can influence change by using the sources of power that are available to them (internally), and how innovation and learning from within the organization are valuable processes that change makers can exploit to implement change. As a result, we aim for change makers to feel more empowered and less frustrated with the often complex or challenging roles they are charged with.

Chapter Summary

- Business strategy is also grounded in the **external environment** in which an organization operates in the form of markets and stakeholders. Political, economic, social and technological (PEST) factors will help the organization to position itself within an external context.
- A wider **stakeholder mapping** can help an organization identify key groups who will influence an organization and also help to determine if the values upheld by its corporate strategy are ethically and culturally appropriate.
- Managing change strategically requires leading two distinct macro-phases which are: (a) developing the **strategic vision of change**; and (b) designing and implementing the **interventions**.
- Often, those responsible for coordinating change management are seldom the same as those who prepared the strategic plan which can be a **source of frustration** for change makers. They may have varying degrees of influence in deciding what change is required but will have a front seat in making those changes happen.

Activity

As we have seen in this chapter, the external environment and organizational strategy have a significant influence on organizational change. Consider the mini-case study (in Box 3.3 below) and discuss the following questions:

1   What aspects of the external environment (e.g. PEST) are driving change in this organization?
2   How does their business strategy inform the change that is taking place?
3   To what extent does the change management programme described follow the macro-phases of strategic change implementation?

Note you can apply these discussion questions to the mini-cases from Chapters 1 and 2 (see Boxes 1.3, 1.4 and 2.2) and to all other examples of change and case studies in this book as a starting point to understand the organization and its change context.

Box 3.3

Schroder and Wendall

The company was set up by two partners in the 1960s and is still owned and run by those two families (now in their second and third generations) and employing around 500 staff. Based in the south of Germany, the company specializes in manufacturing seals for industries such as car manufacturing and gas and water suppliers. The company has two major longstanding manufacturing contracts with major car manufacturers but in the 1990s was struggling to keep up with supply due to some of the more personnel-intensive production steps that it employed. Since then, they have sought to make gradual refinements in these production areas through employee-led innovation and investment in technological automation tools with modest success.

A plan for the future

In 2016 an opportunity emerged to enter into an additional major automobile contract with a specialist in electric transportation. The company identified this as a potentially lucrative market through which they could expand their business; however, the electric car market was still relatively new and the speed and extent of growth was likely to be unpredictable and inconsistent. In order to realize this opportunity, the company recognized that they would need to expand their capacity for production, but also needed enough flexibility to manage potentially large swings in demand. To achieve this, they needed to make some more strategic plans for growth and further efficiency savings over the next five years.

They developed a plan to expand and develop the company by improving their manufacturing processes and capabilities. The overall plan included multinational ventures such as building a new plant in Eastern Europe and extensive expansion with a new partner organization in the Czech Republic. However, the first stage was a manufacturing change based at their existing plant which would improve quality standards to enable the successive stages of the plan to be implemented. The organization was attempting to optimize the production system at their current plant by implementing a lean manufacturing philosophy. The aims of this stage of the project were to increase productivity, lower cycle times, lower goods work-in-progress, increase quality and flexibility in production, and utilize 'process management tools' (e.g. lean production methods, aimed to identify waste and improve the flow of processes). The organization believed that the current plant still held a lot of potential and they wished to offer their employees good job security before beginning the 'riskier' stages of the plan such as the setting up of the new plant.

In 2018 the organization employed a consulting company to assist them in implementing this plan. Together they planned the phases of change implementation,

(Continued)

including an analysis phase (three months); a rough planning phase (two months); a detailed planning phase (one month); pilot projects and further detailed planning (eight months); rollout of new system and training for employees and managers (12 months).

The strategic plan was announced at an employee meeting during the analysis stage of its action plan where the consultants were introduced and employees were informed that they would be visiting different production teams to observe processes and recommend improvements. Following this meeting some concerns were raised by the Works Council (an employee representation group) about anxiety among employees, who felt that they were no longer trusted to make improvements to their own work.

Further Recommended Reading

For an overview of the relationship between strategic management and organizational change, see Zubac, A., Tucker, D., Zwikael, O., Hughes, K. and Kirkpatrick, S. (2022) *Effective Implementation of Transformation Strategies*. Singapore: Palgrave Macmillan.

For an overview on stakeholder perspectives and matrix, see Mitchell, R.K., Agle, B.R. and Wood, D.J. (1997) 'Toward a theory of stakeholder identification and salience: Defining the principle of who and what really counts', *Academy of Management Review*, 22(4): 853–886. DOI:10.2307/259247.

To understand more about digital drivers of change specifically, see Westerman, G., Bonnet, D. and McAfee, A. (2014) *Leading Digital: Turning Technology into Business Transformation*. Boston, MA: Harvard Business Review Press.

PART II

AN APPROACH BASED ON CHANGE MAKERS

4

CHANGE MAKERS AND CHANGE AGENTS

DIVERSE ROLES AND COMMON CHALLENGES

Chapter Objectives

- To explore who change makers are and how they enable change in organizations
- To appreciate the diverse nature of change-maker roles in different organizations and how these might be used in different ways
- To understand the importance of change-maker engagement in the change process
- To discuss the common challenges that change makers face in organizations

4.1 Introduction

In a dynamic business world, organizational change is widely considered a specialism practised by management consultants and organizational leaders. It is also, however, an essential component of managing people in organizations effectively and often the 'nuts and bolts' of change implementation are undertaken by mid- and lower-level organizational members.

Internal change makers are critically important. They work on internal organizational change dynamics, the mechanics of doing organizational change. Internal change makers tackle, understand and solve internal implementation challenges. They identify innovative processes and try to predict the unintended consequences of changes within the organization. Internal change makers use their agency, and a diverse array of other forms of power and influence to work between units from within organizations.

In this chapter we will consider the diverse range of internal change makers in a change management project. Internal change makers are often thought of as the supporting cast in a change project but, in our research, we have found them to be some of the most powerful 'leaders' of change (Tucker et al., 2015, 2022). In the first part of this chapter, we will explore who change makers are, what they do and how this is represented in organizations. We will outline different roles and titles for change makers to help you identify them, discuss how they are created or discovered, and consider the role of project teams and change makers in change.

Organizational change education tends to focus on developing the skills of senior leaders of large corporations or for small business and entrepreneurial start up leaders. In the second part of this chapter, we look at research which has highlighted the importance of mid- and lower-level change makers in the change process, and we discuss how they add value to change through sense-making, managing emotions, diffusing innovations and spanning boundaries.

Change education that focuses on unequivocally powerful leaders makes assumptions about the power and freedom of strategic choice which change leaders have and places emphasis on top-down leader-led approaches to change. So, in the third part of this chapter we will examine how some of these assumptions lead to common challenges which prevent change makers from enabling change. We review some of the key common challenges which are faced by all types of change makers including role ambiguity, disparate power dynamics, managing complex and multifaceted change and the dominance of institutional logics.

4.2 Who Are Change Makers and What Do They Do?

Before we embark on our discussion of change-maker impact it is important to address the diversity of change-maker roles across different types of organization and industries. Academic literature does not have a unified terminology for referring to change-maker roles; therefore, in this section we introduce and explain our definition of a change maker and then discuss how change makers are created in organizations.

Definition of change maker

Throughout this book we use the term 'change maker' to describe organizational members who become the architects and builders of change in organizations. Researchers have criticized change management research for the lack of conceptual clarity around agent roles (Chreim et al., 2012; Parry, 2003; Tucker et al., 2015) and we would argue that part of the challenge of understanding the contribution of change makers is due to the use of different definitions and interpretations of change roles in different organizations, making it hard to gain a clear picture of how they add value.

In a review of change agency literature and a study of hospital transformations, Tucker and Cirella (2018) identify three types of agents who are important for organizational change and innovation:

1   **Champions** – ideological motivators who enthusiastically promote specific innovations and changes based on their strong beliefs and personal commitment to the cause
2   **Opinion leaders** – respected experts with a history of previous successful recommendations who are able to influence the beliefs and actions of others about the change
3   **Integrators** – facilitators who coordinate multiple constituencies within an organization by removing language barriers, linking resources and connecting processes and structures to achieve change outcomes

In terms of our terminology in this book,[1] we use the term 'change maker' here, as opposed to numerous other role titles and terms such as those featured in Box 4.1 to emphasize how all of these roles have the ability to employ creativity to implement change. This is not to say that anyone who holds a job title featured in this list will automatically be a change maker but it would probably be at least part of their role which they aspire to. To 'make' change is to construct, create or concoct something new from the resources available. **Change makers** are proactive and purposeful in promoting and enabling change (Dopson et al., 2010; Greenhalgh et al., 2004; Locock et al., 2001). Change makers imagine and craft innovative solutions to problems and engage in collaborative work and processes of organizational re-design (Mohrman and Cummings, 1989).

We distinguish change makers from other change leaders and external consultants who can draw on perspectives influenced by the external environment to guide decision-making. Change makers are bounded by the ultimate decision-making power of others, who they collaborate with, typically senior leaders, executives or business owners. They also work with colleagues, experts and teams across the organization. They may have little or no explicit or strategic say in the direction of the change and its overall objectives, yet are entrusted with its implementation.

---

[1]In this book, we use the term change makers, but in the literature a variety of terms is used. When we draw from other literature, we sometimes use their terms in order to stay true to the source (for example, change agents is a popular term).

-Box 4.1-

Job titles and labels used for change makers in organizations

Project manager/programme director – designated leader of a package of work

Change agent – facilitates and implements change

Project analyst/assistant – a supporting role, collating or analysing data to support a work package

Integration leader – brings members of disparate groups together to co-create change

Grassroots volunteers – contribute freely with front-line experience

Clinical/product champion – enthusiasm for the cause and a personal commitment to seeing it realized (Howell and Shea, 2001)

Liaison/broker/coordinator – finds, assesses and interprets information to identify questions (Ward et al., 2009)

HR change manager – specializing in human resource management issues with managing change

Change manager/lead – a specialism in change management; this could be a generic role or specific to one change initiative

Implementation expert – a specialism in implementation of change

Process/management engineer – specific business process training such as 'lean' or 'six sigma'

IT project manager – specific information technology skills and responsibilities (e.g. software development, database administration)

Digital services manager – digital project or operations skills and responsibilities (e.g. vendor liaison, customer service manager, digital marketing)

… and many more

Creating change makers

All change projects are different and therefore the way change-maker roles come about is equally varied. In some cases, large organizations, or those with a vast history of change management, may already have individuals who they rely on to create change within certain groups or teams. In other cases, change-maker roles emerge as a need develops in a more ad hoc manner where gaps in change communication emerge. For example, technology experts implementing a new digital system may be struggling with resistance from front-line staff who do not see any value in the system or from technical back-end staff who perceive a loss of power or control over organizational systems. Change makers may be created to bridge the gap in this dialogue and help create a shared understanding of the purpose and benefits of the technology.

In many cases, 'change maker' is a partial role embodied by the individual; for example, a general manager who takes care of a day-to-day line of business but is also restructuring their department. An individual may only undertake a change-maker role for a limited period, returning to their 'normal' role once the change is complete.

A key question, then, is how formal should a change maker's role be? Some research argues that change makers should be left to informally emerge within the organization when a need develops – the argument being that individuals who feel passionate about the innovation or change will take it upon themselves to make it happen (Mantere, 2005; Markham, 1998; Parry, 2003; Rogers, 2003; Schon, 1963). Much of this research, which stems from a diffusion of innovation theories (Rogers, 2003), argues that change makers can only be identified once they make themselves known to the organization.

Other research has argued that individuals should be selected based on skills and attributes that are strategically identified as necessary for change implementation (Chreim et al., 2012; Hanney et al., 2003). Once appointed into a role, change makers can be trained to use these skills to implement change. Challenges for organizations are to accurately understand what is needed from the change-maker role and to predict how individuals will perform (Tucker et al., 2015).

Tucker and Cirella (2018) explore the key differences between informal and formal change-maker positions and when they might be most relevant. **Informal agents** are most effective when left to create influence within their own networks using methods and resources which they already have. Their independence and trustworthiness help to overcome resistance to change. **Formal agents** are better suited when the change maker needs authority to make decisions about change implementation which might be more strategic, or where change might be unpopular. Formal change makers have more power to create consistency across multiple groups who will be differently affected by change. These differences are summarized in Table 4.1.

Table 4.1   Creating different change makers (adapted from Tucker and Cirella, 2018)

Informal agents are identified	Formal agents are appointed
To harness front-line engagement	To align change implementation at a strategic level
To seek innovation and sharing of ideas	To seek consistency or compliance with organizational goals
To create enthusiasm and excitement about change	Need authority to make decisions

(Continued)

Table 4.1 (Continued)

Informal agents are identified	Formal agents are appointed
Can frame change in the language of change recipients	Can frame change to strategic leaders and outsiders
Are allowed to form their own opinion about the change (and change their mind)	The agent is viewed by others as a representation of the organization
Use more informal and personal methods to share information	Use more formal channels to share information

There is often a temptation for organizations to formalize the role of change makers who emerge spontaneously in order to recognize their work. This frees them up from other duties and provides resources to support the 'good' work they are already doing (Hendy and Barlow, 2012), especially when a planned approach to change is adopted (see Chapter 2). However, formalizing a role inadvertently changes the nature of the power bases within the role and this can have unintended consequences. For example, in a study of middle-manager change makers in a healthcare restructuring, Tucker et al. (2015) found that when respected unofficial campaigners for change were given a formalized change-maker role, operational aspects of the project management (e.g. developing procedures and sourcing equipment) physically and psychologically detached them from their former supporters. Once in a formal role, their request for cooperation from colleagues was no longer interpreted as shared empowerment but instead became synonymous with the mandate of the institution. This shift in role formality undermined the integrity of their outlook; as informal agents they were representatives of the wider employee group but as formal project managers they became representatives of the overbearing employer.

Project managers and project teams

One way that organizations may choose to formalize change-maker roles is to create a project team with a specific remit of delivering change. A project team may consist of a project manager/director, various related functional liaisons (e.g. estates/facilities, finance, service teams), other change makers representing lines of business, and administrative or support staff. In general, a **project manager** should have authoritative knowledge and expertise in the area related to the intervention. A common choice is to identify the project manager from the organizational unit most involved in the change. The key responsibilities are planning the project, coordinating its development, and controlling schedule and costs. Overall, the project manager is responsible for the results and should be able to integrate different aspects of the project and solve possible issues during the development.

A specific distinction, typical of the project management field, is between a 'strong' versus 'weak' project manager – this weight depends on the kind of organizational structure related to the project. When different functions contribute to an inter-functional team that is working on the project, this constitutes a matrix organization. A strong matrix means that the project manager gets more power and authority in terms of managing people and resources coming from the functions; if the matrix is weak, usual roles and powers are not modified and the project manager is a facilitator of the project. A balanced matrix is a solution in between, and the project manager can negotiate and make agreements with the functional managers. If the project manager is allocated only part-time to the project of change, it might be important to have some team members who can be full-time on the project, if needed.

Thus, the right combination between project type, organizational structure (and so authority of the project manager), authoritative knowledge of the project manager and their personality is key to the success of the project (e.g. Dvir et al., 2006).

In understanding the role of the project team, it is important to consider three key issues. Firstly, the project management team would need to establish a specific line of reporting and accountability within the organization. In fact, the reporting must be aligned with the matrix solution adopted. For example, a strong matrix solution might report only to the CEO. Secondly, it is important to have a balance of team members with generic project management skills and team members with local knowledge – knowledge of lines of business. Project leaders may have an established career of project management which is detached from business specialty, so it is important that other members can gain the trust of the workforce through appreciation of front-line challenges. Thirdly, there will be a transition period when 'change management' becomes 'management', where some members of the project team will detach from the project, taking with them the knowledge and 'memory' of what happened and why. It will be important to plan for this handover period.

4.3 The Importance of Change Makers in the Change Process

Change makers in mid- and lower-level management roles have received an increasing amount of attention in the academic realm. Wooldridge et al. argue that 'what makes middle managers unique is their access to top management coupled with their knowledge of operations' (Wooldridge et al., 2008: 1192). Essentially they are mediators between the organization's strategy and the day-to-day activities (Nonaka, 1994).

This research has highlighted four key ways that change makers influence effective change management from their position within the organization.

Diffusion of Innovation

The importance of a variety of change makers has been identified in innovation literature (opinion leaders and champions in particular) to act as key informants about networks within organizations and systems, allowing innovative ideas to diffuse across groups (Rogers, 2003). Change makers have been found to be particularly helpful in achieving 'critical mass' – the point at which enough members of a community have adopted an innovation so that further adoption becomes self-sustaining (Rogers, 2003).

Individual adoption is only one part of the assimilation process in adopting process-based innovations in service organizations. Whereas product-based innovations may rely heavily on imitation between individuals, adoption of managerial innovations or change processes may be more top-down and formalized (Greenhalgh et al., 2004). Due to their position in the organizational hierarchy, change makers are well placed to support this process. Within complex systems and organizations, different groups operate in different social structures and have different norms for influence and professional values (Greenhalgh et al., 2004). Some groups respond well to authoritative decisions while others value informal peer influence.

Retaining the core origins of an innovation is important; however, also allowing some adaptability to ensure a 'fit' within the target context is a key factor in innovation adoption (Mathers et al., 2014). The logic and incentive for innovating may need to be translated to different institutional groups within and across organizations. Currie and Spyridonidis (2019) found that powerful change makers influence resource allocation and engage front-line staff in *adapting* innovation within a local organizational context. Therefore, change makers within these networks will likely have the best knowledge of which strategies to assimilate innovation might be most successful with a given group (as we will explore in more detail in Chapter 10).

Sense-making

A significant body of research focuses on the importance of middle-manager change makers in making sense of change, both for themselves (Tucker et al., 2015) and for others (Gioia and Chittipeddi, 1991; Rouleau, 2005). Sense-making is a process of creating mental models of events to act as a basis for behaviour (Gioia et al., 1994; Weick, 1995). This cognitive framework allows organizational members to understand events and form appropriate behavioural responses (Weick, 1995; Weick et al., 2005). Sense-making is especially important during organizational change because when our world shifts, gaps in our understanding are created. By observing the behaviour, actions and storytelling of change makers, employees can re-create a mental model of the new organizational reality (Balogun, 2010).

Balogun and Johnson (2004) found that the lateral social interactions of middle managers, in particular, were highly significant in shaping change, especially where there is ambiguity around organizational objectives about change. Middle managers translate and implement strategic organizational goals at an operational level (Currie and Procter, 2005; Mantere, 2008; Rouleau, 2005; Wooldridge et al., 2008). By knowing who to get in the room and how to speak to them in the right language, change makers were able to influence the organization strategically (Rouleau and Balogun, 2011), across boundaries and by altering change recipient's behaviour (e.g. Dopson and Fitzgerald, 2006).

Managing emotions

Emotions are an embodiment of individual experience, from which meaning is interpreted and behaviour is activated. When an event of significance occurs, recipients of change will experience positive or negative feelings about the event. They will also perform a cognitive appraisal of what the event will mean for them; for example, can I benefit from this or will my job be at risk? (Oreg et al., 2018). These cognitive and emotional dimensions of employee attitudes can differ; for example, on hearing about the withdrawal of a failing product line, an employee working in that department may feel both scared for their own status but also relieved that a strategic direction for the organization has brought clarity at an uncertain time. These mixed feelings may appear as ambivalence but, in fact, represent a complex, multidimensional emotional episode that employees experience (Piderit, 2000). Resolving these emotional paradoxes can generate creative change problem-solving (Luscher et al., 2006); however, without guidance and support, the high level of anxiety created by these 'mixed feelings' can result in inertia and paralysis. Managing emotions in organizations is arguably a key factor in successful organizational change (Ashkanasy et al., 2002).

Change makers are in touch with the core capabilities of the organization and a large part of their role is to shape these. This includes the **emotional resources** of organizational members. Whereas senior leaders are often disconnected from the day-to-day life and experiences of organizational life, internal change makers are not. A study by Huy (2002), of a large IT services company's radical restructuring, describes how change makers can significantly impact the success of change by: (a) personally committing to change projects and championing them to others; and (b) being attentive to change recipients' emotions and helping them to cope with change. Change makers are often the most aware of the atmosphere within the organization and can try to address negative emotions and concerns, often just by being someone to talk to or by explaining things more. This leads to less adverse reactions to change and smoother implementation.

Moreover, change makers may act as mentors or a support system for employees by helping them to interpret and reflect on their emotional experiences. When change recipients face circumstances that may no longer be governed by familiar traditions, the social interactions and internal conversations we have with ourselves, motivated and based on emotion (emotional reflexivity), shape and change our sense of self and our interconnectedness with the organization – identity change (Burkitt, 2002).

Boundary spanning

Extensive bodies of literature on knowledge management and networks found that change makers sharing knowledge and communicating across boundaries is another key way that they can influence effective change management from within the organization. This is often referred to as boundary spanning. Boundary spanners act as a link that bridges and facilitates coordination between organizational members across professional boundaries (Williams, 2002). Complex organizations often operate in siloed groups especially where employees perform different functions or operate under different professional codes of conduct; for example, physicians and nursing staff in a healthcare setting often work under separate terms and conditions, shift schedules and professional regulations (Spyridonidis et al., 2015). It is understandable that such distinct groups develop distinct ways of doing things and find it challenging to make sense of change in the same way. Change makers who focus on facilitating change across these disparate groups have been found to be very successful (Cross et al., 2013; Haas, 2015).

Change makers reduce conflict by identifying and focusing on common-ground outcomes (Richter et al., 2006). In a study of a UK healthcare collaboration initiative to facilitate knowledge translation between academic and clinical partners, Evans and Scarbrough (2014) identify two approaches for enhancing boundary spanning: (i) bridging, facilitating discrete events between groups (e.g. opportunities to come together and discuss challenges) and designating specific responsibilities for sharing to group members to form lasting connections across boundaries; (ii) blurring, which involves de-emphasizing the boundaries between groups by drawing on a range of interpersonal skills to acquire and manage the exchange of relevant information (Haas, 2015; Williams, 2002). Change makers who are especially good at boundary spanning often have dual expertise that allows them to relate to both groups and understand the motives, roles, and responsibilities of others (Evans and Scarbrough, 2014; Williams, 2002).

4.4 Challenges for Change Makers

So far in this chapter we have discussed the diverse nature of change-maker roles in different organizations and explored the importance of these roles. In this section, we will review some of the key common challenges which are faced by all types of change makers, many of which we will explore further throughout this book.

Role ambiguity

A 'role' is defined as an explicit and systematic enforced prescription for how a 'role holder' should think and feel about themselves and their work (Goffman, 1961). Unlike job titles, roles can be more informal and defined by the role expectations of others rather than a formal description (Katz and Kahn, 1978). As we have discussed above, change-maker roles vary in terms of their formality; these positions are often new and ambiguously defined or will change over time as the change progresses (Tucker and Cirella, 2018). Therefore, it is important to know that a role, and the way change makers see themselves, is socially constructed. That is, they work out how to enact the role by observing and learning from other individuals who enact similar or related roles and from the feedback of those they interact with (e.g. a colleague who asks them to work on a particular issue).

Therefore, the roles of change makers are influenced by a diverse range of organizational members who they interact with. As we discuss in this chapter, change makers wear multiple ill-fitting hats and they may be pulled in numerous directions (Tucker and Cirella, 2018). Change management research shows that failing to define a change maker's role in the change may have unintended consequences for the change outcomes (Tucker et al., 2015; Tucker et al., 2022). This may lead to paralysis of activity, when a change maker is not able to get work done because they do not know which role expectations to give priority to as someone is always going to be unhappy with how you are enacting the role (Currie and Procter, 2005).

These tensions can lead to role ambiguity and/or role conflict (Currie and Procter, 2005). Role ambiguity occurs when the *boundaries of a role are uncertain* or ill-defined. For example, understanding the remit and reach of the influence that the role has and the risk of overstepping into the domain of others. Role conflict occurs when *two (or more) opposing role profiles contradict* one another. For example, a bank manager may have a duty to ensure consistency and compliance with lending practices to clients, whilst at the same time trying to change these practices to conform to new regulations. Where the roles are so at odds with one another, it can be increasingly challenging, if not impossible to perform both roles effectively. Role ambiguity can be especially challenging for change makers entering a new role because what is viewed as inconsistent values and behaviour may impact the trust or commitment which they have earned from previous co-worker relationships.

Power dynamics

Change makers work within internal organizational change dynamics. In this space, systemic power structures shape the thinking of organizational members through historically developed discourses and social norms (Clegg et al., 2006; Schildt et al., 2020). Traditionally, these power structures tend to empower senior executives and disempower employees (including lower and middle managers). Therefore, a change maker's methods of influencing and collaborating are different from those of senior executives who leverage hierarchical power and control over communications, policy or other levers of change, from the top of organizations (Smircich and Morgan, 1982) – see Chapter 8 for more discussion of power issues. Change makers often have a more limited sphere of influence and must rely on limited, albeit different, power resources to create or nudge along change. Moreover, in creating transformational change, change makers may be required to disrupt existing power structures; they may have to work against established and externally validated perspectives about what knowledge or evidence is 'powerful' in organizations (Tucker et al., 2022).

As we have described above, the level of formal status a change maker is given in their role will vary. Internal change makers must use a diverse array of other forms of power and influence to work between units from the middle of organizations. Change-maker power is likely to be more relational. They may use linguistic strategies, such as storytelling and sense-giving to influence others (Rhodes and Brown, 2005; Schildt et al., 2020). For example, change leaders may communicate a sense of crisis in order to push through changes (Smircich and Morgan, 1982).

For change makers, decision-making and their ability to influence this involves a struggle with internal politics (Rouleau and Balogun, 2011). They must make creative use of power sources to gain a seat at the table and be able to communicate effectively with authoritative strategic leaders. Change makers also have a role to play in interpreting, understanding, representing and responding to diverse views within the organization (more on this in

Chapter 6). Different groups within the organization will have various definitions on what constitutes change success (e.g. financial success, economic success, values-related success – becoming more sustainable). Similarly, change makers must manage the responses of the inevitable 'winners' and 'losers' in any change scenario. Employees who feel ignored and treated unfairly will become demotivated and this will have consequences for post-change performance (Tucker et al., 2016).

Dominant narratives and resistance to change

Organizational behaviour is largely determined by institutionalized practices which are deeply rooted in an organization's history. These practices are taken for granted by organizational members, often unnoticed, laden with values and assumptions, and are notoriously difficult to change (DiMaggio, 1988). Breaking down existing shared logics is important because, until this happens, it is hard to release the innovative problem-solving energy of a workforce and to diffuse new ideas throughout the organization (Bridwell-Mitchell, 2016).

As discussed in Chapter 1, organizational change leads to disruption of institutional logics (Greenwood et al., 2002). This is referred to by some as a 'sense-breaking' process (akin to unfreezing – see Chapter 2). Change in everyday routines creates a meaning void (Aula and Mantere, 2013; Mantere et al., 2012) which is uncomfortable and anxiety-provoking for individuals. Change makers must convince others to let go of past ideas and embrace discomfort, at least for a little while.

To understand these lived experiences, storytelling research is particularly prevalent in the literature. Stories (Gabriel, 2000) enable us to understand how an individual makes sense of and understands a situation. It helps make clear what is important to an individual (Maitlis and Christianson, 2014). Stories that become shared and which are retold over an extended period can become institutionalized and, as such, not only represent accepted understanding of a topic but because they may be widely shared, significantly impact on and influence broader discourses within the organization (Vaara et al., 2016). Näslund and Pemer (2012) found that dominant stories in organizations shape the meaning and labels that are available for new sense-making, making it hard for organizations to move away from historical positions and new ways of thinking.

Creating a **shared vision** of what change is intended to do is extremely challenging. The creation of a shared understanding amongst organizational peers will be guided by the development of dilemmas encountered by employees in the everyday practice of the changed organization (Bridwell-Mitchell, 2016). Organizational members make sense of the new organizational reality as a collective, influenced by social dynamics in a way that may or may not be aligned with the aims of the change (Maitlis and Lawrence, 2007). Change disrupts the way employees relate to the organization at a very individual level and this can lead to unpredictable reactions (see Chapter 8 for more on resistance to change). In a study of implementation of tele-healthcare innovations in UK social care, Tucker et al. (2022) found that as organizational contexts shift, what is valued and important changes, expectations of implementation evolve, and the goalposts for success move. When this happens, front-line workers will re-interpret their relationship with the organization and if they experience mis-alignment in their lived experience and what they seek, they may become disconnected and begin to take actions that suit their own objectives rather than those of the organization.

Managing complexity and multifaceted change

Transformational change has been found to create significant psychological strain, burnout and exhaustion for employees in organizations and especially those who have a high level of involvement in its implementation (Bordia et al., 2004; Price and van Dick, 2012; Rooney et al., 2010). The more complex a change becomes, the more tensions arise for change makers to manage and, as organizations become more global and integration across systems becomes more important, the likelihood of transformational change which attempts to achieve multiple goals is becoming more common. When multiple changes happen in succession, a lack of time to embed new ideas can create confusion and change fatigue. Tucker et al. (2014) argue that combining change of work practices, which requires change of routines, culture and ideology, with infrastructure changes (e.g. a new information technology system or new facility) creates additional stressors for change makers who need to manage different timelines and switch between different engagement strategies to enable change effectively.

One of the key challenges change makers face in relation to complex change is **information overload**, where change makers act as a communication broker to multiple sub-groups with different needs. Different types of change often have different timelines and tasks for change makers to do; it can quickly become overwhelming when one part of the change has ambiguous, flexible deadlines and targets, and another part has tighter contractual obligations. This usually results in one form of change (the one with the tighter deadlines) being prioritized over another (Tucker et al., 2014).

Chapter Summary

- Change makers hold many different positions, have different labels and play different roles in the organization, but what they have in common is that they are proactive and purposeful in promoting and enabling change. Change makers imagine and craft innovative solutions to problems and engage in process or organizational design.
- Change makers may or may not be in an acknowledged position for their contribution. Informal agents have influence within their own networks using methods and resources which they already have. Formal agents are better suited when the change maker needs authority to make decisions about change implementation.
- Change makers influence effective change by shaping change through sense-giving to others; by helping organizational members manage the emotional upheaval of change; by diffusing innovative ideas through their networks; and by linking different institutional groups across the organization(s).

- Despite the variety of roles which change makers have, they often face the similar challenges of role ambiguity, lack of structural power, re-creating shared meaning and managing complexity.

Activity

Read the two character profiles of change makers (Boxes 4.2 and 4.3) and discuss the following questions:

1   What qualities do these individuals have which make them a change maker?
2   What do you think are some of the challenges they will face?

─Box 4.2─

David – Operations Project Manager, International Bank

Background

I've been in this role for four years now. I was initially offered the role in relation to a specific project – managing the bank's preparation for post-Brexit operations – and this has since been expanded to include a range of projects.

Prior to this role I had managed various teams within the operations department. Although I had no formal training in project management or change management, I had demonstrated adaptability and willingness to embrace change. I had also gained a reputation for analysis and problem-solving within the management team.

Doing the job

The role has no set guidelines as to how many projects I work on or how I contribute to those; it is based on organizational need. I'm usually involved in multiple projects at the same time, in some cases as a lead for my department, and in others as one of several representatives.

Most projects are like a puzzle to be solved. We are usually given a desired end goal, but with little idea of how to achieve it. Finding that solution is very satisfying.

Any given day can look quite different, depending on the nature of the project. Usually, my mornings will be spent on analysis and reports, while my afternoons are usually taken up with meetings, particularly when the project involves my counterparts in other parts of the world.

I regularly interact with operations managers and subject-matter experts within the department; I also work with other project managers and key contacts in departments such as compliance, financial crime, etc. Most projects have weekly meetings, but usually involve multiple email and telephone conversations outside of that. While everybody has their own priorities, especially with limited time available on busy days, it is usually easy enough to find common ground. Having good personal relationships with key partners makes this easier. They don't have to like you, but it helps if they respect you.

Resistance to change is endemic in my organization, as is common within the sector, although the company tries to promote an acceptance of change within their culture. In my role, it can be difficult to persuade individuals of the benefits of trying to do something differently, even if those benefits are obvious. Additionally, a single negative voice can be more powerful than a chorus of positivity.

A big part of my role requires collaboration with key partners. I frequently work across departmental boundaries. I will generally attempt to cultivate a good professional relationship with those departments so that they are happy to work with me. If a department is not receptive, then I will enlist support of senior managers to enforce cooperation. For example, when developing a post-Brexit operational model, there were numerous departments with their own priorities all trying to shape our response. I had to convince key partners of the viability of the new procedures I was developing, creating a base of support within the project.

-Box 4.3-

Lucy – Project Analyst, Local Government

Background

I started at [local government organization] about three years ago as a social care adviser. I've got a psychology degree but I didn't really know what to do with it so I was looking at potential avenues and ended up getting a job in social care. I started out as an adviser and then worked my way up to be a trainer and team leader. There's not much room for progression within that department so I'd got as far as I ever could with that role.

When I was searching internally I came across this role advertised on the intranet. This project was in a different branch of government (community resourcing) but I felt the aims were similar to those I'd been working on in social care (trying to push self-service, encouraging citizens to know their own personal assets). I don't have any formal change management experience, I've not worked on a project like this before, but in social care we have so much change all the time, you're constantly rolling with it and working out the best way to get that working as a service. The job description for this role asked for someone with data analysis experience, which I had not done in my previous roles, but being a psychology graduate meant that I had been frequently working with data to run experiments, so I figured that I would be able to use that within this role. A key motivation for me was that I felt this new element would challenge me. It would push me as a person. I mean the role is very interesting, but I wanted to see also what that role could do for me.

(Continued)

The role is a secondment, so, there's a bit of security there in that they have to find me something else afterwards, but it might not be what I came from. I haven't really got an end-goal at this point. I'm just sort of thinking this is going to open a lot more doors.

Doing the job

The project is about creating a smoother customer journey for local residents as they access local government services, such as library services, welfare support, and volunteer and community provisions. This means getting a range of partners from the different services, as well as external and voluntary sector partners, to work together. Obviously, in the current climate, we are looking to make financial savings too. We are looking for an efficient solution, where residents can have one point of call, to self-serve where possible. This puts less demand on government and promotes independence.

I work alongside the project manager. As the data analyst I help the project manager and the partners to define our version of success. What we are looking to achieve, and for whom. And then work out from that how to measure it using existing data that the government collects, accessing that data and extracting what we need, and maybe collecting new data via surveys or checklists, to show that we are being successful. One of the challenges is that when the other agencies collect their data, it's all different from each other. So, I need to collect that to compile it in a way that's universal to all and still meaningful.

This is an entirely new role, so I'm not stepping into somebody else's shoes who could train me. It wasn't clear for a while and took a little bit of finding my feet to know where I should be going, and how to do it. I know that my role is a little bit of everything. My role was originally conceived of being two roles that were then incorporated together. One was more of a project secretary role, and the other was the data analytics part. It has taken some time to feel relaxed about the whole thing. It was a little bit unsettling because everything was new at once.

I'm still working out where the boundaries are of what I do. I think that's maybe partly to do with the nature of the project being partnership-based. There's lots of people coming in as partners. It's clear that we [local government organization] are the dominant partner. We always prioritize thinking about what we want from the partnership and how it would work for us. Other partners must bring something to the table and it's in our control as to who's in and who isn't and where it's useful. That creates a power dynamic that I need to navigate. At the same time, it's about working together to explore how the partnership can benefit both of us. Other partners don't always understand what my role is. I'm constantly saying this is what I do and this is why I need whatever measurements I need from you. I must explain why I need figures from them so that I can see if things are working.

I expect that my role will change as the project develops because it's deliberately vague. We don't have a complete plan, or even a definite lockdown on who the partnership will include at this stage. The aims of this project are not something that's been put into practice before so there are things that will need to be ironed out. So, I've got to be able to swing with that completely.

Further Recommended Reading

For an overview of different types of change-maker roles, how they come about and what attributes they hold, see Tucker, D.A. and Cirella, S. (2018) 'Agents of change: Insights from three case studies of hospital transformations'. In *Research in Organizational Change and Development*. Bingley: Emerald Publishing.

To understand more about what happens when change-maker roles are poorly defined or change during implementation, see Tucker, D.A., Hendy, J. and Barlow, J. (2015) 'The importance of role sending in the sensemaking of change agent roles', *Journal of Health Organization and Management*, 29(7): 1047–64.

For a comprehensive study of the powerful role that middle-manager change makers play in change interpretation, see Balogun, J. and Johnson, G. (2004) 'Organizational restructuring and middle manager sensemaking', *Academy of Management Journal*, 47(4): 523–49.

For a more focused look at how champions and opinion leaders influence others to take up innovations and change, see Locock, L., Dopson, S., Chambers, D. and Gabbay, J. (2001) 'Understanding the Role of Opinion Leaders in Improving Clinical Effectiveness', *Social Science and Medicine*, 53(6): 745–757.

5
PERSPECTIVES ON DIGITAL TRANSFORMATION

Chapter Objectives

- To introduce digital transformation definitions, history, current models and more diverse perspectives
- To discuss various approaches and concerns about how to implement digital transformation in organizations
- To explore alternative perspectives on digital transformation, which highlight the importance of technologies, social cultural factors and other concerns often missing in popular models

5.1 Introduction

This chapter looks at different perspectives on a significant kind of organizational change today, 'digital transformation'. Digital transformation spans enterprise-wide changes with large infrastructure and budget requirements, plus smaller-scale transformations around organizational capacities, customer services and innovation processes for example. With a constant stream of new technologies and associated disciplines, including artificial intelligence applications or big data, for example, digital transformation is a concept that nicely frames a range of connected business priorities.

In the chapter, we firstly introduce the topic, outline some key terms (see Table 5.1 below), and make a case for the need to include a variety of perspectives on what we mean and prioritize when we are doing digital transformations in organizations. The second section looks at definitions and some of the history behind the term digital transformation. Thirdly, popular views of *how to do digital transformation* are reviewed to support change makers in need of practical models and frameworks. The fourth section explores *alternative perspectives on digital transformation*, including the technological versus sociological determinism debate and hybrid, middle ground socio-technical view. This section incorporates a sample of **socio-technical perspectives**, which differ from traditional, engineering, top-down or project management approaches to change. These alternative views broaden our understanding of transformation processes in both critical, inclusive, and innovative ways, by drawing on lessons from sub-fields, such as human–computer interaction and information systems fields.

Table 5.1 Key chapter concepts

Key concepts used in the chapter	
Digitize	Converting analogue data or media into digital media, e.g. a paper book into an e-book.
Digitalize	Converting a product or service to take advantage of digital channels, media or data, e.g. to run a student test online instead of in a room together with paper tests.
Digital transformation	Comprehensively changing an organization itself or organizational function to become digital, e.g. transforming a school to offer novel digital teaching, learning, enrolment, assessment services
Technological determinism	View that social and economic change is caused by technology
Sociological determinism	View that social and economic change is caused by social relations and culture
Sociotechnical systems	View of how organizations develop through social and technical relations, including the design and ongoing use of technologies
Human-computer interaction	Sub-field in Computer Science dedicated to the design and use of technologies by users
Practice perspectives	Range of approaches used in Organization Studies (OS) and Information Systems (IS) fields, highlighting how people and technologies interact in often complex, everyday work
Socio-digital	View at the end of the chapter emphasizing how social and digital aspects of change impact each other constantly; neither simply causes the other

Widening our views of digital transformation beyond technology-centric or top-down project management perspectives means accepting a challenging but more holistic understanding of technology and change. Wider views acknowledge complexity and ambiguity, question our assumptions and support change efforts which draw on interdisciplinary expertise. Wider views often accept the politics and power inherent in change settings, as well as the diverse impacts and sensitivities often silenced in popular narratives of linear change, simple project stages and the 'evolutionary' view of ever better technological tools.

For organizational change makers, developing digital transformation capabilities internally will be a key concern. The need to be aware of innovations, systems, software, applications, devices and customer trends will be an important element of these capabilities. In this chapter we do not focus on a particular device (e.g. internet of things refrigerators), a single skill set (e.g. data analytics), or services (e.g. cloud computing) – but see Table 5.2 for typical digital transformation technologies and applications. Instead, the chapter reviews different perspectives and priorities, popular views and alternative views, to encourage digital transformations that take into account effective strategies for different stakeholders, users or organizational groups that change makers are charged with supporting and working across during change efforts. We hope this leads to more innovative and inclusive digital transformations.

Table 5.2 Common digital transformation applications

Common digital transformation applications	
Cloud computing	Delivery of remotely hosted services to users via the internet, e.g. data storage, application hosting, email
Big data	Data sets of great variety, volume, and velocity (speed of capture)
Artificial intelligence	Computing systems or machines that mimic human intelligence to perform tasks based on information they collect and interpret
Machine learning	Algorithmic or artificial intelligence application that analyses large data sets to learn, adapt and make predictions
Internet of things	Physical objects with sensors, software, and the ability to process and exchange information via the internet
Data analytics	Data analysis applications and skills used by analytics experts

Popular models give change makers a solid starting point, but a key contribution of the chapter is to show that popular models and recipes are limited, and that bringing in diverse knowledge, experience and perspectives from other fields benefits change makers, transformation processes and ultimately digital transformation impacts. In the last part of this chapter we draw together lessons learned, and argue for a broader, more inclusive lens on digital transformation, which we term socio-digital transformation.

5.2 Digital Transformation: Definitions and History

There have been several trends in recent decades around transformation, such as 'enterprise transformation', 'finance transformation', 'supply chain transformation' and 'marketing transformation', so the transformation buzz is not unique to the digital. Nevertheless, technology corporations such as Salesforce (2022) deploy definitions of digital transformation strategies and solutions that focus on definitions that involve a 'reimagining of business in the digital age', create new 'business processes', 'cultures', 'customer experiences', or meet new 'market requirements'. Others, such as IBM, agree that digital transformation is 'customer driven' and requires a 'digital-first' approach to all parts of the business. Often, companies state that digital transformation involves specific technologies, such as AI, automation, hybrid cloud technologies, and digital data to improve workflows, smart decision-making or real-time market disruptions (e.g. IBM, 2022).

A cottage industry of consultants, authors and bloggers has emerged, who promote, talk, and write about digital transformation. Schmarzo (2017) defines it as the 'application of digital capabilities to processes, products, and assets to improve efficiency, enhance customer value, manage risk, and uncover new monetization opportunities'. McKinsey & Company (2023) define it as building competitive advantage by 'deploying tech at scale to improve customer experience and lower costs'. Definitions often point to organizations becoming more scientific, data-driven, quantified, instrumented, measured, mathematic, calculated and/or automated. The data behind this transformation enables customers to find what they want, share experience, see recommendations and arrange deliveries in seamless ways. Companies that harness digital transformation capabilities gain strategic marketing insights, manage customer life cycles better and reduce inventory costs through data-driven predictive analytics. These are typical elements of digital change.

One key debate is whether digital transformation is digital at all, or even transformational (e.g. Kane et al., 2015; Kane et al., 2019; Visnjic et al., 2022). Most models claim the digital is most important, but some authors argue it is about people adapting to the technology. Another debate concerns whether digital transformation is a single big-bang change event to get ready for, or a continuous, ongoing capacity to keep on changing. These debates affect change makers because continuous adaptation requires constant development of business competencies, strategy, personnel, and an agile organizational identity that is always switched on, primed for continuous adaptation, akin to emergent views of change management. This contrasts with big-bang views and planned change models.

Change makers need to understand these definitions, debates and approaches, plus the digital technologies themselves, organizational capacities, skills, analytics and customer-centric orientations. They must have a level of technology mastery because technologies are seen by many, including leaders, as the backbone of new digital products and services (Saldanha, 2019). Views of technology as driving and ushering in a continual process of change are now core themes in digital transformation thinking.

Firstly, technology is seen to drive change in historical revolutions – agricultural, industrial and information revolutions. Such eras shaped societies, economies, markets and organizations. Brynjolfsson and McAfee (2014) open their book *The Second Machine Age* with this kind of narrative about how we are now living in a new era, *where machines do our thinking work, in contrast to a previous age where machines did our physical work*. Brynjolfsson and Saunders (2009) argue information technologies create new kinds of productivity and opportunities for digital organizations to share information, decentralize decision-making, incentivize change, and invest in training and education. Digital technology thus drives economic, social and organizational change.

In terms of revolutions, a current Fourth Industrial Revolution (4IR) implicates the melding of physical, digital and biological worlds, using cheap digital technologies (Saldanha, 2019) to which

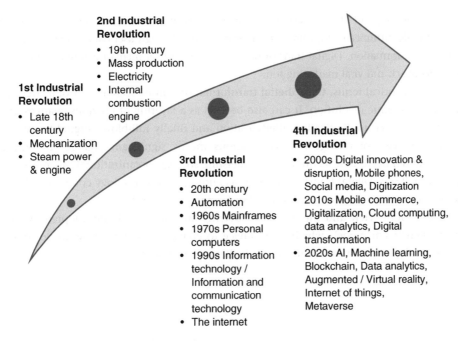

2nd Industrial Revolution
- 19th century
- Mass production
- Electricity
- Internal combustion engine

1st Industrial Revolution
- Late 18th century
- Mechanization
- Steam power & engine

3rd Industrial Revolution
- 20th century
- Automation
- 1960s Mainframes
- 1970s Personal computers
- 1990s Information technology / Information and communication technology
- The internet

4th Industrial Revolution
- 2000s Digital innovation & disruption, Mobile phones, Social media, Digitization
- 2010s Mobile commerce, Digitalization, Cloud computing, data analytics, Digital transformation
- 2020s AI, Machine learning, Blockchain, Data analytics, Augmented / Virtual reality, Internet of things, Metaverse

Figure 5.1 The four industrial revolutions

organizations must adapt. Figure 5.1 shows a 'revolutions' timeline. Here, technology drives evolutionary change, and creates progressive, uniform impacts across populations and organizations.

Yet, change makers must question popular narratives about change, organizations and technology, because variations and bumps in the road are ironed out, flattened or elided. This is a problem for change makers because in *real* organizations with specific digital systems and devices, we encounter *real* bumps, problems, setbacks, inequalities, failures and contradictory impacts all the time. Many researchers see grand narrative perspectives as problematic and overly generic. They ignore real contexts, variations in technology adoption or adaptation, people's own agencies and decisions, resistance, conflicting values, and the complex human and organizational sides of technological change. Pfaffenberger (1992) characterizes the broad, flattening histories as the standard model of technology and, as we shall see, this standard underpins many popular digital transformation views.

A second key theme is that transformation results from layers of expanding, ever more complex processes. Digital transformation today requires previous digitization and digitalization phases. **Digitization** means the conversion of existing information from analogue (e.g. physical photographs, printed books, typed data) into digital formats (e.g. digital images, documents, databases). **Digitalization** follows digitization. In digitalization, already digitized data is used to make processes better, faster, more efficient or simpler, but not to really change products or services. Examples would be using email instead of physical post, replacing paper exams in schools with online exams, replacing paper tax forms with e-forms, or storing photos in an online database to share with colleagues. Lastly, the third layer, **digital transformation**, can finally happen when an already digitalized product or service is completely transformed, and the customer experience transformed too. For example, the shift from Blockbuster as a bricks and mortar store renting out physical VHS movie tapes to Netflix streaming content across multiple devices and algorithmically adjusting customer interfaces through user data is a good example of digital transformation. Digital transformation also uses social media for ranking purchases, product feedback and viral marketing too.

In these historical terms, then, digital transformation can be seen as part of a large-scale social and economic revolution. It can also be seen as a layering of previous changes, from electrification to IT, to digitization, digitalization and finally full-blown digital transformation. This process of change for organizations means significant changes to business processes, and it needs new technologies, leadership, strategy, organizational capabilities and employee skill sets. Digital transformation is also not just for technology companies, but for all kinds of companies and organizations (Westerman et al., 2014).

This revolution view and the historical layering are widespread and adopted by many current mainstream models which offer advice to change makers on how to do, how to implement, digital transformations. And it is these we turn to next.

5.3 Current Digital Transformation Models

In this section, we look at current and popular models of digital transformation, for two reasons. Firstly, these models offer practical, business advice on doing digital transformations, often with a set of steps for planning and implementation. Secondly, these models help us to see popular themes and perspectives on transformation, what they prioritize, miss, or elide. For both these reasons, the section is useful for change makers. We look first at IT project management influences, then technology-centric and technology evolution perspectives, before human-oriented views, and a final review of some lessons for change makers.

IT waterfall and agile models

By the 1960s, experts realized how difficult technology projects were, and in 1968 at a NATO conference the term 'software crisis' was used (Kelly, 2008). Software development was a form of engineering at the time, organized in an expert, technical, rational, scientific manner. Stakeholder communications and customer feedback were not big concerns then. Since then, traditional IT projects have followed **waterfall project management** approaches, which see customers involved early on, but then requirements frozen for most of the development cycle (Hass, 2007). Typical waterfall stages include planning, design, implementation, testing and deployment, in that order. Such stages mimic common project management models such as in 'Project Management Body of Knowledge' (PMBOK) or 'Prince 2', moving from conceptualization, planning and implementation to testing and project closing. Similar waterfall stages are found in other engineering views, such as business process reengineering (BPR), and planned change models covered in Chapter 2.

In the 1990s alternative models emerged, including ones related to lean manufacturing (Dybe and Dings Jr, 2008; Liker and Morgan, 2006). Many of these are now characterized as **agile project management**, an umbrella term covering various more flexible models of change. In agile projects change makers steer teams through iterations, customer collaborations, and face-to-face communication, with each element largely welcoming customer change variations. Although step-by-step engineering or project management assumptions remain (e.g. top-down, linear change processes), digital transformation borrows much from agile approaches too (e.g. customer focus, iterative development). For change makers, this means digital transformations only partly follow traditional, rigid IT project structures.

5.4 Technology-centric digital transformation

Digital transformation is generally centred on organizations deploying and adapting to technologies. This is the mainstream technology-centric view. For example, technologist Thomas Siebel (2019) argues that four specific technologies bring about revolutionary business changes. These are cloud computing, big data, artificial intelligence (AI) and the internet of things (IOT). Change also depends on organizations adapting to technologies (Brynjolfsson and McAfee, 2014) in order to meet customer needs, although there is not always a clear understanding of what drives customer needs beyond the free hand of the market. As such, technology-centric change is a useful perspective, but it can limit our view of what changes and why. Change makers need to be aware of this.

In Westerman et al.'s influential book *Leading Digital* (2014), the first line reads 'Technology is the biggest story in business today, plain and simple' (p. 1). The focus is not on Silicon Valley or start-ups, but on the 'rest of the 90 per cent' of big businesses around the world. After spending years talking to large companies, the authors found many were not ready to transform. To get the most benefit from digital technologies, websites, social media, robots, drones, big data, cloud computing, AI and IOT, companies need to become what the authors call digital masters.

This involves several key steps. They must build digital capabilities, rethink customer engagement, transform business models, and ensure strong leadership (Westerman et al., 2014: 6). These steps require openness, agility and digital skills. Leadership must overcome inertia by driving change from the top down, through 'strong senior executive direction', with 'methods that engage workers in making change happen'. Leadership must push a transformative vision, energizing employees and securing effective governance. Corporate and IT leaders need to come together to drive change. IT is not viewed as a service unit, taking orders from business leaders who do not understand it. It is an equal partner. A key lesson for change makers is that digital technologies drive unstoppable change. Businesses must get on board to survive. The 'longer you wait, the more difficult it will become' (Westerman et al., 2014: 7).

The model provides advice to change makers on how digital transformation is a continual commitment to change, and how business and IT (leaders and teams) must collaborate. Such advice contrasts with traditional views of IT as a service department, or not being a strategic partner. It is different from many agile or similar skunk works models for innovation too, which are project based, ending after a defined period. Westerman et al.'s popular book promotes key steps for digital transformation – see Figure 5.2.

This model explains how good governance, leadership buy-in, making business leaders responsible for IT transformations, new organizational processes, new incentives, rewards, trainings, role

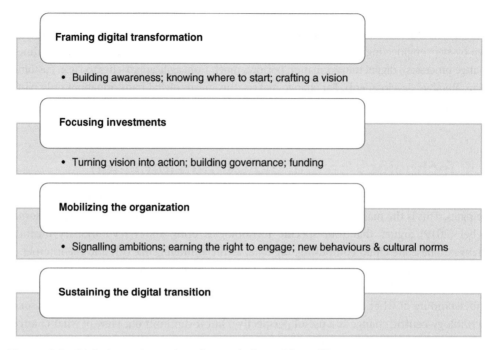

Figure 5.2 Digital transformation phases (adapted from Westerman et al., 2014)

modelling and even gamification can help bring people on board. Digital transformation here is not just a new IT system, but technologies are the centre of the wider changes.

Technology-centric evolution

Technology-centric models often imply an evolutionary view of change, where the organization must 'change or die'. This view is well illustrated in Saldanha's stages perspective (2019) – see Figure 5.3.

In the evolutionary view, the organization keeps evolving, progressing, improving, not just changing, and change is constant, not just single events, or one-off big-bang change projects.

If change then is ongoing and always progressive, resistance becomes a problem for change makers. Middle-level management act like a body's immune system and reject change (Saldanha, 2019), because they find change hard, are inflexible, are the 'frozen middle' (Byrnes, 2005) of organizations. The 'immune system responses can originate at all levels in the organization, but the toughest ones occur at middle management' (Saldanha, 2019: 99–100). This observation is insightful but also a significant generalization. Saldanha also argues it is easy to get senior leadership excited about digital change, and the younger generation gets on board quickly, leaving middle management as the obstacle. This means leaders and change makers must try to get them on board, offer change incentives and make sure the immune system benefits from digital change. Bringing on board the frozen middle is an important task for change makers, involving careful negotiation, collaboration, sharing visions and building trust. Ironically, for technology-centric models, this all requires diverse human, social and organizational factors.

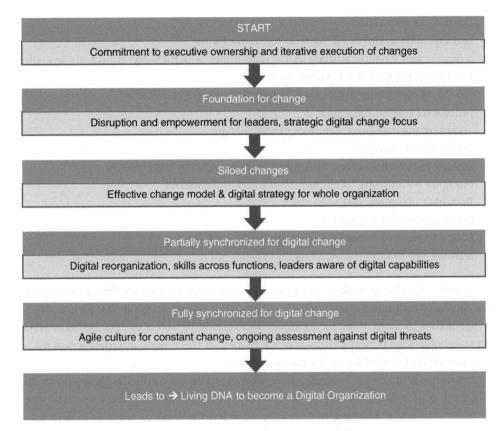

Figure 5.3 Five-stage transformation model (Saldanha, 2019)

The human side of digital transformation

Digital transformation models have emerged which appear to promote more people-oriented, or human transformations. However, when we look closer, many of these perspectives still rest on technologies as driving the need for human and cultural adaptation to the core technologies. For example, models by consultancies such as the Boston Consulting Group (2020) advocate transformation metrics and targets, fail-fast techniques to learn quickly and high-calibre talent management. Microsoft's (2017) five challenges include collaborating not competing, embracing change fears and anxieties, demonstrating digital value through experience, respecting how new technologies fit into the organization, and helping people to be agile and forward-thinking about continuous innovation. There is a clear focus on people in these lists, but each requires people to adapt to and be measured for their technology use, fitting it into their work whilst managing personal anxieties, and so on. These are not people-first, participatory approaches to change, transformation, or wellbeing.

In *The Technology Fallacy*, Kane et al. (2019) highlight how people are the real driver of digital transformation. They have an important chapter on moving beyond the 'digital transformation hype' and they recommend organizations become digitally mature. This maturity involves learning how to innovate through experimentation, collaboration and iterations. They prescribe an organizational DNA to become digitally mature, which includes:

- continuous innovation
- real time data available on demand across platforms
- a flexible and strategic attitude to 'decision rights' which change constantly (e.g. often empowering middle-level change makers)
- flexible or 'morphing' teams for collaboration beyond just sharing
- promoting constant learning
- accepting the disruptive nature of digital changes
- being customer centric
- making information accessible for internal and external stakeholders
- engaging with diverse, often non-traditional, stakeholders
- flattening organizational hierarchies
- being nimble and responsive
- failing forward by testing and iterating
- learning fast to improve processes and products.

This is useful for change makers, practical advice on adapting towards digital technologies, but centring on people and continual business disruption. The advice is valuable for middle-level change makers in many ways; for example, because gaining access to data, decision-makers and stakeholders are typical change-maker activities. In this model, internal change makers are acknowledged as vital for digital transformation.

Unfortunately many of these transformation components conflict with top-down controls, traditional waterfall models or hierarchical power relations in organizations. The model still roots changes in adapting to technologies, when the need to act fast, be responsive, innovate, communicate, collaborate, morph teams, learn, and so on are all very human, social and organizational elements of change.

Furthermore, the needs to disrupt, learn and fail fast, be fluid and flexible, etc. also relate to external issues such as market competition, brand reputation and customer pressures as much as new digital chips, wires or systems. Underneath the focus on people, models such as this still often centre on technologies as driving change, when they should explicitly acknowledge that humans, departments, budgets, internal politics, leadership awareness, staff skills, stakeholder agendas, markets, and many other factors also shape transformation processes and outcomes. Kane et al.'s (2019) model holds value for change makers, but the overriding need to harness the power of technology obscures other factors that change makers are constantly dealing with, such as organizational power, creativity or stakeholder needs.

Some interim lessons for change makers

What can internal change makers take away from these technology-centric digital transformation models? First, without always having senior decision-making power, middle level change makers will need to use diverse skills and resources. Some of these may be digital or technological in nature, such as previous experience of digital transformation, expertise in back-end operating systems, coding, machine learning, data science, system integration, or database administration. Other skills will be more front-end, or user facing, such as functional management, interface design, helpdesk, super-user or training experience. Management domain knowledge of change, strategy and leadership will also be beneficial.

However, what is interesting is that many change-maker skills and organizational processes will not be digital in nature. Communicating change, lobbying for senior buy-in, building consensus, creativity, collaborating, crossing silos, resolving conflicts, understanding users, mapping customer journeys, dealing with internal politics, and working across complex or ambiguous social and digital organizational dynamics – none of these are inherently digital skills or processes. In the technologically heavy transformation literature, these processes and skill sets are there between the lines, but they are often marginalised or dealt with in general terms (e.g. the 'frozen middle', 'information wants to be free'). This is because sweeping evolutionary change claims, urgency rhetoric and adaptation arguments tend to crowd out pragmatic, contextual advice for dealing with subtle, complex change in our own, very specific, change contexts.

5.5 Alternative Perspectives on Digital Transformation

This chapter has so far described the meaning and history of the term digital transformation, and outlined some popular and current models of transformational change processes. We have also covered some of the limitations in these models, their technology-centric biases for example. In addition, IT-driven change and digital transformation have several areas of key challenges or failure points to be aware of. These may concern weak change plans, not taking account of stakeholder needs (Dwivedi et al., 2015) or user work practices, ignoring human factors, or the dark side of technology (Tarafdar et al., 2016). The evolutionary model of digital change is widespread; however, it does not always take account of such failure points well. Therefore, change makers require broader, more nuanced perspectives that acknowledge positive and negative changes, evolutionary change, political shifts, linear plans or creative collaborations, transformation results and multi-stakeholder impacts.

Therefore, this section considers alternative perspectives on digital transformation. Firstly, we compare technology centric and socio-centric change, often characterized in the technological determinism versus sociological determinism debate. This leads us to socio-technical systems, a key theme in digital innovation. We then look at different socio-technical perspectives using examples from computing (e.g. human–computer interaction) and information systems (e.g. perspectives on work practices) to show that technology-centric models are not the only way to encourage positive, inclusive and effective change processes, or digital innovations.

Technological-determinist perspectives

In technological-determinist perspectives a key claim is that technologies cause social, cultural and organizational change. This is assumed in many popular views of historical change (Pfaffenberger, 1992). Digital transformation, innovation, diffusion and disruption models all make this assumption (e.g. Brynjolfsson and McAfee, 2014; Christensen, 2013; Westerman et al., 2014). Scientific innovations occur first, arising from a survival need to overcome existing limitations. Only later do culture, society and organizations adapt, lagging behind technological change. Technology is seen as neutral and apolitical, a linear story of evolutionary progress, from the Stone Age to the Machine Ages.

This view is so popular today that it has been called the standard model of science and technology. Negative impacts are glossed over, put aside as collateral damage. The 'result of the explosion of technological knowledge has been a massive expansion of Man's reach, but with lamentable and unavoidable social, environmental, and cultural consequences' (Pfaffenberger, 1992: 494).

In technological-determinist views, change makers' only option is to follow the technology, adapt and accept inevitable impacts. But there is an opposing, less popular, view where diverse factors, not just technologies, contribute to transformation processes and impacts.

Sociological-determinist perspectives

The opposing view is sociological determinism, a perspective which explains change through sociocultural factors, not technologies. Customs, traditions, education, the profit motive, social norms, human interests and decisions, and diverse work practices cause changes. Technologies result from these cultural ebbs and flows. They don't simply cause them. For example, Green (2002) sees all technologies as born out of social needs, whether they be social, economic, political or military.

This view contrasts with our earlier discussion about digital transformation because it is the social and cultural, meaning the existing business model, strategies, markets, customers, executive politics, departmental conflicts and staff capabilities that drive digital transformation.

For change makers, this view is empowering, emphasizing people's actions, interactions and relationships. However, a problem with sociological determinism is that it gives little agency to technologies themselves, the digital, the internet or the app that stops customers visiting shops. As such, neither sociological nor technological determinism cover all aspects of digital transformation adequately, or give change makers the full set of concepts and tools to navigate digital transformation dreams, cultures, resistance, stakeholders or impacts.

Socio-technical middle ground

A more fruitful middle-ground perspective has grown steadily for decades, initially around the notion of socio-technical systems. The term was first coined by UK Tavistock Institute researchers Trist and Bamforth (1951). The main aspects of the socio-technical system approach began as:

- recognizing the system as a whole, a relationship between *social* and *technical* parts
- designing these two parts together for effectiveness
- relating these two key parts to the work environment around them
- emphasizing the importance of employee involvement and teamwork (e.g. semi-autonomous work groups or self-managed work teams).

It is now a term used across diverse approaches to complex social and technological change. Socio-technical systems have been used in design studies and information systems for many years (Sawyer and Jarrahi, 2014), and are highly relevant to digital transformation. These perspectives ask us to look at real-life situations, and the complex range of human, social and technological factors that contribute to changes and impacts.

Most socio-technical perspectives combine technology with human and social factors more deeply than the popular digital transformation literatures. In fact, in socio-technical perspectives, both humans and technologies have agency, both adapt to each other, and change makers can work with both to promote positive organizational changes. This means when working with internal stakeholders, change makers can appeal to the benefits of new digital technologies, but also to the decision-making power of department heads in shaping how to communicate, implement and operationalize new technologies. This is something that leaders, and those adopting top-down popular transformation models, may need convincing about. Digital transformations are significant change processes and benefit from user and department ideas and input.

Human–computer interaction – the social end of computer science

Computer science has technical and human oriented sub-fields – the back end (infrastructure management, integration, etc., away from users) and front end (web development, helpdesk services, etc., nearer to users) as they are commonly termed (Beynon-Davies, 2009). Both back-end internal systems and front-end customer facing interfaces are researched in **human–computer interaction (HCI)** and **computer-supported collaborative work (CSCW)**, two sub-fields within computer science that focus on how individuals (HCI) or groups (CSCW) behave when using diverse technologies.

HCI examines how interfaces work, and how individuals behave when using digital tools and devices, whether these be mobile phones, laptops, office workstations or controls at power plants[1]. Interfaces help or hinder people's work tasks, whether audio (e.g. alarm bells), tactile (buttons, keyboards) or visual (panels, monitors, phone screens). HCI draws on technical fields like computer graphics and coding, as well as human domains such as communications, psychology and human factors.

Two things are important for change makers regarding HCI. Firstly, understanding users and tasks helps designers create effective technologies and helps administrators manage them effectively. Change makers can promote digital transformation successes by creating spaces for digital/IT teams and functional departments and users to collaborate. Secondly, change makers must be aware that new technologies impact how employees do work, share information or control their data. These issues depend on how services and data sharing are

---

[1]After the 1979 Three Mile Island nuclear accident, a US President's Commission Report (1979) found the plant control panel was huge with hundreds of alarms and hidden indicators. This is a classic example of bad design with high risks (Meshkati, 1991). Our takeaway is that if digital technologies are badly designed or don't align with training, roles or abilities, failures will result.

governed within the organization, and this requires negotiation between IT and functional managers. Change makers can predict opportunities and challenges by learning how well staff or customers adopt, adapt, work around or even avoid new digital systems.

CSCW shares similarities with HCI, but focuses on groups using technologies, rather than individuals. CSCW draws on psychology and social science, and offers change makers lessons on how groups and teams collaborate around technologies. CSCW uses many socio-technical concepts, such as **boundary objects**. These are objects of information (e.g. a physical book, webpage or an idea) that are used differently by different groups, communities, departments or experts. For example, marketing professionals and product development professionals understand products differently, as doctors and nurses understand health records differently (Bossen et al., 2014). Such differences concern how each group uses the product or health record in everyday work. By identifying boundary objects (e.g. reports, indicators, plans) and understanding how different groups use them, change makers can translate or broker digital transformation opportunities.

CSCW highlights other group work lessons, such as how communication quality and ineffective personal relationships can damage virtual teamwork, whereas in contrast kick-off meetings, instant messaging and leadership can mitigate such problems (Thompson and Coovert, 2006). How we present our digital identities is important too. Impression management, a social phenomenon identified in the 1950s by anthropologist Erving Goffman (1978) highlights how we manage people's perceptions of ourselves. It is important today in how we curate our digital selves, whether commenting on LinkedIn (DeVito et al., 2017) or adjusting our Zoom backgrounds before meetings. Complex group dynamics impact on employee and customer behaviours in digital environments, but are rarely prioritized in change plans.

HCI and CSCW emphasize socio-technical change at individual or group levels, and their lessons are insightful for digital transformations. *One limitation, however, is that top management may not always pay attention to low-level user/customer experience, or technology acceptance.* Therefore, change makers should amplify the voices of lower-level groups to minimize resistance, promote sustainable transformations and secure returns on investment.

Information systems and organizational practice

Perspectives adopted in fields such as organization studies and information systems make use of social theory to create innovative ways of understanding the design, use and impacts of technologies for organizations. The section samples perspectives on organizational practice and sociomateriality to help change makers widen their own understand of digital transformations.

Broadly speaking, the practice turn in social science in the early 2000s indicated a shift in focus away from focusing on individuals and ideals of how people should act, towards what people actually do and say within their everyday work (e.g. Miettinen et al., 2009; Reckwitz, 2002; Schatzki, 2000).[2] **Practice perspectives** avoid economic man explanations (homo

---

[2]Practice' does not mean 'practitioners' or 'professionals' in this chapter, or 'practice' as in doing something repeatedly to become proficient. These are separate meanings of the word.

economicus) of rational actors with perfect information, and sociological man explanations (homo sociologicus) about what people *should do* if they belong to certain categories or groups, such as managers and friends (Reckwitz, 2002). It is not the individual CEO hero or troublesome HR middle manager who is responsible for digital change or failure, nor the 'frozen middle' of rigid managers. In contrast, practice perspectives bring into frame the complex mix of people, processes and technologies involved in change. In this sense, practice perspectives welcome people's agency, organizational structures, resistance, power, politics, learning, change and stability to help us understand what people do. This goes beyond simplistic appeals to evolutionary change, technological utopia, or top-down controls and looks at how people react, respond, establish routines or do unexpected things.

Practice perspectives highlight several important elements in organizational changes (Nicolini, 2012). First are the performances of people, their routines and organizational norms. Second is people's ability to affect change, their agency. Third is people's knowledge, expertise, learning, values and the beliefs they follow as managers or front-line staff. Fourth, power and politics are important parts of practice, in contrast to them often being seen as too hard to handle, too risky to discuss in top-down plans or rational models, or taboo in optimistic success narratives about organizational changes. Finally, practice perspectives emphasize materiality, which for change makers means the actual technologies themselves, the systems and tools important in digital transformations. Practice perspectives also allow us to zoom in or zoom out of organizational settings, from actions in an executive meeting on a Monday morning, to how they impact on various departments in the following weeks and months. Practice perspectives look at what people do, not what we expect them to do.

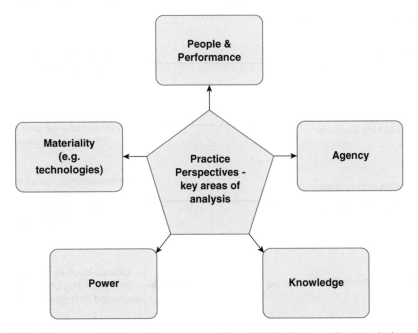

Figure 5.4 Key areas that practice perspectives highlight to understand change

Technology-as-practice

Early social practice theories (e.g. Bourdieu, 1977; Giddens, 1986) were used in socio-technical change and information systems research; however, these were criticized for focusing too much on social factors, and too little on technologies themselves. To overcome this limitation, Orlikowski (2001) developed the technology-in-practice view to help explain how people adopt, adapt and change technologies to fit ongoing work needs after new system installations. In other words, how people and technologies interact together over time shapes work, not just the idealized functions that technology designers plan for. This means change makers must pay attention to what people and departments do with technologies after implementations, not just what we believe will be done according to designers, engineers or senior managers during planning and purchasing. A problem with much digital transformation literature is a focus on the functionality of the system, its intended or imagined use, rather than its later actual use, which the technology-as-practice view embraces.

Orlikowski (2001) argued that we should pay more attention to IT artefacts (e.g. devices, laptops, databases, spreadsheets) after design and installation, because usage changes over time. Received wisdom about technology is just a tool we use. This is myopic, as it does not consider how work practices change, new processes emerge, people innovate with new tools, unintended consequences arise and the background web of computing; that is, the commitments, resources, policies, skills, training, spaces, incentives, and so on change over time (Kling and Scacchi, 1982; Orlikowski and Iacono, 2001). Change makers need perspectives which go beyond the technology-as-tool metaphor to see the bigger picture around digital transformations (see Figure 5.5). Change makers can help promote successes by keeping aware of what goes on around technologies, how practices change, power changes, people learn, new decisions are made and politics shifts.

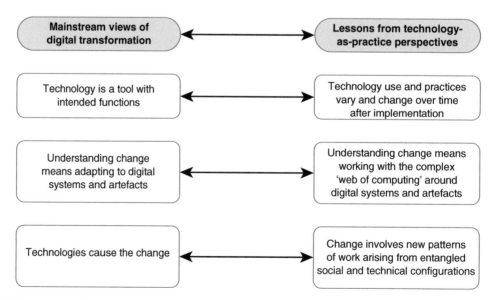

Figure 5.5 Practice perspectives bring into view the bigger picture around digital transformation

Furthermore, in going beyond technology-as-tool views, Orlikowski (2010) argued that technology and management research had failed to see how people and technologies were mixed together or entangled in new, emerging work patterns. Popular views position technology in unsatisfactory ways, as inert or unexplained, as an external force causing organizational impacts by itself (the techno-determinist view), or as a contingent product shaped by human interpretations alone (the socio-determinist view). Change makers can gain insight by seeing not how technologies impact on people, nor vice versa, but how new ways of working emerge, noticing new patterns of behaviour, how business processes shift and change, why people re-purpose technologies, using some and avoiding other functions.

Sociomateriality

Orlikowski and others developed sociomaterial perspectives too (Jones, 2014; Orlikowski, 2010). Material means our interest in digital technologies, systems, wires and devices. In this view, diverse factors get entangled with each other in our daily work (Orlikowski, 2005), or imbricated in layers of change (Leonardi, 2011), re-shaping our work experiences, our organizational norms, how we hold meetings, how we evaluate travel advice (Orlikowski and Scott, 2014), or how we decide on new information systems (Pollock and D'Adderio, 2012).

Sociomateriality helps us see how new digital systems and experiences entwine with workplace norms and behaviours, creating new behaviours or business processes. An excellent example today would be how Zoom meetings are different from face-to-face meetings before the COVID-19 pandemic. Customers, staff and students attend Zoom meetings, but often turn off cameras depending on the specifics of each meeting. A sociomaterial view suggests these new attitudes, behaviours and changes are due to a mix of human and non-human factors, beliefs, attitudes, worries, devices, software, lighting controls, interfaces, camera positions, backgrounds and so forth, and are not simply a technology causing whole new kinds of meetings by themselves. Crucially, this means change is not just people adapting to technology. With digital transformations, work changes, services change, staff and customers change, leaders change, and this brings an array of uncertainties, challenges and opportunities that change makers must keep up with. This is more than just adapting to the new technology. Work is constantly changing, in social and technological ways.

Established technology-centric and project management models find such behaviour changes difficult to explain, often claiming that it is technology that makes us behave in new ways; for example, social media makes us mean, e-commerce produces customer joy or students refuse to engage in Zoom classes. We easily forget that people re-shape software just as much as software re-shapes people. Digital transformation in this sense is not caused by digital boxes, nor cultural attitudes, but is a complex process of change, where diverse people, technologies, choices, ideas and other factors become entangled, leading to new patterns of behaviour. Neither human intentions and plans (our subjectivities) nor objective engineering inventions like apps or devices (objective reifications) determine future changes by themselves (Feldman and Orlikowski, 2011). Sociomateriality resonates with continuous improvement perspectives, but it questions techno-deterministic views, top-down change narratives and claims of constantly better, ever more efficient, evolutionary digital progress. Organizational learning also becomes a key activity in observing and responding to our transformations.

Final lessons for change makers

One important question or lesson stands out at this point – does existing digital transformation literature do enough to support change management in organizations, especially when failure is a possibility and changes impact on wider organizational, social, and environmental domains? The best response to this is that current technology-heavy models have a role to play, but they are not yet mature enough to acknowledge and mitigate against inequalities, or wider organizational, social and environmental problems. Urgent, techno-centric polemics can lead to aggressive, disruptive or even destructive change processes.

Therefore, perhaps we need to supplement 'digital transformation' with something more expansive, something that includes the many non-digital issues we have encountered. Some writers have talked about '**socio-digital**' formations (e.g. Sassen, 2012: 2). Socio-digital indicates wider views, models, worries, sensitivities, impacts, inequalities, and the need for stakeholder negotiations and diverse forms of expertise beyond project managers or technologists alone.

Socio-digital transformation would acknowledge current popular models, but seek more inclusive transformations and broader stakeholder participation on what digitally transformed futures should look like.

─Box 5.1─

Is socio-digital a new term?

'Socio-digital' is not a new term. Microsoft had a socio-digital research group in Cambridge, UK in 2013. Lancaster University has had a research group on socio-digital sustainability from 2013 (http://wp.lancs.ac.uk/sds/).The University of Bristol launched the ESRC-funded Centre for Sociodigital Futures (https://www.bristol.ac.uk/fssl/research/sociodigital-futures/). Saskia Sassen has used the term for years (Sassen, 2012; https://www.eurozine.com/interactions-of-the-technical-and-the-social/). Finally, socio-digital ideas relate to well-established research streams, such as socio-technical systems and sociomateriality (e.g. Leonardi, 2011).

Chapter Summary

- The chapter has reviewed digital transformation definitions, history, popular models and alternative views. Alternative views push back on grand narratives that change is urgent and uniform for all, that it brings only choice and freedom (Brynjolfsson,

2014) or is coming for all (McConnell, 2015). Change makers should consider their context, not grand claims from pundits and vendors.

- Popular models of digital transformation are relatively practical, drawing on management discourse, project controls and simple evolutionary models of technology which promise success if organizations adapt to the technologies.
- Digital transformations are seen as big-bang events to prepare for, or continuous change mandates; however, both forms of change rely on organizational capabilities and social aspects of change.
- Some popular digital transformation perspectives are narrow, eliding social and environmental impacts, organizational power, inequalities, change failures, complexity, ambiguity and interdisciplinary challenges.
- Change makers can broker digital/functional team dialogue spaces and collaborations, using insights from socio-technical perspectives to navigate unexpected impacts, changes after implementations, ethical concerns or changes in organizational power dynamics.
- Change makers should learn about digital transformation models as part of professional development, including popular models of transformation, plus socio-technical perspectives that promote innovative and inclusive change.
- Change makers may adopt balanced views of urgency or success-for-all claims from vendors and leaders, but can remain sensitive to diverse voices and specific groups that may lose out during change. Forming alliances, lobbying leaders and promoting collaborations can help make digital transformations more equal, fair, participatory, user-friendly, innovative, effective and sustainable over the long term.

Activity

Discuss and/or reflect on how internal stakeholders (e.g. executives, IT teams, marketing, product development, customer services, human resources, teachers, doctors, nurses) would be involved or impacted, and which change perspectives (e.g. waterfall, agile, digital transformation, socio-technical systems, technology-as-practice, socio-digital transformations) would be suitable for the following digital transformation scenarios. Think about each scenario, and about why, and how, different groups could be involved, or different perspectives might be more or less effective.

1 Building a new IT hub for a large bank
2 Improving software development at a small digital games company
3 Developing mobile apps for a national clothing retailer
4 Improving dashboards for executive decision-making at an insurance company
5 Supporting new staff work from home policies in local government
6 Establishing a new data analytics team to manage all data for an airline
7 Setting up an innovation unit to trial AI-driven customer services online
8 Funding a drone-based product delivery team in a regional delivery company

9   Finding out how a new HR system is used in practice, post-implementation, at a law firm

10 Moving teaching and learning online at a mid-sized university, and simultaneously supporting all students, from diverse backgrounds, with diverse learning abilities

11 Improving eHealth services for pensioners in a large city hospital

Further Recommended Reading

For more on digital transformation and its 'human' side, see Kane, G.C., Nguyen Phillips, S., Copulsky, J.R. and Andrus, G.R. (2019) *The Technology Fallacy: How People Are the Real Key to Digital Transformation*. London: MIT Press.

For a good practical model to use in digital transformation and innovation processes, see Herbert, L. (2017) *Digital Transformation: Build your Organization's Future for the Innovation Age*. London: Bloomsbury Publishing.

For an excellent introduction to different kinds of practice theories, which uses an accessible case study to show how each approach works, see Nicolini, D. (2012) *Practice Theory, Work, and Organization: An Introduction*. Oxford: Oxford University Press.

Finally, for more on the growing literature around problems with information technologies for our working lives, see Tarafdar, M., DArcy, J., Turel, O. and Gupta, A. (2016) 'The dark side of information technology', *MIT Sloan Management Review*, 56(2).

6

CHANGE AND VOICE

INCLUSIVITY, EQUALITY AND DIVERSITY

Chapter Objectives

- Discuss the importance of including and representing a diverse range of voices in implementing change
- Understand how typical organizational change techniques present challenges in representing diverse voices
- Identify various techniques and practices that managers can employ to enable employees to have a meaningful voice

6.1 Introduction

In this chapter we will discuss the importance of including and representing a diverse range of voices in implementing change starting from the perspective that activities which might be traditionally viewed by change management practitioners as 'resistance' may also be viewed as constructive input into the change implementation process (Connor, 1995; Ford et al., 2008). In this chapter we explore alternative perspectives on diverse consultation and inclusive employee voice mechanisms for change makers.

In the first part of the chapter we will offer a critical perspective on how mainstream processes for managing resistance fail to encourage an inclusive approach, diminishing the voices of minorities within organizations. In the second part, we will dive deeper into the challenges that change makers may themselves face in representing diverse voices within their organization including how the ability to influence others relies on similarity rather than diversity; the complexity of perceptions of fairness and equity; and working within institutional structures that silence marginalized groups. In the final section, we explore the effectiveness of mechanisms for employee voice at ensuring an inclusive dialogue as change develops. We highlight some more inclusive mechanisms for encouraging employee voice throughout the change process, including enhancing recognition of employees' unique expertise and value; and suggesting how meetings, training and other processes of change implementation might become more inclusive.

6.2 Resistance and Voice: A Critical Perspective

Resistance to change is one of the most discussed and examined areas of change management. We discuss issues of power and resistance in more detail in Chapter 8; however, here we will discuss the importance of including and representing a diverse range of voices in implementing change, which may appear in the form of resistance. Kotter and Schlesinger (1979) identify four reasons why employees may resist change.

- **Parochial self-interest** – people believe that they will lose something of value as a result of the change; for example, decision-making power, positive work environment or relationships that they *value*.
- **Misunderstanding and lack of trust** – when there is a lack of information, many organizational members will misunderstand or make assumptions about change. Where trust is lacking, there can be a reliance on rumour rather than trusted sources for sense-making.
- **Different assessments** – employees may be situated differently within the organization and therefore have a different perspective on the cost–benefit of the change. They may see more first-hand some of the costs of change and therefore assess them to be higher than other organizational members. They may or may not be an accurate assessment of the costs/benefits overall.
- **Low tolerance for change** – people fear that they will not be able to develop the new skills and behaviour that will be needed in the changed organization. Even if an

individual is generally supportive of the change, they may resist because it is too much change for them to process in the time given.

Resistance to change is common, but we can see from these reasons that many of them are more about the right information at the right time and place, and the different interpretations of organizational members. Many would argue that the eradication of resistance to change is impossible, and it is generally accepted that the concept of resistance is more complicated and open to interpretation than typically assumed. In their seminal paper, expanding the way we think about resistance to change, Ford et al. (2008) argue that the label 'resistance' is used to interpret the behaviours and communications of change recipients – organizational members who are affected by change – by those who are responsible for the formulation and implementation of change (e.g. change makers and senior leaders). Interpreting behaviour that does not unquestioningly conform to a new organizational reality as 'resistance' positions change makers as 'correct' and 'right' and resisting employees as 'wrong'. This is potentially problematic for organizational change as it may result in diminished employee voice and leader-centric bias about what is fair and ethical business practice.

Traditional resistance to change literature presents change makers as heroic individuals, implementing difficult but necessary business decisions and unpopular truths. Change makers are portrayed as having more access to insight of organizational goals, opportunities and challenges than other organizational members. It is assumed that this knowledge enables them to look after everyone's interests and, in doing so, look after the organization's interests. Where they encounter resistance to this mission, change makers are perceived as the undeserving victims of employee attack and, if they succeed, their victory is more powerful because they endured and overcame defiance, (seemingly) achieving change against the odds (Sveningsson and Sörgärde, 2019). We acknowledge that, in focusing this text on the role of change makers, highlighting the challenges and value of change makers, we may ourselves be inadvertently contributing to this narrative. However, in this chapter we wish to acknowledge that the assumptions of these discourses tend to marginalize the voices of change recipients and examine some alternative perspectives on resistance as a mechanism for employee voice.

These traditional managerial discourses of resistance paint resistant employees as impulsively reacting to change management attempts because they are fearful of the disruption and uncertainty which accompanies organizational change. This assumes a naivety of change recipients and downplays their value to the organization in providing knowledge of front-line issues which could impact on successful change implementation. Contrary to this discourse, we know that change recipients often have complex and ambivalent reactions to change. Piderit (2000) describes three dimensions along which change recipients may react to change: the *cognitive* dimension – beliefs about whether change is positive or negative (change is essential or detrimental to the organization, or to the wider environment or society); the *emotional* dimension – feelings they might have about the change and their personal involvement in it (e.g. excitement, fear); and their *intentionality* towards change – whether they intend their behaviour to support the change or oppose it. Employees may feel differently along different dimensions simultaneously; for example, they may believe that change is good for the organization or for society but also fear the impact it will have on their own experience of work (e.g. Tucker et al., 2022).

Similarly, resistant employees are often portrayed as weak and in need of help and support. Many studies on resistance to change highlight the emotional strain of change on recipients (e.g. Dahl, 2011; Oreg, 2003; Tucker et al., 2014), and/or propose that simple education about the drivers and ideology of change will strengthen their support (Tucker et al., 2013). This is not to say that experiencing change is not difficult, but the focus on vulnerability and helplessness serves as a mechanism to keep change recipients in a position of uncertainty and powerlessness (Sveningsson and Sörgärde, 2019; Theodossopoulos, 2014).

The depiction of resistant employees as irrational and troublesome has been described by some as a *pathologization of resistance* (Sveningsson and Sörgärde, 2019; Theodossopoulos, 2014). This interpretation of change resistance suggests that resistant employees are dysfunctional – their behaviour is viewed as outside of a 'reasonable' parameter of reactions. The assumption that the response is flawed is associated with psychological instability. Symon (2005), for example, notes that so-called 'resistant' reactions tend to be ascribed to the personality of the resistor rather than a legitimate and collective alternative interpretation of change events – for example, identifying unintended consequences or implications of a change decision. A common managerial assumption is that resistance is an isolated and personal interpretation of an individual – that one person has raised an issue due to their individual misunderstanding or unique concerns. This assumption delegitimizes the arguments of the individual resistor and depicts them as a potentially destructive individual who is a threat to the common good rather than a voice representing what others also think and believe. It then follows that these individuals should be cast out or ignored so that they do not cause unnecessary delay or conflict. In this way, change makers undermine the counterarguments of resistors and silence opposing voices (Sveningsson and Sörgärde, 2019). In writings about political resistance, Theodossopoulos (2014) found that narratives of resistance tend to decontextualize the actions of resistors by detaching the actions of resistant employees from the accompanying actions of a collective group (other employees) and situations which led to resistance. This positions those actors as irrational and, in turn, silences them. In an organizational context, resistance may, in fact, be more driven by the quality of relationships between change makers and change recipients (Ford et al., 2008; Furst and Cable, 2008) or the history of change within that organization (Hancock and Tucker, 2020; Mantere et al., 2012) than the instance of change itself.

These mainstream teachings of overcoming resistance to change tend to label a wide range of undesirable behaviour as 'resistance'. As we have seen, this is a mechanism of managerial power and control. Discourses of resistance weaken the contributions of vulnerable employees and give power to change leaders and change makers who are strategically aligned. These leader-centric approaches fail to encourage an inclusive approach to change, diminishing the voices of minorities within organizations. By assuming that resistance to change is the product of individual misgivings, grounded in fear (Connor, 1995) (see Figure 6.1 for a summary of the assumptions about resistant employees), change makers can miss out on potentially helpful contributions from knowledgeable and innovative front-line employees that could be crucial in successful implementation of change. Instead, it is vital that change makers distinguish between what is intentional resistance, aimed to oppose and halt the progress of a specific change, and what is perceived as resistance but is, in fact, useful feedback and critical evaluation.

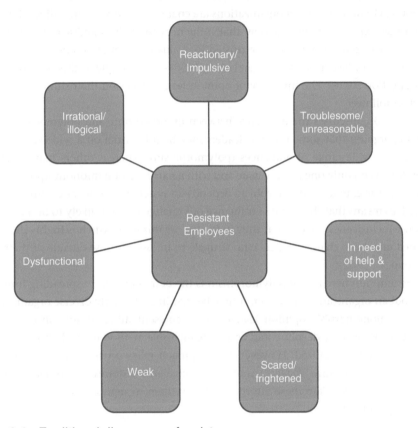

Figure 6.1 Traditional discourses of resistance

6.3 Challenges in Representing Diverse Voices

Above, we have discussed how typical organizational change narratives diminish the voice of employees and their lived experience of change. This is especially the case when we consider those employees from diverse and minority backgrounds who may struggle to make their voices heard in organizations (Wilkinson et al., 2020). In this part of the chapter, we will explore more deeply some of the challenges that change makers may face in representing diverse voices within their organization. This includes the reliance on similarity rather than diversity in trying to influence others; the complexity of perceptions of fairness and equity; and working within institutional structures which silence marginalized groups.

Influencing similar others

Literature on diffusion of innovation reminds us of the tendency towards homophily in spreading change from one individual to another throughout an organization or network. This means that change makers tend to have more influence with organizational members with a similar socioeconomic, educational, professional and cultural background (Greenhalgh et al., 2004). Opinion leaders in organizations are change makers who are influential because they have an expert or respected view that influences the beliefs and actions of their colleagues (Locock et al., 2001). They are trusted to evaluate information and new practices as a representative of local norms (Soumerai et al., 1998) – for example, is this proposed change a good direction for us? The influence of opinion leaders relies on their similarity to a close network of followers.

Rogers (2003) discusses the difference between monomorphic and polymorphic opinion leadership, arguing that some opinion leaders may be influential on a wide variety of subjects and to a wide range of audiences (polymorphism), whereas others may be effective opinion leaders on only one narrow issue and with a narrow group (monomorphism). Rogers suggests that the extent of polymorphism depends on system norms towards innovation and change. This means that the scope of influence of a change maker is likely to be a representation of the inclusiveness values that they hold – an organization which is highly diverse and segregated may have change makers who struggle to influence those outside of their immediate group.

The assumption here is that polymorphism is the best approach to spreading innovation throughout an organization; however, it may be that in particularly diverse organizations, a network of monomorphic opinion leaders, who represent different specialist groups and their specific needs more deeply, could be a more inclusive method to reach groups that have been previously marginalized. However, this approach relies on the presence and recruitment of effective change makers from all groups and requires coordinated, complex mechanisms to consolidate these efforts and allow them to represent their community in boundary spanning ways.

Different notions of fairness

Research into business ethics has revealed that people have many different views about what is 'fair' (Fisher and Lovell, 2009). Adams' equity theory (Adams, 1965) argues that the employment relationship is viewed as an exchange between the employer and the employee. Employees compare their experience of exchange – what they contribute to the organization against what they receive in return (known as the contribution/inducement ratio) against that of comparable others. This exchange is based on their perception of their own inputs (such as time, effort, emotional labour, skills, knowledge and experience) and outputs (rewards, recognition, treatment and experience of work). Figure 6.2 depicts the comparison ratio synonymous with this theory. This individual equity assessment may be based on incomplete information (especially about the inputs and outputs of 'others'), yet it is a powerful determinant of behaviour. It is through this analysis that organizational members make judgements about whether they believe themselves to have been treated fairly. If they perceive inequity, they will adjust their contribution to match the ratio of others.

Figure 6.2 Adams' equity theory, ratio analysis of employment exchange

Equity is an especially important concept in organizational change because many organizational changes include altering tacit or explicit inputs of individuals; for example, changes to reward structures, workload, work hours, effort required or level of responsibility. Employee reactions to changes in equity (whether these are based on perceived or real inequity) are rooted in comparisons between an old and a new reality, the increased salience of their own or other's value to the organization (or lack of), or experiencing inconsistency between effort and outcome – for example, experiencing increased workload as a result of change with no compensation in recognition or reward.

During change, individuals frequently turn to impressions of fair or unfair treatment to decide how to react to change. 'Fair treatment helps people manage their uncertainty ... both because it gives them confidence that they will ultimately receive good outcomes and because it makes the possibility of loss less anxiety-provoking' (Lind and Van den Bos, 2002: 196–7). Research into organization justice explores different ways that employees might examine whether organizations (and those who represent them) are acting 'fairly'. Organizational justice scholars have categorized four different types of justice that employees might examine in an organizational context (Colquitt, 2012; Marks and Mirvis, 2011; Schraeder and Self, 2003):

1   **Distributive justice** – the fairness associated with decision outcomes and distribution of resources. Examples include changes in work practices or restructuring may mean that employees need to work longer hours or expand their skill range/ responsibility or have more or less access to resources. Or decisions to introduce new practice/innovation may impact on some employees more than others

2   **Procedural justice** – the fairness of the processes by which outcomes or resources are decided. This might include the degree of power and control over outcomes employees perceived themselves to have (e.g. were they able to voice their views and were they listened to). For example, were the decision-makers neutral? Were the needs and opinions of certain stakeholder groups ignored?

3   **Interpersonal justice** – the fairness regarding the treatment of the individual during the decision-making process. For example, was I treated with respect and dignity in interactions with the organization?

4   **Informational justice** – the fairness of information sharing and openness. For example, was I kept adequately informed during the change process? Do I know why this is happening?

We can see that there are many different notions of fairness and determining the 'right' and 'fairest' actions to take is a regular part of the change maker role. Change makers can use these different meanings of justice as a framework to understand conflict as different views are put forward and promote dialogue between groups to resolve this as they implement change.

Institutionalized power and silencing

It is important to understand that power and politics play a critical role in deciding which ethical questions are raised and discussed in organizational change. Lukes (2005) argues that power is exercised in three key ways: decision-making power, non-decision-making power and ideological power (see Chapter 8 for definitions of Lukes's (2005) three faces of power). Non-decision-making power is sometimes referred to as '*agenda setting*'. This power allows key individuals in organizations to determine the parameters of discussion, the way actions are evaluated and, ultimately, how actions should be judged, and has been found to be a key means that power influences organizational behaviour during change. Unconscious bias may lead change makers to give priority to agenda items that are important in their eyes, relegating items important to more marginalized groups further down the agenda. Hughes (2010) suggests that powerful change managers tend to focus discussions of organizational change on the treatment of employees in the change process; for example, opportunities for, rather than quality of, consultation; one-way communication strategies, rather than the outcomes and views of change for diverse groups within the organization. This agenda setting may result in a lack of scrutiny over how marginalized groups of employees are being unequally affected by change (Donaghey et al., 2011). A report by UK think-tank Demos (2003) on local government work with communities acknowledges that low-quality consultations and relationships during change processes may hide inequalities and problems if staff or marginalized groups feel they cannot speak out for fear of reprisal.

Change makers may find it difficult to represent diverse voices even where these groups do voice concerns or raise issues through employee voice structures. **Unconscious bias** is when we hold an unfair belief about a group of people, which we are not aware of. This bias can unknowingly affect our behaviour and decisions. In this sense, change makers, ignoring concerns from certain groups, need not be an act of deliberate repression on their part but, rather, a cognitive and unconscious bias leading to the change maker failing to hear the voice. Examples of this could be the **fallacy of centrality** – 'if it was important I would know about it' – or where different groups offer views that contradict each other which overwhelm and can lead to avoidance (Ashford et al., 2009). On other occasions, change makers may hear grievances from minority groups but be unable to act due to lack of time or resources or a lack of power to address wider systemic barriers to change within or beyond their own institution.

There are various reasons why employees may choose to remain silent instead of making their voice heard (Morrison, 2014). Morrison and Milliken (2000) argue that organizational structures such as centralized decision-making, and managerial practices such as a tendency to respond poorly to negative feedback, can lead to widespread withholding of information about potential problems by employees. Change makers may also themselves feel unable to convey messages up the chain to senior leaders where these do not conform with the dominant narratives of the organization. In such cases, employees may not perceive themselves to be powerful enough to be heard (Hendy and Tucker, 2021; Kalfa et al., 2017), or do not have what they believe would be deemed sufficient expertise, evidence or data to put their point across. This may especially be the case where organizational idiom places a high value on professional or scientific expertise over employee lived experience (Tucker et al., 2022).

6.4 Mechanisms for Employee Voice

Promoting equality and diversity in organizations is important for all areas of organization and management to ensure that all employees have adequate voice in how decisions are made and work is done. Institutional arrangements aimed at fostering inclusivity (e.g. gender or ethnicity quotas for employment or promotion; codes of conduct, equality policies, anti-discrimination initiatives) have an important role to play in furthering equality across the organization. Similarly practices to promote whistleblowing or misconduct reporting are essential to avoid organizational silence such as that outlined by Morrison and Milliken (2000). Together, creating a climate where employees from all groups feel able and willing to raise issues and have them listened to is important in creating a readiness for change and underpin employee engagement and flexibility but giving employees the confidence that the organization will have their best interests at heart. In this section, we will explore more specifically some of the voice mechanisms that change makers might embrace in implementing change directly.

Voice mechanisms are important especially during organizational change for four key reasons. They:

- Provide feedback on how change implementation is going and **identify challenges** that might arise. Responses to these challenges can be planned for and give an indication on employee understanding and feeling about the changes.
- **Contribute to learning** and effectiveness of organizations (e.g. problem-solving). It is inevitable that during change unexpected events will emerge, and accessing diverse forms of knowledge and experience can create effective solutions to adapt and innovate changes to resolve these problems (Syed, 2020).
- Provide an **environment of psychological safety** for employees (Milliken et al., 2015). This security improves organizational commitment and also helps to mitigate some of the uncertainty and insecurity that typically surrounds change.

- **Safeguard the rights of employees**, providing a mechanism for employees to express grievances. Employees can raise concerns about the impact of change on their wellbeing, safety, opportunities and freedoms which may allow organizations to address these issues before unresolvable conflicts arise.

Vehicles for employee voice tend to be uniform and assume employees are homogeneous (Bell et al., 2011; Syed, 2020). In practice, the way employees prefer to express their voice and the propensity at which they desire to do so may vary depending on their gender, race, and so on. As a result, diverse employees' insights may remain ignored in organizational decision-making (Syed, 2020). A lack of appropriate vehicles to enhance non-mainstream voices has led to marginalized groups opting for silence in order to protect themselves from potential mistreatment or because they believe that speaking up is futile (Bell et al., 2011; Morrison, 2014).

Academic theory on employee voice conventionally distinguishes between employee involvement (EI) – a more direct form of interaction between the employee and employer – and employee participation (EP) – where voice is provided in a more indirect way via representatives (Marchington, 2007).

Employee participation (e.g. collective bargaining)

Employee participation is a form of employee voice based on a collectivist two-way dialogue between employer and employees. Most commonly, this refers to collective bargaining where employees are represented by trade unions who negotiate pay and conditions of employment with employers. Union representatives are democratically elected by union members to represent the voice of all employees covered by the collective bargaining agreement – including non-members who work for the organization covered by the agreement. This collective representation provides employees with a more powerful voice than they would have individually and can shape broader organizational policies around job security and change management policies, such as fairness of redundancy processes and distribution of resources.

Trade unions, however, have historically experienced problems associated with representative democracy and have been criticized in the past for making little effort to recruit Black and minority ethnic (BME) workers to become union members and to hold leadership positions; for failing to take up grievances of BME workers; and for avoiding race issues on union meeting agendas and manifestos (Syed, 2020). This has led BME union members to feel that unions do not adequately represent their interests, in turn lowering membership and voice within unions and contributing to the institutional bias further. These issues of representation bias also extend to considering the level of engagement that representatives or stewards have with the 'grass roots' membership which has been found to be diminishing along with levels of union membership more generally in many developed countries.

Collective bargaining as a mechanism for employee voice may be a useful resource for change makers because it offers employees a more powerful seat at the table in determining how change impacts on their working conditions. Additionally, indirect voice allows employees a level of anonymity in raising concerns and may offer more security to minority groups within the organization. In the long term, working together with unions to increase the representativeness of union democracy can be an asset to future change management of the organization and improve relations between change makers and employees (e.g. by supporting union leaders from diverse backgrounds and by ensuring that race issues are given adequate discussion). In the shorter term, change makers should, however, be aware of the limits of relying on employee participation mechanisms alone. A more consultative approach, offering a matrix of employee participation (EP) alongside employee involvement (EI) may offer more avenues for inclusive employee voice.

Recognition

Traditional participation and involvement literature advocates for consultation, involvement and participation of employees in proposed changes (Furst and Cable, 2008; Wanberg and Banas, 2000). Managerial initiatives aimed to nurture psychological ownership of change (Dirks et al., 1996; Fuchs and Prouska, 2014) or exchange support for compliance (Cropanzano et al., 2002) are often criticized as 'hollow gestures' or 'tick-box' checklists, merely playing lip-service to real employee voice (Bordia et al., 2011). Furst and Cable (2008) found that where the quality of the relationship between employees and their closest managers was poor (in terms of perceived trust and respect), consultation was viewed as a tactic to shift problem-solving responsibility on to employees. As a result, moves to legitimize change were seen as calculative, and attempts to ingratiate employees were seen as manipulative. This is particularly problematic where historically change has been handled poorly (Bordia et al., 2011).

Recognition theory argues that to feel a worthy part of their group, society or institution individuals need to feel recognized by others. Human beings have a desire for meaningful social relations which leads them to seek interactions with others. Expression of employee voice requires individual autonomy and collective co-interdependence that is only achieved through our recognition of others (Honneth, 1996).

In a study of the introduction of mobile policing technology in the UK, Hancock and Tucker (2020) offer recognition theory as a means to encourage genuine engagement with a change initiative providing 'real' voice to front-line officers. They found that by making genuine moves to understand the demands of the job, particularly under conditions impacted on by a culture of austerity and declining material resources, change makers were able to enhance employee involvement in the pilot project in a way that officers' emotional wellbeing, organizational standing and professional expertise were finally recognized. Moreover, this recognition not only gained support for the focal mobile policing initiative, but also seeded a change in the relationship dynamics between senior police management and those serving on the front line (Hancock and Tucker, 2020). Unlike traditional consultation initiatives, recognition necessitates the emergence of certain sociocultural and political institutions to make deeper changes, creating underpinning systems and norms to act as a guarantor – in other words, it requires a shift in thinking and practice within an institution towards valuing the status and rights of individuals that goes beyond consultation on a specific change initiative or issue (Honneth, 1996; Holtgrewe, 2001; Marcelo, 2013). For example, human resource management practice, whilst often viewed as a managerial control instrument, can be underpinned by an ethical acknowledgement of the right to recognition of employees. Recognition may lead to institutional acceptance of employees as autonomous subjects entitled to dignity and respect, which may, in turn, be borne out through organizational policies and managerial reward structures (Islam, 2012).

Based on Honneth's (1996) system of three distinct, but interdependent, patterns of experience, we offer some practical suggestions of how this could be achieved in Table 6.1.

Table 6.1 Suggestions for improving recognition of employees based on Honneth's components of recognition system

	Description	Practical suggestion
Love/self-confidence	Experience of assurance that a precious other will continue to care when independence is demonstrated	• Work to develop strong relationships between change makers and front-line staff • Allow honest expression of doubts, problems and feedback • Create opportunities for front-line staff to talk to neutral/independent parties without fear of rejection • Adopt a change culture of trial and error, where experimentation is valued
Respect/self-respect	Being institutionally recognized as a legitimate bearer of universal rights and responsibilities	• Make sincere attempts to understand the legitimate needs of front-line staff • Acknowledge the professional status of front-line staff and their expertise • Provide opportunities to participate in planning and decision making • Make front-line staff a part of the conversation
Social esteem/self-esteem	Feeling confident that one's achievement or abilities will be socially recognized as 'valuable' by other members of a society or group	• Develop a high trust culture where front line staff are allowed freedom and security • Give front line staff autonomy to solve practical problems • Demonstrate that the employee voice is being listened to • Acknowledge achievements and give credit to front line staff where it is due

Inclusive meetings and collaborative decision-making

Meetings are a common occurrence during change implementation and an important forum to disseminate information, share ideas, cultivate discussion and build collaboration. Change makers will often be in a position of organizing and leading such meetings depending on the exact remit of their role. Meetings are also an important opportunity for employees to contribute to discussions and debate and provide feedback on how change is going. Workplace inequalities caused by power dynamics and organizational hierarchy can either be reinforced by the conduct and etiquette at these meetings or bring about opportunities to dismantle them through actions and behaviours of organizers and attendees (Henderson and Burford, 2020).

Organizing and leading meetings require lots of decisions that appear to be of little significance; however, these choices can have implications about who can/cannot participate and how engaged they can be. For example, decisions about when and where the meeting is held may exclude workers who work flexible hours around childcare or who may work in different time zones. Other considerations may include accessibility of the venue, parking, availability of visual or hearing support. Where attendance at meetings is voluntary, it is important that the meeting appears welcoming to as diverse a range of people as possible. Communicating the above information and provision will help people decide whether to attend and encourage them to feel welcome and valued.

Unconscious bias can have a subtle impact in everyday organizational life; for example, how comfortable employees feel about speaking up around someone who they believe is similar to them, or less likely to confide in someone they perceive as 'different' from us (ACAS, n.d.). Therefore, it is important that change makers consider this in conducting meetings, choosing items for the agenda and who speaks when. It is important not to relegate items important to more marginalized groups to further down the agenda and then cutting discussion on these short when the meeting has not run to schedule. Preference can often be given to certain employees who are confident speaking in front of the chair and other persons in charge of the meeting and those who wish to offer alternative views or are less assertive may feel frustrated. In this context, change makers have an important role to play in indicating that alternative views are welcome and an anticipated part of the discussion and encourage participation from those who might otherwise have felt excluded.

Essentially, meetings and decision-making activities throughout the change process are an opportunity for change makers to demonstrate through their own behaviour their commitment to inclusivity and representing diverse views. Cultivating these relationships with others will allow them to better represent diverse groups within the organization.

Chapter Summary

- Traditional management narratives pathologize resistance to change. When we assume that resistance is the result of dysfunctional employees, this delegitimizes the arguments of the resistor and depicts them as potentially destructive. It then follows that these individuals should be cast out or ignored so that they do not cause unnecessary delay or conflict. Discourses of resistance weaken the contributions of vulnerable employees and fail to encourage an inclusive approach to change.
- Change makers tend to have more influence with organizational members with a similar socioeconomic, educational, professional and cultural background. They rely on

this influence to engage others in the change process and therefore tend to exclude those from diverse groups not represented in the characteristics of change makers.

- There are various reasons why employees may choose to remain silent, instead of making their voice heard. Sometimes employees may be reluctant to raise issues and concerns because they feel powerful enough to be heard. Agenda setting by managers about what is fair may result in a lack of scrutiny over how marginalized groups of employees are being unequally affected by change
- Unlike traditional consultation initiatives, recognition of employee's unique expertise and value necessitates a shift in thinking and practice within an institution towards valuing the status and rights of individuals that goes beyond consultation on a specific change initiative or issue
- By demonstrating through their own behaviour at meetings and training events, their commitment to inclusivity and representing diverse views, change makers can cultivate relationships that will dismantle workplace inequalities caused by power dynamics within the organization.

Activity

Read the following three scenarios. For each:

1 Identify different individuals or groups (job roles or departments or branches) within the organization that might have varied perceptions of fairness of the proposed change. For each group, consider the change from their perspective – is it fair?
2 Consider how, as a change maker, you might ensure that these organizational members feel listened to, included and empowered. What would you take into consideration to ensure that an inclusive decision-making approach to change is taken?

Scenario A

Company A, a European-based software company, is proposing to move its main customer support service to the Far East. The new support service includes the sales team, after-sales team and a technical support team. A 24-hour service will mean that the sales team can offer customers around the globe more immediate product support. A reduced-size customer services team will remain in Europe to provide strategic oversight and deal with more complex issues. Customer services employees in Europe have always prided themselves in being experts in the complex software products that the company provides and many of them have been loyal members of the company for many years, with an understanding of many iterations of the software currently on the market. With all of these teams moving abroad, the future of the European-based teams is uncertain.

Scenario B

Following the COVID-19 pandemic, Company B introduced a hybrid working arrangement where employees are only required to attend the company offices in person two days a week. However, after two years of hybrid working managers at Company B have become worried that the performance of their office-based staff might have declined. In particular, new staff who have joined since hybrid working began have struggled to learn the procedures and regulations in the role. The company blames a lack of opportunity for in person peer learning and support to be the reason for this downturn. To combat this, the head of the department wishes to require employees to return to the office four days a week, hoping that this will increase the opportunity for employees to work in teams, learn and solve problems together.

Scenario C

Retail Company C has recently acquired a controlling share in a similar industry retailer (Company D). They are in the process of integrating their businesses to ensure efficient use of resources. In some cities across the country, both Company C and D have retail outlets serving overlapping communities – thereby duplicating expenses such as rent, utilities and staffing. It has been proposed that where two stores exist within a 30-mile radius of each other, one of the stores would need to close. The merged company directors are keen to rebrand the retailer as a luxury shopping brand, so where two stores are competing over the same geography, the location in the more affluent area will remain.

Further Recommended Reading

For a different look at organizational narratives of resistance to change and how these reveal organizational power dynamics, see Ford, J.D., Ford, L.W. and D'amelio, A. (2008) 'Resistance to change: the rest of the story', *Academy of Management Review*, 33(2): 362–77.

This edited volume provides the latest research on employee voice. Wilkinson, A., Donaghey, J., Dundon, T. and Freeman, R.B. (eds) (2020) *Handbook of Research on Employee Voice* (2nd edn). Cheltenham: Edward Elgar Publishing. See Chapter 1 for an overview of employee voice challenges and directions and Chapter 28 to understand more about diversity management and missing voices.

For more food for thought on how employee silence can be perpetuated by management practice and institutional norms, see Donaghey, J., Cullinane, N., Dundon, T. and Wilkinson, A. (2011) 'Reconceptualising employee silence: Problems and prognosis', *Work, Employment and Society*, 25(1): 51–67.

PART III
CURRENT ISSUES ON CHANGE

7

LEADERSHIP AND ORGANIZATIONAL CHANGE

Chapter Objectives

- To familiarize readers with leadership literature, concerns, debates and trends
- To compare traditional, contemporary and alternative views of leadership
- To discuss leadership as it relates to organizational change processes, and the work of change makers supporting change efforts within organizations

7.1 Introduction

This chapter features a tour of leadership knowledge and explores how different leadership views and models can inform organizational change management. The chapter does not exhaust the vast leadership literature; rather, it does pay particular attention to how we can lead change initiatives 'from the middle', which means through change makers within internal departments and divisions, rather than through top-level executives. This means highlighting change issues such as negotiating across departments, combining expertise, using leadership approaches to cultivate collaborations, adaptation, innovation sharing, communicating and resolving internal conflicts. As we shall see, leadership approaches have different strengths and weaknesses for supporting change in the middle of organizations.

Firstly, we look at **traditional views of leadership**, largely understood as the qualities of individual leaders as talented, charismatic or special people. Secondly, we explore **contemporary and established views** which are widely used today, such as situational, transactional and transformational leadership. And, thirdly, we look at **alternative or more critical approaches** which are likely to be influential in the coming decades. These include negative aspects of leadership such as toxicity, as well as alternatives such as distributed leadership.

The chapter's main concern is to compare leadership approaches and relate them to organizational change management and change makers working within organizations. Received wisdom and popular beliefs about leadership often implicitly lean on Thomas Hobbes's leviathan (see Hobbes and Missner, 2016) where the 'head' of the body of society (e.g. a queen, king, or state government) is considered sovereign, holder of absolute power, the leader of the state. Traditional leadership emphasizes this hierarchical authority, and how the body (e.g. citizens, workers, professionals) take orders from the head but do not influence key decisions. More recent alternatives to such sovereign power have led to greater roles for middle-level managers, specialists, coordinators and other professionals in organizational change (e.g. Kotter, 2002) and change strategy (Hambrick, 1989; Schedlitzki and Edwards, 2018), and this sharing of power is reflected in how leadership views have evolved over time.

A key theme across this book is that organizational change is often managed and implemented from the middle of organizations, by a diverse array of managers, experts and other internal change makers. In this chapter we consider how these change makers might draw insights from leadership knowledge and approaches. Traditionally, leadership research has largely targeted top level, senior executives; however, we know that leadership occurs in many ways throughout organizations, in following, in groups, teams, and at all levels (Dubin, 1979; Gronn, 2008; Kellerman, 2008; Storey, 2005).

Leading from the middle shares some similarities with leading from the top, with certain skills or processes required. These include planning, communication of the change goals, consensus building and use of different forms of power, such as informational power or technical expertise (French and Raven, 1959; Murphy, 2017), for example. However, there are also differences. For example, firstly, change makers effect change internally within the organization and do not have the authority, seniority, or legitimacy to mandate change from an executive level position. Secondly, as change makers do not have the same authority, seniority, hierarchical elevation or 'sovereign' power as executives, they cannot claim absolute authority to implement change, nor do they have executive level decision-making authority or budget control. These points are important and help change makers to see the insights available from diverse views of leadership.

7.2 Traditional Views of Leadership

Leadership studies emerged in the early twentieth century along with (and sometimes in tension with) management studies. Traditional leadership studies explored what leaders were like personally and psychologically, as individuals. An important debate that has run for decades and influences change processes (Kotter, 1990a) is whether leadership and management are different or not (Bennis and Nanus, 1985; Yukl, 2010). Managing is often seen as technical, mechanical, day-to-day, short-term, routine work. In contrast, leadership is viewed as strategic, long-term, future-oriented and visionary (Kotter, 1990a; Kotter, 1990b; Mintzberg, 1975; Rowe, 2001). These distinctions suggest middle-level change will be more mechanical, like typical managing. However, if change makers are involved in strategy, alliance building and turning visions into pragmatic change, then the distinction becomes blurry. Change makers, in this sense, are not simply undertaking routine work, they are creatively leading change in the middle of organizations.

A second longstanding leadership debate concerns whether leaders are born or made. Are leaders special people who naturally possess innate leadership talents, unique skills and abilities; or do they develop and learn such talents during their careers? Traditional views focus on born leaders with natural talents, such as kings, queens and other historical, social, political or military figures like Napoleon Bonaparte, Catherine the Great or Mahātmā Gandhi (Northouse, 2021). Such examples align with the 'great man theory' of leadership, or 'hero' views of leaders (Carlyle, 1866; Spector, 2016) and these beliefs remain popular today perpetuated by popular narratives of resistance – see Chapter 6. Various individual elements make up this traditional package of the individual leader, including their (i) character traits, (ii) personality, (iii) style, (iv) skills, (v) intelligence and (vi) charisma. Change makers may also have such personal qualities, and work with other unit and team leaders who also do, and this is summarized at the end of this section.

Traits

Character traits or trait theory (Bass and Stogdill, 1990; Jago, 1982; Stogdill, 1948) form a key part of traditional views. Traits are stable aspects of a person's character, existing over time and across situations. Kirkpatrick and Locke (1991) argued that leaders were distinct types of people, different from others. This is still a widely held view today, with popular examples circulated in media, movies, leadership self-help books and even neuroscientific accounts (Goleman and Boyatzis, 2008). Trait views highlight a leader's strength, decisiveness, capability and dominance, for example. Stogdill (1948) researched hundreds of possible traits, and many others have followed suit on traits such as drive, vigour, risk appetite, confidence, ability to accept the consequences of one's own decisions, ability to absorb stress or influence others (Northouse, 2021). Mann (1959) stresses intelligence, masculinity, adjustment, dominance, extraversion and conservatism, and many modern tests, such as the Myers–Briggs test, highlight specific individual traits suitable for leadership roles. Strong traits like these reinforce the 'great man theory' or 'hero' view of leaders described above, even though Stogdill never found a definitive list of traits that all leaders have.

Personality

A leader's personality refers to their character or distinctive ways of behaving. For example, Judge et al. (2002) link the big five personality factors to leaders' personalities. These comprise neuroticism (sensitivity versus security); extraversion (outgoing versus reserved); openness (curiosity versus cautiousness); agreeableness (friendly versus challenging); and conscientiousness (organized versus easy-going). These are seen as part of a leader's personality and extend the trait analysis into more variable aspects of personality. In testing personality, individuals are asked a series of Likert scale questions where they rate answers 1–5. The results show where an individual is on each of the five factors. Judge et al. discuss how effective leadership aligns with secure and confident, extravert and energetic, open and creative, and tenacious and conscientious people, although the level of agreeableness required is not consistently clear. These distinctive ways of behaving impact on change processes, relationships and project success (Dvir et al., 2006).

Style

Leaders have a leadership style and associated behaviours. A leader's style can be more task- or people-oriented (Northouse, 2021). Task-based styles mean leaders emphasize objectives, targets and task completion. People-oriented styles stress relationships with others, care, collegiality, and wellbeing. Task behaviours include more 'directive leadership', where leaders control decision-making. Relationship-based styles have more concern for staff, participation, and shared decision-making.

The well-known Blake and Mouton grid (1964, 1985) illustrates the task versus people spectrum and different leader styles. Change makers can draw on these lessons to better orient their own work in support of change efforts (see Figure 7.1). The original Blake and Mouton work focuses on five forms of management, but their original model can be adapted to focus on how a people- or task-focus can support change makers and change leaders.

The original leader styles result in different support for change, as follows:

- 'Impoverished management' (Grid Area 1) may result in weak change support
- 'Country club management' (Grid Area 2) may result in people-focused support, but lack task-focused support
- 'Authority/compliance' (Grid Area 3) may result in task-focused support, but lack people-focused support

- 'Middle-of-the-road management' (Grid Area 4) may result in moderate people and task focused support for change
- 'Team management' (Grid Area 5) is the most likely to result in more holistic change support, both people and task focused

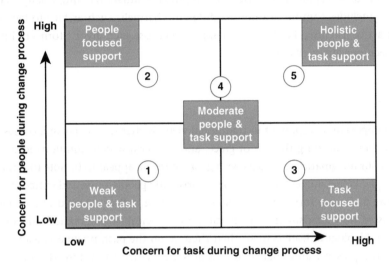

Figure 7.1 Change support grid (adapted from Blake and Mouton, 1964 version)

Skills

Skills refer to a leader's abilities, experience or expertise. Katz (1955) draws attention to human skills, technical skills, and conceptual skills. Human skills include the ability to work in groups and cooperate with others. This is well suited to all levels of leadership. Technical skills were functional to specific problem spaces, such as IT or project management skills. Katz viewed these skills as less important for more senior leadership. Conceptual skills include being able to see and understand the big picture or whole organization. These were the most important at higher levels.

Mintzberg (1980) discusses three kinds of skills too. First are interpersonal skills which are important when acting as a liaison or figurehead. Second are informational skills which are required for monitoring, sharing or disseminating information and knowledge. And third are decisional skills, required for handling problems and disturbances, allocating resources, negotiating or entrepreneurial work. These skills and abilities will shape the contribution that individual leaders and change makers can have on a change initiatives.

Intelligence

Intelligence concerns the ability to quickly understand and use new or complex information. Gill (2006) discusses an intelligence-based approach to leadership, emphasizing different kinds of intelligence. Cognitive intelligence is an individual's ability to understand information and perceive appropriate actions. Spiritual intelligence is the need for meaning, shaping values and a sense of self-worth. Emotional intelligence concerns understanding oneself and the feelings and needs of others. Moral intelligence is knowing right from wrong and being able to articulate and apply moral principles to problem situations. And, finally, behavioural intelligence includes communicating via different channels, such as face-to-face speaking, writing or active listening. Leaders and change makers use such diverse forms of intelligence to make decisions about change.

Charisma

Finally, an important component in traditional views is charisma. Charisma comes from the Greek word *karis*, meaning the gift of grace, and is a term which summons ideas of divine qualities in our imaginations. Leaders with great charisma appear to be able to influence and inspire people. Weber argued, in 1947, that charismatic people possessed extraordinary gifts, inspired awe and came forth in times of crises, offering radical solutions. Some researchers have discussed how charismatic leaders can be ideological or pragmatic leaders (Mumford et al., 2008). Ideological leaders focus their rhetoric on the past, pragmatic leaders focus on actions in the present, and charismatic leaders emphasize the future through visions of change. Charismatic change makers would be useful in negotiations, alliance building and communicating change.

It is worth noting two concerns about charisma. Firstly, charisma today is associated with smooth talk, likeable personalities and style, often expressed via appearance and body language. Popular media often suggests one can learn to be more charismatic by harnessing body language, positive attitudes, oratory, a winning smile or interpersonal skills (e.g. Geoghegan, 2005), but this view is limited, as it does not consider leadership or change contexts, challenges or task requirements for example. Charisma is rarely enough by itself. Secondly, the idea of charisma has a positive aura normally, but charisma can be mobilized for progressive or regressive change, by 'good' or 'bad' leaders. For example, one can argue that Hitler and Martin Luther King were both charismatic, but few would argue that Hitler's charisma produced progressive results for society. Strong, persuasive, appealing, attractive charisma can produce disastrous results.

What these traditional views mean for change makers

Traditional leadership views emphasize individual leaders, their traits, personality, skills, intelligence and charisma, plus (importantly) their positional power in organizational hierarchies. For change makers, one major difference is limited positional power. Change makers will have limited organizational authority in comparison to senior leaders. Internal change makers can still use their own positional authority to build consensus or make agreements with colleagues, but these colleagues may be above, equal or below them in the organization. Change makers can still make use of their individual skills, abilities, traits, intelligence, personality and charisma to support or lead change efforts. However, they will have limited authority to amplify the impact of their individual characteristics.

7.3 Contemporary Views of Leadership

Contemporary views of leadership arose out of dissatisfaction with individual-centric views, and represent a move towards more behavioural, results-oriented, situated concerns and how leaders relate to followers. Contingency views and situated views emerged in the 1960s and 1970s, stressing the environment in which leaders act. Perspectives such as transformational or authentic leadership arose in the 1990s and remain popular today. The focus on relationships between leaders and followers adds value to the work of change makers who need to build internal alliances and consensus with others in the organization to sustain change processes. Traditional views of skills, charisma, and so on remain important but more contemporary views, with roots in contexts, situations and contingencies (or even creative leadership covered in Chapter 9), have become important considerations. The following views are explored below: (i) contingency-based leadership, (ii) situational leadership, (iii) the full-range leadership model, (iv) authentic leadership, (v) responsible and caring leadership, and (vi) corporate leadership and fundamentalism.

Contingency-based leadership

Contingency views departed from individualist accounts of leadership and built on the idea that leader traits or skills are not universal in all situations. From this perspective, effective leadership is specific to contexts. Not all leaders or approaches are suited to all contexts (Yukl, 2011). Leadership behaviours vary depending on task, subordinate needs, leader expertise and stress, and authority. A key assumption in Fiedler's (1964, 1967; Fiedler and Garcia, 1987) contingency theory is that leaders are unable to change behaviours. This means leader–team alignment needs careful planning. Leader behaviour is either task or people-relationship motivated, and surveys are used to determine which approach, task or relationship, is most effective. Contingency views like this highlight the importance of aligning leaders with appropriate contexts. Nevertheless, as contingency views limit ones flexibility, and leaders often need to change and adapt, their usefulness as part of change processes is restricted.

Situational leadership

Situational leadership is closely related to contingency views. Hersey and Blanchard (1977) argue that leaders follow four different behaviour styles according to the context and ability of staff to perform specific tasks. Firstly, in **directing** behaviours, leaders give clear instructions and focus on task completion. The situation, here, is likely to be one involving risks, heavy cost of failure, and new or novice staff members. Secondly, in **coaching** behaviours, leaders offer some guidance and support according to staff needs but keep the focus on instructions and results. Coaching is best suited to when the team has some ability but not enough to complete the task alone. Thirdly, in **supporting** styles, the leader's behaviour supports, motivates and encourages staff to achieve specific results. The situation here is likely to be one where task completion is required but it is not a critical risk, and staff have significant experience already. Finally, the fourth leader behaviour is **delegating**, used when staff are relatively expert and able to take charge of a task. Delegating is still an important, but often underestimated, form of leadership behaviour during organizational change.

In such situational leadership, the leader's behaviours adjust and calibrate according to context, workforce and situational factors or risk levels, making these views suitable for supporting change. For example, training new staff at a fashion store call centre has low risk to customers if advice is incorrect, so leaders may adapt their behaviour from directing to coaching, supporting and delegating quickly. In contrast, training an engineer at a nuclear power plant requires more time, risks and safety procedures, and senior engineer engagement as risk levels are much higher.

Similarly, change makers need to adapt to their situations, to skill levels of collaborators, sometimes leading, training or modelling, sometimes following and learning from expert individuals and teams already implementing change processes.

Full-range leadership model (FRLM)

The full-range leadership model (FRLM) (Avolio, 1999; Avolio and Bass, 1993, 2002), developed in the 1990s and early 2000s, is a model that combines three core styles of leadership: laissez-faire, transactional and transformational leadership, all of which are valuable for organizational change.

Laissez-faire leadership

The first view is laissez-faire leadership. Laissez-faire leaders take a hands-off approach, avoid clear stances, ignore problems and refrain from intervening. This is often seen as a negative form of leadership but does have benefits such as not overreacting to problems, giving others autonomy, and buying time for informed responses later. Leaders may be praised for being careful and shrewd, but history may not be kind to leaders who dismiss new problems that become serious threats (Lodge and Boin, 2020). Being aware and on top of change processes is important for change makers, and this makes laissez-faire leadership potentially risky for change efforts. Still, keeping executives informed and taking no action at the middle level until authorized can be a practical response when change is heavily centralized or change implementations are driven by senior authority figures.

Transactional leadership

Transactional leadership is the second style in FRLM. The transactional style creates an exchange between leaders and followers, where the leader rewards followers for specific tasks or behaviours. A form of punishment or withdrawal of benefits is used to incentivize or penalize followers when behaviour is non-conforming, or tasks not completed. Often, transactional leaders use positional authority in the organization to negotiate the reward/ punishment frame; so, in a sense, the transactional style does not always feature equal leader–follower participation. In change processes, transactional leadership tends to motivate people using rewards and punishments, carrots and sticks, and may reduce the initiative or autonomy of staff, leaving them feeling a lack of control, investment or agency in the change process. Furthermore, transactional leadership has been criticized for not developing people to their potential. Going beyond set tasks may not bring extra rewards.

Transformational leadership

The third style in FRLM is transformational leadership. This is the most popular and most change-relevant of the three. Transformational leadership is about change, vision and reconstructing a process, product, service, unit or whole organization (Avolio, 1999; Avolio and Bass, 1993, 2002). Transformational leadership comprises four components:

1 **Individualized consideration** – leaders show concern for individuals, carefully pitching challenges for people's development, learning and feedback
2 **Intellectual stimulation** – leaders stimulate follower interest and imagination, provoking change-oriented mindsets, encouraging creativity, and the use of intuition and logic to achieve change goals
3 **Inspirational motivation** – leaders inspire followers by articulating exciting possibilities, communicating a vision, aligning organizational goals with personal goals, treating threats, problems, and mistakes as opportunities for learning, often using inspiring language and symbolism
4 **Idealized influence** – leaders display a charismatic appeal, expressing confidence in the change, taking personal responsibility, displaying a sense of purpose, persistence and trust, emphasizing wins and accomplishments along the change journey, and securing the respect, trust and confidence of followers by personally demonstrating exceptional abilities

Many of these qualities are popularized in a wide range of change leadership books, texts and programmes to support organizational change. However, these often represent an ideal view of change, and do not always support a more practical implementation perspective, i.e. the mundane actions of being a transformational leader of change at any level within the organization (Alvesson and Sveningsson, 2003). Nevertheless, transformational leadership can be used in a positive manner by change makers to show care, build engagement and motivate followers or change partners.

Authentic leadership

Another well-established view of leadership is authentic leadership. Authenticity for leaders, personally and professionally, is a popular concept today, referenced and reinforced in the media, and included in many leadership development programmes. This view of leadership grew out of the transformational paradigm (Bass and Steidlmeier, 1999; Price, 2003), and highlights a leader's own conduct and ethics (Avolio et al., 2004; Avolio and Gardner, 2005; Caza and Jackson, 2011; Gardner et al., 2011). Authentic leaders are understood to have certain tendencies, for example towards self-awareness, genuine representations of themselves to others ('relational transparency'), and the use of objective evidence and information ('balanced processing') in decision-making (Schedlitzki and Edwards, 2018). Different definitions of authenticity have arisen and, despite its ongoing popularity, there remain questions about who gets to define, construct and tell the stories of authenticity in the leadership context (Liu et al., 2016). Its focus on conduct and ethics offers a positive model for change makers working at different levels in an organization, and authenticity can support effective communications, trust and alliance building.

Responsible leadership and caring leadership

In the mid-2000s Maak and Pless (2006) created the notion of responsible leadership which stresses not the leader–follower core relationship, but relations between leaders and multiple kinds of stakeholders. In this multi-stakeholder view, responsible leadership highlights the social and ethical responsibilities that leaders have to stakeholders, who may be internal to the leader's organization or external to it. To achieve social and ethical ends, Maak and Pless argue that leaders need to take on a variety of roles, such as being a visionary, a servant, a coach, a change agent or a storyteller. The focus on roles, stakeholders, and the need to adapt and be flexible is valuable for internal change makers who need to be flexible and attentive to internal partners' needs.

A closely related concept is caring leadership, where leaders take care of others, performing a duty of care in their organizations (Ciulla, 2009; Gabriel, 2015; Tomkins and Simpson, 2015). In this caring approach, leaders face problems such as the high expectations of followers who demand caring, competent and moral leadership, equal treatment and recognition that they work collectively, even in quite individualizing work environments (Gabriel, 2015). Tomkins and Simpson (2015) discuss 'leaping-in' and 'leaping-ahead' as kinds of caring. Leaping-in is a dominating type of care concerned with more immediate action. Leaping-ahead is about the future and involves anticipating changes. Caring leadership aligns with responsible leadership, can support effective change, but may face practical challenges in terms of strict deadlines, over ambitious plans or limited resources for change.

Corporate leadership and fundamentalism

Another theme in contemporary leadership relates to corporate leadership and what Western (2019) terms corporate fundamentalism. Western suggests religious antecedents have helped form a leadership culture evident in many large organizations around the globe where management texts are circulated and followed, promoted in business schools and popular media, and adopted by large organizations. This can seem like a spiritual activity, with sacred reverence for cultish management fads and ideas. Similarities between religion and corporate cultures include the appeal of charismatic and transformational leadership, the conviction that liberty and free markets drive corporate culture, intolerance of alternatives to head office plans, zeal for new markets and new followers, and the use of teams and dispersed leadership held together by strong corporate cultures. Western argues the Protestant work ethic, meritocracy and light governance all contribute to this modern, globalized form of leadership. The idea has intuitive appeal for the way it provides a clear and idealistic vision for change but can limit participation and creativity from staff. In fact, it presents challenges for internal change makers or units who wish to contribute, alter or adapt change processes because corporate vision and culture often marginalizes specific group needs (see Chapter 6).

What contemporary views of leadership mean for change makers

To summarize, contemporary views have evolved from contingency and situated models which take account of context, to FRLM, responsible, caring or corporate models which highlight leader–follower relations. Although not reliant on the hero leader as much as traditional models, contemporary views share some similarities. The leader who transforms, is responsible, cares or drives corporate culture remains the central figure. These approaches focus on how the change maker impacts on others, how they get a good deal in transactional exchanges, or how they are inspired in transformational or quasi-religious visions of change. What these models marginalize is the negative repercussions of leadership, damage to followers or stakeholders, or how leadership is arguably more dispersed across organizations than leader-centric models still presume.

7.4 Alternative and Critical Views of Leadership

This section looks at alternative views of leadership, particularly views that focus on negative impacts and those that avoid seeing leadership as concentrated within the bodies and minds of individual leaders. These views are growing in importance and scope and give us new conceptual resources with which to understand organizational change and support change makers. Many of these ideas point to the importance of critical ways of thinking which have significant value for leadership and organizational change but which remain marginal in popular leadership literature and media. We discuss alternative views and concerns including: (i) follower-centric leadership, (ii) distributed leadership, (iii) inclusive leadership and diversity, and (iv) toxic, bad and destructive leadership.

Follower-centric leadership

One alternative view of leadership is when the leading is done by the followers. This more recent follower-centric view relates to leader–member exchange (LMX) ideas

(Anand et al., 2011; Bauer and Erdogan, 2016). Kellerman (2008) argues followers are becoming more important than leaders in creating change and identifies five types of followers who interact with each other as much or more than they do with their leaders. These are **isolates, bystanders, participants, activists** and **diehards**. Each of these is more or less engaged with their organization, and more or less willing to participate in or support the strategy and change process. It is worth noting that follower-centric models align well with the dynamics of supporting or leading change from the middle of organizations, not just from the top. Follower-centric approaches empower change makers in the centre of organizations, recognizing the important work they do and the challenges they face. Follower views and the distributed leadership ideas, discussed next, offer substantial alternatives to traditional models of hero leaders and concentrated power. Followers, experts, groups and change makers also have more influence over change than traditionally assumed.

Distributed leadership

There is an increasing concern today with how leadership is more distributed than previously thought. The focus on followers is part of this movement away from the hero leader. Distributed, network or community approaches (Gronn, 2008; Schedlitzki and Edwards, 2018) can be insightful, and emphasize the complex array of stakeholders, agents, experts and groups involved in leadership. In distributed leadership, leading and following become key parts of the leadership conundrum, not the whole of it. For example, power is distributed (Gordon, 2011) across people, departments, roles and resources in organizations, and even outside of organizations such as in the case of doctors, lawyers and academics who belong to professional communities who adhere to agreed values, methods and principles (Currie et al., 2009). Distributed leadership is an old idea but is maturing in leadership and management literature (Rose and Gordon, 2015), accompanied by an increasing range of models. Distributed perspectives help change makers see, map out and respond to the many people, groups and factors involved in organizational change (Canterino et al., 2020).

Inclusive leadership and diversity

Alongside awareness of how leadership is distributed comes increasing awareness of diversity and inclusion. This is particularly true when the traditional hero leader often reflects masculine characteristics, or is stereotypically represented with male, white imagery (Ford, 2010). Organizations and leaders need to be more aware of diversity and inclusion than before, and these sensitivities are important for change makers too (Kelan, 2023). Understanding how diverse kinds of leaders lead and how leaders impact on diverse groups in organizations is important when implementing change. Gender is one key area of concern (Kelan, 2020, 2022), as are race, age, ability/disability, ethnicity, sexual orientation, educational and socioeconomic status, or class (Yukl, 2010). With gender relations, previous studies have argued women possess the feminine advantage (Carli and Eagly, 2011), are more democratic leaders than men

(Eagly and Johnson, 1990), are more transformational (Eagly and Carli, 2003) and are often devalued when adopting directive (typically male) leadership strategies (Eagly et al., 1992).

Women also face the **glass ceiling** which hinders their advancement (Hoyt, 2007), and the glass cliff (Haslam and Ryan, 2008) which sees them promoted in times of crisis and later blamed for organizational failures. Women are also over-represented in roles that do not have career pathways to leadership positions (Hoyt, 2007). Concerns like these about gender inequalities are often similarly experienced by people of different racial backgrounds, socio-economic status, sexual orientation, age or ability. Despite benefits of greater organizational creativity and progressive ethical results for having diverse leaders, workforces, change makers and teams, diversity can bring greater distrust and more conflict (Yukl, 2010), requiring further sensitivity, planning, communication and better listening during times of change. The question that change makers must ask is to what extent units and teams leading or impacted by change processes are ready to benefit from inclusion and diversity.

Toxic, bad and destructive leadership

Specific concepts have emerged in recent decades that explore what we might call the dark side of leadership. They offer an explicit alternative to the more widespread positive, optimistic or populist accounts of heroes, inspirational transformation and charismatic awe. These concepts are described below and have a place in how we see, lead and implement organizational changes, define their impacts, and how we think about change resistance and power.

Lipman-Blumen (2005) describes how toxic leaders charm, manipulate and, eventually, leave followers in a worse-off state than when they found them. Toxic leaders either deliberately or unintentionally harm followers, acting in careless ways, or through a focus on themselves rather than those around them. They can exhibit destructive behaviour, dysfunctional personal qualities and/or narcissistic tendencies (Kets de Vries, 2003). One must bear in mind that one person's toxic leader, may be a hero to others and that toxic behaviour can change, alter, grow or dissipate over time. Also, toxicity may be linked to personal character traits or behaviours (an individualist/psychological view), but also to situational or contextual factors and pressures, in a change environment (a sociological/organizational view).

Bad leadership, according to Kellerman (2004), involves incompetence, rigidity, intemperance, callousness, corruptness, insularity and, potentially, evilness. Incompetence means the leader may lack the will, skills or ability to be effective. Rigidity relates to a lack of flexibility. Intemperance means the leader lacks self-control, is aided and abetted by followers, and is unwilling or unable to intervene effectively. Callous leadership is unkind, uncaring and fails to acknowledge the challenges followers face. Corruptness means lying, cheating or stealing for one's own benefit at the expense of the organization, followers or stakeholders. Insularity means the leader and some followers minimize or disregard the wellbeing, health or welfare of others, particularly those not considered to be in the leader's own insular group. Finally, evilness relates to leaders who commit atrocities. Bad leaders exhibit some of the characteristics, and are empowered by followers, other leaders, or established institutional norms that fail to limit them.

Destructive leadership (Krasikova et al., 2013) is harmful or damaging to the interests of an organization or its employees. It involves behaviours such as abusive supervision, petty or managerial tyranny, personalized charismatic leadership, strategic bullying or pseudo-transformational behaviours. Destructive leadership considers a leader's personal characteristics, organizational goals and the scarcity of resources to achieve those goals. One example of destructive leadership would be in an organization where safety procedures are paramount, but leaders prioritize product sales and tolerate faster, yet unsafe work practices. This would go against the legitimate interests of the organization and would be destructive (Krasikova et al., 2013). In organizational change processes, establishing new safety procedures in such a context would require efforts from the leaders and change makers, to avoid destructive leadership and negative impacts. Furthermore, pseudo-transformational plans can lead to destructive leadership, harm to the organization or staff, and strategically impact on organizational change processes. Destructive leadership, as well as toxic and bad leadership, are all concepts which help us understand the negative side of leadership. Each can arise before, during or after change processes.

What alternative and critical views mean for change makers

The alternative views of leadership contrast with traditional views, particularly in the attention to how leadership is distributed and shared in an organization, and how the impact of leadership on inclusion and diversity, for example, is now considered at least as important if not more important than the older concern with a leader's personality, character or skills. Similarly, the more recent attention to negative, toxic or destructive aspects of leadership also emphasizes newer anxieties about leadership impacts and inequalities. This does not mean traditional views have gone away, just that newer concerns are in focus today, and that change makers, professionals and managers need to be aware of these concerns and sensitivities when leading or supporting change efforts today.

7.5 How Leadership Views Support Change Efforts

Themes covered in this chapter relate to formal authority, clear communications and collaboration, and how traditional, contemporary and alternative views of leadership can help us to understand these aspects of change. Figure 7.2 provides an overview, showing how traditional leadership aligns well with seniority, executive charisma or formal policy to support change, for example. On the other hand, alternative and critical views of leadership help us understand collaborations and boundary crossing work between departments to support change, more than traditional leadership views do.

It is worth noting two caveats about leadership and change. Firstly, the shifts from traditional to alternative, old to new, individual to distributed, or autocratic to more participatory or democratic leadership do not guarantee leadership or change effectiveness. Change makers must be aware of the complexity of their own change contexts which may involve diverse

Change themes	Leadership views		
Centralized control of change e.g. formal hierarchy, status, position, compliance, expertise as authority, central policy, control of finances, technologies, spaces, schedules	Traditional views align with authoritarian leadership and centralized control of change; Change makers may have important roles but less decision-making power, and more of a message conveyor role	Contemporary views do make use of centralized controls for change; change makers will be important in the leader-follower alignment, e.g. in corporate, responsible or transformational leadership types	Alternative and critical views can be sceptical of centralized controls, but do not dismiss hierarchy, expertise or compliance; change makers will have a larger role in monitoring problems and benefits for followers
Communication e.g. storytelling, sense-making, persuading, champions, opinion leaders, inspiring, knowledge transfer, overcoming ambiguity	Traditional views will likely use central control over communications; change makers will have a largely one-way communication role, from leaders to followers	Contemporary views will use more two-way communication, to include staff and stakeholders, but still prioritize central messaging, plans, values, visions, etc.	Alternative or critical views require effective two-way communication; change makers may be facilitators, e.g. supporting inclusion systems or agile change feedback collection
Collaboration e.g. networking, boundary work, integrators, combining expertises, adaptation, conflict resolution, co-production, overcoming silos, negotiation	Traditional views may not always align with more open collaborative views of change; change makers may need to lobby for the benefits of collaboration	Contemporary views will use more two-way communication, to include staff and stakeholders, but still prioritize central messaging, plans, values, visions, etc.	Alternative or critical views align well with collaborative initiatives, distributed leadership, etc.; change makers have active roles and can support inclusive collaborations too

Figure 7.2 Leadership views and change themes: control, communication and collaboration

people, skills, resources and agendas. This means a **hybrid** or **menu** view of leadership sensitivities and approaches may be most effective for supporting change, responding to new challenges and being agile. Internal leaders and change makers can choose which leadership models and sensitivities are most relevant for given change goals, projects or environments.

Secondly, popular leadership industry (Ferry and Guthey, 2020; Guthey et al., 2009) claims, memes, celebrity 'hero' personas, success narratives or sleek digital videos, encountered face-to-face in workshops, or online in social media feeds, often paint a picture of simple, universal, empowering forms of leadership. They do not account for complex settings, stakeholders, the potential to harm or failing to achieve change. They do not do negative. What change makers and change leaders must do, then, is ask to what extent insights from different approaches, sensitivities to potential harms, or mundane, everyday skills and behaviours such as walking around, listening, and talking with teams and partners (Alvesson and Sveningsson, 2003) might help them lead effective change. For leading change, we need more than a hero.

Chapter Summary

- Traditional views of leadership have concentrated on individual leaders, their character traits, personality, skills, intelligence and charisma, in what may be considered a 'hero' view of leaders as special people. This view is useful for thinking about leading organizational change; yet change makers may not have the authority to amplify their individual characteristics in supporting change.
- Contemporary views such as situational leadership, transformational leadership, authentic leadership and responsible leadership have shifted the focus on to the leader's relationship with followers but have not jettisoned the individual hero halo. These views remain relevant to organizational change, transformation and how change makers relate, connect with and impact stakeholders during changes.
- Alternative or critical leadership views sensitize us to leadership being distributed across individuals and groups, being potentially damaging, toxic or bad, and being important for diversity and inclusion. These views take us beyond the individual leader to leadership as a complex phenomenon in organizational life.

Activity

Discuss and reflect on the following questions:

1   Do you agree there are core leadership traits and skills; or do you think it varies by context, people, change goals and situations? Say why you think so.
2   What kind of leadership plans or approaches have you seen in your life and work? How do they fit with the models and concepts discussed in this chapter?
3   Are some leadership models suited to specific kinds of change? For example, transformational change, continuous improvement change, change in different organization types, sizes or sectors.
4   What is your preferred leadership style, and what would you like to learn more about to improve how you lead change in future?

Further Recommended Reading

For a comprehensive book on leadership and change, see Beerel, A. (2009) *Leadership and Change Management*. London: Sage.

For a comprehensive textbook on leadership, see Schedlitzki, D. and Edwards, G. (2018) *Studying Leadership: Traditional and Critical Approaches*. London: Sage.

To learn more about the full-range leadership model, see Avolio, B.J. (2010) *Full Range Leadership Development* (2nd edn). London: Sage.

For a critical article on the ordinary, simple and mundane things effective leaders do, see Alvesson, M. and Sveningsson, S. (2003) 'Managers doing leadership: The extra-ordinarization of the mundane', *Human Relations*, 56(12): 1435–59.

For an article on leadership, change and power through meanings, see Smircich, L. and Morgan, G. (1982) 'Leadership: The management of meaning', *Journal of Applied Behavioural Science*, 18(3): 257–73.

8

POWER AND RESISTANCE IN ORGANIZATIONAL CHANGE

Chapter Objectives

- To introduce traditional, contemporary and emerging views of power
- To explore resistance, different dimensions, rationales, and how it can be re-interpreted to support change
- To consider ways in which awareness of different aspects of power and resistance can aid change makers and organizational change efforts

8.1 Introduction

The fundamental concept in social science is power, in the same sense in which energy is the fundamental concept in physics. (Bertrand Russell, 1938: 12)

This chapter focuses on **power** in organizational change efforts. Power relations are critically important because they are complex and encountered during change efforts. Power intersects with key themes in this book, from project management, to inclusion, innovation, digital transformation and leadership. It is also important because it is often misunderstood, viewed as evil, illegitimate or a taboo problem we should not talk about. In contrast, we think discussing power provides change makers with new ideas for innovative plans, resources for relationship building and sense-making, plus such awareness makes change efforts 'power-sensitive'.

The topic of this chapter, then, is power, social power and its sister concept, resistance. Power concerns the ability to influence, persuade, normalize, regulate, build consensus and alliances, coerce people, dismiss alternatives, adopt new ways of thinking and working, empower others, and stifle or unleash creativity. Resistance takes place at different levels, from individual to group or unit levels. It draws on a range of more or less legitimate rationales, that change makers may at times struggle to interpret, despite pursuing positive change for diverse stakeholders. Understanding resistance is important for change makers who need to influence, build consensus, empower others and make sense of resistance.

Some simple questions can help us orient ourselves to power and resistance:

- How can change makers recognize power and use it to promote change?
- What are the different kinds of power evident in organizational contexts?
- Is power always about the boss, money, coercion and control?
- What do change makers need to learn to be power-sensitive?
- What is resistance to change and what are its key dimensions and rationales?
- Can 'resistance' benefit change efforts? If yes, then how?

The extent to which power is perceived as legitimate, good or bad will vary depending on whose view you take. We often see power differently, good for me, not so good for you. This is its **relational** aspect, meaning power is understood differently across people, places, and time. An example of this is 'hate speech' on social media. It can be profitable for social media companies and advertisers as it generates engagement and advertising revenue. It can be empowering for influencers, increasing their followers. But it can be exploitative for citizens and users, polarizing debate. In change efforts, power will be seen differently by different leaders and stakeholders, so making spaces for dialogue and understanding, for sensitively discussing power, can be highly beneficial, even though this can be very hard to do. Understanding power and resistance helps change makers build stronger change efforts, and stronger relationships with internal leaders, experts, employees, teams and units.

In this chapter, we cover traditional and contemporary views of power, before highlighting hot-button issues involving power that have become more heated in recent years. Following this, we look at the dimensions and reasons for resistance to organizational change, before unpacking a more collaborative, sense-making view of resistance that supports change processes.

─Box 8.1─

Change, power and resistance at AssureCo

This box features a case scenario. As the chapter progresses, we refer to this case, asking how topics and issues help us better understand the case. The case is a tool to stimulate learning and reflection through the chapter. It helps us, as change makers, build our awareness of power relations, politics and resistance during change processes.

AssureCo is a leader in insurance, pension and annuity products. At the HQ in London is the Complaints Department. They are a team of 25 people, who have been struggling with increasing complaints volumes over the last year.

AssureCo's Executive Team recently appointed an ambitious albeit autocratic high-flyer to be the new Complaints Manager, Eric, replacing the previous well-liked, but under-performing female manager, Sarah. Also new, is a young, graduate trainee from a top UK university, who is acting as the Assistant Manager, Ross. A new Complaints Information System (IS) has been introduced to modernize complaint responses and boost performance metrics. In the past, the department was measured by the number of complaints dealt with by the whole team each week. Now the measure is daily, individual and shown on a large screen in the office.

Senior team members see Eric and Ross as ushering in a welcome change, more direct, more efficient and more fun – if you work hard and can take both pressure and the occasional joke. Other staff, older team members, younger new hires and temporary staff find the new managers hard to deal with, uncaring and even toxic. There is current talk of firing slower staff. Group meetings are held every day at 9.00 a.m. Friday night is drinks night, when team members are expected to meet at a local bar. Ameena is a Senior Trainer from People & Culture. She visits often to coach and train on services, regulations and systems. She is well liked. However, given product, system and procedure complexity, newer team members feel training is not enough. A Change Maker, Siri, supporting the new IS is also in the team. She meets regularly with IT Services, Digital Strategy and People & Culture task forces. She represents the Complaints Department on progress being made with the new IS.

Questions

1   How will the system and management changes unfold?
2   Who has power?
3   Who is resisting?
4   How can topics in this chapter help us understand the case?

8.2 Aspects of Power and Change

Power is a part of many aspects of organizational change, such as political shifts, power wielders and receivers, change models, work roles, and people's attitudes or behaviours. These issues are explored below.

Power and politics in organizational change

Firstly, power is a sensitive issue in organizational change because it is part of political shifts that happen during changes. Political acts can include questioning, avoiding, resisting, blocking, bullying, causing fear, arriving late, lobbying, and so forth (Buchanan and Badham, 2020: 267–9) and these can all happen during change processes. Power relations can be observed in conflict, resistance, strikes and budget or personality clashes, but power and politics are also evident in less visible, everyday activities, for example 'foot-dragging, evasion, false compliance, pilfering, feigned ignorance, slander and sabotage' as well as 'rumour, gossip, disguises, linguistic tricks, metaphors, euphemisms, folktales, ritual gestures, anonymity' (Scott, 1985: 137).

Changes are a time when stable power balances are disrupted, when new settlements emerge, new policies or human resources are set up, or new controls established over units or technologies (e.g. Markus, 1983). To help support changes, change makers should observe who is gaining or losing political influence, and which new ideas, change or business models, or leaders are attracting or losing advocates.

Power as possession or relational, wielders, receivers and cultural norms

Secondly, in traditional views of power (discussed below), power is seen as a resource or possession. It is controlled by the person who has that power – **the power wielder**. A wielder can use different kinds of power. Agent A can act in more or less coercive ways to get B to do something. A **power receiver** then reacts to the wielder and can attempt to steer them towards a positive outcome for themselves. In this sense, even traditional forms of power are perceived in different ways by receivers and wielders.

Contemporary views of power see power as a cultural norm, part of rules, roles, schedules, interfaces or other arrangements. For example, letting gold-level gym members see extra times and services at the club, more than silver members, enacts a power relation through the digital booking form, based on membership payments and earlier service designs.

Norms and cultural forms of power are relational, experienced by some people, in some situations, not all. This contrasts with hierarchical and possessive forms of power, which suggest an individual has power in all situations e.g. bosses in company hierarchies, personal strength or wealth. Power is part of relationships between people and groups (Buchanan and Badham, 2020; Crozier, 1973), wielders, receivers, and all of us following or resisting cultural norms.

Power in concepts and in work roles

Thirdly, power is in the concepts and models we use to understand, plan and implement changes, as well as organizational roles and positions. For example, power is part of Lewin's (1952) three-step model or Kotter's (1995b) eight-step model. In such models, setting up a new vision, finding and supporting change makers, implementing change, celebrating wins and sustaining change with new institutional norms are all important sites of authority, negotiation, expertise and meaning. This means they are places where power is evident, people influence each other, new networks and alliances are established.

One typical conflict often experienced during change is between the two roles of leadership and management. Leaders are charged with changing organizations, and establishing long-term visions to sustain and grow the organization. This clashes with the roles of managers who are charged with the everyday stability of tasks and roles, and sustaining short-term results (Kotter, 1990b). Change makers may become caught between these roles and, as such, benefit from being aware of different forms of power and resistance used by leaders, managers and other influential roles.

Power in behaviour

Fourthly, power is also in our behaviours and psychology. A valuable, sometimes controversial, example of this is **nudge theory** (Thaler and Sunstein, 2009). Nudge is a popular term in behavioural psychology methods that seek to change people's behaviour through small adjustments to their environments, which cause significant attitudes or behaviour changes. One example is how popular foods such as bread are placed at the back of supermarkets to encourage shoppers to buy other foods as they journey around the store. Nudge and behavioural psychology have been used by governments to influence public opinion on change issues, and by commercial and non-profit organizations. Change makers, by making small changes to wording, plans or arguments, may be able to nudge change recipients towards adopting and promoting intended changes. As adjustments are almost imperceptible, some consider nudge a less ethical form of change power.

Power and change makers

Finally, in terms of how power relates to aspects of organizational change, it is important for change makers to realize that their power may not be the same as the power senior leaders wield. Middle-level change makers may not have the status, positional power, financial control over budgets or hierarchical legitimacy that leaders have. However, change makers can generate power relations, using their independence, ability to work without consistent managerial support, self-confidence, humility, neutral position, ability to build collaborations, capacity to develop high-trust relationships, and ability to work across silos and business functions, being ambidextrous in their dealings (Kanter, 1984). These are not traditional 'big boss' forms of power, nor financially intensive, yet they are still considerable change-maker assets. Power is not all about heroic or despotic individuals, but is about change-maker confidence, awareness, perspectives, psychology, different roles, shifting politics and, not least, different kinds of power relations, as discussed below.

The **AssureCo Case** (see Box 8.1) demonstrates how change efforts take place in environments where power relationships exist. Consider the following:

1   What power relations do you see in the AssureCo case? (Consider roles, concepts, technologies or the abilities of individuals in the case.)

2   What scope is there to negotiate with people in the Complaints Department, around management or technology changes, performance and efficiency goals, or training efforts for example?

8.3 Traditional Views of Power

Power has traditionally been understood as hierarchical, concentrated, constraining, and as a resource or possession of controlling, bad, destructive, dark or evil individuals (Keen, 1981). Such bad people exploit weaker people. Strong companies crush weaker companies competitively. Powerful leaders use their knowledge and personal networks to outmanoeuvre other executives. Control over authority, finances, and force come under this traditional perspective, as well as power in individual skills and abilities.

Authority and hierarchy

Authority is a key component in traditional views of power, and it comes with a level of legitimacy, gained through legal position, knowledge, expertise, but most often seniority in a hierarchy. We follow leaders because they are a legitimate authority. In change processes, it is important for leaders to support or sponsor change strategies, to speak up for them and take action to encourage change. Change makers may have some authority due to position, but this is often a key difference in comparison with senior leaders or the boss. Change makers must establish legitimacy in other ways.

A good example of authority due to hierarchical position is given by Western (2019) in his book on leadership. He discusses the football club manager André Villas-Boas during his time managing an English Premier League team. Villas-Boas sought to exert power over the players by calling upon his hierarchical authority, saying: 'My authority is total. … They [the players] don't have to back my project, it's the owner who backs my project.' In this example, the leader claims total authority over subordinates (the players) due to position. Western goes on to discuss several kinds of leaders who use different modes of authority, for example the Quakers, anarchists and contemporary social movements such as Occupy Wall Street. These all avoid basing power on hierarchical authority and legitimacy, seeking more participatory or consensual forms of legitimacy.

Coercion, remuneration and normative power

Another traditional view of power was outlined by Etzioni (1961) who viewed power as coming from coercion, remuneration and normative strategies (see Figure 8.1). Examples of coercion include threats, sanctions, force or intimidation. This form of power can lead to resistance, alienation, legal, ethical or other problems for change makers. Remuneration is a very common, accepted and transactional form of power. It is financial in most cases, although related more broadly to exchanging gifts. It is instrumental, contractual in modern business, and balances power between the employee and the company, with the former offering labour and skills, and the latter offering remuneration and other benefits.

For a change maker, this kind of power can be used either through offering new agreements or contracts to change supporters for taking on new project roles, by appealing to people telling them the changes are part of their existing duties, or by saying changes will improve people's work, work experiences or effectiveness. Finally, normative power comes from symbolic rewards and cultural norms. This kind of power includes offering symbolic roles to people as part of changes, praising them for good practice.

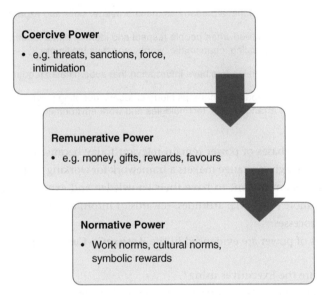

Figure 8.1 Coercive, remunerative and normative power (adapted from Etzioni, 1961)

Influence and persuasion

Other kinds of power that fit with the traditional resource view, where individuals have power because of their resources, for example personal status or individual skills, is power as influence, persuasion or authority (Schedlitzki and Edwards, 2018). Influence and persuasion are useful for change makers who lack authority. Influence is having the ability to impact on other people's behaviours or attitudes. It is an essential leadership skill, used to encourage people or groups to achieve goals. Persuasion is a little different. It is convincing people to act or change their thinking or beliefs in particular ways. It is, in a sense, a kind of influence, which deploys reasons, claims, arguments or political tactics. Change makers often need to use influence and persuasion to get stakeholders to support changes.

The seven bases of power

Another traditional resource and individualist view on power comes from French and Raven's (1959) popular model (Table 8.1). Over time, they identified seven bases of power.

Table 8.1 Bases of power (adapted from French and Raven, 1959)

Bases of power	Definition
Rewards	When material, financial and symbolic rewards are given to followers
Coercion	Force and pressure, involving punishment that followers try to avoid
Legitimacy	Followers believe in leaders, accepting their claims, justifications, etc.
Expert	Belief that a person has the knowledge, skills and experience to lead
Referent	Achieved when people respect and identify with a leader, seeing them as appealing, charismatic, worthy and thus legitimate
Information	When leaders have information that subordinates require
Ecological	A broad and perhaps blurry category, denoting power over physical arrangements, technologies and work environments

French and Raven's bases of power remain relevant today because using different power bases at different times gives change makers a framework for working with diverse stakeholders. Some stakeholders may want to have their knowledge and expertise recognized, while others may prefer more referential attitudes, rewards or information exchanges to agree and support change processes.

Different forms of power are evidenced in the **AssureCo Case**. Consider:

1 What power are the Executives using?
2 The old Manager, new Manager or new Assistant Manager?
3 How about the Senior Trainer?
4 The senior department staff, older staff members or newer trainees?
5 The change maker and task forces?
6 How might they use authority, persuasion, coercion, group affiliation, social and cultural norms, expert or information power?

8.4 Contemporary Views of Power

Popular views of power often rely on the idea that financial control, heroic skills and abilities, the big boss and violence are the most important forms of power. However, contemporary views enable us to see a wider range of power dynamics that are less reliant on individuals, position or concentrated resources. These views see power as part of more distributed relationships, such as meaning, discourse, communication, frameworks combining different power forms, or broader work from sociology or philosophy that help us see that power dynamics have changed through history, how power can be positive and productive rather than only destructive or evil (Clegg, 1989). Below are some of the most relevant contemporary views of power.

Meaning and power

One interesting view of power in this more distributed sense is the spread of meanings in an organisation, and people's sense-making around shared meanings. Sharing new meanings is a core leadership function (Smircich and Morgan, 1982), commonly used in the early stages of change efforts. It is an important part of change-maker tactics too. Power through shared meaning involves defining key terms, goals, values and managing communications. It involves shaping people's thinking, establishing shared visions, framing plans, milestones and journeys, building new capacities and connections. So, power is not only controlling budgets or having an executive role but also creating, sustaining and negotiating meanings across departments.

The three faces of power

Another contemporary model of power is Lukes' (2005) three dimensions of power, often called the 'three faces' of power.

- The first dimension is **decision-making** power. This is reliant on formal authority and hierarchical position, and draws on traditional power forms.
- The second face of power is **agenda setting**. This is having influence over what topics are prioritized, managing an agenda to influence others. This form of power can marginalize opposing, critical or minority views, keeping them 'off the agenda'.
- The third dimension is **institutional** power. This is found in everyday actions, established norms or values, such as how patients wait for doctors, or how teachers have the right to assign homework, not students. Such norms are cultural, taken for granted, institutionalized in education, healthcare, business or government, and willingly followed.

Change makers may face problems with this third face of power because organizational change involves disrupting and changing norms which employees have become accustomed to. Other forms of power such as expertise or rewards may be useful in changing such norms.

Power-over, power-to, power-with and power-within – an accessible framework

An easy-to-understand, accessible model is power-over, power-with, power-to and power-within. This framing can be traced back to Follett (1940). Power-over is related to force, coercion, discrimination or abuse. Those who control resources and decision-making in an organization have power over others. This aligns with traditional views of power. Power-with involves sharing interests and capabilities to work together and collaborate with others. This is power as participation. Power-to involves helping people realize their potential, through support, training or education. This is empowerment. Finally, power-within signals each person's self-worth, self-respect and fulfilment. It is a self-determined form of power and needs to be grasped by individuals themselves.

For change makers working across different groups and stakeholders, this is a practical and easy-to-explain framework, but the easy labels can, at times, blur more complex distinctions hidden under the seemingly clear labels (Pansardi and Bindi, 2021).

Three circuits of power

Comprehensive frameworks on power have been developed through the years. For example, Clegg's (1989) circuits of power comprise episodic, social integration, and systemic integration circuits (Figure 8.2). The word circuit signifies how individual actions are curtailed by agreements and resources, similar to how electrons are shaped by the laws of physics in an electrical circuit. This framework is useful because it shows how we are not completely free to do anything. Electrons are not completely free, and neither are we. We have to follow organizational rules and use organizational resources.

The **episodic circuit** is where the actions of leaders, managers or influential people are acted out. This power is active, **causal power** according to Clegg. It is easily seen and provokes resistance, such as when a project manager demands overtime to deliver a milestone at short notice. The **social integration circuit** involves capacities or **dispositional power**. Clegg uses the example of a police officer who can stop traffic, but generally does not. This dispositional power depends on existing social agreements that allow the police to legitimately stop traffic, but only under certain conditions. Organizations have similar agreements on who can do what. Change makers will need to negotiate their dispositional power, given their roles can be temporary, informal or dependent on the authority of more senior leaders.

Finally, the **systemic integration circuit** explains how power is facilitated using existing resources and techniques. **Facilitative power** is used here, involving technologies, policies, rewards, resources and sanctions. A traffic police officer may have the dispositional power to stop traffic, but what laws are they following? Do they have a car and flashing lights to block the road or a team and information system to monitor traffic and issue cautions? These are facilitative powers. For change makers, this circuit explains how the change maker will be able to use their power, what support they have from organizational strategies, rules, rewards, sanctions, technologies and other human resources.

Foucault's work on power

Perhaps the most controversial, expansive and influential writer on power has been Michel Foucault. It is beyond the scope of this chapter to look extensively at his work but change makers can gain many insights into power in organizations by reading his work. Foucault's biggest insight is how power has shifted over centuries in many developed nations, from the ancient **sovereign authority** of kings or ruling elites to how power is more distributed

Episodic Circuit

- Actions of leaders, managers and influential people
- **Causal power** - actions taken; can lead to resistance

Social Circuit

- Organizational agreements in place to support use of episodic power
- **Dispositional power** - capacity to act based on agreements

Systemic Circuit

- Organizational resources, systems and techniques to support actions
- **Facilitative power** - resources/techniques facilitate episodic or social power

Figure 8.2 Circuits of power (based on Clegg, 1989)

today. Distributed power includes schedules, timetables, building layouts, expertise, targets, and plans that govern our daily work, or even how flexible workplaces that care for employees are themselves a kind of **pastoral power** (see Leclercq-Vandelannoitte, 2021). Flexitime, a pool table and pizza are designed to make us loyal, to work harder and better.

Change makers can benefit from engagement with Foucault's work by seeing that power is not simply loud and obvious, a resource or individual skill, nor always destructive, as in

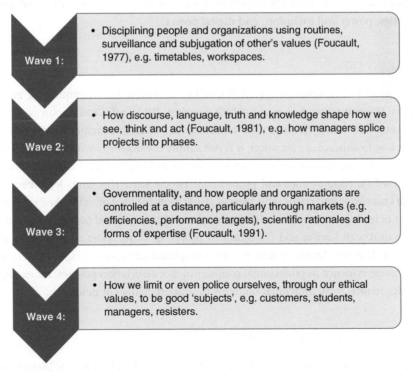

Wave 1:
- Disciplining people and organizations using routines, surveillance and subjugation of other's values (Foucault, 1977), e.g. timetables, workspaces.

Wave 2:
- How discourse, language, truth and knowledge shape how we see, think and act (Foucault, 1981), e.g. how managers splice projects into phases.

Wave 3:
- Governmentality, and how people and organizations are controlled at a distance, particularly through markets (e.g. efficiencies, performance targets), scientific rationales and forms of expertise (Foucault, 1991).

Wave 4:
- How we limit or even police ourselves, through our ethical values, to be good 'subjects', e.g. customers, students, managers, resisters.

Figure 8.3 Four waves of power in Foucault's work

traditional views. It can be quiet, soft, mundane, normalized in routines, silent, unnoticed, freely accepted and even welcomed by those under control. It can be productive, progressive and beneficial for diverse stakeholders in organizations. Four broad waves of Foucauldian influence have been identified and are shown in Figure 8.3 (Clegg et al., 2022: 211; Raffnsøe, 2019).

Meanings are used by leaders in the **AssureCo Case** to establish power relations, for example on performance standards. Consider:

1   Might lack of training be re-interpreted as an explanation for weak performance, instead of blaming inefficient employees?
2   Are power-over, power-to, power-with or power-within evident in the case?
3   Thinking of facilitative or dispositional power, what systems would AssureCo need in order to safely expose unfair use of power?
4   Finally, would Foucault's waves of power be relevant, for example regarding care or targets?

8.5 Emerging Views: Distributed Power, Inclusion and Digital Change

In addition to the traditional and more contemporary views of power, there are emerging concerns and new ideas about power in organizations that draw on existing perspectives and highlight specific hot-button issues. This section outlines some of these to inform change makers because these are critically important today. They include power as distributed or in communities, power and inclusion, and digital power.

Distributed power

Firstly, power can be distributed, spread out, diffused, often across communities, groups and professions. Power is networked across people (Gordon, 2011), roles and resources in organizations. Power is also held by professional bodies and knowledge hierarchies (Currie et al., 2009), such as in law, healthcare or education. It is not simply the doctor's own knowledge that gives them power, but the role of a doctor, their position in hospitals, and their membership of esteemed medical communities and professional associations. This lends legitimacy to their individual knowledge and status. This view of power as distributed or networked contrasts with hero views of leaders, and traditional 'big boss' views of concentrated power. Although change makers do deal with leaders and concentrated power, ignoring wider communities and networks in which power functions and becomes amplified limits our perspective. Looking for positive change evidence in professional communities or association policies, for example, can help change makers sway individual opinions to support change in new ways.

Power, inclusion and diversity

Secondly, power is seen as part of problems to do with social and economic inclusion, diversity, wellbeing and equality. These are increasingly important elements of organizational change processes and influences. They often make up rationales for change, alongside typical justifications such as efficiency or competitiveness. Unfortunately, traditional organizational change narratives and project plans can diminish the diversity of voices contributing to change efforts, potentially silencing employees' voices, and their lived experience of changes. Minorities may find it hard to have their voices heard (Wilkinson et al., 2020), and this may contribute to forms of resistance (see Chapter 6 for more on this issue).

Change makers may influence organizational members who share similar demographic, educational, professional, cultural and socioeconomic backgrounds and experiences (Greenhalgh et al., 2004), but it may be challenging for them to represent different voices (e.g. Kelan, 2023). Change makers may also be limited in their abilities to support minority needs or concerns if power structures are in place (e.g. policies, technologies, hierarchies, ways of working) that marginalize unfamiliar, difficult to deal with, hidden or non-incentivized non-targeted concerns. Project metrics can render complex needs silent because such needs cannot be counted or turned into metrics. Change makers may not be supported to work with different groups whose views clash or contradict each other (Ashford et al., 2009). These issues of inclusion, diversity, equality and wellbeing are becoming increasingly important in organizational changes. However, these issues throw light on some of the most important impacts of unequal power dynamics in organizations.

Power and digital change

A third growing concern for change and power is the increasing ubiquity of digital technologies, systems and devices, and **digital transformations**, even within non-digital change strategies (see Chapter 5). Technology–power relations have been researched over many decades (e.g. Markus, 1983; Zuboff, 1988, 2019) and, despite being a marginal issue in most technology fields, a focus on power offers a strong corrective to some of the more breathless and utopian talk about the digital economy or digital change (Willcocks and Lioliou, 2011). If data are the new oil, as proclaimed at the World Economic Forum in 2011 (Schwab et al., 2011; see also Taffel, 2021), we must pay attention to unequal power relations regarding digital data. Such power dynamics are found in open arguments and explicit resistance but often with digital data and technologies such inequalities are quiet, embedded in mundane work tasks, opaque algorithms, data analytics (Beer, 2018), surveillance systems or complex global data flows between organizations (P.R. Kelly, 2018, 2019). With smart watches, clothing, objects, environments and the internet of things, it is doubly important to pay attention to things, places, buildings, rooms and so forth, as these also convey technology–power relations.

Such digital-power issues are part of wider concerns about non-human objects because the design, use and management of these objects and systems creates new power dynamics around them. Change makers are increasingly planning and implementing change programmes which incorporate new digital systems and digital work practices, and as such being aware of these power relations, the quiet ones and the loud ones, is important for effectiveness, efficiency and performance but also for inclusion and business sustainability.

These issues (distributed power, inclusion and digital change) are evident in the **AssureCo Case**. Consider:

1   Are any of these issues important for the change process and change maker in the
     AssureCo case? For example, is power distributed?
2   Is it just dominant new managers who have power?
3   Are there any inclusion, wellbeing or diversity issues in the case?
4   And is power related to digital systems or new digitalized work practices?

8.6 Traditional Views of Resistance

There are many power responses to organizational change efforts, including agreement and
consensus building but also resistance, from individuals, leaders or units. **Resistance to
change (RTC)** has often been framed as coming from 'the baddies', the stubborn, irrational
or dysfunctional change recipients who do not want to get on board with change plans. As
such, popular management texts include definitions of resistance as something like the following: 'Resistance to change consists of those organizational activities and attitudes that
aim to thwart, undermine and impede change initiatives' (Clegg et al., 2022: 13).

Ford et al. (2008: 362) disagree with this view: 'Prevailing views of resistance to change
tell a one-sided story that favors change agents by proposing that resistance is an irrational
and dysfunctional reaction located "over there" in change recipients.' They suggest, firstly,
that change makers themselves sometimes provoke resistance and, secondly, that resisters
can bring change benefits.

As such, this section outlines some of the traditional ways of understanding resistance,
and the following section looks at alternative, more recent and more positive interpretations
of resistance. As we shall see, resisters are not always simply 'screwing up' change efforts
(Dent and Goldberg, 1999; Klein, 1976). For more on how resistance relates to voice and
inclusion, see Chapter 6.

Change receivers may resist change for many reasons and in many ways. Researchers have
explored resistance at different organizational levels, for example individuals or departments, and in the different dimensions, such as cognitive, emotional or intentional
resistance. **Cognitive resistance** concerns people's beliefs and thinking processes, particularly whether they see change as negative for themselves, their unit or their organization.
Emotional resistance concerns people's affective response to change efforts, for example
excitement or fear of change. **Intentional resistance** contrasts people resisting for no clear
reason, versus those whose thinking is focused and intentional, for example if they support
alternative change strategies. People can also be **ambivalent to change**, holding contrasting thoughts about change at one time (Piderit, 2000).

Wanberg and Banas (2000) looked at individual factors (e.g. self-esteem, optimism and
perceived control) and situational factors (e.g. level of participation, social support) to better
understand resistance. Resistance takes form through diverse **resistance actions**, such as
tardiness, criticism, scepticism, refusing to cooperate, strikes or even revolts. People can resist
change because of what is being changed, for example a new HR policy, or because of how
change is being introduced, for example without consultation.

Resistance as psychological responses to change

There are benefits to understanding resistance to change in psychological terms. Constant change may lead to employee confusion, **change fatigue** or the creation of **survivor syndrome** where workers who have survived previous changes or lay-offs remain in the organization, and require extra investment around trust and relationship building to get them on board for future changes. Management and change makers have roles to play here, building trust, communicating change clearly and mitigating resistance risks.

People may tend to resist or avoid change according to factors identified by Oreg (2003). Firstly, people prefer steady routines. Secondly, people may wish to avoid stress when facing new situations. Thirdly, people may be distracted or confused by the short-term inconveniences that accompany changes. And fourthly, people may be cognitively rigid, unable to change their minds easily, and as such they may want to minimize the frequency of changes.

Change processes may be voluntary, innovation based, or imposed. Those with high cognitive rigidity will be less likely to volunteer to change or try out new innovations. Those seeking safety in routines and emotional stability may find change stressful or even sad (Oreg, 2003).

Resistance and leadership

Furthermore, leadership styles and follower input into change processes can influence levels of resistance. Transformational leadership seeks to include followers in change processes by motivating and inspiring them. Transactional models of leadership focus more on incentives and remuneration to promote change. In the leader–member exchange model, the relationship between leaders and followers is paramount, so different strategies or sanctions, legitimizing change, consulting with followers, or ingratiating followers through praise can be used to manage resistance (Furst and Cable, 2008).

However more authoritarian, coercive and even transactional forms of leadership do not highlight ways of dealing with follower attitudes, confusion or stress related resistance for example (see Chapter 7 on leadership).

Resistance and identity

Reasons for resisting change may include people's own view of themselves, their work and careers, or their own identities. People will wonder how the changes benefit them, and whether they have been consulted sufficiently in change planning. Most people build skills and identity over time in their careers, and change can threaten their identity, leaving them 'walking naked into the land of uncertainty' (Quinn, 1996: 3). Identity is another concern, alongside psychological views, levels of resistance and different dimensions of resistance that helps change makers to better understand where resistance is coming from, its different causes, and how it influences people's identities.

Resistance due to threats and fears

Traditional views of resistance to organizational change have often focused on threats and fears arising from problematic groups or individuals. They resist change because they think it will not benefit them, nor be good for the company.

Some typical reasons for resistance (Connor, 1995; Schedlitzki and Edwards, 2018) include:

- Limited trust between stakeholders
- Belief that change is unnecessary or not feasible
- Economic threats or perceived high cost of change
- Fear of personal failure, loss of status or loss of power
- Threats to ideals or values
- Resentment that others may interfere in work responsibilities.

To be fair, each of these reasons speaks to very real issues that change makers often encounter. They may come up against a lack of trust, perhaps because previous projects and change efforts have failed. They may come up against threats to beliefs in how work should be done, how services should be provided, and so forth. In this sense, Connor's list of reasons is both useful and practical, representing a good starting point for change makers when facing resistance to change. However, as discussed in Chapter 6, attributing belief and fears can lead to assumptions embedded in a dominant, silencing, resistance narrative. It should not be the end point of the resistance conversation.

At the **AssureCo Case,** resistance may arise in the Customer Complaints Department. Consider:

1 Can you see any potential for any types of resistance discussed so far, for example emotional resistance, preference for stable routines, change ambivalence, or any other strong rationales for resistance?
2 How do you think the change of management and information system change might influence people's identities in the unit?
3 How can change makers alleviate potential problems?

8.7 Alternative Views of Resistance

Resistance has traditionally been framed from the change maker's point of view (Ford et al., 2008). Treating resistance as wrong, or irrational, can lead to the increased use of authority to fix it, which puts both sides in a vicious cycle of power dynamics. Resistance myths can become self-fulfilling prophecies, generating more evidence for managerial control and more reasons to resist (Fleming and Spicer, 2008). This explains why resistance is a widely observed phenomena in many organizations (Clegg et al., 2022). It also means those who resist change efforts may come to be perceived by change makers, whether senior leaders or middle-level officials, as problematic, stubborn or inflexible. In this view, leaders and change makers are seen as innocent, not a cause of or at fault for resistance. Resistance is presumed to be 'over there', in problematic units, attitudes and the erroneous thinking of change recipients.

Going beyond this change advocate bias can help us see resistance in a new light, as potentially valuable for change processes. The following section looks at how change makers may inadvertently provoke resistance, plus how they can re-interpret resistance as potentially beneficial for change processes.

Overcoming the 'resistance is bad' view

Whilst real issues may be raised by employees, there are also problems with the way that these issues are perceived due to assumptions that we make about employees who are resisting. Seeing resisters as purely bad or irrational may be how change makers make sense of encounters that resemble conflict, but resisters often act in specific, objective ways (Ford et al., 2008: 364) that are not bad or irrational. When we assume resisters are bad, we miss opportunities for engagement, resolving problems or strengthening change.

Two issues are important for re-interpreting how we traditionally see resistance. Firstly, change makers should try to understand *how they themselves can be implicated in exacerbating resistance*. Secondly, change recipients should look deeper into *how so-called resisters can support change processes*.

Firstly, how might change makers contribute to and provoke resistance? Change makers, through their own work or following leader decisions, may break agreements, promises or violate trust with organizational units or individuals, or be perceived to have done these things. Approaches to organizational justice suggest trusting relations and positive encounters build successful change orientations (Cobb et al., 1995), whereas injustices reduce cooperation, and can even provoke retaliation (Benisom, 1994). Change makers can contribute to resistance through communication breakdowns, failing to communicate change plans, and failing to promote buy-in and acceptance (Rousseau, 1989; Rousseau and Tijoriwala, 1999). People must be given time and space to review and engage with, even question, change plans as part of their process of sense making about new changes. Figure 8.4 reviews ways that change makers can provoke resistance.

Change makers should share justifications and benefits to promote change and overcome resistance, providing clear counterarguments for recipient fears, or else risk inoculating change receivers against change efforts, making them immune to change because they lack appealing justifications to consider and adopt (McGuire, 1964). Being ambivalent and not caring about change, misrepresenting benefits or dangers, failing to clarify the need for action, blocking change by refusing counteroffers or alternative proposals (Ford et al., 2008) – these are all examples of the ways in which change makers can themselves provoke resistance.

Re-interpreting resistance as beneficial to change

Secondly, how can change recipients and resisters help improve change efforts? The presence of resistance suggests existing values and conversations are evident, which need to be

Figure 8.4 Ways change makers can inadvertently contribute to resistance

engaged with to achieve successful change. Without open complaints or criticism, existing values are hard to tease out and engage with, and so, opening up debate and conversation can help surface alternative change interpretations. In this sense resistance can, perhaps counter-intuitively, support change success. In fact, change efforts may die out if people stop talking, caring, or engaging completely (Ford et al., 2008).

Engaging with resistance rationales can lead to deeper acceptance over time, mitigating the risk of passive responses or apathetic acceptance of change. Change recipients who have resisted, engaged and then influenced change can become active advocates of final agreements, which contrasts with unthoughtful agreement that dissipates over time (Duck, 2001). Recipients who have a strong connection and identity with their organization, may resist aspects of change, but support the wider development and improvement of the organization. These motivations can support change processes and help organizations overcome specific points of resistance.

There is also a further strengthening value to resistance. This occurs when conflict is treated as part of a defence mechanism against too much directionless change. Here, resistance protects the organisation against potentially damaging changes. This means careful, strategic, justified engagement on points of conflict can lead to stronger changes, thereby generating more committed advocates. Change makers though, should distinguish between task-oriented conflicts, and more emotional conflicts that can become contagious (Hatfield et al., 1994).

In reconstructing our idea of resistance, Dent and Goldberg (1999) argue that resistance has, unfortunately, come to be interpreted as a psychological resistance within change recipients' bodies, rather than a broader organizational phenomenon in more systemic terms (Lewin, 1952). This myopic focus on troublesome individuals means change makers have few tools to work with when they encounter resistance, to repair damage from broken agreements, to admit mistakes or to bring closure to historically unjust outcomes. Developing tools for these, in contrast, can support change processes.

Constructive engagement and shared sense-making

Ford et al. (2008) propose constructive engagement in cases of resistance. Although we should acknowledge people's internal thoughts and feelings about resistance and change, we should focus most intently on people's public actions and behaviours. This allows change leaders, change makers and facilitators to bring out old assumptions, values, angers, etc., into dialogue, to help generate resolutions, stimulate sense-making and reach closure (Isaacs, 1993). In this way arguments become open, not hidden, dialogue can proceed, and change recipients are given a voice and role in improving changes.

Additionally, dialogue between change proponents and change recipients should not include freezing others' views or actions under a resistance caricature but should be about shared sense-making. This means becoming more aware that when we assign something with the label 'resistance', we are missing an opportunity for understanding, collaboration and innovation. We do not all label the same actions resistance, so diverse perspectives can lead to opportunities for consensus and innovation. Resistance can, at times, simply mean alternative ways of achieving positive change.

Finally, Ford et al. (2008) argue that resistance is part of ongoing organizational relationships, and is necessary for working life. This depends on the nature of the relationship between the change maker and change recipient. This relationship must be cared for, cultivated and developed. In short, a better way to view resistance is to see it as opportunities for communication, engagement, dialogue, negotiation, offers, counter-offers, generating a deeper understanding of change and building stronger connections. Not all conflicts can be turned into collaborations, but labelling resistance as 'over there' in the minds and bodies of troublesome individuals or units is a negative tactic, and minimizes positive resolution pathways. Change makers don't simply support change, they cultivate change relationships with diverse stakeholders in contrasting contexts. This sense-making can help mitigate change resistance.

Readiness for change, motivations and outcomes

Forms of resistance also allow change makers and leaders to understand when an organization is ready for change or not, as resistance can arise out of organizational imbalances or contradictions, rather than simply irrational individuals. A readiness lens can be a constructive way to view what may unfairly be labelled resistance (Choi and Ruona, 2011). Factors that affect readiness for change include:

- low trust between stakeholders and leadership
- low tolerance for change due to a lack of capacity or emotional reluctance to change
- different estimations of cost and benefits attached to change processes
- parochial self-interest and fear of loss.

Part of the response to readiness issues is found by promoting motivations for change. Ways of promoting positive motivation include:

- training and education
- persuasion and argument
- dialogue and negotiation
- feedback

- engagement and involvement
- facilitation and support
- dramatization of the need for change
- co-option, for example giving group leaders or resisters desirable roles in change processes
- setting clear goals for change
- coercion, although this can backfire if authority comes into question.

One can also use outcomes to mitigate resistance. Desired outcomes vary across teams and individuals as we all want different things. Examples of desired outcomes include the following identified by Hayes (2022):

- Better team relationships, a stronger sense of belonging, job security or autonomy
- Improved career development, professional development or change to gain expertise
- Job satisfaction, more meaningful or more interesting work, or greater work challenge
- Opportunities for creativity, collaboration, engagement or new achievements
- Improved pay, work conditions, chance to establish more flexible working
- Recognition of work, effort or role; improved status, power or influence

These desired outcomes can help balance political tensions and motivations during change efforts. Offering better pay, conditions, career development, status, power or creative opportunities, for example, may appeal to different change recipients.

Resistance, power and better change processes

In relation to power, resistance has at times been found to be the product of very thoughtful consideration (Knowles and Linn, 2004). Dissent has also been beneficial in management too (Nemeth et al., 2001; Schulz-Hardt et al., 2002). Given how power is concerned with agreement, disagreement, consensus, persuasion and influence, such observations suggest two-way power, inclusive of the views and concerns of resisters, can be a place to explore further change successes. The first step is not to label change recipients as resisters without understanding each other. Constructive dialogue must come first.

In sum, resistance can be politically mobilized to slow down, change or defeat organisational change efforts that leaders, managers and change makers are promoting. However, much of what might be perceived as resistance, can have functional value (Ford and Ford, 2010). In this sense, resistance constitutes a form of feedback and, when leaders genuinely encourage feedback, there is a good chance that the eventual vision, change or transformation will end up more robust and effective than it would have been with zero feedback (Hayes, 2022). Change makers would do well to consider resistance as part of the sense-making that takes place between organizational groups. It is a part of normal power relations and politics in organizations. Resistance is not always irrational, destructive or unjustified. It is often useful, if challenging, in the pursuit of more robust, and even innovative, change successes.

Is anyone provoking resistance in the **AssureCo Case**? Consider:

1 How could managers communicate better with the department?
2 Is the change maker able to engage staff who may be starting or thinking of resisting the management or information system changes?
3 Is the organization, at all levels, ready for these changes?
4 How might their readiness be improved?

Chapter Summary

- Power and resistance can be complex and entangled, but they are normal parts of organizational life. They are not simply activities done by bad people. They are part of activities and norms followed by us all
- Traditional views of power (e.g. hierarchy, coercion) focus on power as a resource, possessed by the powerful. Contemporary views (e.g. power as meaning, distributed, circuits) see power as relational, experienced differently by different stakeholders, fluid and changeable. Power and resistance can lead to loud conflict (e.g. explicit demands, strikes), or silent, mundane activities (e.g. measuring or foot dragging)
- Increasingly, power relations involve issues of diversity, inclusion, equality, wellbeing, distributed power across groups and systems, plus digital change or transformation
- Resistance comes in many varieties (e.g. emotional, intentional) and is based on diverse rationales (e.g. fear of change, of failure, or lack of trust). Resistance can offer a chance for shared sense-making, collaboration, innovation, and more robust long-term change, instead of short-term conflict and blame
- Change makers (leaders and those in the middle of organizations) can inadvertently provoke resistance (e.g. by not communicating clearly or breaking promises)
- By learning about power, politics and resistance, change makers can become more adept at power-steering, influencing stakeholders, decisions or agendas, and creating spaces for dialogue and discussion. Being aware of power and resistance is, in itself, a 'super-power' that strengthens change-maker skills and change effort results

Activity

In this activity, there are four dilemma scenarios to prompt reflection in light of the topics, models and issues covered in the chapter. Use the prompts that follow to reflect and discuss each dilemma.

Dilemmas

1 An elite **university** adopting new digitalized teaching and learning services in a post-COVID-19 environment of intense market competition.

2   A large regional **hospital** dealing with unaffordable strikes from doctors and nurses who are paid below market value.

3   A successful **bank** that has suffered a recent publicity scandal because of improper conduct, corruption, racism and sexism at the level of board members and senior division heads.

4   **Your own experience and career** in respect of organizational changes that you have seen, observed, followed, participated in, led or acted as a change maker.

Prompts

1   **Change context**: What is happening in the dilemma? What is the change process about? Who are the key people, change makers and other stakeholders? What systems, processes, work norms or technologies may be part of the change context?

2   **Power**: What power relations might be evident in the context? What kinds of power would different stakeholders be able to use? Are they used in productive ways, or destructive ways? And for who? Could any of the following arise: coercion, empowerment, power-over, power-within, agenda setting, cultural norms, expertise, distributed power, etc.? Who might wield or receive different power strategies?

3   **Resistance**: What kind of resistance issues might emerge? What rationales for resistance might be justifiable? Who is resisting? Who is dominating? Would resistance be psychological, emotional, intentional? Are there mechanisms or opportunities to re-interpret resistance and use it to promote more robust long-term understanding and change successes?

4   **Change makers**: What should change makers do? Is there scope for change makers to provoke further resistance? What roles might change makers adopt to promote change successes or minimize risks? What do change makers need to do or clarify to bring different stakeholders into greater consensus?

5   **Your views of change, power, resistance:** What do you think of this dilemma, in terms of how you would approach it? Who is 'right' or 'wrong'? How might you reflect on the chapter topics, the questions and dilemmas below, and your own experiences, to further develop your own views of power, resistance and change?

Further Recommended Reading

For a comprehensive review of power and politics in relation to organizational change, see Buchanan, D., and Badham, R. (2020) *Power, Politics, and Organizational Change*. London: Sage.

For a comprehensive set of articles on power relations see Clegg, S.R., and Haugaard, M. (eds) (2009) *The SAGE Handbook of Power*. London: Sage.

For an overview of the move from more traditional to more positive views of resistance, see these two articles: Ford, J.D., and Ford, L.W. (2010) 'Stop blaming resistance to change and start using it', *Organizational Dynamics*, 39(1): 24–36; and also Ford, J.D., Ford, L.W. and

D'Amelio, A. (2008) 'Resistance to change: The rest of the story', *Academy of Management Review*, 33(2): 362–77.

An excellent section on power relations in organizations is found in Chapter 19, pages 459–83, of Bratton, J. (2020) *Work and Organizational Behaviour*. London: Bloomsbury Publishing.

For a list of different kinds of insurgency games and reasons for doing politics deployed by weaker power agents against more dominant ones in organizations, see Chapter 7, pages 209–10 of Clegg, S.R., Pitsis, T.S. and Mount, M. (2022) *Managing and Organizations: An Introduction to Theory and Practice* (6th edn). London: Sage.

9
CHANGE AND CREATIVITY

ENHANCING THE POWER OF COLLECTIVE CREATIVITY

Chapter Objectives

- To introduce key perspectives and dynamics around creativity and creative processes in organizations
- To explore individual creativity, team and group creativity, and organizational creativity
- To discuss the notion of collective creativity as a way to develop ideas, solutions and improvements together
- To examine the different drivers for supporting creativity as a truly collective effort

9.1 Introduction

Creativity plays an increasingly important role in organizations, especially with regard to a variety of types of change, especially continuous change and innovation of products, services, processes and business practices. People and interactions between people are the basis for a continuous development of new ideas and, in turn, sustaining change. Therefore, the aim of this chapter is to understand how to enhance creativity among people and teams.

This chapter will first provide an overview on different definitions of creativity and describe the creative process in general. Then, the chapter will move to analyse the key perspectives on creativity, focusing in particular on **individual, team** and **organizational creativity**. We argue that these perspectives represent different levels of creativity that change makers need to consider all together to appreciate the interrelated dynamics of creativity. Team creativity techniques will also be presented. They represent practical tools for change makers to involve individuals in generating ideas and solutions.

The last part will discuss the notion of **collective creativity**, a comprehensive concept that emphasizes the plural and collective view on creativity and how it builds up. Following the key view of this book, collective creativity will be discussed emphasizing the role of all employees, change makers, experts and managers at all levels as agents for creativity. This approach to collective, continuous creativity can support mobilizing, making improvements and developing change. Finally, we will discuss the challenges for collective creativity, in terms of organizational mechanisms and leadership.

9.2 What Is Creativity?

In our previous experience of teaching around creativity, we have often asked students, 'How do you perceive your creativity?' Approximately, and without any statistical significance, 2 per cent of students said very low, 40 per cent low, 42 per cent high and 16 per cent very high. Often, we do not perceive ourselves as 'creative', as happened for the 42 per cent of students in our sample, most likely because we are involved in contexts and tasks that don't require to be creative or, in any case, because we don't have the opportunity to express our creativity with some regularity. Even in this case, with some resolution and some exercise, for example practising *lateral thinking*, we can easily 're-discover' our creativity. We don't forget how to ride a bike – the same for creativity. Back to the initial question, the answer should be that 'we all are highly creative', as creativity is a brain function that is typical of human beings. There are many other myths around creativity, often associated to something magical or heroic. On the contrary, creativity is quite practical as we will discuss in this chapter.

There are many definitions around creativity, but a common point is that it is a mental process that involves the generation of new ideas or new concepts or the generation of new associations between existing ideas and concepts. German psychologist Wolfgang Köhler was the first to add the element of insight, or intuition, to the concept of creativity. In one of his famous experiments with apes, as described in his book on problem-solving titled *The Mentality of Apes* (1917), Köhler put a piece of banana out of an ape's cage, positioned out of their reach. He then placed a very short stick next to the ape and a longer one next to the banana. Initially the ape tried, unsuccessfully, to take the fruit with the short stick. After a pause, the ape suddenly decided to use the short stick to drag the long one towards them and then use the long stick to drag the fruit towards them. This sudden insight into the 'right thing to do' refers to the aha or eureka moment.

Building one of the first models on the individual's creativity, social psychologist Graham Wallas, in his work *The Art of Thought* (1926), explains the generation of a new thought through a four-stage process:

- **preparation**: the preparatory work that focuses the individual's mind on the problem and explores its dimensions;
- **incubation**: when the problem is internalized in the unconscious and nothing seems to be happening at the conscious level;
- **illumination**: when the creative idea arrives, bursting from the unconscious into awareness;
- **verification**: the process of conscientious verification of the idea, followed by elaboration and application.

This approach is widely recognized, although various researchers have suggested different variants, especially in the number of stages and their names. It is also well recognized in the workplace, with many professional roles particularly aware of it. For example, architects make and re-make projects, expanding the creative options at their disposal, and judges take some time for incubation before making decisions, letting ideas and insights rest for a while. All individuals naturally and spontaneously develop this creative effort, but awareness can increase its effectiveness.

At the same time, creativity cannot exist in a vacuum. For this reason, interactionist models of creative behaviour were proposed on the assumption that creativity is the complex product of a person's behaviour *in a given situation*. Social and contextual influences can therefore facilitate or hinder creative outcomes. Vice versa, each person can influence and enrich their context thanks to their cognitive and non-cognitive abilities and their personal traits.

Creativity can be defined from different perspectives. For example, we have already discussed the person(s) developing creativity, some key stage of a creative process, the 'place' that represents the context relevant to creativity and the product of creativity in terms of new ideas. These aspects actually relate to the popular **four Ps of creativity**: person(s), process, place and product (Rhodes, 1961). In particular:

- **person-oriented approach** studies individual characteristics and behaviours;
- **process-oriented approach** examines the development of new ideas and the relevant dynamics;
- **place-oriented approach** focuses on the interplay with the context, including resources, climate and situations;
- **product-oriented approach** focuses on the outcome in terms of new ideas generated by an individual or a group of individuals working together.

To fully understand creativity, it is fundamental to integrate all these orientations – and this chapter will be integrative in nature. Extending the view to the organizational contexts, individuals and groups should be first of all aware of the creative process, making a systematic effort to fully implement it. The next section focuses on the creative process and its key characteristics.

9.3 The Creative Process

This section discusses the creative process, outlining key phases and characteristics with particular reference to the organizational context.

The first aspect is the **input** of the creative process. In psychological terms, the input of the individual's creative process would be a 'temporary absence of the object' (following psychoanalyst Wilfred Bion), perceiving something missing in our mental map and triggering our creative effort to fill it. Similarly, in organizations, the input for the creative process is the perception of a problem or a gap (for example, a lack in the commercial offer) or, conversely, the perception of an opportunity to grab. In other words, it refers to so-called 'problem-solving' in organizations.

The 'perception of the problem' means that we are talking about subjective perceptions; thus, the way in which the problem (or the opportunity) is perceived affects a possible different drive to find a solution and therefore the subsequent development of the entire creative process. For example, if we perceive the problem as irrelevant or impossible (impossible is a creativity killer), we will not be motivated to make any effort to do it; on the contrary, if we perceive the problem as challenging, even quite difficult, but 'workable', we will be motivated to embark on a creative process towards a solution.

Then, the creative process includes two fundamental **macro-phases**: firstly, the identification and focus on the problem/opportunity (problem-setting); secondly, the generation of alternative solutions and identification of the final solution to the problem/opportunity (problem-solving).

Problem-setting is the macro-phase in which the work is set up and structured, the problem is defined and understood in-depth and in all its dimensions, objectives are defined, available resources are analysed and, in case of teamwork, roles and contributions expected from team members, as well as possible working methods of the group, are discussed. Also, relevant data are collected and all available resources are analysed. In this phase, it is essential to involve all individuals who have relevant skills and high levels of involvement. Referring to the Wallas model on the individual's creative effort, problem-setting mostly overlaps with the first two stages of preparation and incubation.

Problem-solving is the second macro-phase, where creativity is developed in the most distinctive sense. In fact, it includes the generation of alternatives and the search for a solution. These two macro-phases are not strictly in sequence. For example, if we obtain new data during problem-solving, we might need to return to problem-setting and revisit some aspects. Problem-solving mostly overlaps with the other two stages from the Wallas model, illumination and verification. In problem-solving, two different types of thinking emerge as fundamental – divergent thinking and convergent thinking:

- **Divergent thinking** refers to the generation of *many* ideas; it is pure creative thinking and focuses on the *quantity* of ideas generated. Through divergent thinking, individuals or teams create new connections between ideas (e.g. developing metaphors) and reflect on various possibilities and alternatives (e.g. brainstorming). With divergent thinking, no idea is subject to restriction, suppression or censorship.
- **Convergent thinking** refers to the evaluation and selection of ideas; it is the most rational part of the overall creative process and focuses on the *quality* of the ideas developed. In particular, it involves comparing and contrasting the ideas generated as a result of divergent thinking, improving and refining them, analysing, judging, selecting and making decisions about the idea(s) that are most suitable to solve the initial problem or to catch the initial opportunity and that can be successively implemented.

Problem-solving involves the combination of both types of creative thinking, usually in sequence, starting with divergent thinking to open up the spectrum of ideas and continuing with convergent thinking to select, improve, test and finalize those most relevant. In fact, although divergent and convergent thinking are both in place throughout the process, usually the initial stage of problem-solving is associated with divergent thinking (generating numerous ideas and alternatives, supporting imagination and expression of the 'impossible') and the successive stage of problem-solving is associated with convergent thinking (evaluating and selecting ideas until identifying the idea, or the package of ideas, leading to a practical, final solution). Figure 9.1 offers a visual illustration.

Some incubation between divergent and convergent thinking might be particularly helpful as it can provide space for further development of ideas and also offer some emotional distance from the ideas before assessing them. At the same time, individuals and teams can move back and forth between these two types of thinking, as needed. Thanks to teamwork, individual team members can contribute offering their complementary divergent and convergent-based skills.

The **outcome** of the whole process is a creative idea. During the process, and in particular with divergent thinking, we can generate magical ideas – 'magical' because they might be perfect, beautiful but impossible. By the end of the process, generating more and more magical ideas and then continuing to work on them more rationally, the final outcome will be a truly **creative idea** – an idea which is new, original, still beautiful, but also effective, workable and doable. For example, if the objective is to fly, the divergent thinking might suggest, for example, the magical idea of a human being with wings. Then, thanks to convergent thinking, this idea should evolve and improve until developing a creative idea; for example, the design of an aircraft. The magical idea thus becomes a creative, practical, effective idea.

The actual **implementation** of the creative idea is the next step to the creative process as described. Once the creative idea has been developed and verified, it might become a significant part of the organization, involving all the relevant change dynamics and processes. In particular, the creative process often represents a central phase of a broader innovation process (see Chapter 10).

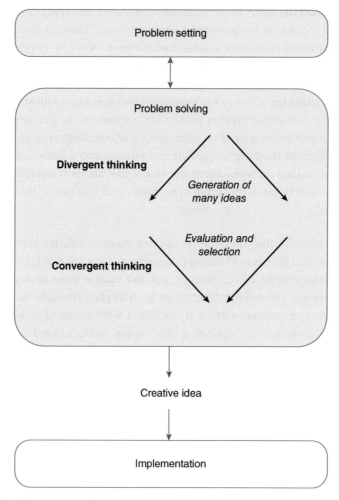

Figure 9.1 An illustration of the creative process

Creativity and creative processes can be analysed at three relevant **levels of analysis**:

- *Individual* creativity
- *Group* or *team* creativity
- *Organizational* creativity

Although the next three sections, for the sake of clarity, will illustrate separately what creativity looks like at these three levels of analysis, the different levels are actually all interconnected, in particular when we consider creativity within organizations and change processes.

Since the historical background of creativity mainly stems from the discipline of psychology, the literature was heavily dominated by individual creativity at least until the early 1990s. Organizational scholars argued that remaining mostly at the individual level of creativity was not really addressing the nature and complexity of the phenomenon and that more attention needed to be paid to creativity occurring in different collective contexts, such as small groups of individuals, project teams, cross-functional teams, units and divisions (Amabile, 1983; Bissola and Imperatori, 2011; Kurtzberg and Amabile, 2001). The relatively recent expansion of research on creativity within organizational studies is surely relevant and impactful. In fact, theories of organizational creativity tend to be integrative, incorporating individual and group-based elements.

The last part of the chapter will discuss the challenge of collective creativity, where the interrelation of different elements is even more crucial to develop creativity in a purposeful, continuous way. Coherently with the view offered in Chapter 6, collective creativity refers to developing creativity *through* collective change and involvement of an inclusive group of organizational members.

9.4 Individual Creativity

When we think of a creative person, we might imagine an eclectic individual far from common, such as a mad scientist, an eccentric artist or a computer guru. Are these stereotypes really valid? Although the literature has studied particularly creative people to determine their common traits, research does not clearly identify a precise set of characteristics that immediately identify a creative person.

On the contrary, what we can reinforce is that all human beings are creative, by nature. Cognitive psychology considers the human brain a creative entity that continuously processes data for problem-solving, understanding and reacting, and this happens, most of the time, on an unconscious level. Since the brain is creative, we are all truly creative.

Thus, being creative means processing data to find a new answer, whether it is an unconscious reaction (for example, intuitively saving oneself from a danger) or includes some conscious response (for example, analysing a problem under different aspects). The field of individual creativity was greatly supported by the efforts of Guilford (1950) and Torrance (1962, 1974), psychometric theorists, who focused on measuring individual creativity from a psychometric perspective.

Traditionally, neuroscience offered a view on the brain based on the two hemispheres, left and right, suggesting that, for each individual, one of the hemispheres is dominant over the other. However, in reality, creativity is such a complex function to be in only one particular part of the brain, or even in only one half of it. Neuroscience has extensively confirmed that creativity involves all the parts and regions of the brain working together, from both hemispheres. In simple words, creativity comes from the constructive 'dialogue' between the left and right hemispheres.

Many studies have examined individuals who have experienced damage in a specific area of the brain, to identify functions that have been lost in relation to that. Often, this 'retrospective' approach is a very helpful way to find the associations between areas of the brain and functions. Thanks to this approach, and along with brain mapping (e.g. fMRI, functional magnetic resonance imaging), the studies on different parts of the brain overall showed that many areas (for example, frontal cortex and hippocampus) are heavily involved in creativity.

In particular, creativity seems to emerge when two important brain networks 'talk' to each other. They are the default mode network and executive control network (e.g. Beaty et al., 2015). The **default mode network** tends to be active when our mind gets 'lost' (internally directed), coming up with sudden, surprising, interesting ideas or reflections. It might happen, for example, while we are walking, running, or when we are half asleep, or having a shower (always have a post-it note to hand!). The **executive control network** tends to be active when our mind focuses on a task (externally directed), directing our thinking to the task or activity and evaluating it. People who more often express their creativity are those where these two networks are more connected. In fact, combined together, the default mode thinking makes new connections (divergent thinking) and the executive control network can channel and evaluate the ideas.

Moving to the organizational context, Henry Mintzberg (1973, 1994), studying the role of managers, suggests that planning, involving analytical skills, and implementing plans, involving synthesis and intuition, are both fundamental. Similarly, creativity refers to ample and various sets of abilities related to acquiring and processing data with the aim of solving problems through questions, answers, actions and new ideas. This involves both conscious and unconscious mental processes. Conversely, some attitudes certainly hinder creativity, in particular the so-called creativity killers; that is, attitudes that inhibit the development of creative efforts, such as 'I am not capable' or 'I am not creative'.

If everyone has potential for creativity, organizations dealing with creativity-related efforts (solving problems and generating new ideas) should involve members from all levels and areas. Managers might believe that creativity is something rare (e.g. Catmull, 2008) and might be in desperate search for 'creative' people. But, actually, a creative workforce is already there. Following the main assumptions of this book, the most useful ideas most likely come from change makers, middle managers, experts and 'normal' employees within the organization. The following is the powerful incipit of an article on collective creativity in Pixar, authored by Ed Catmull, co-founder of Pixar and former president of Pixar and Walt Disney Animation Studios, and that highlights the importance of normal, 'good' people for developing creative ideas:

> A few years ago, I had lunch with the head of a major motion picture studio, who declared that his central problem was not finding good people – it was finding good ideas. Since then, when giving talks, I've asked audiences whether they agree with him. Almost always there's a 50/50 split, which has astounded me because I couldn't disagree more with the studio executive. His belief is rooted in a misguided view of creativity that exaggerates the importance of the initial idea in creating an original product. And it reflects a profound misunderstanding of how to manage the large risks inherent in producing breakthroughs. (Catmull, 2008: 65)

The American psychologist Sternberg, in his studies in a factory context (e.g. Sternberg and Lubart, 1991), found that workers continuously develop new procedures to improve their workload. Analysing other similar studies, Sternberg concludes that the acts of creativity are continuous and, even in a situation of apparent adaptation, new ways of managing old and new problems continue to be invented. From a change-related perspective, change makers should therefore 'recognize' creativity in everyday, practical activities of problem-solving. Creativity can be expressed in different ways and, if neglected, demotivated individuals could find ways to resist or even sabotage change – potentially, and paradoxically, through creativity itself.

In conclusion, it is true that some people have more new ideas than others, but it is also true that management often mistakenly underestimates the great creative contribution that all people in an organization have to offer (Cirella, 2015).

9.5 Group Creativity and Team Creativity

Research on teamwork widely suggests that, under certain conditions, groups can achieve relevant synergies and come up with better solutions than those that an individual could find alone. A key reason is that the knowledge of the group is usually much broader than that of a single individual. This becomes even more evident when considering creativity developed in a group setting: individuals can work on the ideas of others and, building on these, develop new ones. Based on this, Box 9.1 offers an example from the arts.

Box 9.1

Le cadavre exquis

French surrealists in the 1920s created a parlour game named 'the exquisite corpse' (from the French *le cadavre exquis*). It is an artistic, historical example of a creative outcome collectively assembled. Each person starts drawing on the top part of a new sheet of paper, whatever comes to their mind, then folds the paper (to cover the drawing, just leaving its edge visible) and passes it to the next person, who, starting from the small visible sliver of the previous drawing, would 'continue' the drawing on the next part of the paper. So, going on, each person in turn would make additions until the round is complete. At the end, the full sheet will be filled. Then, it will be unfolded to discover the 'magic' illustration, mostly incongruous but certainly original and surprising, that the collective has put creatively and unexpectedly together. Another variant of this game would follow the same methodology but with pieces of text. Each person, at each turn, would write a part of a sentence, answering a specific question at each turn, for example 'who?', 'what did they do?', 'how?', ... (or calling for adjective, noun, adverb, verb, ...). At the end, again, the paper will show a full, new, unexpected story.

Moving back to organizations, several factors are relevant to group and team creativity, including for example workspace, interaction patterns, role and experience of team members, time pressure and, above all, communication (see for example Cirella et al., 2014, for a literature review on the many variables potentially involved in team creativity).

Communication that happens in a group can facilitate, or hinder, group creativity. In particular, communication in teams has three key functions: interaction (for socialization), information (for sharing knowledge and methodologies) and transformation (for creative efforts). The last function is crucial for a creative team. In groups focused on creativity, it is essential for change makers to build a **dialogue** even more than usually, including how to listen and, at the same time, how to gain attention. Team creativity techniques (see later in this section) can help create space for all these aspects. Ad hoc team exercises can enable a group creativity experience and afterwards give the opportunity for debriefing and reflection – see for example the activity suggested by Desplaces, Congden and Boothe (2007) proposing building a tall, free-standing tower only made of newspapers.

Building a collaborative climate within a group is fundamental, referring to a context where the contribution of each individual is genuinely welcomed. Some dynamics and behaviours seem to be particularly important to create such a climate, in particular those linked to asking for help and offering help (see last part of the chapter on collective creativity).

The advantages of creative teams reside in the possibility to put together multiple perspectives, increased influx of information, better understanding of the problem and increased motivation and enthusiasm. In other words, the **plurality** of perspectives and points of view represents one of the most precious resources and allows the group to multiply its energies and results. Therefore, change makers should turn to teamwork when they need to analyse complex problems in a creative way or to develop and refine creative ideas.

Creativity in groups can develop when there are very different ideas from different proponents. In fact, a contrast based on different ideas can be managed in a constructive way (conversely, a relational conflict would be problematic). In this situation, it is important to, first of all, acknowledge the existence of a conflict, then give each person, in turn, the opportunity to express their idea. Next, the other team members should try to develop *more* alternatives, to get out of the initial contrast and, building on new ideas and alternatives, it will be possible to develop a shared, common project and work towards reaching an agreement (a synthesis).

Creative groups can be disadvantaged by some critical dysfunction of a team, i.e. the absence of trust, the fear of conflict, the lack of commitment, the avoidance of accountability, and the inattention to results (Lencioni, 2005). Another potential issue in creative groups is groupthink – see Box 9.2.

-Box 9.2-

Groupthink

Groupthink is a mode of thinking that individuals engage in when pressures towards conformity become dominant in a group, overriding the appraisal of alternative courses of action. Conditions that can trigger groupthink include high cohesiveness, insulation of the group from outsiders, lack of methodological procedures for search and appraisal of alternatives, and directive leadership.

Change makers can prevent groupthink as a result of some steps, for example:

- Appointing a devil's advocate – a role that, by design, challenges the decisions made
- Bringing in outside experts
- Testing group ideas on outsiders
- Having the leader(s) refrain from stating their position before the group reaches a decision
- Re-examining the alternatives after the decision has been made
- Alleviating time pressure (if possible)

Thus, change makers have the crucial task to provide the best conditions (in terms of work context, contents and processes) for teams to develop their creativity and solve problems more effectively. For example, management literature suggests different principles, such as protecting the team from the criticisms of others in order to preserve the creative process, promoting creative language into the organizational vocabulary, and managing the equilibrium between routine and exception, and between art and business.

Team creativity techniques

This section illustrates some examples of creative techniques, particularly useful for groups and teams in the *divergent phase* (generating ideas). Change makers can adopt these techniques to encourage adopting different points of view and breaking pre-established structures and patterns. In fact, these creative techniques represent practical tools for change makers to deal with teamwork oriented to creativity.

Brainstorming – brainstorming is one of the best-known methods for developing ideas through group participation. Everyone, within the group participating in a brainstorming session can freely express their ideas, without worrying about how daring or peculiar they might be. Usually, a facilitator keeps track of the ideas, writing them down on a board. The ideas shared belong to the group, so all members are encouraged to further develop ideas from others as well. During a brainstorming session, no idea should be judged or suppressed.

Brainwriting – brainwriting has the same logic as brainstorming but, in this case, the ideas are written by the participants, for example on papers or post-it notes. It might give more space to participants to elaborate ideas than brainstorming, and the use of post-its allows, for example, to group different kinds of ideas into clusters. Brainwriting can be very successfully developed by virtual teams using an online platform that allows simultaneous writing and interaction by participants on the same virtual board (Jamboard from Google is a popular example for this kind of platform).

A specific and popular technique based on brainwriting is **6-3-5 Brainwriting** (Rohrbach, 1969). This technique is also known as the '6-3-5 Method' due to the structure of the process; that is, involving six participants where each person generates three ideas every five minutes. After explaining the topic or the problem to solve, each participant receives a paper on which to write three ideas in five minutes. After this time, each will pass their sheet to the next person (e.g. the person on the right). So, each participant can read the ideas on the sheet received and, taking (or not taking) inspiration from these, three other new ideas are added to the same sheet in the time again of five minutes. The technique continues with further rounds, passing the sheet to the next participant, for a total of six rounds, so that everyone has the chance to read and write on all the sheets. Thus, in 30 minutes, 108 ideas will be suggested as a result of the contamination of ideas made possible by continuously passing the sheets with the ideas. Other variants, in terms of number of participants and methods, may be envisioned as well.

Nominal group technique – this is a highly structured group technique in which the main focus is the rational process of problem-solving (Delbecq and Van de Ven, 1971). The basic rules for his technique are:

1   Each member of the group writes down their ideas individually and silently.
2   Each group member takes turns sharing their ideas with the others, one at a time. All ideas are written by a facilitator on a board, so that they can be seen by everyone. No discussion of ideas is allowed at this stage.
3   Group members discuss the ideas only with the intention of clarifying them. No criticism is allowed at this stage.
4   In order to reduce the alternatives, the group proceeds with a preliminary vote in which the most valid alternatives are selected.
5   These alternatives are therefore discussed with greater attention.
6   Each group member votes individually and silently for the idea that best fits the original problem, so that the most voted idea can be selected.

Overall, the nominal group technique represents an orderly and rational process that still encourages discussion and participation in some of the phases. This technique can be useful in situations of stress or conflict but, at the same time, the final selection phase (phase 6) may seem too restrictive.

Catastrophe technique – the catastrophe technique (or reverse brainstorming) is a variant of traditional brainstorming. The initial brief or problem is translated into its opposite; that is, into a negative objective. For example, if the real goal is generating ideas to double sales, the catastrophe technique would transform it into the goal of generating ideas to halve sales. Then, a 'normal' brainstorming is developed on this new objective, generating ideas as specific and detailed as possible. After this brainstorming, the challenge will be to transform the ideas generated back into their opposite; that is, related to the real, positive objective. The advantage of this technique is the greater freedom the participants might perceive. In fact, they can generate and express ideas about a fictional goal (the negative, catastrophic one), favouring the generation of original and unusual ideas, generally in a more relaxed climate.

Mind maps – mind maps are a traditional, visual way to represent information and concepts. They were made popular by the British psychologist Tony Buzan in the 1970s. There are different ways to develop a mind map (for example, it can be integrated with pictures and illustrations), but the key point is to create associations between different concepts, creating space for expanding the connections and links to further concepts and ideas. Usually, it starts with a central key concept (or problem, or challenge) positioned at the centre of the space and then connections and sub-connections are generated. Figure 9.2 shows a simple example of mind map. It is a flexible tool that can support the creative work of individuals and groups – it can support brainstorming/brainwriting as well. For example, people can prepare individual mind maps and then share them to create an integrative, comprehensive mind map. Or, people can jointly work together from the beginning on a common, shared mind map.

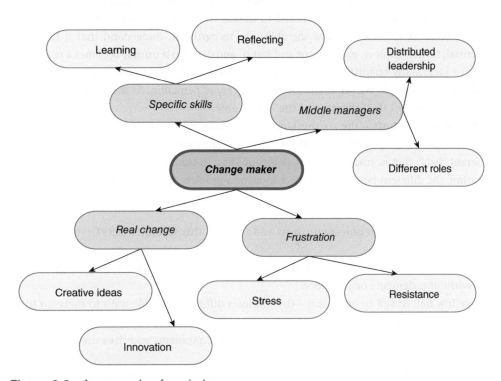

Figure 9.2 An example of a mind map

Analogies and metaphors – working by analogies and metaphors can also help generate creative ideas and solutions. Analogies and metaphors allow us to get out of the schemes or frames within which the initial problem has generated. If we remain attached to the initial schemes, it is certainly possible to generate good solutions, but the risk is that these solutions are too tied to the formulation of the problem itself. Analogies and metaphors, to use for brainstorming, allow 'forgetting' about the original problem in its original formulation.

Changing roles – in the context of teamwork, when the roles are quite distant from each other, a possible way to generate ideas more collaboratively involves changing roles in the team, for example with an exercise of **role playing**. For example, for some specific time, the marketing expert in the team might swap roles with the operations manager in the team. The goal is to allow each person to 'play' (and better understand) the roles of other team members. In terms of advantages, fresh eyes for each role can bring more original ideas. Also, this is particularly useful when there are conflicting objectives or different ways of interpreting the same initial objective.

Serendipity – serendipity (from a Persian fairy tale situated in Serendip, the classical name for Sri Lanka) is a popular term that represents an unplanned, fortunate invention or discovery. Serendipity means obtaining a discovery unintentionally, for example by chance or by mistake. But, developing a creative idea from serendipity doesn't just mean to be 'lucky'. Some good luck is surely needed to obtain the initial, unexpected 'discovery', but then it becomes essential to have the ability to recognize it, understand that it has some potential, further explore, experiment and test it, and develop it until it becomes a real, solid, creative idea. Many scientific discoveries come from serendipity, at least in terms of the initial hint – for example, we can mention the discovery of penicillin. At the end of the chapter, Box 9.3 will present the invention of the Post-it note.

Six thinking hats – the six thinking hats technique was proposed by Edward de Bono (1985), writer and expert in lateral thinking. The technique suggests facing a problem with different 'hats'; that is, under different points of view. In teamwork contexts, team members, 'wearing' the different hats, can discuss a topic or a problem from different perspectives. The hats are:

- white hat: linked to objectivity, facts and figures – this separates facts from personal interpretations;
- red hat: linked to emotions and feelings – this gives free expression to feelings without judgments or prejudices;
- yellow hat: linked to optimism – this explores different possible ways to make an idea work positively;
- black hat: linked to pessimism – this indicates the problems and risks that may be encountered;
- green hat: linked to creativity in a strict sense – this offers new ways of seeing things to generate more effective ideas;
- blue hat: linked to synthesis – this is focused on managing and concluding the whole process, also managing the use and sequence of all other hats.

Angel's advocate – the angel's advocate is a technique proposed and mentioned by different authors (for example Hubert Jaoui, a French writer and expert of creative thinking). It suggests a constructive attitude in relation to ideas proposed and shared. In particular, the angel's advocate is ideal when a proposal or an idea seems not particularly convincing to us. In fact, there are four main steps for conducting a dialogue when we play the angel's advocate role:

- Fully listen: listening is the essence of any affective interaction, so it is important to 100 per cent listen to the idea that is proposed and shared with us.
- Reformulate: after listening, we can reformulate the idea (e.g. 'if I understand correctly, your idea is ...'); this helps to signal our interest and to clarify any possible misunderstandings.
- Congratulate with sincerity: after making sure we have understood well, it is time to identify at least one positive aspect, even a small one, of the proposed idea and underline it with sincerity (e.g. 'the aspect that I like about the idea is ...').
- Ask questions: at this point, a brilliant way to understand (and make others understand) both strengths and weaknesses of the idea is to ask questions and try to find answers that, in turn, can bring improvements to the original idea.

These steps make it easier to creatively improve the initial idea (instead of rejecting it) and find a common synthesis. In fact, the technique, if implemented genuinely, favours mutual listening and collaboration.

Team creativity techniques are surely important, but the organizational context is fundamental to make them work. The next section will discuss organizational creativity.

9.6 Organizational Creativity

The need to examine creativity from a more comprehensive level strongly emerged thanks to the research of Teresa Amabile (1983, 1988, 1996), the American academic and expert of creativity who led the way into organizational creativity in the 1980s and 1990s, and who was among the first scholars to broaden the view on creativity to the social and organizational level. Organizational creativity represents an ongoing and lively academic area, as relatively little attention has been paid to creativity occurring at the collective level (Kurtzberg and Amabile, 2001), due to the traditional (mostly psychological and psychometric) focus on individual creativity.

The two main, seminal, theoretical models of organizational creativity are the componential model by Amabile (1988) and the interactionist model by Woodman et al. (1993). The **componential model** of creativity (Amabile, 1988) encompasses a view that positions individual and small group creativity in the context of organizational innovation. Assuming a two-way influence between individuals and organization, creativity takes place at the intersection of intrinsic motivation, task domain skills and creative thinking skills (at the individual/small group level) and, in relation to organizational innovation, motivation to innovate, task domain resources and innovation management skills (at the organizational level). Figure 9.3 illustrates the componential model of creativity.

Undertaking a similar view, Woodman and colleagues (1993) proposed an **interactionist model** of organizational creativity, one of the first multilevel models of creativity, linking individual, group and organizational variables to creativity. The authors have also

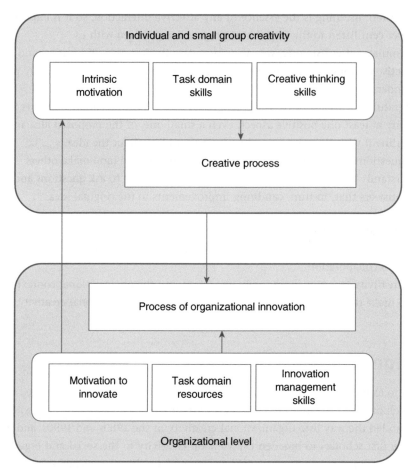

Figure 9.3 A simplified version of the componential model of creativity (adapted from Amabile, 1988)

translated this into a system model that represents a useful, practical framework to appreciate the multidimensional view of creativity. This seminal framework is presented in Figure 9.4.

These two frameworks not only represent an original theoretical contribution, but also offer important guidance for change makers and creative leaders to systematically manage creativity across an organization. Change makers should aim to take into consideration the components and characteristics highlighted in the models if they want to promote change that is enhanced by widespread, organizational creativity.

Creative climate

A specific organizational feature that is widely studied in relation to creativity is the climate in which it takes place. In fact, the organizational climate – the set of attitudes, emotions and behaviours that emerge daily in the context of that organization – can promote or inhibit creativity. Measuring the creative climate of an organization is, however, rather complex. Yet,

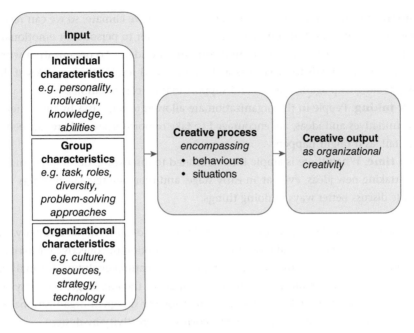

Figure 9.4 A simplified version of the organizational creativity framework (adapted from Woodman et al., 1993)

researchers, through the use of questionnaires and interviews, were able distinguish favour-able and unfavourable work climates to creativity. Three relevant large research projects by Amabile and Gryskiewicz (1989), Isaksen et al. (1995) and Ekvall (1996) were able to develop specific questionnaires, respectively work environment inventory, situational outlook questionnaire and creative climate questionnaire.

In particular, Swedish psychologist Goran Ekvall (1988, 1996) has developed a creative climate questionnaire to measure how conducive the climate is for creativity. It emphasizes ten climate dimensions that characterize a creative climate:

1   **Challenge**: Organizational members care about their work, are proud of it and take responsibility for what they do.
2   **Freedom**: People in the organization are independent and feel free to find new ways to develop their work.
3   **Idea support**: People listen to each other and encourage each other when new ideas are suggested.
4   **Trust and openness**: People feel comfortable discussing their ideas with others.
5   **Dynamism and liveliness**: People feel that working in the organization is dynamic and exciting, with high pace of change.
6   **Playfulness and humour**: The atmosphere is relaxed and allows people to laugh, joke and enjoy their work.
7   **Debates**: It is normal for people to discuss their ideas, hear different voices and debate different approaches.

8 **Conflicts**: Conflicts negatively correlate with a creative climate, so we can reverse this dimension to low level of conflicts. Here, *conflicts* refer to personal or emotional conflicts, as opposed to *debates* around contents and ideas. An organization with a low level of conflicts tends to avoid personal conflicts and resolve them quickly if they do arise, avoid gossip against others and support mature conversations.

9 **Risk taking**: People in the organization are allowed to take risks by implementing new initiatives and ideas, are encouraged to take opportunities and are not penalized if they fail, as it might happen.

10 **Idea time**: When there is ample time dedicated to discussing, developing and undertaking new ideas, even at an early stage, and there are regular meetings where people discuss better ways of doing things.

Many frameworks have been developed in recent years on organizational creativity. Integrating the group and organizational levels of analysis, the notion of collective creativity, with a reinforced focus on the collective strengths, represents a natural evolution for analysing and enhancing creativity in organizations. It also emphasizes the challenge, nowadays increasingly relevant for change makers, related to intentionally designed organizational systems that support and enhance everyday collective creativity (creativity-by-design).

9.7 Collective Creativity: Empowering People as Agents of Creativity

Different organizational factors and contexts can support creativity as well as pose some constraints, exerting forces in different directions, and determining a certain variability in creativity (Cirella, 2021). In practice, creativity is not guaranteed even when some enabling conditions are present. A fundamental tension refers to 'the paradox that creating something novel in a continued way requires balancing and combining creative workers' freedom with stability/structure in the process [...] Thus, supporting creativity, especially in creative industries, involves not only providing freedom to groups of creatives but also intentionally designing structures and routines at the collective level' (Cirella, 2021: 404). This refers to a **design approach of collective creativity**, which offers insights on the challenge of enhancing creativity in organizations by design.

Collective creativity can be applied to any collective aspect of an organization, most importantly groups and teams but, also more generally, any 'micro social system' (Quinn, 1992), nested within the organization and comprising individuals cooperating in some way to develop a common creative effort (Cirella and Shani, 2012). Thus, collective creativity incorporates both group and organizational elements. For example, Figure 9.5 shows an illustration of a collective entity which entails members belonging, at the same time, to different groups (with each group working around a specific project or task).

For example, in Pixar, the development department focuses on assembling 'small incubation teams', including a director, a writer, some artists and storyboard people. This happens

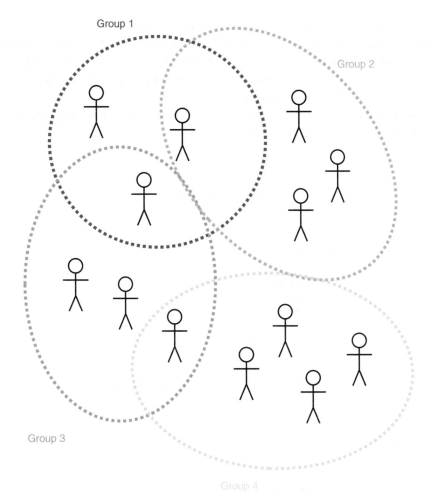

Figure 9.5 An illustration of a collective entity (adapted from Cirella and Shani, 2012)

not only for refining ideas for a possible new movie, but also for seeing whether the team works well together (Catmull, 2008).

A useful framework to understand the key interactions that build up and characterize collective creativity entities is suggested by Hargadon and Bechky (2006). Studying different groups involved in activities of problem-solving, the authors propose a framework on precipitating moments of collective creativity in organizations. The authors suggest that 'collective creativity has occurred when social interactions between individuals trigger new interpretations and new discoveries of distant analogies that the individuals involved, thinking alone, could not have generated' (Hargadon and Bechky, 2006: 489). Their data suggest that four sets of interrelating activities play a role in triggering moments of collective creativity. These activities are help seeking, help giving, reflective framing and reinforcing – as illustrated in Figure 9.6. In particular:

- **help seeking** means actively seeking the help and assistance of others;
- **help giving** represents the attention and effort to assist with the work of others;
- **reflective reframing** represents the 'mindful behaviours of all participants in an interaction, where each respectfully attends to and builds upon the comments and actions of others' (Hargadon and Bechky, 2006: 489);
- **reinforcing** the organizational values that support individuals as they engage in help seeking, help giving and reflective reframing.

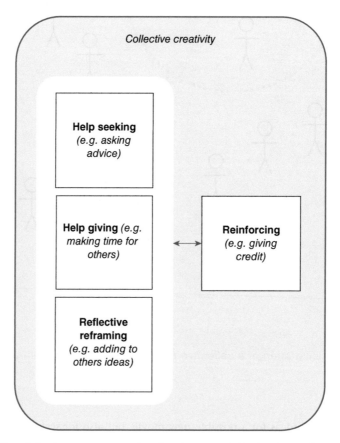

Figure 9.6 Precipitating moments of collective creativity (adapted from Hargadon and Bechky, 2006)

Overall, these activities reinforce the idea of collective creativity based on a widespread, plural, frequent, proactive and constructive collaboration within the organization and throughout different collective entities, most importantly teams and team-based structures, but also informal groups, people in an office, networks, units or the whole organization. Thus, change makers should support and empower people to *collectively* contribute to creative outcomes. Such an approach is coherent not only for developing specific creative ideas in relation to the outcomes of the organization (products or services), but also for improving processes and supporting change.

A relevant debate is about how to support collective creativity and, in particular, how to develop an organizational design that can purposefully take collective creativity into account. A recent framework (Cirella, 2021) suggests specific organizational variables to support collective creativity when developing teamwork design – as presented in Figure 9.7.

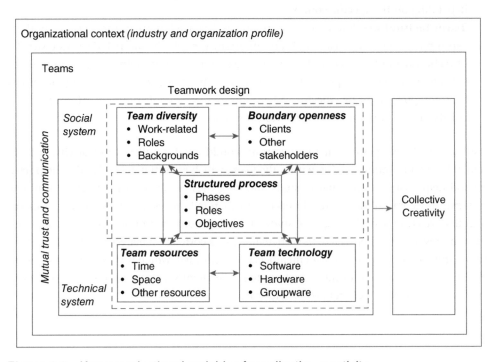

Figure 9.7 Key organizational variables for collective creativity

Source: Cirella, S. (2021) 'Managing collective creativity: Organizational variables to support creative teamwork', *European Management Review*, 18(4): 404–417.

The five organizational variables for collective creativity are:

- **Structured process**: Although it seems a paradox, supporting collective creativity requires some structure, finding an equilibrium between freedom and structure; the most important elements for structuring the work creative process relate to defining some key phases, identifying key roles within the team, and sharing and clarifying the objectives;
- **Team diversity**: This has always been an element associated with creativity; in the context of this framework, team diversity that can support collective creativity is specifically related to diversity of work experiences, roles and backgrounds of team members, more than other dimensions (e.g. demographic dimensions);
- **Boundary openness**: This variable refers to the possibility for the team to involve other external factors, such as client(s) and other stakeholders. This possibility can reinforce the exchange of points of view, which is essential to any form of collective creativity, most likely through actions of help seeking and help giving;
- **Team resources**: The variety of team resources that can support collective creativity within teams is often underestimated. Depending on the characteristics of the creative

process and its objectives, possible important resources are time, physical (or virtual) spaces, or other ad hoc resources. For example, in some contexts or organizations, availability of a generous timeframe is important, but in others not. Similarly, the availability of proper spaces (e.g. brainstorming-friendly) might be important depending on the specific context;

- **Team technology**: Similar to team resources, the availability of the technology that can support collective creativity is an important variable. It can include a wide variety of technical and technological resources, such as appropriate software (e.g. up-to-date software related to the specific task), appropriate hardware (e.g. 3D printing machines if prototyping might be crucial), and groupware (e.g. suitable online platform for collaboration, even more often relevant nowadays).

The framework also points out two necessary conditions for collective creativity, namely mutual trust and communication within the team, which are intimately related to help seeking and help giving. A quantitative study adopting these variables (Cirella, 2016) was able to statistically confirm the positive impact of a structured process and technological support on collective creativity. Although the study didn't find confirmation for the other variables, other interesting results emerged. In particular, while a correlation between collective creativity and individual creativity of team members was confirmed, which was expected, a negative relation (although minor) of individual creativity on client satisfaction (one of the outcome variables) was unexpectedly found – as illustrated in Figure 9.8.

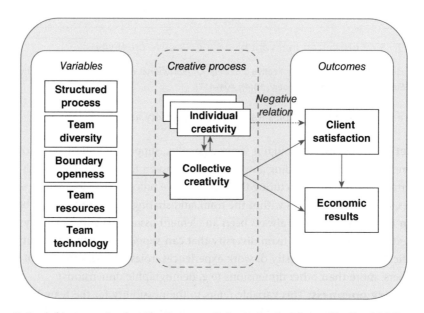

Figure 9.8 A framework of collective creativity (adapted from Cirella, 2016)

We can observe that collective creativity is much more important than individual creativity to support outcome variables. Collective creativity includes individual ideas but, thanks to the collective dimension, it takes more carefully into consideration the process and its objectives. The risk for the individual creatives is to 'fall in love' with their own ideas, even when they are actually out of scope. Conversely, these ideas should be further developed and transformed (convergent thinking) to achieve creative, useful ideas. And this becomes easier with the creative collaboration between different people.

This framework suggests that change makers should take into account the five organizational variables, and also consider having teams discussing and developing ideas even when some (seemingly) great ideas come from single individuals. Of course, this applies to a great variety of situations, while, on some occasions, creativity might be redundant. For example, the creative process at IDEO, a popular design consultancy company, is highly collaborative and democratic but, for a very brief, specific moment in the process, top management kicks in to consolidate the creative vision out of few alternatives.

Finally, we will discuss more in detail two key challenges related to collective creativity: (i) developing it as an organizational capability; and (ii) leading for collective creativity.

Developing collective creativity as an organizational capability

It is regularly observed that organizations keeping their creativity over time are those that have collective creativity built into their DNA; that is, in their culture, tradition and routines. It is a capability that needs to be cultivated purposefully over time, with a consistent series of changes and improvements that embed collective creativity as the 'normality'. This aspect makes creativity and change even more interrelated.

A useful view is about organizational learning mechanisms to build collective creativity as an organizational capability. As we will see in Chapter 12, **organizational learning mechanisms (OLMs)** are defined as institutionalized arrangements that allow organizations to systematically collect, analyse, store, retrieve and use information that is relevant to the performance of the organization (Popper and Lipshitz, 1998). Adopting the work of Shani and Docherty (2003, 2008), there are three key categories of OLMs: cognitive, structural and procedural. They will be fully discussed in Chapter 12.

In relation to collective creativity, **cognitive mechanisms** provide values for thinking, reasoning and understanding issues that are consistent with collective creativity; **structural mechanisms** encourage interactions between members, stimulating the collective development of new insights or providing access to useful sources; **procedural mechanisms** include routines and methods, for example post-project reviews, that can be institutionalized to promote learning about collective creativity.

Cirella and Shani (2012) suggest that a purposeful mix (a 'tapestry') of OLMs can support the development of collective creativity as an organizational capability (Figure 9.9). This tapestry should include mechanisms that:

1   include elements from all three categories;
2   are coherent with each other;
3   are related to collective creativity skills, processes and structures;
4   are overall intentionally designed to support the development of collective creativity.

A quantitative study (Cirella et al., 2016) was able to determine the positive relation of the three categories of OLMs (cognitive, structural and procedural) with creativity.

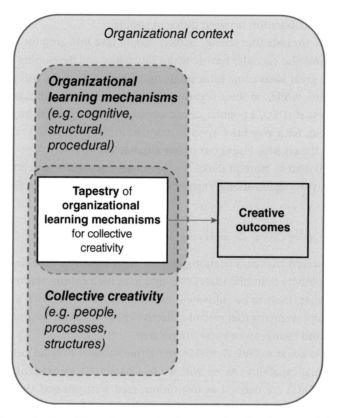

Figure 9.9 Organizational learning mechanisms and collective creativity (adapted from Cirella and Shani, 2012)

Back to Pixar as an example, they adopts different OLMs to enhance collective creativity (Catmull, 2008), illustrating well the idea of a 'tapestry' of OLMs. Based on the article by Catmull (2008), in terms of cognitive mechanisms one of the key values in Pixar is, for example, *combining art and technology*. In fact, technological innovations can inspire artistic choices, and art challenges technology to evolve. In terms of structures, for example, Pixar has a 'creative brain trust' comprising a team of senior managers (mainly senior directors) that is available to provide support when a director and producer working on a movie feel in need of assistance about a specific problem. The team provides support for problem-solving, offering possible advice – and the director, along with their team, will be free to decide what to do with the advice. In addition, the 'dailies' refer to a daily review process, where people show incomplete work to the team to obtain constant, constructive feedback and support. The team is encouraged to give comments and feedback and, in this way, people inspire each other. In relation to procedures, for example, Pixar adopts 'post-mortems'; that is, a post-movie review of what went well and what went wrong, to identify some key lessons learned. People are asked about the top five things that they would do again, and the top five that they wouldn't. Also, quantitative data are used in the review to further stimulate discussions (Catmull, 2008).

Analysing cases from different industries, from different cultures and with different characteristics (for example, size), we can still observe that OLMs adopted for collective creativity are quite similar (see, for example, Pixar, Box 9.3 and Case C in Part IV of this book). Recurrent examples of OLMs in relation to collective creativity, and that we can recommend to change makers, are about defining a mission or vision centred on creativity, and promoting the value of creative culture (cognitive mechanisms); making the most of databases and archives using them in a purposeful and sustained way, establishing a team of senior staff to provide creative support, and holding periodical staff meetings focused on creativity (structural mechanisms); adopting post-project review procedures to identify improvements, and establishing procedures for disseminating learning (procedural mechanisms).

In conclusion, creativity in organizations is not (or not only) a 'romantic' inspiration, but relates to a process of change, that is centred on learning (see Chapter 12) and which can be planned and designed with the support of OLMs (Cirella et al., 2016).

Leading for collective creativity

A specific notion to examine leadership within a creative context is creative leadership, referring to the creative function of leadership. Adopting the work of Mainemelis and colleagues (2015), the industry/sector has a major impact on determining the 'way of leading' that is most appropriate or suitable for creativity in that context. For example, the context of haute-cuisine chefs is very different from the context of theatre directors, with the former being a more directive context and the latter a more participative context.

Mainemelis et al. (2015) propose a framework that envisages three different contexts of creative leadership: directing, facilitating and integrating. They are positioned against two dimensions, namely the role given to the leader's creative contribution and the role given to the followers' (collective) creative contribution. The authors define and position these contexts as follows (see also Figure 9.10):

- **directing** context of creative leadership: 'leading by materializing one's own creative vision through the work of others' (high leader's creative contribution; low for followers' creative contribution);
- **facilitating** context of creative leadership: 'leading by fostering the creativity of others in the work context' (low leader's creative contribution; high for followers' creative contribution);
- **integrating** context of creative leadership: 'leading by synthesizing one's and others' heterogeneous creative contributions' (p. 401) (high leader's creative contribution; high for followers' creative contribution).

The integrating view is certainly fascinating but challenging. In particular, the need for *balancing* one's own creative contribution and followers' creative contributions

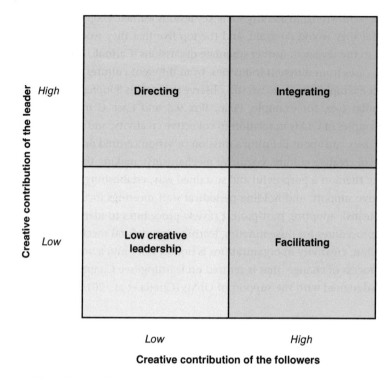

Figure 9.10 Creative leadership (adapted from Mainemelis et al., 2015)

resonates with the need for *balancing* structure and freedom that we discussed in relation to collective creativity. More generally, it resonates with the need for *balancing* the leader's focus on task and focus on people/relationships, which is a typical duality of leadership (see Chapter 7).

Although the context is usually quite specific, at the same time we note that, given a specific context or industry, different leadership styles and approaches are still observable. For example, Flocco et al. (2018), reviewing the context of movie directors, identify examples of movie directors (creative leaders) who adopt leadership approaches positioned very differently in the *continuum* between the two opposites of autocratic and democratic leadership. For example, still adopting the work of Flocco and colleagues (2018), Lars von Trier is associated with an autocratic approach and Richard Linklater with a democratic approach. Other movie directors (such as Christopher Nolan and George Lucas) are positioned in between, as they try to integrate different aspects of control and freedom. This symbolizes the challenging 'need for balancing' related to creative leadership and to collective creativity more in general.

Chapter Summary

- Creativity refers to an effort to generate new ideas and concepts or generate new associations between existing ideas and concepts. Change makers should be aware that all people in organizations are creative by nature and creativity may be triggered by problems and opportunities.

- The creative process involves both divergent thinking and convergent thinking. Change makers may generate many ideas and options and then iteratively develop, recombine and select until they identify the appropriate creative idea(s).
- Creativity develops at individual, team and organizational levels. Each level involves different modalities and different factors. For example, different team creativity techniques can support the exchange of ideas and perspectives that is the essence of creativity at the group level.
- Organizational creativity offers an integrative perspective of creativity. Collective creativity represents a further development that emphasizes the collective power of creativity in organizations. Change makers can enhance collective creativity thanks to specific design variables, such as structured process and technological support.
- Two challenges related to collective creativity are developing it as an organizational capability and leading for creativity. Two key frameworks, respectively, refer to organizational learning mechanisms and creative leadership.

Activity

As we have seen in this chapter, creativity develops in different ways and at different levels. Considering the case in Box 9.3, discuss the following questions:

1 What are the key features of creativity in the specific case?
2 What elements and practices from the case are associable to three categories of organizational learning mechanisms (cognitive, structural, procedural) in relation to creativity?
3 What is the role of organizational culture/environment in relation to creativity?
4 What are possible weaknesses related to creative development within the case?
5 What kind of leadership is needed to support creativity, given the specific case?
6 How does creativity-by-design relate to serendipity in the context of the case?

You can also repeat this exercise using the example of Pixar presented throughout this chaper.

Box 9.3

The story of Post-it

The 3M Post-it case is particularly popular, given the intriguing story that shows the invention and development of such a famous product.

The original adhesive used in Post-it was invented in 1968 by Spencer Silver, a 3M researcher. He was actually working on developing stronger and more resistant

(Continued)

adhesives, so initially this new adhesive found was of no use. Silver was still looking for an application for this adhesive and, for years, was talking of his invention to colleagues – his nickname became 'Mr Persistent'.

Only in 1974, a colleague of his, Arthur Fry, thought about a possible use. In fact, he was singing in the church choir. At the practice on Wednesdays, he used to put little pieces of paper into the hymn books to mark the pages with the hymns for the upcoming service. But, by the Sunday, the bookmark papers were often lost, falling off the book. Something to keep the bookmark papers in place was needed. He remembered a talk by Silver about his invention and had a eureka moment. They started to work together, developing these new bookmarks. While they were collaborating, they started to write some notes on these papers and they soon realized that this product could be much more than a bookmark, but a new tool to communicate.

The first prototypes were available in 1977. Fry prepared and spread them at the 3M headquarters to promote the potential product and check the reaction. It was a success. 3M decided to launch the product into the market. The product was able to easily gain attention: when a user started to adopt it, for example putting it on papers to pass to colleagues, it was easily visible to more people.

This case is an excellent illustration of the different 'ingredients' with which creativity can be developed in an organizational context. In fact, the Post-it case is associated to a series of inventions and creative ideas that, along with persistency, helped create a product that no one knew to need, until it was invented. Many sources describe and discuss this famous case in depth. We have used, and suggest, Nayak and Ketteringham (1986) for a detailed account, and the website https://www.post-it.com/3M/en_US/post-it/contact-us/about-us/ (accessed 28 November 2023) for a brief summary.

Further Recommended Reading

For a comprehensive book exploring different key aspects of group creativity and its context, see Paulus, P.B. and Nijstad, B.A. (eds) (2003) *Group Creativity: Innovation through Collaboration*. Oxford: Oxford University Press.

For a paper reflecting on the intimate relation between individual and collective creativity, see Chaharbaghi, K., and Cripps, S. (2007) 'Collective creativity: wisdom or oxymoron?', *Journal of European Industrial Training*, 31(8): 626–38.

For a paper discussing the obstacles of creativity in organizations, see Amabile, T.M. (1998) 'How to kill creativity', *Harvard Business Review*, 76(5): 76–87.

For an intriguing book illustrating how the society and its changes are related to a 'new' social class of people who share commitment towards creative work and values (first original edition from 2002), see Florida, R. (2019) *The Rise of the Creative Class*. New York: Basic Books.

For a book on creative leadership, focusing on the challenge of leading for creativity and including theoretical insights and empirical studies, see Mainemelis, C., Epitropaki, O. and Kark, R. (eds) (2018) *Creative Leadership: Contexts and Prospects*. London: Routledge.

10

CHANGE AND INNOVATION

EXPLORING COLLABORATIVE MODELS

Chapter Objectives

- To introduce key perspectives on processes of innovation in organizations
- To examine the key challenges of innovation management
- To explore the most relevant models of innovation involving collaboration in different forms
- To discuss innovation models involving different agents, such as interpreters, users and lead users

10.1 Introduction

The concept of change is intimately linked to that of innovation. Whenever there is innovation, it affects organizations and generates changes. Vice versa, innovation is always based on change: change makers, or innovators in the innovation field, view any change not as a threat, but as an opportunity to innovate. Innovation is a very broad concept but, above all, it refers to the opportunity for creating something new, different and better. Usually, innovations emerge in organizations as a challenge to pursue or as a necessity for change.

A full, comprehensive discussion on innovation and innovation management is outside of the aim of this chapter (see Further Recommended Reading at the end of the chapter). On the contrary, our aim, after a general introduction to innovation, is to focus on theories of innovation that emphasize **collaboration** and the active role of agents, experts and innovators. They represent models that are useful for change makers who are developing innovations and who wish to make the most of agency and collaboration. Put simply, we expand on the view of collective creativity from the previous chapter to consider inter-organizational collaboration.

Thus, this chapter will introduce the notion of innovation, briefly defining the key types of innovation and underlying some distinctions between creativity and innovation. The chapter will also outline key characteristics around managing innovation and the role of technology, to provide the context in which innovators and change makers operate.

We will explore the importance and complexity of inter-organizational innovation efforts based on **networks** of various agents, by adopting theoretical perspectives on open innovation and collaborative innovation. Here, innovation develops thanks to the collaboration taking place between agents from different organizations, such as partners and intermediaries.

Then, we will discuss theory and practice on design-driven innovation, focusing on the role of **interpreters** in developing successful and impactful innovation. Lastly, the chapter will present user innovation, highlighting the key role of **users** and lead users. Both approaches emphasize the importance of collaborating with key agents of innovation.

10.2 What Is Innovation?

Innovation is a broad term that includes different kinds of efforts and processes that are related to *developing and implementing something new, leading to improvements*. This can apply to products, services, technology, processes and complex systems. Research and development (R&D) activities are strongly associated with innovation, as they are a key source of innovation, ideas and problem-solving frameworks. At the same time, R&D activities represent only one of the activities taking place during the different stages and within the different aspects of an innovation effort (OECD, Frascati Manual, 1992). In fact, innovation overall includes research, production (including technological, organizational and financial activities) and marketing/commercial activities.

There are various ways, often dichotomies, to frame and classify different types of innovation. First of all, product (or service) innovation introduces something new into the market; process innovation supports the change and improvement of internal processes of the organization. Then, technological innovation specifically brings technological modifications to products or processes, based on a specific technology or invention; social innovations are even more relevant and pervasive, as they refer to changes in systems, environments and societies – for example, the impact of social media on societal dynamics, telemedicine in healthcare or hybrid working in post-COVID-19 work settings. Innovation can also refer to business models; innovating a business model successfully happened, for example, with Google (their revenues model based on advertising), Epic Games (their games, like Fortnite, mostly based on a free-to-play business model with revenues coming from in-game purchases), Zara (their lean and agile supply chain model based on fast fashion) and Apple (their Apple-centred ecosystem based on the integration between different Apple products).

Then, a key dichotomy refers to **incremental** and **radical innovations**, based on the degree of novelty of the outcome. They overlap with the characteristics of respectively continuous improvement and transformational change (see Chapter 1).

Finally, a typical distinction in the innovation field is between **sustaining innovation** and **disruptive innovation**. The former refers to the creation of better-performing products/services (adopting incremental and/or radical innovation) to sell with higher profit margins to the most demanding customers. The latter refers to the creation of 'good enough' products, for example simpler, more user-friendly and cheaper, to sell to less demanding customers. For example, making smartphones cheap and accessible for many, in the mid-2010s, was an important disruptive innovation.

There are two types of disruptions: low-end disruption, when an *entrant* uses a low-cost business model to enter at the bottom of an existing market, and new-market disruption, when an *entrant* creates a new segment in an existing market by targeting a new, wide customer base. More in detail, disruptive innovation unfolds when a company with fewer resources moves upmarket and challenges the incumbent company. The incumbent company (relying on an innovation strategy based on *sustaining innovation*) would probably move to a new segment to keep higher profit margins, focusing on even better products to sell to unsatisfied customers. For example, this happened when Apple extended its market upwards and launched the Apple Watch in 2015, when the market of smartphones was already very populated at that point. Initially, smartwatches were not very common and took a few years to take off. This dynamic shows that technological progress is often even faster than the ability of the market to adopt it.

Managing innovation helps companies understand when it is the right time to change, and how. Even great innovators (for example, Xerox, Polaroid, Nokia, Volvo, Sony, Olivetti) had major crises when they kept doing the same thing for too long, due to the inability to change. This reinforces the importance of managing innovation.

10.3 Managing Innovation

Making innovation is difficult, but it is inevitable for an organization's survival and sustainability. If an organization does not change, the context will make it change. Managing innovation should be a competence widespread in the organization, not simply for top managers or R&D practitioners, but involving all individuals, such as middle managers, change makers and any teams. As mentioned earlier, innovation envisions the implementation of new and improved solutions. Coherently, and for the sake of conciseness, we will discuss innovation management around three relevant key features: novelty, improvement and implementation. We will then focus the relation between innovation and technology.

Novelty

Innovation refers to something new, but not necessarily entirely original. For a company, innovation can be launching a product completely new to the market (differentiation), but also imitating an existing product and producing it for the first time (adaptation). Actually, Schumpeter (1934) suggests that innovation refers to new combinations of material and cognitive elements that already exist. Generating something new (in general or specifically for a company) requires an ongoing, well-balanced combination of incremental/continuous improvements and radical innovation. Thus, the degree of novelty of innovations is not always the same. Figure 10.1 suggests that incremental innovations are beneficial when they can notably improve the performance of the product (or service) but, at a certain point, the improvements will become more limited. That is the time for something completely new (radical innovation), which needs to be planned well in advance.

A successful innovation strategy would consist of inevitable cycles of incremental and radical innovations. In particular, the need for the next radical innovation is often much closer than companies perceive, as radical innovation is often overlooked. Companies often consider radical innovation as too challenging, and come up with objections and excuses such as:

- 'It's difficult'
- 'We need new skills'
- 'It's risky and costly'
- 'It's not invented here' (Not Invented Here syndrome)
- 'We've always done it this way'
- 'Our best customers don't ask for it'
- 'Our competitors are doing as we are'
- 'We would cannibalize our current offer'

That's true: innovation and, in particular, radical innovation, *is* difficult. But the opportunity cost for not changing, not innovating, might be much higher, and even undermine company survival.

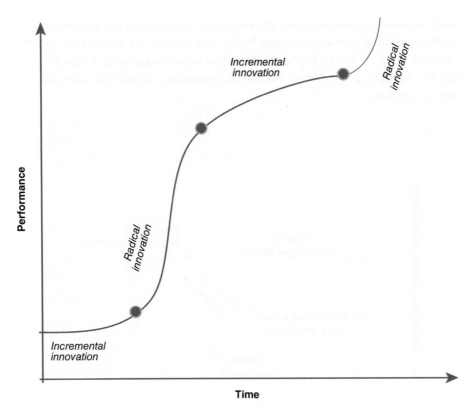

Figure 10.1 Incremental and radical innovation

Improvements

Improvements from an innovation can be for the users and/or for the company; respectively, they are innovation in value creation and innovation in value capture. **Value creation** refers to creating value for the users while **value capture** means to capture the value created and turn it into profit margins. Value capture is obviously key to the sustainability of a company but tends to be overlooked as the focus is often on value creation only, with the assumption that value capture will follow (Michel, 2014). This is often true, but the two aspects should both be managed by design. For example, Nespresso successfully managed to combine value creation for the customers (offering a new, handy coffee machine) with value capture (thanks to the high pricing of the exclusively brewed coffee).

There is often a trade-off between performance variables of a product. In other words, improving one variable means another getting worse. For example, a trade-off problem for a smartphone can be about compactness and screen size/visibility. A simpler innovation can focus on improving either dimension, but it means worsening the performance of the second dimension. Figure 10.2 shows that innovation A can improve performance P1 but worsen performance P2 (and vice versa for innovation B). A deeper and more complex innovation is brought with an innovation that rethinks the product and pushes the trade-off relation forward, meaning better performance for both variables (innovation C in the figure). For smartphones, this may mean introducing a new smartphone design, for example as a result of the recent inventions of foldable smartphones and rollable smartphones.

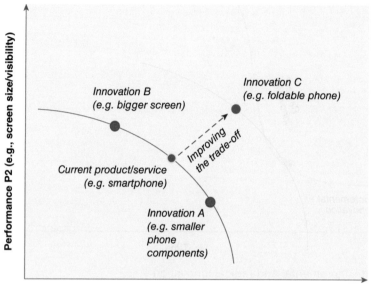

Figure 10.2 Improving a trade-off

The diffusion of the improvements establishes a new normality, so users' expectations about the level of performance change over time. Following the Kano model – a product development theory developed by Japanese Professor Kano in the 1980s – we can highlight that a product's attributes, which are initially 'delighters', then become normal performance needs over time, and then basic needs in the end. For example, this happened with some features of smartphones, such as satnav and high-quality cameras. Initially, they were features for top smartphones, nowadays they are normal features for all smartphones.

Implementation

An idea doesn't automatically become an innovation. One of the major differences between creativity and innovation is around the actual implementation of ideas, which is characteristic of the innovation process (see Box 10.1). From an economic perspective, Freeman (1974) sees innovation as the first *commercial transaction* of a new product or process.

─Box 10.1─

Creativity and innovation

In many contexts, 'creativity' and 'innovation' are often used in generic terms and interchangeably. It is quite understandable, as the two areas are very close, share various activities and partially overlap. However, it is important to distinguish these terms as they point out different key aspects. Creativity is seen as the part that achieves the vision of what can be done, while innovation usually refers to the implementation process through which the vision leads to practical results (Amabile, 1996). Creativity focuses on problem-solving that can lead to the development of a creative idea. Innovation more properly relates to decision-making processes, including the decision to look for a new and effective idea, to choose the most effective idea and to determine how to implement that idea.

Creativity often depends on an incredibly wide variety of factors and, at times, also on serendipity which is why creativity-by-design (see Chapter 9) remains a relevant challenge for many organizations. Innovation still involves many factors but requires organizational choices and changes that can be planned slightly more predictably. Furthermore, as already discussed in this chapter, innovation doesn't necessarily refer to unique and original ideas. For example, a successful innovation can, in fact, derive from imitation or adoption from other external sources.

Innovation refers to a process starting with knowledge (research) and then moving forward generating a set of ideas, then a vision and a specific invention (development), until reaching its full implementation with the launch of the innovation into the market. In practice, from many creative ideas, only some are moved to development but, then, only a few are actually implemented and launched. Even if research is the first phase of the process, it can be intentionally oriented, already up front, around implementation and the needs of users.

The process of innovation is often called the innovation funnel, as it progressively narrows ideas down until an innovation is launched (Figure 10.3).

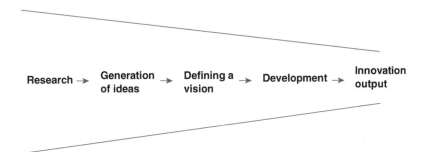

Research → Generation of ideas → Defining a vision → Development → Innovation output

Figure 10.3 Innovation funnel

To summarize, managing innovation includes designing an innovation strategy and an innovation process that are coherent with the overall business strategy and change orientation. In terms of innovation strategy, it is essential to think about cycles of incremental and radical innovations (novelty), and jointly manage value creation and value capture (improvements). In terms of innovation process, it is key to employ the innovation funnel and its phases towards the innovation output (implementation) consistently with organizational structure and culture.

Innovation and technology

The interplay between change, innovation and technology is relevant and complex. In this section, we will review several key theories to highlight the variety of views on the role of technology (see Chapter 5 for more on these perspectives in relation to digital transformation).

The key assumption of **technological determinism** is that innovation in technology causes social change, as happened for example with the steam engine (industrial revolution), manufacturing line (mass consumption) and computer (information age). Technological determinism sees technology as an autonomous force and so companies are primarily driven by technological competitive imperatives that represent *the* direction to innovate if companies wish to survive (McLoughlin and Harris, 1997). So, work and change need to be organized to meet the requirements of the technology.

Critiques on technological determinism include the debate on workers robbed of their production process knowledge due to the **scientific management** (Braverman, 1974). The technology-led innovations increased regimentation of work to align with technologies, and de-skilling of workers, meant people's critical judgement lost its central role (Blauner, 1964). Already in the early nineteenth century, the Luddites represented an association of textile workers in England who rebelled against manufacturers adopting textile machinery and destroyed the machines. Nowadays, the term 'Luddites' represents, in general, opposition against new technology. For example, a Luddite Club of young people in New York became popular in 2022. They decided to abandon smartphones and social media and chose to simply use old flip phones and meet each other in the park.

The critique of Foucault (1977) specifically concerned the information technology used as a *panopticon*; that is, a constant, intrusive observation and control. Many studies on call centres have highlighted the use of information technology as management control and surveillance (e.g. Bain et al., 2002).

Positive views on technological determinism include the possibility of new jobs and new skills (re-skilling) with potentially more empowerment and critical judgement and less repetitive tasks, in the age of the 'smart machine' (Zuboff, 1988).

A different theoretical view, the **socio-technical systems** (STS) approach (e.g. Rice, 1958; Trist and Bamforth, 1951), supports the idea of the 'best fit' between technical and social elements. Organizations do have a choice and can innovate the work system by jointly considering technology and people. Technical and social aspects have a reciprocal relationship: social systems necessarily engage with technology, but technology is part of a wider social context.

Social construction of technology (SCOT) views suggest that creating technology is a multi-actor and multi-directional process (e.g. Scarbrough, 1996). The meaning of an innovation is key (see the section on *design-driven innovation*) and, in particular, a new technology can have a different meaning from different groups or individuals (Michalski, 2014). Technology is not an autonomous device, but an artefact which reflects social norms (see Chapter 5).

Differently, from a **power perspective**, technology can reflect a dominant ideology and the views of *elites* in power (see Chapter 8). So, technology can limit individual agency but, at the same time, technology can also enable change in power dynamics, away from elites who traditionally have the control. For example, apps that promote peer-to-peer services and collaborations reshape the power dynamics, promoting social values and giving more knowledge and power to users (for example, volunteers in Italy have created an app on the occasion of a major flood in 2023, and the app made it possible to match the availability of volunteers with the needs of those seeking help; another app in the UK tried to promote sharing extra portions of homemade food with neighbours). In summary, technology innovation can be seen as a conflictual and contentious process, rather than the implementation of a rational and neutral tool (e.g. Michalski, 2014). This discussion also highlights the important relation between innovation and knowledge (see Chapter 12).

10.4 Innovation and Collaboration

Discussion on the key characteristics of the innovation process showed the importance of gaining new skills to support cycles of incremental and radical innovation and mastering technologies. Organizations often access external sources to gain relevant knowledge, specific technology expertise, or to deal with challenging time (or cost) pressures. This reinforces the need for collaboration, strengthening the relationships with universities, clients, suppliers, organizations from different industries and even competitors. In this context, the concepts of open innovation and collaborative innovation are particularly relevant.

Open innovation

Open innovation is a pivotal approach to innovation focusing on collaboration across organizational boundaries. In the book *Open Innovation: Researching a New Paradigm* (2006), Henry Chesbrough coined and defined this term:

> Open innovation is the use of purposive inflows and outflows of knowledge to accelerate internal innovation, and expand the markets for external use of innovation, respectively. [This paradigm] assumes that firms can and should use external ideas as well as internal ideas, and internal and external paths to market, as they look to advance their technology. (Chesbrough et al., 2006: p. 1)

Open innovation opposes 'closed innovation', which refers to the view that innovations are exclusively developed by the organization alone and the innovation process (including research, generation of ideas and development) takes place only within the organizational boundaries. Figure 10.4 visually illustrates the open innovation paradigm.

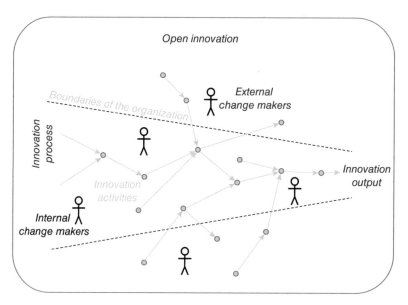

Figure 10.4   Open innovation paradigm (adapted from Chesbrough et al., 2006)

The open innovation paradigm requires the creation of networks of innovation that allow different types of actors to make dynamic connections. These networks can help gain complementary resources and competences, improving the organization's flexibility and, in turn, increasing its innovative capacity. Open innovation is a complex paradigm that requires some degree of investment, creating collaboration with other actors; consequently, it is not appropriate for all kinds of innovation efforts. When considering adopting the open innovation paradigm, an organization should identify the projects where access to external sources of competence is specifically required and, in those situations, what contents and phases of the project and what partners need to be involved in the collaboration. Then, a coherent form of governance for the collaboration should be established, along with management, monitoring and control tools.

A common motto for open innovation is about 'doing the right alliances and doing the alliances right'. 'Doing the right alliances' means identifying appropriate partners and content for the collaboration; 'doing the alliances right' includes managing the collaboration properly, with ad hoc managerial tools, monitoring and control activities and, if needed, corrective actions.

Following Chesbrough et al. (2006), doing the right alliances consists of four key factors:

1   **Identifying benefits and risks**: Potential benefits for innovation-centred collaborations are many. They all rely on the advantages made possible by the combination of knowledge and competences, integrating different scientific and/or technological expertise. On the one hand, advantages might involve sharing (and so minimizing) the costs and uncertainty of the innovation efforts. On the other hand, advantages might concern increasing creativity and innovation outcomes. This refers, for example, to fostering knowledge and technology transfer, catching market opportunities (for example, entering new markets or going international), responding to environmental and technological changes, improving time to market, increasing flexibility and pace of technological change, and better meeting the customers' and suppliers' needs (for example, broadening the products' range). Potential risks are related to a potential loss of control over strategic assets, spill over (passing knowledge to other actors) and loss of competences (as they are developed externally). Opportunistic behaviour by partners is a risk common to any relationship or collaboration. Furthermore, the organizational complexity of the collaboration could lead to increased time and costs. Some cultural barriers can also inhibit collaboration and its values. For example, the so-called Not Invented Here (NIH) syndrome or bias refers to the tendency to reject external ideas that have been generated elsewhere.

2   **Focusing the contents of the collaboration**: If the collaboration, considering benefits and risks, is appropriate, the following step is to focus more in-depth on the specific contents of the innovative project. In particular, a collaboration is set up to exchange and integrate different sources of knowledge and technology. Key elements to consider are the strategic relevance of the contents/ideas, appropriability (capacity to appropriate the benefits from the innovation) and familiarity. Other aspects, for example maturity of the technology and its potential applications, should be assessed.

3   **Defining potential partners**: Once the collaboration is deemed appropriate, with contents well focused, identifying the right partner(s) is crucial. Information about potential partners should be collected to allow an appropriate assessment. Partner(s) should be assessed in terms of tangible resources that they can provide, intangible competence and know-how that, again, they can provide, fit in terms of culture and values (in particular around collaboration) and in terms of management style. Also, other aspects, such as reputation, track record of previous experiences of collaborations, and possible contractual power, should be considered.

4   **Establishing the collaboration governance**: The elements discussed until here can provide the input to identify the most adequate form of governance for the specific kind of collaboration. In general, many different forms of governance can be adopted, for example consortia, outsourcing, alliances, joint ventures and acquisitions. The different forms of governance can be classified in respect to the level of integration required; that is, the level of internalization of activities and resources involved in the collaboration. There is a *continuum* of the different forms of

governance, where the two opposite areas comprise equity alliances (involving some forms of shareholding; e.g. acquisitions represent the highest level of integration) and non-equity alliances (without sharing equity or creating separate entities; e.g. loose agreements represent the lowest level of integration).

Based on these factors, change makers should adopt and tailor open innovation models to open up innovation efforts, in consideration of the external context (sociocultural context, industry context) and internal context (size, strategy and culture of the organization).

Collaborative innovation

Within the area of open innovation, the concept of collaborative innovation emphasizes the aspects related to the collaborative relationships. Collaborative innovation can be defined as the 'phenomenon in which organizations' activities are virtually co-designed, implying a coordination of decision making across organizational boundaries' (Ollila and Yström, 2016: 365). Exploring the concept of collaborative innovation requires an emphasis on the importance of 'soft' features, intended as features related to people's behaviours (change makers, middle managers, practitioners from different organizations) within inter-organizational and multi-actor innovative efforts.

This focus requires an integration of different scientific disciplines. Traditionally, *innovation management* literature broadly covers the technical and business aspects of a firm engaging in these kinds of collaborations; *organizational behaviour* mostly focuses on the influence and roles of individuals in relation to creative processes in a specific firm, organization, team or micro-social system (Chapter 9). Differently, understanding multi-actor collaborative innovation requires combining different lenses (Cirella and Murphy, 2022), as it usually takes place in inter-organizational collaborative spaces, **spaces in between**, that are quite difficult to explore (Ollila and Yström, 2016).

Collaborative innovation fits particularly well with our emphasis on the role of change makers, as behaviours and dynamics related to collaborative innovation refers to exploring what actually happens between the different actors (change makers from different organizations) as they interact in the context of the collaboration. In fact, each of the multiple actors involved brings their own view on innovation and a specific representation of the collaboration (Cirella and Murphy, 2022). The key implication for change makers is to recognize that 'opening up the innovation process to partners outside the organizational boundaries is likely to be difficult, as it challenges established practices, norms and organizational cultures, which can result in a perception that the innovation process has become more "messy"' (Olilla and Yström, 2016: 363). Put simply, the **messiness** of the collaborative spaces-in-between is not only normal but even beneficial to develop innovation. At the same time, dealing with this messiness requires specific practices and roles that can make the most of the collaboration.

The role of intermediaries

When exploring multi-actor collaborations, the role of a possible intermediary is crucial, as it can promote collaborations between organizations that otherwise would not have been collaborating, for example because they are competing in the same industry, not being linked to a network or, more in general, missing the opportunity of collaboration (Cirella and Murphy, 2022). O'Malley et al. (2014) offer an example from the Irish pharmaceutical industry. Competition between Irish subsidiaries of global pharmaceutical companies is very intense but, at the same time, major collaborations are now ongoing. This was made possible by the Solid State Pharmaceutical Cluster (SSPC), a national hub (intermediary) created with the specific purpose to support collaboration between pharmaceutical companies.

Innovation intermediaries are described with various terms, for example brokers, bridgers, networkers, consultants, third parties, platforms (e.g. Bessant and Rush, 1995; Hargadon and Sutton, 1997; Trabucchi and Buganza, 2022). In the collaborative innovation context, intermediaries represent 'an active role in the process of joint exploration and creation of knowledge' (Agogué et al., 2013: 1). In fact, an intermediary is a 'co-creator and enabler of collective knowledge creation' (Agogué et al., 2013: 2) who actively 'explores' the collaboration, providing guidance to the organizations involved on how to approach complex issues (Cirella and Murphy, 2022).

In this context, a relevant example of intermediaries consists in universities, university-based institutions and research-based institutions. Examples are various, such as university hubs, ad hoc divisions of universities, technology parks and scientific parks. University-based intermediaries are in the best position to activate dynamics that enhance collaboration between different actors. In fact, this falls within the role that university usually plays in innovation-related collaborations with the industry, as highlighted in the popular triple helix model, envisaging triadic relations between academia, industry and governments, and its further developments, such as the quintuple helix model (e.g. Carayannis et al., 2012; Etzkowitz and Leydesdorff, 2000) which also includes civil society and environment.

Developing practices of collaborative innovation

The paradigm of collaborative innovation emphasizes the importance of developing practices (or micro-practices) of collaboration. For example, the study of Cirella and Murphy (2022) examines the practices of collaborative innovation emerging when the university is the intermediary actor that promotes the collaboration and creates and protects a collaborative space for companies to become, at least partially, partners.

First of all, two general features emerge as key to successful collaborative innovation: the identification of specific objectives and the presence of trust. The identification of specific objectives refers to the importance of setting the objectives (end purposes) of the collaboration. Objectives should be consistent with the different expectation of the actors involved and share the risk of the innovative project. They are often related to obtaining funds to develop innovative ideas. From the perspective of the intermediary, funding opportunities represent a trigger (a 'Trojan horse'), as they can facilitate engagement with new, potential collaborators (Cirella and Murphy, 2022). Trust is consistently associated with the success of collaborations (e.g. Salampasis et al., 2014). Trust is important in all relations, for example university–firm, firm–university, firm–firm, but all actors should really trust 'the third party'; that is, the university in the role of intermediary.

The study (Cirella and Murphy, 2022) then furthers the understanding of practices of collaborative innovation taking a *practice theory* perspective (e.g. Nicolini, 2012; Reckwitz, 2002), as it sheds light on organizational dynamics as they are made and re-made in routine everyday practices (Nicolini, 2012). The four emerging micro-practices comprise networking, partnering, culture making and supporting, and they are presented in Box 10.2 and in Figure 10.5.

─Box 10.2─

Collaborative innovation practices

These practices of collaborative innovation are based on an Italian university-based institution committed to building more effective relationships between the university itself, the industry and the public administration (Cirella and Murphy, 2022). The practices are described presenting the goal towards which they are directed:

- **Networking**: 'the practice of networking is associated with the teleological goals of identifying, managing and matching a network of contacts in order to facilitate the initiation and updating of innovation-related collaborations. This practice impacts particularly on the probable success of collaborations and on speeding up project team composition' (pp. 7–8).
- **Partnering**: 'as an essential component of initiating and updating the collaboration, the practice of partnering is directed towards the teleological goal of deep relationship building and maintenance. Its impact relates to encouraging ambitious and innovative projects, as well as encouraging longer-term collaboration goals' (p. 8).
- **Culture making**: 'the practice of culture making is directed towards agreeing on shared values, establishing shared principles and, ultimately, supporting a shared identity for the established group of collaborators. Its impacts are to bring different points together, foster innovative ideas and overcome obstacles (e.g. different attitudes) that limit collaboration' (p. 9).
- **Supporting**: 'the purpose of the practice of supporting relates to the joint development of activities with an emphasis on seeking and giving help. It has an impact on developing project content, promoting best practices, giving visibility to results and improving their impact' (p. 10).

The implication for change makers is about the need to develop practices of collaboration at the micro-level and in greater detail. This allows to understand better what actually happens when different actors deal with a collaboration and make the most of elements that, although not original, are usually underestimated, for example:

- everyday mundane activities (chatting with colleagues, word of mouth …);
- physical face-to-face interactions;
- visits to collaborators;

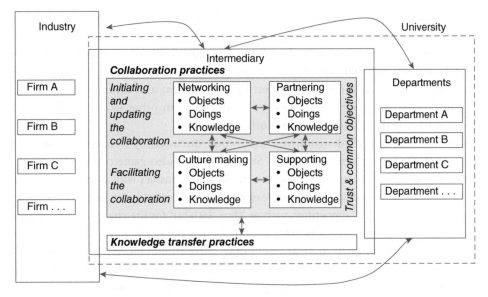

Figure 10.5 Practices of collaborative innovation

Source: Cirella, S., and Murphy, S. (2022) 'Exploring intermediary practices of collaboration in university–industry innovation: A practice theory approach', *Creativity and Innovation Management*, 31(2): 358–375.

- use of physical space of collaboration;
- involvement of previous collaborators;
- use of background knowledge.

This approach can help change makers appreciate the value of everyday basic activities and 're-interpret' them as added-value practices for change and innovation.

10.5 Design-Driven Innovation: The Role of Interpreters

Design-oriented views of innovation and change call on better understanding of stakeholders, as leaving out key stakeholders from innovation processes limits results and obscures potential impacts. For example, users should be part of a more nuanced, user-centric view of change, as we will discuss in the last part of the chapter on user innovation. Yet, it is not only users who influence innovations but also a range of relevant experts and innovators, called 'interpreters' in the work of Verganti (2009) on design-driven innovation.

Design is key in the context of change and innovation. For example, many companies involve design consultancy firms (e.g. IDEO, frog and EPAM Continuum) in their innovation processes to develop solutions that can more likely meet customers' needs. Design is not only (and not mainly) about aesthetics, it is also about the development of new meanings.

The traditional view of design includes the combination of *technology*, which supports the functions of the product, and *style,* which gives form, in order to meet user needs. This view, centred on the form/aesthetics, was dominant in the 1980s and

1990s. Then, design management in the late 1990s shifted to a focus on problem-solving to develop creative solutions (see Chapter 9). From the 2000s, a new stream of design management increasingly focused on the innovation of meanings, creating products and services that are able to change their own use, purpose and values. *Design* comes from the Latin *designare* (based on *signum*, or *sign*) and means marking/distinguishing by a sign – giving some specific significance. In other words, design can be seen as *making sense of things* (Krippendorff, 1989).

A popular example of design-driven innovation discussed by Verganti (2009) is the Nintendo Wii (now evolved to Nintendo Switch). It is a video game console launched in 2006, and still represents one of the top five home game consoles with more than 100 million units sold in the world. The main reason of the success did not lie in the technical characteristics (like main competitors such as Xbox 360) but for the change of the meaning of gaming. The Nintendo Wii innovated gaming from a physically passive immersion in a virtual word for game experts towards a physically active entertainment for everyone.

Combining the dimensions of *function/performance* of the new product or service (supported by technology) and *meaning* (supported by new languages and values), we obtain different possible spaces for innovation strategy, as illustrated in Figure 10.6 and, in particular, we can identify the space for design-driven innovation.

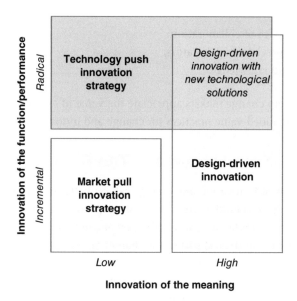

Figure 10.6 Spaces for an innovation strategy (adapted from Verganti, 2009)

The focus of design-driven innovation is generating new meanings. This can refer to both incremental and radical improvements. In fact, every product or service has a meaning – innovators and change makers who do not realize this simply cannot manage or innovate it.

Even if the key focus is on new meanings, technological research still plays a crucial role. When moving from ideas to manufacturing aspects, the difficulties might be challenging. This can require research from an engineering department or support from specialized technology companies. For example, the plastic materials used for the iconic furniture items by Kartell (for example, the popular Kartell Bookworm) need to have the right technical characteristics and the right mould, thus the research carried out on the plastic materials is usually very complex. Back to the example of Nintendo Wii, the new functions of the console were made possible by a so-called *technology epiphany*; that is, a new technological solution. In this case, a new semiconductor sensors solution, developed by STMicroelectronics for Nintendo, was essential to make the console. The collaboration with STMicroelectronics is so important that it is still ongoing for the Nintendo Switch console.

Box 10.3 offers additional examples of innovation focused on new meanings.

Box 10.3

Innovation and new meanings

This exercise will give you the opportunity to reflect on the change of meaning that is embedded in the development of some products and services, successfully launched into the market.

Consider the examples of innovation from the list below. Identify and discuss the change of *meaning* (i.e. from old meanings to new meanings) associated with each innovation.

- Example 1: Innovating from iTunes to Spotify
- Example 2: Innovating from YouTube to TikTok
- Example 3: Innovating from Booking.com to Airbnb
- Example 4: Innovating from Blackberry to iPhone
- Example 5: Innovating from a chocolate bar to Kinder Surprise
- Example 6: Innovating from a traditional fuel car to Tesla

Interpreters and design discourses

Generating new meanings definitely requires an understanding of *future* user needs. For example, user innovation (next section) focuses on users in a specific context of use. Conversely, design does not necessarily imply getting closer to users. In fact, design-driven innovation takes advantage of agents and experts, **interpreters**, who have some knowledge, views, opinions on people, behaviours and trends – even from different industries and sectors.

A variety of designers, managers and key stakeholders should be involved; this, in turn, leads to a network view of design and innovation of meanings. Chesbrough (2007) argues that traditional businesses often create obstacles for innovation, but Verganti (2009) reminds us it is important to involve a range of agents from the design discourse, including users, experts and some novel stakeholders. Verganti recommends change makers contact what he calls 'lead informants'. These are well-connected people who can help an innovation network grow. Accessing a relevant design discourse, and its network of interpreters, can help develop visions related to future user needs (Figure 10.7).

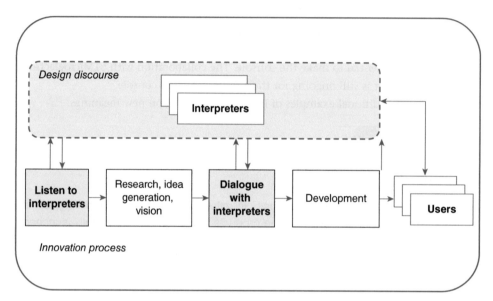

Figure 10.7 Innovation process involving interpreters (adapted from Verganti, 2009)

In Verganti's design-driven approach, change makers should focus on how meanings are attached to new technologies, products and services, and seek out relationships with, and advice from people who can interpret these meanings. These can be technology or culturally oriented experts from academia, the media, communities, different industries, technology, artistic or cultural sectors. For Verganti (2009), they are usually external, but change makers may find effective interpreters also from functional groups or specialist teams within their organization (Figure 10.8). In any case, interpreters add novel ideas, new meanings, nuance and novelty to innovation and change efforts.

For example, the pasta maker Barilla engaged with a range of interpreters, including winemakers, professors of customer experience, a catering entrepreneur, a food historian, a food critic and a chef with expertise in molecular gastronomy in seeking new ideas for pasta products. Similarly, digital transformation requires novel perspectives to innovate and appeal to different groups and stakeholders, which are not always found in project management or computer science.

Thus, in the design-driven approach, interpreters are seen as important parts of innovation, 'mediators' who connect interpreters together and 'brokers' who know the language of innovation in sectors where companies wish to borrow ideas from. Along with

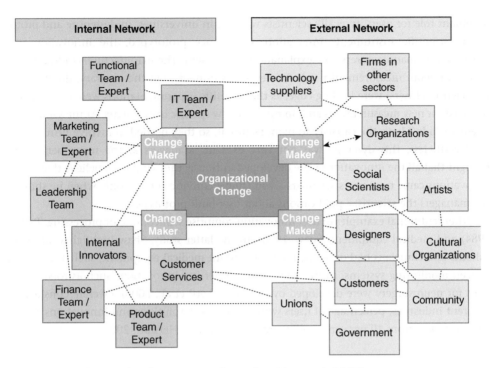

Figure 10.8 Innovation interpreters (based on Verganti, 2009)

interpreters, users themselves can be excellent sources of innovative ideas, as we discuss in the next section.

10.6 Innovation and the Role of Users

External tinkerers, or 'lead users' according to von Hippel (2005), or simply users (even internal to an organization) who find new workarounds or hacks, can play a relevant role in generating innovation and help drive industry ideas forward.

The traditional model of the innovation process envisages the sequence of *invention, commercialization* and *diffusion*. In this view, innovation diffuses to (and within) the market with no further changes, and the user is simply a passive consumer. Conversely, many examples show that the *use*, and so the user, is a potential source of innovation. Even if innovation management literature has focused on user innovation only from late 1990s, it is not really a new concept. For example, Adam Smith (1776), talking about the division of labour, highlights that 'a great part of the machines made use of in those manufactures in which labour is most subdivided, were originally the inventions of common workmen, who, being each of them employed in some very simple operation, naturally turned their thoughts towards finding out easier and readier methods of performing it' (Book one, Chapter I).

The seminal study of von Hippel (1976) on innovations in scientific instruments, such as nuclear magnetic resonance spectrometry and transmission electronic microscopy, found a dominant role for users, typically scientists working in universities, in designing and proto-typing scientific instruments innovation. Only once prototyped, the innovation was transferred to manufacturers. The explanation was evident. The manufacturers didn't have a clear idea about measurement needs for newer instruments. On the contrary, the needs of the scientists (users) were leading edge, as the scientific experimentations were highlighting the need for new measurements and, in turn, for new specific instruments. At the same time, scientists didn't have the capacity to manufacture it, so they needed to involve firms.

Nevertheless, this dynamic was not very evident. Managers at the instrument firms thought that all the innovations were developed in-house; they could not believe that many innovations came from users/scientists – von Hippel convinced them only when he showed the managers the scientists' publications about user-built prototypes.

Other traditional examples of user innovation comprise semiconductor processing (Pavitt, 1984) and medical equipment (Shaw, 1998). In the latter study, Shaw highlights that consultants and clinicians had developed new, important medical equipment, such as neonatal oxygen monitoring systems. In the same sector, other key innovations such as robotic systems for neurosurgery were developed by users (e.g. Lettl et al., 2006). Overall, considering different industries, percentage of users who develop new solutions and innovations ranges approximately from 10 per cent to 40 per cent (Lüthje and Herstatt, 2004).

User innovation

Von Hippel (1994, 1998, 2005, 2007) associates **user innovation** with the locus of problem moving away from a specialist supplier and going 'towards those who directly benefit from a solution such as the direct users of a product or service' (von Hippel, 1998: 630). Two aspects characterize user innovation.

First, manufacturers benefit from innovation by selling it, so they tend to 'create solutions that are "good enough" for a wider range of potential users'; users, in terms of individuals or firms, have a motivation to innovate more specifically as they will benefit from *using* that innovation. In fact, 'direct beneficiaries will be motivated to create a solution that will be exactly right for their own very particular circumstances' (von Hippel, 1998: 630). Manufacturers are also users, for example in terms of components or equipment they need to make their final products.

Second, information is asymmetric and tends to be 'sticky'. Users (often, niches of users) have information about advanced needs and context of use; manufacturers have information about generic solutions. All needed information should be brought together at a single locus, but it is costly to transfer information from one locus to another in a useable form – that represents the stickiness of the information (von Hippel, 1994). In technology transfer projects, information is highly sticky and cost of information transfer, in particular when technology is new, accounts for a large part of project costs (e.g. Teece, 1976).

A popular example showing the power of user innovation is the invention and development of the mountain bike. Mountain bikes were invented by users in early 1970s.

Cyclists in Marin County (California) started assembling 'clunkers' using old paper boy bikes. To improve performance, for example in downhill races, users modified commercial bikes with motorbike tyres and drum brakes. A cottage industry flourished in the mid-1970s, with users making bikes for others. But they were expensive. The technology continued to move forward in the following years and, in the early 1980s, the first mass-produced mountain bike was finally produced by Specialized, a Californian bicycle company. By the early 2000s, mountain bikes accounted for more than 60 per cent of the US market, showing how user innovation can be commercially relevant.

The characteristics of user information are very evident in this example (Lüthje et al., 2005). **Tacit knowledge** (see Chapter 12) was a clear feature of a rider's knowledge and needs, for example around specific feats such as aerial stunts and pedal-spin. Also, extreme riders (for example ice-bikers, downhill and jumping bikers) tended to innovate more, showing that user-innovation information is 'sticky' and context-specific. Similarly, more frequent riders tended to innovate more. Repeated personal experiences, which deepen the embodied and tacit knowledge, facilitated the identification of problems and generation of new product solutions.

Regarding the manufacturing of mountain bikes by users, prototype innovators were able to manufacture the products as well, as they often had some technical knowledge from their professional background (for example engineering for the bicycle suspension. or medicine for the body armours) or from another sport (for example motocross). Having all the information at one single locus (as they were user innovators) reduced solution stickiness. For similar reasons, we can track similar user innovations in different extreme/specialized sports, such as canyoning, gliding, boardercross and handicapped cycling (Franke and Shah, 2003). Compared with 'normal' users, user innovators often had a more central role in their community and spent more time on the sport/activity.

The role of lead users

Lead users are users who innovate more than the norm and represent the portion of users who are active innovators. As depicted in Figure 10.9, lead users, compared to experts and user innovators, are ahead in terms of envisioning market trend and simultaneously are particularly motivated to innovate, as they would anticipate higher benefits from innovations that meet their needs (Hienerth and Lettl, 2017; Lüthje and Herstatt, 2004; von Hippel, 1986).

In some cases, lead users are easier to identify. For example, in the case of innovation of PC-CAD software, lead users, dissatisfied with the packages available on the market, were able to develop their own software or customize existing packages, clearly bringing better solutions into the market. In contrast, in the example of mountain bikes, it was impossible to predict that some users would have launched such a successful trend.

Lead users have developed innovations that are important and, in some cases, even revolutionary, such as the World Wide Web, or simply Web, Free/Libre Open Source Software (FLOSS), Wikipedia and many others (see Box 10.4).

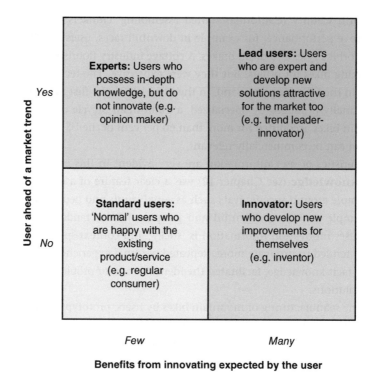

Figure 10.9 Different types of users (adapted from Hienerth and Lettl, 2017)

—Box 10.4—

Examples of user and lead-user innovation

This box offers a variety of examples of innovations created and developed by users and lead users:

- World Wide Web: Tim Berners-Lee did not expect to invent anything revolutionary; he said that it was just something he needed in his work (Hienerth and Lettl, 2011). He wanted to solve a problem that was hindering his efforts as a consulting software engineer at CERN, the European Organization for Nuclear Research. His innovation was to adopt the idea of hypertext and apply it in the context of networked computers. He further expanded the idea he had developed at CERN and finally made it available exactly on the internet in 1991.
- Free/Libre Open Source Software (FLOSS): This represents free/open access software with source code openly shared, e.g. Linux, Apache, Open Office, Mozilla Firefox. Each project refers to an 'innovation community', which is organized very openly but formally. In fact, participants work on module- or problem-based projects, and modules combine to create the final product. They are organized

over the internet (virtual communities) and the products are distributed not-for-profit. The projects are often pioneered by small groups of lead users.

- Wikipedia: This is similarly the result of a large, virtual innovation community. In fact, the articles are written and edited by volunteer editors. In 2023 Wikipedia sees the active involvement of about 290,000 editors, includes around 61 million articles (source: https://en.wikipedia.org/wiki/Wikipedia; accessed 28 November 2023) and appears to have similar accuracy rating as the Encyclopaedia Britannica (e.g. Giles, 2005).
- LEGO case: LEGO Mindstorms was a new toy created by LEGO in 1998 and eventually discontinued at the end of 2022. It represents one of the best-selling products in the LEGO Group history (https://www.lego.com/en-gb/themes/mindstorms/ev3; accessed 28 November 2023). Mindstorms was a robot made of LEGO bricks, featuring a computer brain, stepper motors for movements, and sensors for light, touch and temperature (Hienerth et al., 2014). Some users discovered how to hack and program the robot and, based on that, more users started to create their own Mindstorms tools and variations. These communities grew rapidly, without any company involvement. In fact, the company became unsure about how to respond for around a year, as LEGO executives didn't know what to do with such a new situation (Hienerth et al., 2014). Eventually, LEGO management came to understand the power of community-led innovation and explicitly allowed users to develop their inventions. This experience helped LEGO to enhance their other ongoing initiatives to involve users. For example, LEGO still continuously engages with innovators, professional users, and fans, in particular LEGO Certified Professionals and AFOL (Adult Fan of LEGO) communities, to develop new ideas, networks and platforms.
- Hasbro case: In January 2023 news broke that Wizards of the Coast, a subsidiary of Hasbro, the global games company, were about to change copyright agreements for the popular role-playing game Dungeons and Dragons. The planned change caused an uproar because fans, players and lead users had been making adventures, characters, images, spells, weapons and other paraphernalia for the game for decades. They had been allowed to make game elements and sell them. The community responded with threats to leave the game and fight back. Eventually, Wizards of the Coast shelved their plans, and the community can still make and sell Dungeons and Dragons products. The case shows how over decades, lead users can drive and benefit from innovations. It remains a bone of contention as to whether Wizards of the Coast will try again in the future to regain control over all these user-created products, through copyright law.

A common form of lead-user innovation is user-to-user collaboration and refers to innovation communities. In fact, lead-user innovation tends to be distributed amongst a large number of lead users, as individual users rarely have the capacity to produce complex, multiple innovations just by themselves. Innovation communities represent direct, informal, user-to-user cooperation and, when increasing in complexity, they can become organized cooperation networks, for example as in the case of FLOSS projects and Wikipedia.

From a company perspective, the process associated with the **lead-user method** (Lüthje and Herstatt, 2004) represents a good example of a tool to identify and integrate lead users into innovation projects. The four main steps are about: (i) launching a lead users project; (ii) identifying key needs and trends; (iii) identifying lead users and ideas; and (iv) designing a new concept thanks to a lead users workshop (Lüthje and Herstatt, 2004). This process exemplifies a structured way to identify and actively involve lead users by design. Examples of companies who have engaged with this method are 3M, Johnson & Johnson and Hilti (e.g. Herstatt and von Hippel, 1992; Lüthje and Herstatt, 2004).

In conclusion, Lettl et al. (2008) identify some key managerial implications related to lead-user innovation. Firstly, it is essential to constantly screen for potential lead users and lead-user activities. Then, change makers should create new ways of integration with lead users, developing models of cooperation with them. Sponsoring (external) lead-user activities is also a way for risk reduction, in particular for parts of the new product development process. Finally, organizing and using hybrid community forms helps change makers to sustain and institutionalize sustainable knowledge transfer with lead users. These actions are helpful for change makers to proactively manage and benefit from lead-user innovation. In fact, lead users can help change makers build new organizational forms of innovation based on sustainable co-creation between lead users and organizations.

Chapter Summary

- Change is intimately linked to innovation. Whenever there is innovation, it generates changes. And innovation is always based on change: change makers view any change as an opportunity to innovate. It is important to proactively manage innovation to make sure to change at the right time. Radical innovation is often needed much earlier than expected.

- Open innovation emphasizes the importance for organizations of opening up their boundaries and collaborating with companies, partners, institutions – creating a network of change makers.

- The role of the university is key to promote innovation at the cutting edge. Universities, university-based institutions and science parks can play an intermediary role to make different change makers becoming partners for innovation. Nevertheless, collaborative spaces-in-between are often very 'messy'. This messiness is not only normal, but even beneficial to develop innovation. It implies that specific micro-practices – often mundane practices – are needed for change makers to make the most of collaborations.

- Thinking about new meanings (design) is essential to develop successful innovations. It often requires an intense, ongoing dialogue with influential actors mostly outside the organization, the so-called interpreters.

- Innovation doesn't end with diffusion, or even consumption, and doesn't only happen in R&D labs. Innovation is a cycle of change. New products (or services) lead to new possibilities and new uses. In turn, new uses can unveil new problems and new needs, leading to new products. So, innovation can arise from collaboration with and between experts, users, lead users. Tacit knowledge of users and lead users is key to many innovations and change makers should be actively open to that.

Activity

Science parks are often considered important actors in the innovation ecosystem. Traditionally, their relevance is related to the physical proximity that they can offer to the organizations involved. But, more recently, it was widely argued that science parks can play a much broader role than simply as a physical platform. For example, the case on Area Science Park (Trieste, Italy) offers some insights about the role of a science park in promoting a creative and collaborative climate. Considering this case (Box 10.5), discuss the following questions:

1   How do the aspects presented in the Area case have an impact on promoting collaboration and innovation?
2   What are other aspects that can further promote collaboration between different actors in Area? And with external innovators?
3   What are possible obstacles that can limit collaborative innovation in a science park like Area?

---Box 10.5---

Area Science Park

Area Science Park, based in Trieste, Italy, and established in 1978, is a national research organization managing one of the most important science and technology parks in Italy. Area hosts approximately 75 R&D centres and high-tech companies, along with public research institutions, for a total of approximately 2,600 employees, most of them researchers.

Four aspects critical to a creative and collaborative climate can be identified in Area, adopting the study by Cirella and Yström (2018):

- The promotion of a **shared identity**: Area identity is based on the importance of scientific research. When a new firm wants to move to Area, they need to submit an innovative three-year research programme. Also, 'the strategic orientation of the park is to strengthen its role of socio-economic engine of development at national and international level taking advantage of three core competences, i.e. scientific network management, training, and technology transfer' (p. 10).
- The design of **structured work processes**: Structured processes can help team up different actors for combining the competences needed to develop an innovative project. 'Most of Area Science Park work processes, related to the services of the science park, mainly focus on matching the entrepreneurial needs with research opportunities and include a creative effort to deeply analyse what research can offer and understand which are proper ways to value it' (p. 11).

(Continued)

- Use of **communal spaces**: The use of communal space can enhance formal and informal dynamics of communication. 'Some communal spaces are obviously related to informal interactions, such as coffee shops, restaurants and outdoor areas. These spaces, positioned at the centre of the main campus, facilitate informal interactions. Respondents highlight that these interactions, in quite unpredictable manners, are at the end triggers for informal exchange of ideas. The science park also promotes frequent meetings on campus (including meetings between Area management and tenants and meetings between tenants) using work-related branded spaces, such as laboratories and meeting rooms' (p. 11).
- Use of **internal communication technology**: Area adopts an intranet platform and an extranet platform for the organizations hosted in the park. 'This system was designed to facilitate communication within teams and between different actors in the park. Although some respondents highlight this system is underutilised, they identify its potential as a trigger for sharing knowledge and ideas in a systematic way' (p. 11).

Further Recommended Reading

For a comprehensive textbook focused on innovation management, see Tidd, J. and Bessant, J.R. (2014) *Strategic Innovation Management*. Chichester: Wiley.

For a seminal book on open innovation, as discussed in the chapter, see Chesbrough, H., Vanhaverbeke, W. and West, J. (eds) (2006, 2008) *Open innovation: Researching a New Paradigm*. Oxford: Oxford University Press.

For collaborative innovation, see a comprehensive special issue from the *Creativity and Innovation Management* journal, 29(1): 141–91 – the introduction to the special issue is Yström, A. and Agogué, M. (2020) 'Exploring practices in collaborative innovation: Unpacking dynamics, relations, and enactment in in-between spaces', *Creativity and Innovation Management*, 29(1): 141–5.

For an essential book on design-driven innovation, as discussed in the chapter, see Verganti, R. (2009) *Design Driven Innovation: Changing the Rules of Competition by Radically Innovating What Things Mean*. Boston, MA: Harvard Business Press.

For an important and comprehensive book on user and lead user innovation, see von Hippel, E. (2005, 2006) *Democratizing Innovation*. Cambridge, MA: The MIT Press. (An electronic version of this book is available under a Creative Commons licence.)

11

EVALUATING CHANGE

FROM METRICS TO NETWORKS

Chapter Objectives

- To familiarize readers with perspectives, terminology and approaches for evaluating change in organizations
- To review practical aspects of change evaluation, such as the use of indicators and metrics, and models which stress formative evaluations of change or innovation
- To discuss broader, network-oriented and stakeholder-sensitive approaches that support both formative and summative evaluations

11.1 Introduction

Throughout this book, we have explored methods to increase the likelihood of successful change in organizations. But, how do we know if change has been successful? How do we know what has changed and what impact this has had on the organization, its performance and the experience of those who work within it? This chapter explores how we might evaluate transformation efforts, and how best to understand the range of factors, metrics, agents or 'networks' involved in achieving organizational change.

It is worth noting early on that an established canon of evaluation has taken hold in recent years in many fields. This view contains four key components (see Figure 11.1). Firstly, project or change **inputs** such as cost, time, effort, expertise, etc. Secondly, change **outputs**, for example profitability, numbers of customers or other measures. Third is **outcomes**, which are more descriptive and contextual behaviour changes such as the way employees or customers behave following a change to services. Finally, there are **impacts**, which all change makers hope to achieve. These are behaviour changes of significant value or duration, covering longer terms and wider groups of people. Table 11.1 shows an overview of some of the key language of evaluation and terms used throughout this chapter.

Figure 11.1 Key elements underpinning contemporary evaluation

We draw on literature and examples from technology-driven change and digital transformation. This helps us illustrate opportunities and challenges that are important for organizational change evaluation across diverse sectors and goals. Technology-driven change is itself a key area for organizational change today, and boasts many evaluation methods and models. As such, this relatively mature evaluation area is an effective resource for us to draw on when discussing how to evaluate change in its broader sense, spanning different sectors, kinds of organizations or change objectives. The approaches which we identify in the chapter apply equally to other types of strategic and planned change (e.g. restructuring outcomes, new services, facilities or system performance) where an organization wishes to understand the impact of actions taken to transform itself.

The first section is on traditional evaluation approaches, and these emphasize measures, engineering style goals, performance and what we understand today as indicators or metrics. Examples here include project management indicators, User Acceptance Testing (UAT), Critical Success Factors (CSFs), and a focus on innovation processes. This is followed by a second section which makes the case that change management generally lacks comprehensive approaches to evaluation or impact and often focuses more narrowly on formative evaluation and monitoring during change processes rather than significant impacts after changes have happened.

The third section explores network views for use in evaluations and includes a look at design networks together with two socio-technical network approaches, Activity Theory (AT) and Actor-Network Theory (ANT). These take account of social and organizational change, using qualitative methods and multi-stakeholder perspectives. They contrast with evaluations that depend on the priorities of powerful or influential change leaders, executive project managers or metrics analysts. Network evaluations are more sensitive to complexity, power, ambiguity and collaboration in and across units with diverse needs and values. As such, they offer a wider frame for understanding change results, failures and impacts at organizational, social, economic, business and environmental levels. However, they can be more challenging to perform than well-established indicator or metrics-based formative evaluations.

Table 11.1 Important evaluation terminology

Term	Meaning
Inputs	Resources, finance, skills, etc. that are allocated to change efforts
Outputs	Measurable results following change efforts, e.g. increased hits to a new website, number of trainee participants, number of new customers
Outcomes	Description of how change efforts influence new behaviours, e.g. increased customer purchases, fewer complaints volume/severity
Impacts	Longer-term or significant changes in behaviours over time and across groups, more permanent and compelling than outcomes
Formative	Evaluations undertaken during change efforts to learn and assess progress
Summative	Evaluations undertaken after change efforts to assess results, outcomes, impacts
Monitoring	Ongoing data collection during change efforts, often part of formative evaluations, but more regular and routine
Indicator	A short description of what is to be monitored or measured, e.g. trainee numbers can be an indicator for programme success
KPI	Key performance indicators, a popular term in indicator-based approaches
OKR	Objectives and key results – an indicator approach using incremental milestones
CSF	Critical Success Factors – an approach focusing on specific success indicators
UAT	User Acceptance Testing – a methodology for testing if users accept a new technology or if it requires further development
Metrics	Measurable sets of indicators which can be digitized, collected, analysed and used to create performance media such as dashboards for analysts
Stakeholder	A person/group with an interest in, or affected by, change efforts
Beneficiary	A person/group who is a key target recipient of change benefits
Evidence based	Rationale used to justify data collected in support of strategies/decisions
Performative evaluation	Evaluations or metrics that cause people or groups to adapt behaviour, regardless of later change outcomes, e.g. units begin to 'game' evaluation KPIs

11.2 Evaluations as Performance and Metrics

This section first looks at widespread, often standard and assumed, ways of evaluating change. These draw on engineering and project management but also incorporate views from technology evaluation and computer science. Many of these evaluation frames rely on reducing the number of variables and the complexity of the change to make it manageable. This reduction process often ends up with two categories or clusters of factors, such as the user and the technology. We characterize these pairs as evaluation dyads, a theme which recurs through this section.

Evaluation in project management

Practically speaking, evaluation of change in organizations normally revolves around evaluating whether specific project goals have been achieved, or whether project scope, timeframe and resources have been successfully adhered to. It is often represented by the project triangle, or what some have called the **iron triangle** (e.g. A. Kelly, 2018).

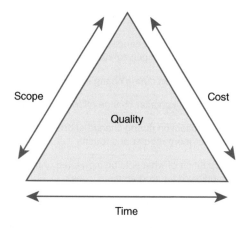

Figure 11.2 The project management 'iron triangle'

From a classic project management perspective, if a change initiative comes in on time, on budget and on scope, it is deemed successful. If it comes in over budget, delayed or does not meet the original scope of work, it is deemed unsuccessful or even a failure. As we have seen in previous chapters, many organizational change projects fail to meet the objectives which they set out to. This 'projectified' view is the most common method of how changes are evaluated in practice and follows well-established project management models such as Prince 2 or Project Management Body of Knowledge (PMBOK). Delivery of scoped requirements, in line with cost and time, are paramount and indicate success.

To handle complexity, project models and evaluations often use indicators of different sorts, such as **key performance indicators (KPIs)**. These measure progress during a project. More recently **objectives and key results (OKRs)** have become popular with many organizations, especially technology developers having been championed by Schmidt and Rosenberg in 'How Google Works' (2014). OKRs are like typical management objectives, but they embed highly measurable key results in the process of achieving objectives, similar to project milestones. Evaluators would consider these as part of 'formative' evaluations or 'monitoring' because they happen during the change process, and they focus on delivering already established goals, rather than assessing their value, or wider impacts. Technology-driven change methods, such as **user acceptance testing**, follow a similar delivery focus (see below).

Critical success factors

Critical success factors (CSFs) are developed in diagnostic phases of projects to identify requirements. Typically, they are built by first identifying perceptions of success from different organization units. These are then compiled into a list or matrix of factors, which are monitored during change efforts to assess progress. As such, they are like indicators or OKRs, but emphasize gathering unit inputs early on. System developers often see management and user inputs as critical for success (Larsen et al., 2009), but team characteristics and project methods are important too (Kim and Peterson, 2000). Other typical factors include communications, product innovations, managing expectations and various metrics.

DeLone and McLean (1992) originally proposed a CSF model with six factor groups: system quality, information quality, system use, user satisfaction, individual and organizational impact. Later, others developed new models, which focused on areas such as perceived usefulness (Seddon, 1997) or service quality (DeLone and McLean, 2003; Wang, 2008).

CSFs help organizations create shared goals and monitor changes. They prioritize timebound delivery first and foremost, with less attention to impacts beyond project cycles. In sum, CSFs are development focused, and foundational for the metrics and data analytics common today. Such indicators and metrics are valuable sources of data for senior decision-makers, but risk eliding employee and customer contexts, power and politics, ambiguities or cultural aspects of change (Klein and Myers, 1999; Monod and Boland, 2007; Remus and Wiener, 2010). Conflicts, complexity, contested views, capacity development, big picture or long-term changes are rarely metrics-oriented priorities.

User acceptance testing

Software is a big part of change efforts today, particularly innovation and digital transformations. Up to 50 per cent of time and cost can be spent on software testing, early software design, code walk-throughs, inspections, test cases, testing of modules, routines, integration, applications and usability (Myers et al., 2011). User acceptance testing (UAT) is a method used late in the development cycle before software is released to market, users, clients or online. This is also called beta-testing, or end-user testing. Essentially, UAT assesses whether a new technology is acceptable to users and customers.

UAT is well established in engineering and computer science, and widely adopted by software developers and technology vendors. UAT assesses how users interact with new technologies, such as a machine, a smartphone or new digital service. Tests are designed to mimic real user environments and are often done with experienced testers or business clients who help design the testing process. Multiple tests are conducted, and test results are compared with expected results to assess functionality, quality and error rates. Usually test items are pre-designed in advance and testers go through required, fixed steps to complete tasks, such as accessing data from a new database or placing an order on an e-commerce site. Typically, UAT validates whether business requirements are met, identifies bugs, reduces the risk of defects and ensures functionality meets user needs (Testing Experts, 2020).

There are many UAT models, developed across fields such as behavioural science, psychology, social cognition and innovation. Venketesh et al. (2003) used eight such models to develop a unified UAT approach but today there are many end-cycle tests under the broad UAT umbrella, including module testing, security testing and performance testing. Overall, in terms of evaluation, UAT centres on the dyad mentioned earlier – the user and the technology. If the user accepts the technology, the technology is good. This risks leaving other concerns and impacts that change makers will encounter, out of the evaluation equation.

Relying on metrics for evaluation

Traditional, metrics-centred evaluation and project evaluation methods focus heavily on performance, business growth, profit-orientations and monitoring *during* change efforts, not wider outcomes or impacts after changes happen. This is formative, not summative evaluation.

Evaluation metrics increasingly capture raw data in real time, via special software. Such data follows already pre-defined goals and indicators. One challenge is that such 'evaluation-as-metrics' backgrounds the importance of diverse opinions, negotiating, discussing and interpreting data and results. It suggests all valid data must be like this; that is, factual, discrete, objective, incontestable, certain and error free. It also prioritizes customer and client data used for ranking algorithms or advertising services, plus employee and project data used for performance management. Evaluations, arguably, should look beyond simply marketing and performance alone.

Innovation, performance and priming the pump – but unclear evaluation?

Another key concern in organizational change is how to develop innovations within continuous transformation processes. Visnjic et al. (2022) explain how Sandvik, a Swedish mining equipment company, based their innovation strategy on mixed teams of business leaders and subject matter experts working together. They were given freedom to experiment and fail, to explore and collaborate with real customers, on genuine problems. This problem-first approach meant teams focused on practical work with partners to create innovations. This kind of complex innovation model is valuable but cannot be evaluated using metrics alone.

Herbert's BUILD model (2017) uses evaluation to monitor emerging innovations, holding leaders responsible for the indicators used to evaluate maturing innovations. The word evaluate is used generally, denoting departments working together, understanding competitor strengths, even reviewing literally everything. Decision-making criteria are suggested for estimating the future potential of an innovation, its customer value, business impact, feasibility and scalability. Metaphors are also used frequently, such as how evaluations should be like a 'military fitness course' weeding out weak innovations, or how evaluations should not simply be 'run of the mill digital metrics' for performance, but must support impacts, brand awareness and even consumer attitudes to refugees in one example. Employee performance should be translated into metrics, despite Herbert's acknowledgement that heavy-handed metrics can create panic and chaos. In this model, evaluation is quite general but also metrics-based, emphasizing innovation, performance and brand. There are no specifics on how to do this evaluation, how challenges are faced or how impacts diverge across stakeholders.

Approaches to organizational transformation often focus on being committed, agile and meeting success metrics. These supersede evaluating wider outcomes, impacts, staff wellbeing or learning from internal department worries. For example, Saldanha (2019) offers pointers at the end of each chapter. Is your transformation about exponential technology ecosystems, 10X efficiency gains or a perpetual transformation culture? Is it about leaders owning the transformation, having 'primed the pump', with their own 'skin' in the game? Companies are advised to reach 'innovation velocity', and to evaluate a large, fast, low-cost funnel of innovation ideas using metrics, although the author says large organizations may have problems with speed, and start-ups may only have 'one big idea', not a funnel of many ideas. Therefore, it is unclear what kind of organizations these innovation metrics, funnels or 10X gains suit, or how change makers can evaluate leadership, innovation or ownership.

Evaluating learning during change

Popular digital change models (e.g. Westerman et al., 2014), promote test-and-learn approaches. These often require clear success measures, small pilots, assessing results, refining the approach, and sometimes using control groups or A/B testing to discover which changes or innovations work best. These are formative kinds of monitoring, occurring during change processes, not ways of evaluating outcomes or long-term organizational change. Regular monitoring helps organizations to learn, assimilate new knowledge and build 'absorptive capacity'; that is, their ability to adapt.

However, being ready for continuous improvement is not uniform across an organization. It varies across units and tasks. Talking to individuals in different units reveals these differences. Basic evaluation techniques such as talking, interviews or walkarounds (Kane et al., 2019) can be rich, practical steps for change makers. Leaders and change makers can create 'game plans' and these can be incorporated into evaluation discussions and goal-setting with internal units.

Summarizing metrics-based views

In sum, organizational change must be regarded as more systemic than innovation of products alone. Organizational change happens at a greater scale involving organizational structures, practices, values, roles, skills and cultures (Gimpel et al., 2018). This means evaluation is a greater endeavour than monitoring innovations. Some of the metrics-based views considered offer a narrow view, where evaluation is focused on innovation or individual performance rather than organizational change itself. Table 11.2 offers advice for change makers thinking about developing indicators and metrics for evaluation purposes.

Table 11.2 Key questions for evaluators designing indicators or metrics

Key questions	Examples
How do we translate needs into metrics?	What metrics might assess leaders owning change, innovation funnels or a unit's learning culture?
How do we evaluate learning?	What is the learning focus – a new finance system, HR policy, customer service platform, or a change towards agile and collaborative working?
What is the scale or scope of evaluation?	A single unit, a pilot project, an innovation funnel, a division re-structure or new enterprise strategy?
What techniques and methods should be used?	Performance management data, digital system data from customer facing websites, walking around departments, talking, interviews, surveys, observations, collaborations?
What are the evaluation sensitivities?	Who designs the metrics? Who is excluded from this? Who gains? Who loses? What new risks arise? How will KPIs or metrics shape behaviours, independent of the planned changes? Do metrics lead to problematic performative results?

Much evaluation talk in change literature remains formative and therefore limited. Metrics and KPIs for innovation are good, practical starting points. However, organizational culture, interdisciplinary and stakeholder views, complexity, power (e.g. who decides the metrics?), ambiguity and resistance to change are part of transformations too, parts that change makers and leaders should acknowledge. They require interpretation, beyond metrics alone.

11.3 Beyond Metrics, Towards Networks

Organizational change lacks a mature view of evaluation and methods for evaluation. It depends largely on aspects of project management and engineering approaches, with a narrow focus on metrics and innovation potentials. The literature frames evaluation as a formative assessment of how well innovations are going, rather than a post-hoc review of changes and impacts across the organization and stakeholders. As such, we suggest that change management evaluations need to take account of broader and deeper organizational, human and social factors, such as how particular evaluation methods are used, how views of **success** can change across time, across stakeholders, or how change risks, conflicts, paradoxes, and project phases can distort evaluation processes and metrics.

As discussed in Chapter 1, the nature of success is not clear in organizational change literature. Scope, cost, time, growth and profit are often put forward as simple, central concerns; however mastery, customer focus, employee empowerment, success factors and user acceptance models suggest understanding success is not that simple.

Success will be defined differently by different stakeholders, users, teams, professions, or partners, and can even vary over time (Ralph and Kelly, 2014). Such variance is common, for example with iconic buildings like the Sydney Opera House, which was originally considered a failure because of delays, investment overrun and weak performance on traditional project measures such as those in the iron triangle. Nevertheless, it later came to be seen as iconic and judged to be a success. Architectural projects have a lesson to teach us, where bridges, developments for Olympic Games, new parks and towers can be evaluated differently at different times. Rational evaluation of success and perceptions of success may differ.

We saw earlier how the use of technologies changes over time. It is not fixed by designers or during implementations (Orlikowski, 2001). This means formative metrics, popular in traditional evaluation models, only tell half the story. Post-hoc evaluations can show how success and impact interpretations change over time.

A more complex range of factors and variables belies the 'simple model/urgent action' arguments in many popular change texts. In contrast, change makers should be paying attention to organizational dynamics. For example, are organizations:

- ready to acknowledge new risks that emerge due to new changes or technologies (Ciborra, 2006)?
- aware of the non-linearity of change, how views of success ebb and flow (Iannacci and Cornford, 2018)?
- able to see the conflicts that transformations bring (e.g. efficiencies versus innovations, standardization versus differentiation, agility versus planning, control versus autonomy) (Gregory et al., 2015), or tactical responses to these conflicts (Wimelius et al., 2021)?
- effectively responding to metrics and performance management, with an appreciation of the organizational politics or ethical dilemmas involved (e.g. keystroke surveillance, work diary systems, Amazon worker 'e-bracelets' (Kretschmer and Khashabi, 2020)?
- able to see how evaluations and metrics can change during project phases (e.g. initiation, development, implementation, exploitation) because each phase involves different people, alliances and processes, etc. (Kohli and Melville, 2019)?

Unfortunately, metrics and dyads alone can obscure other outcomes and side effects. New risks, out of scope changes, unexpected changes, staff wellbeing (Tarafdar et al., 2016), power shifts due to new units owning new data, environmental impacts, gender inequalities, new inefficiencies, etc. are rarely included in narrow dyad views or innovation funnels. An expansive view of evaluation, beyond metrics and the iron triangle, is required.

11.4 Evaluation with Stakeholders and Networks

Network views have value for helping change makers cultivate change relationships in organizations. Network views cover broader terrain than popular, project management views of evaluation. They acknowledge that organizational change is complex, involves many agents, stakeholders, interpretations, activities, values, conflicts and processes. This section introduces several network approaches that expand our view of evaluation and bring into focus sense-making with different actors as important change maker concerns.

Evaluations need to take account of how change spreads or diffuses. Rogers (2003) identifies five groups related to innovation-based change: innovators at the start of the diffusion process; next early adopters; then the early and late majorities of adopters; and, finally, laggards who are slower or resistant to change. In evaluating change, it is useful to consider which of these groups have adopted the change, and where the change process is along the diffusion curve from innovators to laggards. One must bear in mind that so called 'laggards' may be resisting a new innovation or change process. Rather than dismissing their concerns, change makers and evaluators would do well to understand the causes and nature of the resistance (see Chapter 8).

As discussed in Chapter 3, understanding how different organizational stakeholders will view change can help us to judge how change has been received.

Firstly, some stakeholders stand to gain more from a change than others, and this can be understood through the ideas of concentrated benefits and distributed costs (Wilson, 2019). Stakeholders who benefit from organizational change will likely support the change. Those who bear the costs of it may be more resistant. Setting up a new well-funded division for research and development, for example, will likely be supported by researchers, trainers and knowledge exchange professionals in the organization. If this means taking skilled people out of existing departments, then some resistance from those departments may be expected, as they are losing specialist talent from their own teams and services.

Stakeholder mapping (described in Chapter 3) is a popular activity for better understanding the stakeholder groups, and their levels of power and interest in the change project. Stakeholders probably have different views of change successes, and talking to them about their interests and agendas can help change makers plan, troubleshoot and evaluate progress or success.

Boundary partners, spheres of influence and spheres of interest

Evaluation approaches such as outcome mapping (Earl et al., 2001) use the idea of boundary partners to understand who a change programme can directly influence and who it can only indirectly influence. Boundary partners are groups we work closely with, who are in our sphere of influence. More distant stakeholders may require us to work through intermediate boundary partners in order to influence them indirectly, as we cannot do this directly ourselves. In a digital transformation programme, for example, some stakeholders will be closer to us, for example the IT unit and power-users in our departments. However, some stakeholders will be more difficult to influence and control, because they are further away from us, for example corporate vendors or citizen groups impacted by our change projects.

When evaluating organizational change, focusing on how it is viewed by and how it impacts on different stakeholders is a good way to frame diverse outcomes and impacts. Understanding who we can influence, and who we need to work with to influence others is important for change efforts. Determining our sphere of influence and boundary partners is best done near the start of change programmes, as such concepts can strengthen change strategies. Figure 11.3 illustrates these spheres and boundary partners in a digital transformation programme.

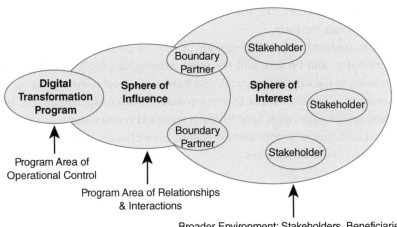

Figure 11.3 Boundary partners, and spheres of influence and interest

Design networks

Design-oriented views of innovation and change also call on better understandings of stakeholders, as well as more collaborative or engaged forms of evaluation. Leaving out users and stakeholders from design processes or evaluations limits results and obscures potential innovations and insights. For example, Kyffin and Gardien (2009) argue that user studies must be undertaken by innovative technology builders, and this is a view championed by authors such as von Hippel (2006). Users, such as staff or customers, must be part of more nuanced views of change, although it is not only users who influence change and innovation.

Designers, managers and key stakeholders should be included which, in turn, leads to a broader, network view of design or evaluation. Chesbrough and Appleyard (2007) argue that traditional businesses often create obstacles for innovation, but Verganti (2009) reminds us it is important to include a range of people in the design of innovations or change processes, including users, businesses and novel stakeholders. Verganti recommends change makers contact lead informants or interpreters; these are connected people who can help innovation networks grow (see Chapter 10 for a full discussion on design-driven innovation and the role of interpreters).

Furthermore, in such innovation networks there are **mediators**, people who contact and connect interpreters together. Also, there are **brokers**, people who know the language of innovation and change, often after working in sectors that have already made changes that our companies wish to learn from. Expert users of new technologies featured in change processes, for example new information systems or mobile apps, can also be creative 'tinkerers' or **lead users** (von Hippel, 2006), who can drive industry ideas forward (see Chapter 10). Equally, users in an organization who create new processes to do work faster, or new workarounds to avoid obstacles, can also contribute to change, if change makers are able to find them and advocate for them.

For evaluators, understanding the designerly or creative people, identifying interpreters, informants, mediators and brokers, and the wider network of people who drive change is important. It helps us see what is successful, and how groups pool talents to support change efforts. For example, a transformation to develop new customer experiences (e.g. increased joy from a new service offering) is hard to assess using old metrics alone, as they probably do not focus on customer meanings and experience. New changes require new metrics and new sense making around the changes.

Activity networks

Activity theory (AT) is a socio-technical approach to change and learning across stakeholders. It emphasizes the technologies, work rules and norms, community and people in organizations. It analyses the change and learning that result from group activities, and the networks of such activities that intersect and overlap with each other, such as how designers, managers, staff and customers use a new technology. Engeström (1987) adapted early work on AT, and others have extended AT over the years (e.g. Allen et al., 2013; Blackler, 1993; Engeström et al., 1999; P.R. Kelly, 2018, 2019; Korpela et al., 2002; Nardi, 1996).

An AT analysis starts by identifying work activities taking place. Each activity, represented typically by triangle figures (see Figure 11.4 for an example), involves groups working to achieve shared goals. To analyse work or evaluate change, AT looks at specific elements, including:

- **Subject**: The people your activity analysis is focused on, for example leaders
- **Tools**: Tools, technologies, or concepts used, for example software, devices
- **Rules/Norms**: The incentives, instructions, orders, or work norms, for example top-down control versus open, collaborative environments
- **Community**: The wider group of people who work with and around the subjects
- **Division of Labour**: How tasks are divided across groups, for example marketing, leading
- **Object of Work**: Collective goal/objective guiding the activity, for example improving a service
- **Outcome**: The results of work done by subject and community, for example the changes that result, both expected and unexpected
- **Transformation**: The change of the activity and work, from before to after achieving the object of work, for example moving from offline to online services for staff and customers
- **Contradiction**: Systemic problems or conflicts in single or multiple activities, for example marketing converts customers by over-promising what product teams can deliver
- **Activity System**: A single focus of activity with each of the above elements
- **Activity Network**: Multiple activity systems interacting together

---

—Box 11.1—

Activity system example

Figure 11.4 shows a single activity system on the left, the leadership in a retail company who have a new data centre and wish to migrate customer services onto digital cloud services, away from telephone services and branch offices. On the right are connected network activities from the IT Unit, Marketing Team Unit and Customers. The figure shows a digital change effort by the company, but the effort is hindered by having an authoritarian leadership style, rules and norms (bottom left corner) that conflict with collaboration, service experimentation and knowledge sharing between IT and Marketing. Units get punished if they fail; thus, they are afraid to experiment and collaborate. This is a contradiction in AT, between the rules and norms, and the shared object of work. This is experienced as conflicts between leadership and units, a slow transformation process and lower-quality new services. AT helps us think about and identify these problems and organizational learning needs.

(Continued)

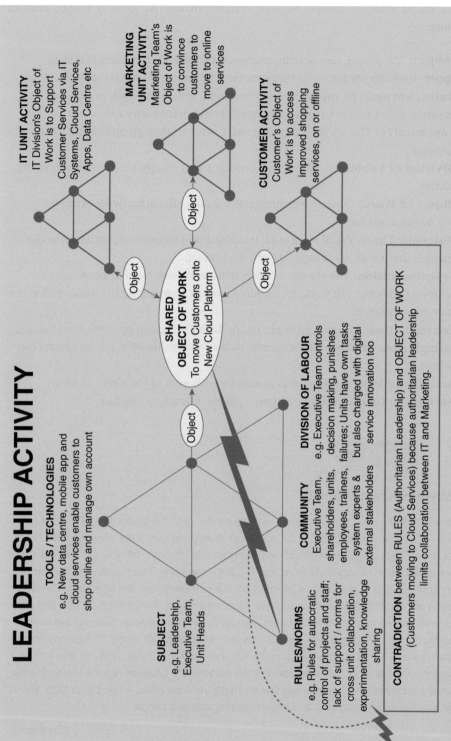

Figure 11.4   Leadership and unit activities in a cloud services change project, featuring a problem as an AT contradiction

Evaluators or change makers can use AT to map out, identify and locate what is happening where in an organization, to understand the key activities, people, technologies, rules and networks that help or hinder change efforts and learning. AT can act as a framework to help change makers and evaluators identify change requirements, impacts, learning journeys and capacity development needs.

Actor networks

Actor networks, often labelled Actor-Network Theory (ANT), emerged out of sociological studies of science and technology projects in the 1980s and today is applied to a wide range of research sites, often drawing on work from key scholars such as Latour (1987, 2007), Callon (1984) and Law (1992).

ANT opposes traditional dualisms, such as nature versus culture, body versus mind, or technology versus users, preferring instead to see these as networks of actors. In this view, change is not the simple impact of *an innovation on an organization*, but the combination of ideas, designs, relationships, people, organizations, finance, sales pitches, customer desires, organizational needs, project politics, and so forth. To use ANT to evaluate change in your organization, means to ask what happens, to who, how, what follows and how does this lead to different views of change. It involves talking to people and observing how changes, strategies, or accounts of success or failure emerge over time.

One controversial aspect of ANT is that it considers humans and non-humans (e.g. buildings, policies, technologies, nature) as important agents of change. A second novel idea is the ANT process of 'translation', whereby networks emerge, grow and become stable, for example around a new team, a new leader or a new digital system. Translation involves four stages: problematization, interessment, enrolment and mobilization.

1 **Problematization** – where an individual or organization defines a problem that others recognize as a problem they also face
2 **Interessment** – where new actors adopt the shared problem frame and begin to build solutions or responses to it
3 **Enrolment** – where many new agents adopt the solutions developed earlier
4 **Mobilization** – where actors do further work to sustain and stabilize the network

A network could be how COVID-19 vaccinations were created, or how a new inclusion policy ripples through an organization. Over time and through these translation stages, we go from an innovation or change with potential, to a successful, sustainable change with buy-in from other actors, groups, units, departments, customers, partners, policies and technologies. This buy-in establishes the network. Of course, a new actor network or policy can fail and fizzle out, but ANT helps us analyse and see why this happens, perhaps during a particular stage.

In evaluating change, ANT helps the change maker or evaluator see the importance of tracking who and what happened during a transformation, as it develops from an idea or spark held by few people to a network of changes that impacts on many.

Box 11.2

Actor network theory example

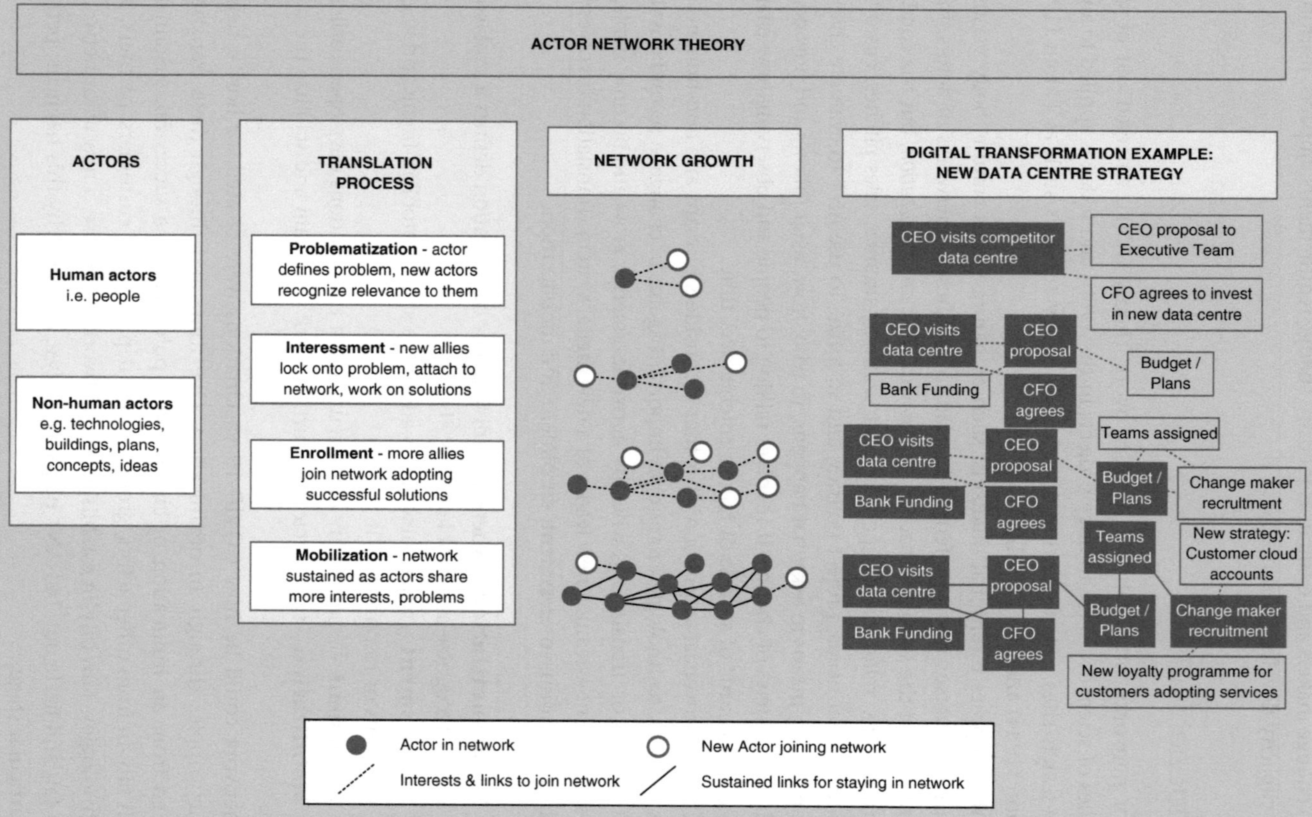

ACTOR NETWORK THEORY

ACTORS

Human actors
i.e. people

Non-human actors
e.g. technologies, buildings, plans, concepts, ideas

TRANSLATION PROCESS

Problematization - actor defines problem, new actors recognize relevance to them

Interessment - new allies lock onto problem, attach to network, work on solutions

Enrollment - more allies join network adopting successful solutions

Mobilization - network sustained as actors share more interests, problems

NETWORK GROWTH

DIGITAL TRANSFORMATION EXAMPLE: NEW DATA CENTRE STRATEGY

CEO visits competitor data centre

CEO proposal to Executive Team

CFO agrees to invest in new data centre

CEO visits data centre

CEO proposal

Bank Funding

CFO agrees

Budget / Plans

CEO visits data centre

CEO proposal

Bank Funding

CFO agrees

Teams assigned

Budget / Plans

Change maker recruitment

New strategy: Customer cloud accounts

CEO visits data centre

CEO proposal

Bank Funding

CFO agrees

Teams assigned

Budget / Plans

Change maker recruitment

New loyalty programme for customers adopting services

Legend:
- ● Actor in network
- ○ New Actor joining network
- ---- Interests & links to join network
- / Sustained links for staying in network

Figure 11.5 ANT actors, translation, network and example

Figure 11.5 illustrates an ANT analysis of change when a company sets up a new data centre. It has four columns. Column 1 shows the actors involved, Column 2 the translation stage, Column 3 the network growth and Column 4 how a digital transformation network can grow from the original data centre idea. In the network growth, more and more actors, people and objects join the network until it becomes relatively stable, spawning new cloud services for customers in the later mobilization stage.

ANT offers a complex view of networks, but contains novel and radical ideas, giving change makers and evaluators appealing concepts for understanding organizational change.

With both AT and ANT, it is not only new innovations that impact on people and organizations, but combinations of factors, configurations and relationships, which produce changes, outcomes, impacts and opportunities.

These network views differ from metric-based views found in project management literature, which frame change as caused by a specific infrastructure catalyst, single hero leader or single technology, not the array of concerns, plans, resources, people, decisions, norms, politics and desires embedded in real life change processes. Evaluators and change makers can draw innovative ideas from AT, ANT and other network views of change.

11.5 Comparing Metrics and Network Approaches

This chapter has discussed two broad paradigms of evaluation and how they apply to evaluating organizational change. A central theme has been the move from practical project management indicators and transformation metrics to more complex and inclusive views of evaluation networks.

Table 11.3 summarizes key differences between metrics-based views of evaluations (left column), and stakeholder, network and socio-technical/socio-digital views (right column).

It is important to highlight that adopting a typical metrics-based approach to evaluation is practical, but not sufficient for seeing deeper, wider or longer-term changes, new risks, relationships or impacts on diverse stakeholders. Expert data analytics and metrics is only as good as the width of its gaze. It can elide problems, or submerge them under expert data or digital dashboards, de-legitimizing marginal voices, resistance to change or unexpected opportunities for learning, innovation and collaboration.

Network views on change evaluation can sensitize us to and mitigate such problems through exploration, collaboration across units or between experts and less powerful groups. Network views offer more inclusive approaches to what change really means for different stakeholders, beyond the claims of technology-centric 'progress for all' stories.

Table 11.3 Summary of key evaluation differences in approaches covered

Metrics-based evaluations			Network-based evaluations		
Project Management views	Computer Science views	Digital Transformation views	Stakeholder Analysis	Design views	Socio-technical (AT, ANT)
EVALUATION PURPOSE Formative & Monitoring Delivery of Pre-set Goals Innovation filtering Focus: Metrics, Performance, Outputs			EVALUATION PURPOSE Formative for planning & delivery Summative for Impact analysis Focus: Outcomes, Impacts, Complexity		
EVALUATION STAKEHOLDERS Organization/Project Leadership as primary, dominant stakeholder			EVALUATION STAKEHOLDERS Single or Multiple Stakeholder views, particularly in socio-technical analysis, e.g. internal & external stakeholders		
EVALUATION DATA Mostly quantitative data, and metrics for digital transformation, e.g. budgets, project KPIs, OKRs, metrics (on system/web/users/staff), plus user feedback			EVALUATION DATA Mostly qualitative, also collaborative, e.g. interviews, meetings, observations, co-design insights, dialogue between stakeholders		
OVERALL ADVANTAGES Technology-centric focus Practical focus on delivery			OVERALL ADVANTAGES Socio-digital scope, sensitive to diverse factors, views, stakeholders Inclusive and more participatory		

Chapter Summary

- Popular ideas such as the project iron triangle or the 'technology causes change' idea are intuitive, but miss many factors, outcomes and impacts.
- Project management and digital transformation often prioritize pre-defined metrics and measurable factors to understand progress, success and failure.
- Metrics oriented evaluations are formative, happening during projects, emphasizing powerful actor views of change, e.g. project managers, leaders.
- Network views are useful for monitoring, formative and summative evaluations.
- Network views are largely qualitative, but are flexible, and can incorporate quantitative data, participatory or collaborative kinds of evaluation, multi-stakeholder dialogue, relationship building or co-designed evaluations.
- Network views are more sensitive to complexity, contexts, inclusion, marginal views, social and environmental impacts and employee wellbeing.

Activity

To review themes in the chapter, discuss and/or reflect on the following questions:

1   What kinds of evaluations have you been involved with in the past?

   a   Think about what the evaluation was about, what sector you were working in, whether changes and evaluation involved many people or few, what change goals and challenges were, etc.

   b   Were they more summative, formative, quantitative, qualitative?

   c   Who defined change goals, evaluation indicators, success or failure, and final reports? Who provided data for the evaluation too?

   d   Were evaluations controlled in a more closed or open way, by influential stakeholders? Was this beneficial to the evaluation process?

2   How do you think evaluations should be done?

   a   With metrics and indicators?

   b   With networks and stakeholders?

   c   Using specific methodologies e.g. the iron triangle, boundary partners, activity theory?

3   Consider your own preferences and biases.

   a   How can you make your own views of change evaluation more effective, more open, more sensitive, and innovative?

4   How might you promote the need for change evaluations in your own workplace?

   a   Who would you need to convince?

   b   How would you convince them to take evaluations seriously?

   c   What kinds of evaluations would you argue for?

Further Recommended Reading

For more on change failure, evidence, and the importance of context and evaluation, see Hughes, M. (2011) 'Do 70 per cent of all organizational change initiatives really fail?', *Journal of Change Management*, 11(4): 451–64.

For more on digital transformation evaluation and metrics, see Kotarba, M. (2017) 'Measuring digitalization: Key metrics', *Foundations of Management*, 9(1): 123–38.

For an overview of the Critical Success Factors, see DeLone, W.H. and McLean, E.R. (1992) 'Information systems success: The quest for the dependent variable', *Information Systems Research*, 3: 60–95.

For more on activity theory, see Kaptelinen, V. (2011) *Activity Theory: The Encyclopaedia of Human Computer Interaction* (2nd edn). M. Soegaard and R.F. Damm (eds). Interaction Design Foundation. Available at: https://www.interaction-design.org/literature/book/the-encyclopedia-of-human-computer-interaction-2nd-ed/activity-theory (accessed 28 November 2023).

To review actor networks, we recommend Cresswell, K.M., Worth, A. and Sheikh, A. (2010) 'Actor-Network Theory and its role in understanding the implementation of information technology developments in healthcare', *BMC Medical Informatics Decision Making* 10(67). DOI:10.1186/1472-6947-10-67.

12
LEARNING, COLLABORATIVE RESEARCH AND KNOWLEDGE SHARING

Chapter Objectives

- To understand how learning takes place in organizations to help change makers to support professional and organizational development
- To explore action and collaborative research approaches to support change in organizations
- To examine approaches to knowledge sharing and development, including knowledge brokering, and developing communities of practice, and to understand how and when these might be adopted
- To acknowledge the dilemmas involved in learning, such as issues of power, resistance and the problem of balancing innovative ideas with pre-existing knowledge of what works in change initiatives

12.1 Introduction

The ability of organizations to harness learning from their own and others' experiences is essential to successful organizational change. We have seen from the rise of a focus on organizational development (see Chapter 2), and drawing from the increased popularity of learning and development strategies in human resource management, how a focus on capturing and implementing learning in organizations has become key to success. Organizational change is an important time for learning, where a large amount of new knowledge is created and new ideas are experimented with.

We describe **learning** as a relatively permanent change in knowledge, skills, attitude or behaviour that comes through experience. Learning is driven by curiosity, recognizing where gaps in knowledge, or the implementation of knowledge, exist, and is shaped by social interactions in the workplace. In managing organizational change, change makers may work with an organization's human resource development (HRD) team. This team will be primarily concerned with organizational development that is aligned with achieving the organization's objectives (Wilson, 2005), so it is important that change makers demonstrate the connection between change objectives and organizational objectives to ensure engagement from these professionals.

In relation to change, organizations may ask the following questions:

1   What can our organization learn from our past experience?
2   What can members of our organization learn from each other?
3   What can we learn from those outside the organization?
4   Where can we look for or acquire the skills, knowledge or data needed to inform our organizational improvement?

This chapter will present an overview of the common approaches and ideas about knowledge and learning during organizational change. Our aim is to introduce some of the key terminology and processes that learning involves as encouragement to make learning and development a key part of the change journey. We begin with a brief look at the history of learning in organizations. This reveals contrasting views around how learning takes place in organizations and focuses on the level at which learning takes place. We argue that learning across all levels, from individual to organizational learning is key to managing organizational change. Understanding these views helps change makers to support learning in organizations, professional and organizational development, and quality learner experiences. We then explore different forms of **collaborative research**, where external (often academics) and internal (researchers within organizations) come together to create knowledge and learn about organizational change through processes such as action research.

The next part of the chapter examines ideas from the academic field of **knowledge exchange**, a highly popular and growing discipline in change management theory. This includes looking at different types of knowledge and knowledge sharing, developing communities of practice, and the important role as knowledge brokers that change makers can play in this process. We compare these approaches from the perspective of the change maker and discuss how and when each might be adopted or adapted.

In the last section, we acknowledge the dilemmas involved in learning. Many of the issues throughout this text have an impact upon the success of learning and development but here we focus on two challenges which are specific to learning and knowledge from the perspective of change makers. The first relates to the value that is placed on knowledge in an organization; focusing on the relationship between power and knowledge we consider how the value attributed to different types of knowledge and the sharing or protecting of knowledge might impact change. Secondly, we explore the problem of balancing pre-existing knowledge when trying to distribute new knowledge as part of change initiatives.

12.2 Learning in Organizations

This chapter begins with a brief look at some of the key theories of the relationship between learning, knowledge sharing and change in organizations. These reveal contrasting views around how learning takes place in organizations and at what level. Understanding these views helps change makers to support learning in organizations, professional and organizational development, and quality learner experiences.

Individual learning

A good starting point to understand learning in organizations is to review how individuals, within organizations, learn. Individual learning refers to skills, ideas, knowledge, attitudes and values that a person acquires, for example through individual study or experience.

When we consider learning in adults we refer to a kind of complex learning. Unlike simple learning – which occurs by adding new elements (information, knowledge, skills) – learning in adults occurs mainly through changes and reorganizations of the person's cognitive space. Learning therefore requires an interplay between 'old' knowledge and new elements placed in front of us by lived experience. Often, learning is a matter of giving a new meaning to elements that we already know within our mental schemes.

Kolb's learning cycle

The foundational ideas of Kolb's learning cycle are helpful here to focus on the internal cognitive processes of the learner. Kolb stated that, 'Learning is the process whereby knowledge is created through the transformation of experience' (Kolb, 1984: 38). This statement highlights the view of Kolb that learning and experience go hand in hand. As individual learners, we embark on a process where we acquire abstract concepts, and through our reflection and experimentation, we generate our own knowledge of how these can be applied and adapted flexibly in a range of situations.

In Kolb's theory, learning is effective when an individual develops a **reflective competency** and progresses through a cycle of four stages. The first is known as the 'concrete experience'. Here, the learner performs an action, has a social interaction or encounters a situation. The learner will then reflect on the experience using their existing knowledge of the world; this is called 'reflective observation'. In this reflective process, individuals will particularly highlight any gaps in their understanding of the experience, or any differences between what they would have expected to happen and the reality of that experience. They will draw from these reflections the new information that they have learned and will engage in 'abstract conceptualization' – a process used to assimilate this new learning into their understanding of the experience. Finally, they will apply this new understanding to the world around them through 'active experimentation' to test the validity of the modified theory. They then seek new 'concrete experiences' beginning a new cycle of reflection and learning (Kolb, 1984).

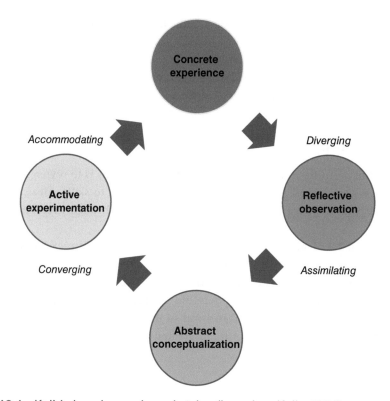

Figure 12.1 Kolb's learning cycle and styles (based on Kolb, 1984)

Kolb (1984) also explains how individuals move from one stage to another by using different learning styles:

- **Diverging** – gathering information to examine things from different perspectives
- **Assimilating** – organizing information into a logical format or general theory

- **Converging** – applying learning (abstract concepts or theories) to practical situations, for example making plans and solving problems
- **Accommodating** – using intuition to seek out and engage in new experiences, for example executing projects ('accommodating' a plan into the reality)

Figure 12.1 shows the relationship between the different stages and learning styles. Whilst individuals will often have a preferred learning style, most people can adapt and use all four styles to have an overall effective learning experience, especially when guided by educators or, in the case of change management, change makers and other organizational members.

Adults undertake this learning journey because they *want* to learn. This desire is a necessary condition, but not sufficient on its own. Other important elements are needed to facilitate learning; these include the presence of an experiential or practical opportunity and time for reflection to allow the possibility of reconnecting with previous experiences and enhancing them. Consequently, learning of organizational members cannot be completely planned (for example, requiring employees to read a handbook). It is also related to an unforeseen experience, to an enlightenment, to a spark (for example in relation to the desire to explore a challenge or solve a problem).

Organizational learning

Organizational learning refers to principles, mechanisms and activities that allow the organization to create, acquire and transfer knowledge to continuously improve products, services, practices, processes and results. In this chapter, we focus on double- and single-loop learning; the learning organization; and organizational learning mechanisms – to offer an insight into the variety and richness of possible relevant perspectives on organizational learning.

Double- and single-loop learning

Argyris and Schön (1978) distinguish between single-loop and double-loop learning, related to Gregory Bateson's concepts of first- and second-order learning. In single-loop learning, individuals, groups or organizations modify their actions according to the difference between expected and obtained outcomes. For example, change makers may attempt to share updates about a change process to organizational members via an email newsletter but, in realizing that most employees were not reading the emails, they modify this and instead arrange a quarterly town hall meeting to deliver key information.

In double-loop learning, the learner (individuals, groups or organization) questions the values, assumptions and policies that led to the actions in the first place; if they are able to view and modify those, then second-order or double-loop learning has taken place. Double-loop learning is the learning about single-loop learning. To use the same example, on discovering that employees were not reading the update emails, a change maker might question why there is a lack of engagement in the change process and conclude that employees do not feel consulted in the process and instead examine how they can make the change more meaningful to different organizational groups. This may involve revisiting the change strategy overall, its aims and their implementation plan. Figure 12.2 offers a visual overview of double-loop learning in opposition to single-loop learning.

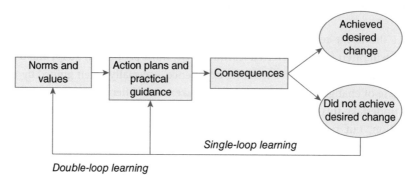

Figure 12.2   Single- and double-loop learning (adapted from Argyris, 1993)

It has been argued that the high incidence of change project failure is perpetuated by the conventional response to re-initiate change management efforts retaining existing norms and working assumptions about how the desired changes might be achieved.

In fact, double-loop learning means reflecting not simply on fixed organizational objectives but on whether a given objective is the right one to pursue. Double-loop learning (Argyris and Schön, 1978) requires re-evaluation of the values and norms against which a particular change management initiative is judged. This means that it is important that change makers have the scope to do this within their role, that they have the critical thinking skills to do this, that they critically think and potentially reconsider organizational culture, sub-cultures and traditions, and that they feel empowered to ask these critical questions and propose solutions.

The ability to carry out double-loop learning at an organizational level is a learned process in itself; that is, learning how to modify and develop values, objectives and reference models. This can be developed by individuals and organizations and it is sometimes referred to as triple-loop learning (Tosey et al., 2012).

It is worth bearing in mind that, in some change initiatives, change makers may not feel empowered to really drive change. This may be because of existing rules, work norms, roles, hierarchies, policies, resources and so forth. In this sense, power, empowerment, and resistance need to be carefully considered. Why are changes happening or not happening, and what kind of learning is required by who? Such critical questions, support double- and triple-loop learning, empowerment and, thus, more effective change.

The learning organization

The concept of the learning organization was first popularized by Senge (1990) as a strategy of placing knowledge creation and learning at the centre of organizational culture. The argument was that learning more quickly and effectively than competitors would provide a competitive advantage and increase creativity. From this perspective an organization's success depends on engagement and learning at all levels of the organization and is essential to provide rapid continuous change.

In his book *The Fifth Discipline*, Senge (1990) makes a case that systems thinking allows change to emerge in accordance with the processes of the natural and economic world (see Chapter 2 for a more general overview of systems thinking in change management). Senge argues that the first four disciplines help to create a systems thinking approach to organizational learning; they are:

1 **Personal mastery** – engaging people within organizations to increase their personal capacity, building knowledge and skills.
2 **Mental models** – encouraging organizational members to rethink the way we see the world through reflection on experiences and studying the best practices of others (Garvin, 1993).
3 **Shared vision** – engaging a group (organization) towards an agreed future to guide learning.
4 **Team learning** – working together in ways so that the individual talents of each employee are enhanced when combined with other members of their teams.

This approach is not without its limitations; becoming a learning organization is a significant transformation for most organizations and one that requires cultural change. It is important that the vision and objectives of learning are aligned to the organization's needs because it is easy for the pursuit of knowledge to become unwieldy if not guided by strategy. Becoming a learning organization is not a 'quick fix' and requires significant investment in time given to employees for learning activities, knowing that, to avoid superficial implementation, it may take time before the benefits of learning can be seen (Senge et al., 1999).

Organizational learning mechanisms

We can define learning mechanisms as the organizational characteristics that favour learning processes and that are proactively planned in order to allow and encourage organizational learning. The underlying assumption is that the ability to learn can be designed rather than left to evolve through the ordinary activities of the organization. Thus, learning mechanisms are deliberately designed to support the development of new organizational skills (such as collective creativity as discussed in Chapter 9).

Organizational learning mechanisms should be practice-based, multilevel, systemic and integrative. Shani and Docherty (2003) identify three types of learning mechanisms:

1 **Cognitive mechanisms** are related to organizational language, concepts, symbols, theories, models of reference, values and reasoning that are consistent with the new capabilities. Cognitive mechanisms are closely linked to sense-making processes, as defined by Weick (1995), supporting the sharing of meanings in the organization. For example, these mechanisms can include the organization's values, mission and business plans.
2 **Structural mechanisms** include all the organizational, physical and technical infrastructures of the organizational system that can promote learning. The structural mechanisms allow collaboration and collective learning about new capabilities or

practices. Structural mechanisms include, for example, the creation of communication channels, changes of work organization (for example the definition of new roles or creation of teams), formal and informal forums to share ideas, even the physical structure of the organization (for example a 'square' in the middle of the premises) and, at the technological level e-learning, databases and knowledge management systems (see later in the chapter) for sharing documents and data.

3 **Procedural mechanisms** concern the rules, routines, methods and tools that can be institutionalized in the organization to promote and support learning. Possible examples are assessment procedures, guidelines and methodologies supporting collective learning, such as post-project review practices.

These three types of organizational learning mechanisms should be jointly designed and combined together to stimulate learning and change at different levels of the organization. For promoting a real change, these mechanisms must therefore concern and include different competences, experiences, values and professional identities.

In this section we have explored a variety of theories about how individuals and organizations learn in order to help change makers support professional and organizational development, and provide quality learner experiences. A recent development that is particularly relevant to learning during organizational change is that of collaborative research, which we will consider next.

12.3 Collaborative Research for Change

Beyond the application of theories and models, such as those presented in this book, research can provide a more direct impact on organizations directly supporting change as a result of learning and knowledge generation. Collaborative research can be seen as a broad family of research approaches that actively involve an organization to develop a research study. Overall, the focus is on combining research rigour and relevance to the organization involved, taking a proactive stance, and developing collaboration between researchers and individuals from the organization (e.g. Hatchuel, 2001). At the same time, each specific research approach usually differs in terms of process implementation, topics studied, and disciplinary backgrounds of the researchers who developed them. For example, **intervention research** is an approach, often related to organization design, focused on developing managerial knowledge that is both con-textualized (therefore useful for the system analysed) and formalized (therefore contributing to the theoretical development of managerial disciplines). Yet, many others are part of this family of research approaches, such as appreciative inquiry and action science (for a comprehensive review see, for example, Reason and Bradbury, 2012). The next two sections will focus on action research, insider action research and collaborative management research.

Action research and insider action research

Action research is a popular method of collaborative research. We have previously discussed Lewin's action research model (Lewin, 1946) in Chapter 2. Action research is a **collective**

approach to solving social and organizational problems. In particular, Lewin stresses the creation of a learning community comprising of representatives from the organization (usually a senior manager), subject specialists charged with implementation (e.g. change makers), and someone who can offer a broad and independent view (known as the external change agent).

Together, this learning community carries out research aimed at solving the organization's problems. They will form plans based on this research – *based on a process of learning* – and action will be taken based on these decisions – as *change requires action* (see Chapter 2, for a more comprehensive review of these two main assumptions). Figure 12.3 offers a visual representation.

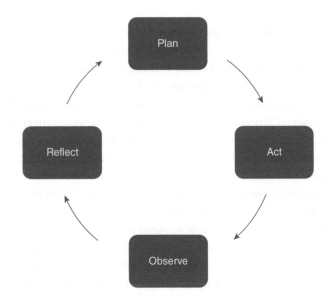

Figure 12.3 Action research model (based on Lewin, 1946)

The action research model emphasizes the process of reflection as an activity separate but related to action. For example, a learning community might propose an action based on their research, but having attempted implementation, their learning has revealed that this approach is failing to engage individuals in some parts of the organization. Based on this improved understanding they will change or adapt the plan before trying again with these groups.

Action research literature usually refers to the researcher as an external agent (usually a researcher from academia) or a 'friendly' outsider (Greenwood and Levin, 1998) and, traditionally, has limited consideration of research developed by a permanent insider (Coghlan and Brannick 2001). Organizational members doing research in their own organization is specifically referred to **insider action research** – a specific type of action research in which the researcher is a full, permanent member of the organization and intends to continue to be a member (Coghlan, 2001). A further variation is *participatory* insider action research. In this case, people taking part in the research are participants in the research, rather than simply subjects of the research (Brannick and Coghlan, 2007), meaning that they are involved as well in selecting the research topic, data collection and analysis, and defining courses of actions (e.g. Kenefick and Kirrane, 2022).

Change makers who have a role in developing action research in the organization can be very grounded and powerful. Doing research means adopting rigorous scientific methodologies (qualitative, quantitative, mixed). It combines a very privileged access to participants and inside sources of information and with the possibility to draw on in-depth background knowledge (for example, drawing from latest theoretical ideas to probe in interviews). At the same time, the duality of the role (i.e. practitioner/manager and insider researcher) and power dynamics (e.g. how the research is commissioned) can become key challenges (e.g. Coghlan and Casey, 2001). We provide two practical examples of insider action research:

- **Professional/practitioner doctorates** undertaking action research. These happen when a practitioner, a middle manager or a top executive joins a doctoral study programme (typically part-time, i.e. still keeping their usual job) and develops action research in (and on) their own organizations (Coghlan, 2007). Doctoral programmes are usually related to management, business studies, education, government/political sciences or nursing. Change-related topics, such as systems improvement, change management, organization development and organizational learning, are valuable subjects for such a doctoral study since '(a) they are real events which must be managed in real time, (b) they provide opportunities for both effective action and learning, and (c) they can contribute to the development of theory of what really goes on in organizations' (Coghlan, 2007: 294).
- **Nurse-researchers**. Nurses are often engaged in learning and study initiatives to improve nursing practice and nursing management and, in turn, contribute to the development of their profession. Among these initiatives, nurses are increasingly undertaking action research projects as a way to plan and study planned interventions as they occur. Doing action research in their own hospital, nurse-researchers are in the position to be 'already immersed in the organization and have a pre-understanding from being an actor in the processes being studied' and engage individuals, teams, interdepartmental groups and the organization in change processes (Coghlan and Casey, 2001: 674).

Collaborative management research

Collaborative management research (CMR) belongs to the same family of approaches, but the emphasis is placed on collaboration between academia and organizations. The motto of CMR is studying *with* the partner organization, rather than studying *on*, paving the way for organization change and development. The aim of CMR is to improve performance within an organizational system as well as adding to a broader knowledge base in the field of management (Pasmore et al., 2008).

Research is developed as a result of an intense interplay between **insiders and outsiders**, respectively inside practitioners who are actively involved in the CMR and outside researchers from academia (we will discuss later about hybrid research teams in CMR).

Following the approach established by Shani in different works (e.g. Shani et al., 2007; Shani et al., 2014), the term 'collaboration' in CMR refers to joint efforts of inside practitioners and outside researchers typically in relation to:

- developing a research programme, focusing on an organizational issue of common interest and defining the boundaries of the research;
- searching and selecting appropriate research methods, for example jointly developing and refining questionnaires for interviews or surveys;
- interpreting the results and developing implications for (managerial) action.

Collective inquiry is at the heart of this collaborative effort. It means jointly seeking answers to questions of mutual interest through dialogue, experimentation and review of prior knowledge. More precisely, management of the partner organization, seeking a better practical understanding of a specific phenomenon within their organization, benefits from the scientific knowledge and method brought by the researchers. At the same time, researchers benefit from knowledge deriving from managerial practices to achieve a better scientific understanding of a specific phenomenon.

If the two parties don't share any interest in *learning*, any joint effort and any collaborative research are impossible. The aspiration to learn must be there, even if the two parties generally have different motivators. This process of collective inquiry resonates with double-loop learning as framed by Argyris and Schön (see above). Here, researchers will try to provide knowledge that is not easily accessible to the organization and that comes from scientific literature and empirically leading to a wholesale change in thinking about the problem.

CMR develops as a process that integrates scientific knowledge, methods and values with practical knowledge and ways of working. The outline of the CMR process includes four interrelated clusters of activities (adapted from Cirella et al., 2012), as illustrated in Figure 12.4:

1 **Preliminary activities based on the contextual factors**. This includes initial contacts and preliminary dialogue between researchers and management of the prospective partner organization. This will help explore areas of common interests and understand whether a collaborative research orientation can be of added value for both parties. This part of the process is highly influenced by contextual factors and, in particular, the external context (such as state of economy and industry characteristics) and organization features (such as strategy and culture).

2 **Developing high-quality collaborative relationships**. This focuses on nurturing a collaborative climate, based on a learning approach, and establishing a collaborative relationship, based on a shared vision for the research project. The highlight of this part of the process concerns establishing a joint, **hybrid research team**. It is composed of both researchers and representatives of the organization, typically change makers and middle managers involved in the areas and topics to be researched. As for any type of small group, research teams usually have an overall team size of four to eight team members. The first step of the research team is to define a shared vision for the research project and review roles and resources.

3   **Undertaking high-quality process of collaborative research.** This focuses on the design of the collaborative research process and development of the research. This includes data collection, data analysis and interpretation of data in order to understand and learn more about the phenomenon under inquiry. Again, the research team is the lead actor for collaboratively designing, refining and developing the research in all its key aspects, including theoretical framework, methodology, data collection and analysis, interpretation of results. Based on the results, a coherent course of action should be defined.

4   **Achieving the outcomes of the collaborative effort.** This refers to the outcomes of the collaborative research. The organization can proceed with implementing the change; that is, a course of action defined on the basis of the actionable knowledge generated through the collaborative process. At the same time, the researchers can proceed with the scientific production based on the new scientific knowledge created. It is also important to evaluate how the research project went (post-project review) and consolidate collaborative research protocols and tools for the future. In fact, if the collaboration is mutually successful, the collaborative efforts usually do not stop and, indeed, can continue – for example with new projects/cycles of research, potentially involving new actors from the organization and academia.

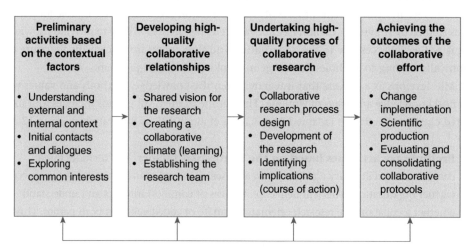

Figure 12.4   A process model of collaborative management research (adapted from Cirella et al., 2012)

12.4 Knowledge Sharing During Change

This next part of the chapter examines approaches to knowledge sharing during change. This includes looking at knowledge brokering and developing communities of practice. We explore different positions and ways that this might be achieved from the perspective of the change maker and discuss how and when each might be adopted or adapted.

Knowledge and knowledge sharing

Studies of knowledge management focus on how different forms of knowledge are circulated and shared within (and between) organizations. Research has shown that there is a strong link between high levels of professional knowledge and high levels of innovation within organizations (Swan et al., 2016).

Different **types of knowledge** include know-what (e.g. notions, facts), know-why (principles and cause–effect relations between different phenomena), know-how (how to work, how to accomplish a job) and know-who (sources of experience and information). A common distinction is made between explicit (or descriptive) knowledge and tacit knowledge (Polanyi, 1966). Smith (2001: 314) defines these in relation to how they might be used in the workplace:

- **Explicit knowledge** – academic knowledge or 'know-what' that is described in formal language, print or electronic media, often based on established work processes.
- **Tacit knowledge** – practical, action-oriented knowledge or 'know-how' based on practice, acquired by personal experience, seldom expressed openly or difficult to express, often resembles intuition.

How, when and what knowledge is shared depends on social interactions. It is found that informal channels of communication may offer a more positive environment for knowledge sharing than formalized channels and this can be facilitated by bringing together different stakeholders within an organization to create knowledge communities that support the integration of previously separate learning within the organization.

Creation of new organizational knowledge is intimately related to continuous transformations and combinations between tacit and explicit knowledge. Nonaka et al. (2001) identify four modalities of knowledge conversion that sustain cycles of knowledge creation:

- **socialization (from tacit to tacit):** combining tacit knowledge from different people through social interaction, e.g. dialogue, collaboration, shared experiences;
- **externalization (from tacit to explicit):** creating concepts and descriptive notions based on the know-how acquired through experience;
- **combination (from explicit to explicit):** combination and re-organization of knowledge from different areas or disciplines, resulting, for example, in manuals, documents, databases;
- **internalization (from explicit to tacit):** internalization of explicit knowledge (from manuals, documents), through communication and experience (**learning by doing**), into individual ideas, approaches and ways of doing things.

An example of the above process comes from research conducted by Easterby-Smith et al. (2008) on knowledge management within a hospital in the UK. The study showed that information exchanges between groups consisted mainly of managerial data and clinical information on patients. However, observations of cross-disciplinary meetings later showed that different groups of clinicians interacted in ways that allowed them to build shared understandings of how the service interfaces may be redesigned. Employees working on common operational problems in different groups later collaborated on developing new working practices based on this informal knowledge sharing. This example suggests that useful knowledge may take quite different forms.

Whilst information is important, we can usefully distinguish between syntactic, semantic and pragmatic approaches to knowledge exchange:

- **Syntactic** approaches to knowledge exchange assume that innovations are achieved through the transfer of formalized knowledge and information that is embodied in routine data and statistical measures
- **Semantic** approaches to knowledge exchange assume that innovations emerge as previously separate groups of employees develop shared understandings of how work can be redesigned
- **Pragmatic** approaches combine both above approaches, bringing formalized knowledge and shared understandings together as new practices are developed and embedded within the organization.

Building organizational capacity for effective knowledge management requires all three of the above approaches to work together. Box 12.1 also offers a focus on knowledge management and technology.

─Box 12.1─

Technology, knowledge management, and the DIKW problem

The management of data, information and knowledge each have their own fields of study. Data management is now seen as a technology-oriented form of expertise, discussing key issues around data security, storage, and database administration. Information management has focused more on how data are processed, organized, accessed, interpreted, shared amongst stakeholders and managed strategically in organizations. Knowledge management therefore should include collaborative work between managers, technologists and experts in health, education, sales or product design for example, depending on the nature of the collaboration. Most change makers not specifically working in a data centre or IT role will likely benefit from familiarity with how knowledge management is seen to be closely linked to digital technologies.

Technologies in broad use today include back-end infrastructure and front-end user-facing systems and interfaces. The back end includes networking architecture, storage and security systems, digital identity management, databases or warehouses plus database management layers, applications, and integration components. General user-facing front-end systems include internal portals and intranets, document and content management systems, public facing internet sites, and dedicated applications for different experts, analysts or work roles. This array of systems, expertise and options poses many knowledge management and knowledge sharing issues for organizations, which are often overseen by human resources or IT services, or sometimes change project teams themselves. Change makers who have familiarity with more than one of these technologies or organizational areas can be valuable interpreters or **boundary spanners** (Evans and Scarbrough, 2014) within change efforts.

So, how can we best understand this range of processes, roles and technologies? One way is to use knowledge management models. For example, Dalkir (2011/2017) creates a broad model that covers the integration of a series of processes, including but not limited to: capturing, selecting, codifying, refining, sharing, accessing, applying, evaluating and reusing knowledge. For Dalkir, managing this knowledge entails, adopting a model, capturing knowledge assets and codifying them, accessing and sharing knowledge across roles and groups, applying knowledge in decision-making and work tasks, taking account of organizational culture, setting up appropriate technologies, putting teams in place and finally guiding all this through effective strategy and success metrics (Dalkir, 2011/2017). This kind of model helps in practical terms, for change makers wondering who to contact about access to information, for leaders trying to understand the complex big picture of information and knowledge management, or for units and departments in seeing where their work fits into the wider picture and diverse functions.

To understand these shifts towards digital systems, there are, in fact, many data, information and knowledge models, old and new (e.g. Dalkir, 2011/17; Williams, 2014). However, many models rely on the foundational ideas in one particular model, the pervasive and implicit **data, information, knowledge, wisdom (DIKW) pyramid** or hierarchy (Ackoff, 1989; Rowley, 2007). In the DIKW pyramid, data (D) are the factual, objective foundation. Organizations need to base learning and knowledge on data and metrics stored in digital systems. The next level up is information (I), which is data that have been stored, processed and rearranged, such as how web data on customers are sorted into user profiles, geographic regions, age groups, and so on. Next, is the knowledge (K) level, where information is used, applied, or activated in specific work contexts. Web-user information is used in executive meetings to argue for new digital services, or employee performance information reviewed during performance evaluations. In this way, objective data are step by step, rearranged, interpreted and applied to create new knowledge. Wisdom is often included in the pyramid, but rarely explained well, and has not featured heavily in the use of DIKW in organizations around the world.

The DIKW pyramid is now a core part of managerial, folk and system views of knowledge. However, change makers should be careful. DIKW does not account for social learning processes or collaborative sense-making. It excludes marginal voices, people who may not have the access, ability, power or legitimacy to create data, interpret information or pitch new knowledge in organizations. Data are not always objective or the foundation of knowledge either, as previous knowledge, assumptions, hunches, feelings

(Continued)

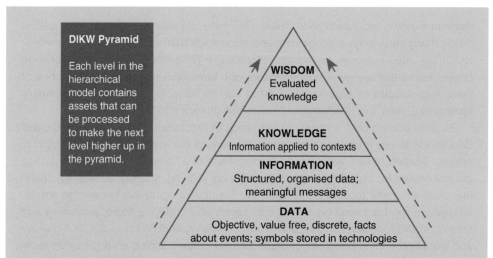

Figure 12.5 The widespread, but problematic DIKW pyramid

Source: Kelly, P.R. (2019) *Power, Data, and Knowledge in Development Sector Impact Evaluation Activities: Critically Engaging with the Impact Iceberg*. Lancaster University.

and biases can all be key ingredients that come together in how new data or knowledge are made (Tuomi, 1999).

Alternative models of knowledge management emphasize social or organizational activities more, and don't see digitized data as the only legitimate foundation for knowledge or learning (e.g. Williams, 2014). There are also less well known but more sensitive views of knowledge work that include how knowledge can be contested, temporary, changeable or dependent on agendas and situations (e.g. P.R. Kelly, 2018; Suchman, 1987). These are good antidotes to the problematic overreach of DIKW.

In sum, DIKW is simple and widespread, but it elides power, participation and the diverse factors involved in shaping data, knowledge, sharing and learning in organizations. These issues are touched on in our chapters on inclusion and power and are critically important for how change makers see knowledge in organizations – either as practical, data-based knowledge products we simply digitally send to each other, or as nuanced processes involving sharing, learning, politics, consensus building, socio-technical systems and negotiation between different stakeholders.

Communities of practice

The notion of community of practice was developed by Lave and Wenger (1991) and Wenger (1999) to mean a collection of people who engage on an ongoing basis through interaction (community) in some common learning endeavour to accumulate and disseminate knowledge (practice). These practices provide value for the organization(s) that can include problem-solving, requests for information, seeking experience and advice, developing strategies and synergies, mapping knowledge and identifying gaps (Wenger et al., 2002). Table 12.1 summarizes the key aspects of communities of practice. This could also relate to groups attempting organizational development and change.

Table 12.1 Key aspects of communities of practice

Shared domain	- Common interest for a subject - Understanding of domain problems - Adopt the same or complementary approach(es)
Community	- Regular interaction between members - Help each other to solve problems - Wide and high-quality communication between people and teams
Knowledge practices	- Practice of accumulating and disseminating knowledge - Sharing information and best practices - Development of database of resources and methodologies

Having a successful community or network that connects and bridges boundaries between and/or within organizations can play a significant role in absorbing/mitigating the demands of knowledge sharing to support change (e.g. Schenkel and Teigland, 2008; Wenger et al., 2002). Lesser and Storck (2001) identify four areas of organizational performance that can be improved through communities of practice:

1   decreasing the learning curve of new employees;
2   responding more rapidly to customer needs and inquiries;
3   reducing rework and preventing 'reinvention of the wheel';
4   spawning new ideas for products and services.

In addition, an important aspect and function of communities of practice is increasing organizational performance through the creation of a shared identity and purpose.

Communities of practice gained popularity in the 1990s due to their capacity to transfer knowledge between and within organizations which was crucial for maintaining competitive advantage, especially for knowledge-intensive firms (Hadjimanolis, 2011) where the benefits that tacit knowledge bring to businesses are central. Communities of practice are frequently related to positive organizational performance (Maurer et al., 2011).

The concept of communities of practice provides an approach that is focused on people and their social structures that enable them to learn with and from each other. Communities of practice are social configurations (Roberts, 2006). As such, they provide a context for the creation and leveraging of **social capital**. Social capital can be defined as 'the actual and potential resources provided by and derived through actors' social relations' (Maurer et al., 2011: 159). Gooderham et al. (2011) found that hierarchical mechanisms (authority, rules, regulations) had a negative effect on social capital formation. Instead, trust in knowledge sharing and prioritization of social interaction is found to be important (Roberts, 2006). To enhance knowledge at an organizational level, communities of practice require managerial coordination, yet communities and networks of practice cannot be directed, only enabled, facilitated or supported (Bate and Robert, 2002).

Knowledge brokering

As highlighted above, effective knowledge sharing involves a combination of formal and informal practices in organizations, on the one hand allowing employees space to explore and reflect on experiences in order to learn, whilst also guiding knowledge generation in a way that ensures that best practices that can help the organization achieve its goals are captured and shared in an evidence-based way.

Naturally, this creates an inherent tension between management involvement and emergent learning processes implicit in organizational use of communities and networks of practice to distribute knowledge (Agterberg et al., 2010). Soekijad et al. (2011: 1005) find that to 'cope with [the] learning tension, [leaders enact] two strategies: brokering and buffering or conducting and controlling'. A brokering and buffering strategy is a combination of mediation within and across networks and shielding network members from negative effects of different levels of learning on each other. A conducting and controlling strategy comprises top-down directives intended to control network activities and hence institutionalize learning.

We discussed in Chapter 4, the important role that change makers play in facilitating knowledge exchange across inter-organizational boundaries – boundary spanning. Boundary spanners act as a link that bridges and facilitates coordination between organizational members across professional boundaries (Williams, 2002). This is particularly the case for change makers who perform an **integrator role** (see Chapter 4) – one who facilitates and coordinates multiple constituencies within an organization by removing language barriers, linking resources, and connecting processes and structures (Tucker and Cirella, 2018).

To reduce conflict and focus on mutual outcomes, two approaches have been identified to enhance boundary spanning (Evans and Scarbrough, 2014):

1 **Bridging** – where a change maker facilitates events between groups (e.g. working groups come together and discuss challenges) or creating specific responsibilities for knowledge sharing for organizational members.
2 **Blurring** – where the change maker draws on a range of interpersonal skills to encourage the exchange of relevant information and de-emphasize boundaries between groups.

In this way, change makers become brokers of knowledge within organizations. Change makers who have expertise that allows them to relate to more than one group within organizations and understand the motives, roles and responsibilities of others make excellent knowledge brokers (Evans and Scarbrough, 2014; Williams, 2002). The work of social network theorists Gould and Fernandez (1989) has explored more fully the range of different types of knowledge broker that may exist within a network, as shown in Table 12.2.

Change makers may be chosen due to their existing positioning within a network, or can have a position formalized by the organization; however, they will need to use their own interpersonal skills to encourage and facilitate trust to enhance knowledge sharing in a way that is non-threatening to organizational members (more on this in the next section).

12.5 Challenges for Learning and Knowledge Sharing

In the final part of this chapter, we acknowledge the dilemmas and challenges involved in learning. We will focus specifically on two key issues. The first considers issues about the

Table 12.2 Types of knowledge broker (based on the work of Gould and Fernandez, 1989)

Type of broker	Network position*	Description
Liaison	B-->A-->C	Between different groups, neither of which they are a member
Representative	A-->A-->B	Acts as nominated group member to broker knowledge to those outside of the group
Gatekeeper	B-->A-->A	Screens external knowledge to distribute within their own group
Co-ordinator	A-->A-->A	Circulates knowledge within their own group
Consultant or Itinerant	B-->A-->B	Mediates between actors in the same group; however, the broker is not part of the group
*where the broker is the middle A		

value placed on knowledge generally, but also specific types of knowledge within an organization and how this influences knowledge and learning during change. Secondly, we focus on the issue of **balancing** the need to build on pre-existing knowledge while also trying to distribute new knowledge as part of change initiatives and consider what it means to be an ambidextrous organization.

Power and the inclusive valuing of knowledge

Power, trust, inclusion and voice are important aspects of learning to change, and we focus on these in other chapters. However, as we have seen, a variety of contextual factors help shape the interpretation and processes of organizational change. This also goes for the role of knowledge and learning within organizations. What type of knowledge and how it is used by organizational members is value-laden and the extent to which having knowledge is a valuable attribute within an organization's culture can vary. For example, in some organizations, being the individual who is coming up with new innovative ideas for new products or services can be a means to rapid promotion and performance incentives (e.g. bonuses or commissions) whereas, in other organizational cultures, the development of others through sharing knowledge and mentoring can make employees valuable assets to the organization. Being in a position to teach or educate others can be powerful.

These values can shift over time and are influenced by a range of factors including leadership within the organization and factors in the external environment. In a study of the implementation of a telehealth innovation in the UK social care sector, Tucker and colleagues (2022), document how, at the beginning of the change initiative, local authorities valued the tacit, experience-based knowledge of change makers who helped to develop the new technology – they received government funding and awarded resources on the basis of this knowledge; however, as the change progressed, value shifted to prioritize explicit, evidence-based knowledge that could show economic benefits of the practices. This shift in values was problematic for change champions who saw power and resources stripped away from them and the knowledge that they had worked hard to acquire became devalued in the eyes of senior leaders. In organizations where *knowledge equals power*, having the right type of knowledge, and the means to demonstrate it, becomes an important motivator for organizational members and change makers alike. Who you share it with (or not) influences the relational power that you have over others and your value to the organization and the change project.

Related to this issue of value is the relationship between trust and knowledge sharing. Trust has been found to be important in offsetting the negative effect of hierarchical mechanisms of social governance (Gooderham et al., 2011); providing a foundation for communities of practice (Roberts, 2006); and lowering the transaction cost – time and energy costs associated with social exchange – of learning and innovation (Sako, 2006). Trust takes time to develop and must be facilitated by the encouragement of collaboration and collective success (Roberts, 2006).

In Chapter 6 we explored some of the challenges of ensuring that voice is given to employees in an inclusive way. Organizational members from a diverse range of backgrounds and experiences may have important knowledge and learning to share so it is important to ensure that appropriate processes for them to share this knowledge exist, and that they feel motivated to do so. Effective **employee voice mechanisms** can contribute to learning and effectiveness of organizations (e.g. problem-solving). It is inevitable that, during change, unexpected events will emerge and accessing diverse forms of knowledge and experience can create effective solutions to adapt and innovate changes to resolve these problems (Syed, 2020).

Change management literature encourages participation and involvement of employees in proposed changes through consultation (Furst and Cable, 2008) to nurture psychological ownership of change (Fuchs and Prouska, 2014). However, in practice these initiatives are often criticized as 'hollow gestures', merely paying lip-service to real employee voice (Bordia et al., 2011). Furst and Cable (2008) found that, where the quality of the relationship between employees and their closest managers was poor (in terms of perceived trust and respect), consultation was viewed as a tactic to shift problem-solving responsibility on to employees. As a result, moves to legitimize change were seen as calculative, and attempts to ingratiate employees were seen as manipulative. Vehicles for employee voice tend to be generic and assume employees are homogeneous (Bell et al., 2011; Syed, 2020). In practice, the way employees prefer to express their voice and the propensity at which they desire to do so may vary depending on their gender, race, and so on. As a result, diverse employees' knowledge may remain hidden in organizational decision-making (Syed, 2020).

If non-mainstream groups do not perceive that appropriate vehicles to contribute their knowledge and experience exist, they may instead opt for silence, protecting themselves from potential mistreatment because they believe that speaking up is futile (Bell et al., 2011; Morrison, 2014). Therefore, fostering an environment where sharing experiences and knowledge is free from judgement and valued for its learning potential is important for change. Change makers have an important role to play in creating opportunities for this and responding in a way that is encouraging and open.

In their book *Ending the Blame Culture*, Pearn and Mulrooney (1998) promote the idea that encouraging intelligent mistakes in the pursuit of change and improvement can help organizations to learn more effectively. This requires systems to manage mistakes that involve being able to capture the knowledge gained and understand the context of a mistake (rather than blaming the individual), and the promotion of a culture which supports and fosters experimentation and some degree of risk taking.

Balancing what works with new ideas

Another key challenge for learning during organizational change is finding balance between building on what works based on knowledge that we already have, and the active exploration to find new and innovative knowledge that can help develop new ideas. Organizational practices that are currently working well, or represent a version of best practice in the organization, can hold a lot of esteem within the organization and therefore individuals may be reluctant to disrupt what is working to continue to change or adapt. **Exploitation** of existing strongholds of knowledge, and the **exploration** of alternative ways to do things, require different techniques, different mindsets and different resources and it is challenging to know which to focus on at any time, or to try to tackle both simultaneously as an organization.

The importance of solidifying knowledge and learning about change is a key focus of change management theory. Already in earlier chapters of this book (e.g. Chapter 2) we discussed the importance of refreezing (Lewin's three-step model) where we focus on taking steps to stabilize and reinforce the change, learning what worked, applying knowledge to solve persistent problems and solidifying best practice. It is likely that a change evaluation may be performed at this stage of the change process, as covered in more depth in Chapter 11. Evaluation is important because it provides four different sources of learning:

1   **Formative/Developmental:** How to improve?
2   **Summative:** What was achieved?
3   **Scientific:** Why were particular outcomes achieved?
4   **Strategic:** Were the goals/aims of the change appropriate for the organization?

Despite its importance, comprehensive evaluation is rare in practice. This is because evaluation can be a complex and highly political process. Reflection on success may deliver 'bad news' in that change was not as successful as anticipated. Therefore, evaluation has a tendency to over-emphasize implementation of change rather than more strategic reflection.

On the other hand, as discussed in Chapter 10, innovation is usually difficult, and knowledge is at the centre of this challenge. To stay innovative, new skills are needed, investments need to be made, and psychological barriers need to be overcome (e.g. 'We've always done it this way'). To develop cycles of incremental and radical innovations, organizational efforts are, in any case, centred on knowledge and new skills. For example, it means discovering new meanings for products we already know, relying on external interpreters, or developing new technologies, investing on internal engineering departments or, again, radically improving a product or a service as a result of the involvement of users and lead users.

In the knowledge management literature, theory distinguishes between exploration and exploitation activities (March, 1991):

- **Exploration activities** involve learning that is centred on identifying new ways to create value for customers through technology and better delivering on customers' requirements, including their latent needs.
- **Exploitation activities** involve learning that is centred on identifying how best to improve current product quality and functionality, and the processes used to develop them.

Arguably, attempting both types of learning at the same time is extremely challenging; however, the concept of **ambidextrous organizations** seeks to achieve just that. Ambidextrous organizations are good at balancing exploration and exploitation activities (Tushman and O'Reilly, 1996). They tend to be adaptable and their people very creative.

Ambidextrous organizations can balance exploration and exploitation because they possess two distinct learning systems. Exploration necessitates double-loop learning while exploitation may be served by single-loop learning.

These two learning systems are best to develop separately because the organizational members utilizing them tend to have different mindsets and may be best supported in different structures. Exploration teams usually work best in decentralized structures, use discretionary processes and have loose cultures. Exploitation teams are normally more centrally situated within the organization. Their dynamics tend to be more prescriptive and less discretionary processes tend to be used (Gupta et al., 2006).

Ambidextrous organizations encourage their people to experiment, learn continuously and take risks. Those working on exploration projects can do so more freely if their units are protected and legitimized. The **entrepreneurial work** they do should be kept 'physically, culturally and structurally separate' from the other parts of the organization (Tushman and O'Reilly, 1996: 11). Exploration teams tend to develop architectural or radical innovations while exploitation teams tend to innovate incrementally. Hence, exploration teams focus on the longer term while exploitation teams focus on the short- or medium-term future. Ambidextrous organizations are good at managing the tensions that arise when distinctly different structures, capabilities and cultures must operate side-by-side concurrently (Tushman and O'Reilly, 1996). They enable the organization's people to sense opportunities and threats, seize opportunities and mitigate threats, and reconfigure or transform the organization as this becomes necessary (Teece, 2017). More mature organizations and those operating in fast-moving markets are more likely to be ambidextrous organizations because competitors put them under pressure to build a stock of exploitable opportunities (Mathias et al., 2018).

Establishing an ambidextrous organization is likely a strategic aim beyond the scope of one change maker; however, change makers will contribute to the leadership that is required to be able to align strategy, structure, culture and processes, required by discontinuous and multifaceted change. Attention should also be paid to how best to integrate the diverse capabilities developed within these different groups of employees. Those guiding exploration projects must be able to articulate a compelling vision for the future to ensure focus. Moreover, whether concentrating on exploration or exploitation, it is important to ensure teams are supported, their members incentivized appropriately and a culture exists where diversity and creativity is valued. It is critical to ensure everyone understands when fast decision-making and flexibility is required and when it is not (Tushman and O'Reilly, 1996).

Chapter Summary

- Theories of learning (e.g. Kolb's learning cycle) demonstrate that the learning of organizational members cannot rely on formal planned learning activities (for example, requiring employees to read a handbook or attend a training course), reflection and experience is also needed for an effective learning experience.
- 'Double-loop' learning requires re-evaluation of the values and norms against which a particular change management initiative is judged. This means that it is important that change makers have the scope and critical thinking skills to do this within their role.
- Research approaches based on action and collaboration can provide a solid, scientific support to generate knowledge and promote change. Action research, insider action research and collaborative management research are key examples. In this context, researchers and change makers build collaborative relations and jointly develop research- and change-related activities.
- Change makers can use bridging (facilitating knowledge exchange) and blurring (de-emphasizing boundaries between groups) strategies to facilitate knowledge sharing across boundaries.
- A key challenge for change makers is understanding the value placed on knowledge generally, but also specific types of knowledge within an organization and how this influences knowledge and learning during change. Building trust, inclusive voice and encouraging intelligent mistakes can help to understand issues of power in learning and knowledge sharing.
- It can be challenging to balance the need to build on pre-existing knowledge when also trying to distribute new knowledge as part of change initiatives. Some research has found that becoming an ambidextrous organization can help to balance exploration (identifying new ways to create value) and exploitation (how best to improve current value propositions) activities.

Activity

We discussed in this chapter the importance for change makers to develop a reflective competency and engage in a systematic effort of learning by doing. A possible way to support this effort is the journaling technique, composed of four main writing areas: *experiencing, reflecting, interpreting, taking action* (Coghlan and Brannick, 2001). They resonate with Kolb's learning model and are based on the work by Coghlan and Brannick (2001) on doing action research in one's own organization, as an internal action researcher.

This activity gives you the opportunity to practice journal writing. Identify a relevant **change-related experience**, activity or challenge you were directly or indirectly involved in recently. Considering the following four areas, which are based on Coghlan and Brannick (2001) and Shani et al. (2009), write down your insights and details. This is also an opportunity to use some of the models and frameworks offered throughout the book.

1   **Experiencing:** Change makers go through many different kinds of experiences. They can be planned or unplanned. Some represent the impact of their actions; others relate to others' actions. They can refer to cognitive activities (e.g. thinking, understanding), feelings (e.g. sense of achievement, frustration) and even body awareness (e.g. feeling sick). Consider a change-related experience that was relevant to you. Write down the essence of what took place, like a journalist would report on an event, focusing on the crucial facts and avoiding any personal opinion or judgement.

2   **Reflecting:** Reflecting requires you to step back from the experience, process it and understand what the experience means. Reflection enables change makers to expose what they discovered and achieved in practice. Reflect on the experience, focusing on its meanings and dynamics. For example, some probes for your writing are: How was the decision-making? How were leadership dynamics? What about interpersonal dynamics (e.g. communication, participation, conflict, subgrouping)?

3   **Interpreting:** Interpreting allows change makers to understand the deep reasons for the emerging reflections and dynamics. By adopting some relevant theories, models, frameworks or concepts, change makers can make sense of their experience. Identify some relevant patterns from your reflections. What theories or concepts can be relevant to explain these patterns? Drawing on those theories/concepts, what interpretations and insights can you develop?

4   **Taking action:** Taking action refers to identifying and developing actions as a result of experiencing, reflecting and interpreting. In a cyclical perspective, new actions will lead to new experiences and thus to new cycles of learning. Based on your interpretations, list some possible specific action ideas that could help you (and others) improve your way to work together, develop change and, in turn, improve performance.

Further Recommended Reading

For a general overview, or an introduction to learning and human resource development, see Wilson, J.P. (ed.) (2005) *Human Resource Development: Learning & Training for Individuals and Organizations*. London: Kogan Page.

For more about the challenges facing learning organizations, see Senge, P., Kleiner, A., Roberts, C., Ross, R., Roth, G., Smith, B. and Guman, E.C. (1999) *The Dance of Change: The Challenges to Sustaining Momentum in Learning Organizations*. New York: Doubleday.

For a stimulating book focused on collaborative management research, see Shani, A.B., Mohrman, S. A., Pasmore, W.A., Stymne, B. and Adler, N. (eds). (2007) *Handbook of Collaborative Management Research.* London: Sage.

For a comprehensive book on action research approaches and practices, see Reason, P. and Bradbury, H. (eds) (2012) *The SAGE Handbook of Action Research: Participative Inquiry and Practice* (2nd edn). London: Sage.

For an overview of different types of knowledge in organizations, see Smith, E.A. (2001) 'The role of tacit and explicit knowledge in the workplace', *Journal of Knowledge Management.* 5(4): 311–321.

To understand more about different modes to use knowledge and ideas underpinning ambidextrous organizations, see Gupta, A.K., Smith, K.G. and Shalley, C.E. (2006) 'The interplay between exploration and exploitation', *Academy of Management Journal*, 49(4): 693–706.

PART IV

INTEGRATED CASE STUDIES

How to Use the Case Studies

Organizational change management is a complex and contextually grounded subject. Based on our extensive experience of teaching and research in this area, we have found that case studies of real organizations are the most effective way to educate others about the management of organizational change. A deliberate feature of this book is to provide materials which can be used flexibly, repeatedly and authentically to understand the interdisciplinary nature of change concepts and the richness of each organization's own contexts, dilemmas and change opportunities.

Therefore, we include five integrated case studies which can be used to study cross-cutting themes. These cases come from a variety of country contexts, industries and organizational forms. Longer case studies allow us to appreciate the interconnectedness of dynamics and decisions, and the holistic and longitudinal nature of change. Each extended case study will include two to four general discussion questions and further alternative questions relating to topics covered in this book. Table 13.1 show which topics are covered in which case study.

- **Case Study A:** Queen Elizabeth Hospital
- **Case Study B:** Building an Entrepreneurial Social Enterprise with Wellbeing in Mind
- **Case Study C:** Leading a Turnaround and Empowering Creativity in Soft Silk
- **Case Study D:** A Global Development 'Knowledge Platform' – What wins when long-term capacity building clashes with short-term results?
- **Case Study E:** Zwilling – Merging two family firms

Table PIV.1   Case study topic breakdown

Themes	A	B	C	D	E
Drivers of change	X	X	X	X	X
Approaches to change	X	X	X	X	X
Change context	X	X	X	X	X
Collaboration		X	X		
Digital change				X	
Employee voice	X	X			
Leadership	X	X	X	X	X
Power		X	X	X	X
Resistance to change	X			X	X
Creativity		X	X		X
Innovation	X		X		X
Evaluation	X				
Learning and knowledge sharing	X		X	X	

CASE STUDY A

QUEEN ELIZABETH HOSPITAL

Danielle A. Tucker

'I'll miss this place,' Eric said, packing another file into the storage box. 'It seems strange that they'll knock it down once we're gone.'

'You'll get used to it,' James replied. 'It comes with the project manager lifestyle. It's best not to form attachments or you'll end up like Rachel.'

'Hey!' Rachel called, feigning annoyance.

James smiled at her. 'You know you'll be missed, really. I'm just trying to make a point.'

Rachel nodded, hefting a storage box and carrying it from the office. James watched her go and then turned back to Eric.

'Seriously, though, you have to be willing to keep moving. Our job is to come, see and conquer. Then move on with a trail of happy clients in our wake.'

'Well, we certainly managed that here,' Eric mused. The project had just wrapped up and, from what he could see, everything had gone really well. The Queen Elizabeth Hospital would be a success story they could tell future prospective clients about.

'We sure did,' James agreed. 'We knocked this one out of the park.'

Background

Queen Elizabeth Hospital[1] is one of a number of facilities belonging to a provincial health authority in North America. The health authority provides health services for 765,000 people and employs more than 18,000 healthcare professionals, technicians and support staff across a network of hospitals, clinics, centres, health units and residential facilities.

---

[1]Queen Elizabeth Hospital is a pseudonym, and the names of individuals have been changed but the case is based on a real process of change. Some details are modified for didactic reasons.

In the early 2000s the health authority invested in a new centre for advanced diagnostics and treatment at Queen Elizabeth Hospital but, after its construction, patients undergoing treatment still had to be cared for in an outdated building which was overcrowded and run down. The physical environment in the old hospital was rapidly deteriorating and the cost of maintenance and renovation to maintain a safe working environment was escalating. Staff were very loyal to the health authority, but actively avoided work placements at Queen Elizabeth Hospital because they felt that the cramped conditions prevented them from providing the best care to their patients, preferring to work at other more modern facilities. In 2010 the health authority embarked on a $350 million project involving the construction of a new 500-bed inpatient building to replace the old one.

Demographic changes within the province were a key driver for the new facility which was located in an area popular with the retirement community. The increasing age of the population meant that elder-friendly facilities were needed to provide the best care possible – including easily accessible inpatient rehabilitation support to improve reablement. The senior management of the health authority decided to build an innovative state-of-the-art facility which would replace the typical 4–6-bed bay ward layout with single-occupancy inpatient rooms. Single-room accommodation has been found to reduce infection rates and medical errors and also provide increased patient comfort, privacy and improve recovery rates. However, it also requires healthcare workers to change the way that they work; to have different relationships with patients and their families and communicate differently with colleagues due to reduced patient visibility (see Maben et al., 2015). The new hospital building was to be arranged into 15 wings. Each wing had 30 single-occupancy rooms, a central clinical station, a localized rehabilitation facility and a patient lounge. Each room was equipped to deal with a range of medical and care needs, had its own ensuite bathroom and in-room technology for staff to record patient information digitally, rather than having to return clipboards to the nursing station.

Managing Change at Queen Elizabeth Hospital

Change was managed in this organization in a very top-down manner. The organization was keen to manage the change using a dedicated project team, who would absorb most of the burden of change management, including designing the infrastructure and training and educating clinical staff who would work there. The project team were separate from the main organizational structure, reporting solely to the executive team.

In recruiting project team members, the organization sought a combination of external and internal expertise. The project director, James, was brought in as an external hire with previous project management experience in construction. James then selected two long serving employees to join the project team, Eric who focused on the facilities and infrastructure, and Rachel who focused on the clinical decision-making. Eric had worked in the estates team at Queen Elizabeth Hospital for 15 years, managing a team who maintained equipment across several hospital sites. He was looking for a new challenge, with around ten years until retirement; he was looking to build a legacy and leave something behind that he was proud of. Rachel was a registered nurse with 12 years of experience in clinical practice. For the last two years she had taken on several roles seeking to enhance clinical practice. This meant she was spending less time working directly with patients and more time facilitating training and working on projects. She enjoyed this part of her work and loved being at the forefront of change and innovation. At a later date additional members joined as more resource was added to the project. The approach was to prioritize planning and organizing skills and the ability to communicate and lead professional groups including both managerial and clinical staff. Its focus was on strategic aspects of project management, rather than the construction and physical infrastructure. Most of those working in the project office had previous experience of managing organizational change or building new facilities.

In 2012 the new inpatient facility opened to the public. The health authority claimed that the new project was a complete success, that the building was completed 'on time, and on budget' and reported lower rates of hospital-acquired infection among patients and safer working conditions for staff were apparent within the first few months of opening.

Three Months After Opening

'This is ridiculous,' Mary sighed. 'What are we supposed to do?'

Sharon shook her head. She had no answers. As a physiotherapist, she knew that clinical protocol required post-operative heart patients to walk up a flight of stairs to assess their readiness to be discharged, but the doors to the stairs were all fire doors, connecting to the fire alarm system. If they entered the stairwell with a patient, an alarm would go off across the whole floor.

'Oh, there's Lisa,' said Mary.

'I heard someone calling my name,' the ward manager replied. 'How can I help?'

'We're discussing the protocol for assessing post-op cardio patients on stairs,' Mary replied. 'The paperwork requires we test them on a flight of stairs, but all the doors are alarmed. We can't discharge anyone if we can't complete the assessment.'

The ward manager frowned. 'I thought we were going to have everything we need in the new rehabilitation rooms.'

'We were,' replied the physio. 'But the rooms are full of boxes so there isn't space to do anything, and there are no stairs in the rooms.'

'I don't know how this was missed by the design team,' the ward manager sighed. 'I'm sure the use of the stairs was included in the design requirements. I'll ask maintenance to remove the alarms from the stair doors for now, but there are obvious safety issues with that, so it will only be a short-term fix. I'll also flag it with hospital management so they can look for another solution.'

Rachel stalked the corridor, her anger evident. She had just left her first Facilities and Operations board meeting in her new role as clinical adviser, and the meeting had devolved into criticism of the project – of her old role. She was confused, and not a little humiliated. The project had accounted for the need to use stairs in assessments.

They had purchased stepping machines for each rehabilitation centre, there was no need to use the actual stairs, but now the ward staff had created a safety issue by disabling fire door alarms and, worse still from her perspective, accused the project of not accounting for this requirement.

She was determined to find out why these accusations were being levelled at the project team, and headed to the ward. As she pushed open the doors to the rehab centre, she felt her heart sink. The stepping machines and other equipment were all here, still in their boxes. The room was cluttered with unopened packaging, leaving hardly any space. A physio was making the best of what little space there was, guiding an elderly patient through some stretches.

'Excuse me,' Rachel called.

'Hi,' the physio smiled.

'I thought this was the rehab centre, so why does it look like this?' she gestured to the packaging.

The physio grimaced. 'Yeah, it's supposed to be, but it's full of these boxes that nobody seems to get around to moving. So right now we can't use it for much.'

'But these boxes are full of equipment for this room,' Rachel replied.

'What do you mean?'

'These boxes are in here because they contain the machines that are needed in this room. Stepping machines, things like that.'

The physio stared blankly at her.

'Has anybody ever looked at what was in the boxes?' Rachel asked, exasperated.

The physio continued to stare.

'So nobody's using these rooms the way they were intended?'

'Can't,' the physio grumbled. 'Those boxes are in the way; we always used the hallways before and it worked just fine.'

Rachel left, wondering how this had gone so wrong; they had worked so hard to engage front-line staff.

Stakeholder Engagement Strategy at Queen Elizabeth Hospital

By establishing an independent and dedicated project office at Queen Elizabeth Hospital, the organization wanted to create a direct link between those designing the hospital and front-line staff who would work in it. Whilst designing the new hospital, mock-up single-occupancy rooms were set up in high staff traffic areas and staff were encouraged to explore it and offer suggestions on how it could be improved. An external training consultant was hired to design and deliver customized training on how to use clinical technology and in-room equipment in the new hospital. Tours of the new facility were arranged and staff visited the new building in groups three to six months prior to opening. The project team encountered challenges along the way; for example, at the time when training and tours were conducted, not all equipment had arrived and not all parts of the hospital were accessible. However, the project team viewed this more as a motivational exercise, arguing that much of the detailed information would be forgotten in the intervening period anyway. Managers also received the same training but, otherwise, had very little involvement in the design decisions. This deliberate circumvention of lower and middle managers aimed to relieve the workload of operational middle management staff who are traditionally burdened by change implementation whilst also struggling with the day-to-day running of the hospital.

The project office acted as champions of change – their strong personal commitment to the project was evident and infectious. In the run-up to the opening of the new hospital, front-line staff were excited and motivated to start working in the new facility. For middle managers, they were about to take advantage of a complex change initiative without experiencing as much work overload or stress as they had expected. Everyone was positive and upbeat. To all intents and purposes, this organization appeared to have been effective in creating enthusiasm and momentum from front-line staff and there was good coherence between the strategy from top and bottom. However, once the facility was built the project team disbanded, problems with the new building or service design became the responsibility of the operational middle managers to solve.

'Why are we going backwards?'

'Thank you for coming,' Rachel began, nervously. Around her the physio staff had gathered, their expressions ranging from dislike to catatonia. 'I understand there has been some confusion about the provision of the rehab spaces, which has led to further problems, so I wanted to clear this up.'

'You're going to move those boxes?' one of the physios asked hopefully.

'No,' Rachel replied. 'We're going to unpack them.'

'We don't have time,' another physio interjected. 'Why do you think we reverted to our old methods? We haven't got time to rummage through those boxes and pack away whatever's in them. We need to be dealing with our patients.'

There was a general murmur of approval from the other physios, and Rachel nodded encouragingly.

'I completely agree,' she smiled. 'And the content of those boxes will help you do just that. They contain machines to help with rehab. Stepping machines so you don't need to use the stairs, things like that.'

This time the murmur was one of surprise.

'Nobody told us that,' the first physio declared. 'That makes sense, but you'd think somebody would have told us. How were we supposed to know?'

'There was a training session a while ago in the rehab centre. We talked about how the rooms would be used. I realize some of you may have missed that, though ...' Rachel began, trying to avoid any accusations.

'I remember that,' the first physio nodded. 'But the room was empty at the time. We thought you were talking through the options for the room, but we already know what we need to do. You show us an open space, we think of how we'll use it. The trouble is that what we got was a room full of boxes instead.'

'Because that was the equipment that we were talking about in the session,' Rachel sighed.

'We haven't used that sort of thing before, though,' the physio continued. 'We didn't know it would be large equipment in those boxes, and we didn't have time to look. We had protocols that said patients needed to walk up stairs, and no access to stairs, we needed to fix that before we started rummaging around in boxes.'

'But we had explained what was being delivered,' Rachel tried not to shout. 'Didn't somebody think there might be a connection, that the boxes might have been left there for a reason?'

'I know how to walk a patient up the stairs, I don't know who stores what or where in the hospital. If somebody buys a load of equipment, that's their responsibility, not mine,' another physio volunteered, his colleagues nodding along.

'But this machinery is *for* you. Or rather, your patients,' Rachel cried.

'How were we to know that? You didn't come and unpack it, and nobody else was taking responsibility for it.'

'You knew that we were buying machines for this room, though.'

'It was mentioned, but the protocol says to walk up a flight of stairs. That hasn't been changed to refer to any machines, so we have to walk the patient up a flight of stairs.'

'But the machine is easier, and safer too if the patient has issues!' Rachel exclaimed.

'We've been walking patients up a flight of stairs for as long as I've been doing this job,' an older physio cut in. 'Why would we stop if it works?'

Rachel shook her head. She felt overwhelmed. 'OK, I see the misunderstanding,' she said through gritted teeth. 'If we get the machines unpacked and I put in a request to change the protocol, will you start using them?'

The assembled physios nodded, confirming they couldn't see why that would be a problem, provided the protocol also changed.

She thanked the physios and disbanded the meeting. She can at least take comfort that this mess will be resolved and the machines used properly, but what else is waiting for her?

Would the boxes have been left here indefinitely if she hadn't investigated? What if she had moved on with Eric and James? What if she got hit by a bus on her way to work? Would the physios have just ignored the boxes until years later when another refurbishment might happen? It isn't her job to explain everything in detail. She provides people with the information they need, and points them to further sources if available, but something like this – something relating to why things are the way they are – is too much. She can't be responsible for that across the whole hospital, every time there's doubt.

Discussion Questions

To understand the context and key features of this change, answer the following questions:

1   What are the key drivers for change?
2   What approach to change has the organization taken? To what extent has that worked for them?
3   How have employees been impacted by the changes. Why do you think they have reacted to change in the way they have?
4   What are the key challenges the organization faces now?

Below are four other topics from this book that you might explore within this case study.

Resistance to change

1   Why were the physio staff resisting change? Is their resistance understandable or are they being awkward?
2   Did the change makers on the project (including Rachel) do a good job of providing opportunities for voice during the change? What could have been done differently?

Innovation

1   The design of the new hospital is very innovative. How would you describe Queen Elizabeth Hospital's approach to innovation and how has it worked for them?
2   As interpreters of innovation, what role do the physio staff play in implementing and evolving the processes of working in the new hospital?
3   Has Queen Elizabeth Hospital maximized the potential of this group in creating innovation?

Evaluation

1   How was successful change evaluated at Queen Elizabeth Hospital? Do you agree with James and Eric's assessment that the change was a success?
2   Perform a stakeholder analysis for Queen Elizabeth Hospital. How would you design an evaluation that can assess the outcomes for all of these stakeholders?

Knowledge exchange

1   What do you think Rachel should do to ensure that her knowledge of the project does not disappear?
2   How might the learning experience at Queen Elizabeth Hospital have benefited from collaborative research?

CASE STUDY B

BUILDING AN ENTREPRENEURIAL SOCIAL ENTERPRISE WITH WELLBEING IN MIND

Danielle A. Tucker and Neha Gopinath

Introduction

Wellbeing in Mind[1] is a social enterprise started in 2003 by Oliver. As a former life-coach Oliver was passionate that mental health and wellbeing at work should be a key focus for UK society. He created Wellbeing in Mind with the aim to raise awareness of mental health issues and to build a more resilient and happier society. The company provides bespoke training programmes and offers consultation to organizations on wellbeing strategy.

After ten years as a solo entrepreneur, Oliver's business is reaching increasingly more organizations and the campaigns he has run are attracting a lot of attention. Suddenly, the demand for his services from clients has dramatically increased and he cannot take on any more contracts by himself. A key selling point of his services is the bespoke and innovative nature of the work that he undertakes. By working closely with clients, he works hard to understand their needs, the nature of their business, and helps them to develop tools that are unique to their requirements. He is struggling to dedicate the time needed with each client to uphold his commitment to this model and feels his ideas are lacking the innovative nature that they once had due to being so overstretched. To avoid having to change his business model to offer more off-the-shelf products and services, he needs to expand the business and bring some additional employees on board to provide support and work with clients.

Over a period of two years, he expands the business to hire a team of eight employees, including a personal assistant who will also help with the day-to-day management of human resource issues, a financial specialist, and several project managers to help produce innovative and bespoke products for clients.

---

[1]Wellbeing in Mind is a pseudonym, and the names of individuals have been changed but the case is based on a real process of change. Some details are modified for didactic reasons.

Developing a Strategy and Organizational Structure

Initially, as employees joined Oliver's business he uses ad-hoc methods and quick fixes to deal with issues of employing people but, as the team increases, he decides it is time to create a strategy for how he wants his organization to operate. He emphasizes that this strategy should be considered as an 'ongoing process' to maintain adaptability and agility in the business as expansion will require iterative changes to the internal structures and processes. He therefore defines some guiding principles to outline the priorities of the organization. These are to:

- Put people at the centre of everything that we do
- Provide a work environment that supports physical and mental health
- Focus on open communication by establishing cordial relationships at work
- Provide peer support with a focus on wellbeing
- Allow space for growth and creativity
- Ensure clear job roles and responsibilities to improve the relationships between managers and their team

As his business expands, Oliver is keen that everyone who comes to work for the organization understands the basic ideology of how one should act and perform at work. He believes in freedom of action and encourages the new employees to think liberally and use their best judgement. In keeping with the firm's ethos of mental health and wellbeing, rather than traditional systems of performance management, Oliver communicates a 'code of honour' which makes rules about flexi-timings, dress code, compulsory lunch breaks, clean desk policy (every night the employees need to clear their desk and recycle where possible) and allows employees to spend a maximum of 15 minutes a day in the meditation room.

Initially, Oliver wanted the organization not to have an organizational hierarchy; however, as more employees joined the team it becomes necessary to divide employees as per different functions to guide how relationships, roles and responsibilities are understood. However, Oliver is keen to maintain the ethos of free-rein and flexible structures within the organization so that anyone can go to anyone else for support regardless of formal status.

His priority is to create a workplace culture that is flexible, free-rein, open, inclusive, creative, innovative and creating value. He describes wanting a family-like culture, where it feels as though the team is close-knit and able to share their personal lives with people at work and that if someone has an issue with someone else, they can fight or argue and sort things out because they know it is coming from a good place, much as members of a family do.

Creating a Work Environment to Promote Wellbeing and Creativity

A key constraint is the lack of office space to accommodate the growing workforce. The new employees associate the lack of physical space with the lack of mental space which hampers their ability to think creatively. Therefore, to create space for more employees, the company moves into a new office, extending the space that they have to work. This move is greeted with excitement from employees. Previous space restrictions had stopped them from having effective brainstorming sessions or meetings or even simple interactions with the team.

The new office space is also an opportunity for Oliver to enact his commitment to improving organizational effectiveness and high performance by providing facilities to support physical and mental health. These facilities include the firm's open layout office with one closed meeting room and a wellbeing room which is used for meditation by the staff. They have a kitchen where there are facilities to heat food and make hot beverages. The office is meat-free because of Oliver's dietary preference and the wish to keep the office 'pure and clean'. Oliver encourages healthy and nutritious eating habits by providing healthy breakfast goodies, fruit and nutritious snacks for the staff to enjoy. He believes in Feng Shui, so crystals are placed within the office to 'maximize positive energy and balance'. There is a shower room for the staff 'to encourage them to cycle or jog to/from work or during their lunch breaks'. Oliver has a pet dog who is referred to as the 'office pet'; who visits the office occasionally because Oliver believes that 'pets can help employees relax, and are often found to reduce heart rate and lower blood pressure'. The office layout and the plants within this space 'help reduce anxiety/tension, depression/dejection, anger/hostility, and reduce fatigue'. The office has a centralized audio system which plays music 'because studies have found that listening to music improves one's mood and overall wellbeing which, in turn, increases productivity'. These are only some of the facilities that the firm provides to the staff in the new office space. Since Wellbeing in Mind works to overcome mental health problems and promote wellbeing, it encourages its own employees to be healthy, both physically and mentally. Oliver believed that the new space would afford 'breathing space' for creativity.

A Great Place to Work?

On the surface, Oliver's organization seems like a great place to work; the family-like environment enables positive emotions, motivation and a sense of sharing and engagement. Employees spend a lot of time together as was intended, but only within the workplace setting. Outside of work, they have their own lives and families. A few employees express some frustration with the blurring of personal and professional boundaries and casual nature of workplace communications. In reality, there is a fine line between 'banter' and bullying, and a few instances arise where an employee expresses that it is sometimes difficult to handle the joking around if they took something personally and there is little support in resolving conflict. A common area of frustration is the lack of accountability to follow routines for common tasks and actions; this sometimes means leaving others to fill in gaps or leaving others to carry the load on some tasks that fall between the job roles of the small workforce.

Over time, there are also some negative comments about Oliver's leadership style. Previously, having only himself to worry about, when Oliver makes decisions about the business and the workplace, these are expressed as, and considered by employees to be, 'final decisions'. They perceive Oliver to be 'two-faced', meaning he tends to say one thing but act in another way. While he encourages employees to voice their opinions or views, this does not lead to any changes in what he is going to do. This negatively affects their ability to be creative at work and to create value for their clients, as most of their unique ideas are rejected either due to lack of resources or because the entrepreneur has a better idea. Some employees feel that they have low autonomy, relatively low engagement levels and a sense of frustration because their ideas are not accepted.

Over time, employees begin to stop questioning Oliver's authority and if they raise contrary opinions, these are ignored. Oliver's control of all the firm's resources means he has the ability to shut down any creative ideas that do not align with his own way of doing things. There seems to be inconsistency in Oliver's mind about whether he wants his employees to act as creative agents or, rather, to execute and implement *his* creative ideas at work. Some employees complain that he would conjure up new ideas regularly and expect them to develop and implement them immediately. Such expectations frustrate them because they cannot complete their day-to-day work in these constantly changing circumstances.

Constantly Changing

Working in an environment where structures and policies are constantly shifting and adapting can be exhausting. Some of Oliver's employees begin to show signs of stress, anxiety and lack of confidence as they struggle to cope with the constantly changing situations and lack of stability. The lack of formal policies and continuously evolving culture of the firm is anxiety provoking for new employees especially because it takes them a while to understand their job and to do the tasks in a particular manner, and then when it suddenly changes again they become stressed. However, at the same time, some employees are highly driven by this continuous change. These employees perceive themselves as agile and flexible individuals who are positively motivated and engaged at work because of the diverse and versatile range of activities they are exposed to there. For them, change is good and it means they can learn more skills and thrive at work in terms of self-development and personal growth. Some of these employees also believe that the dynamic nature of the organization is an explicit tool for creativity. Innovation is only possible when it is accepted that change is inevitable and important not only for continuous improvements but also for ground-breaking innovations.

Discussion Questions

To understand the context and key features of this change, answer the following questions:

1   What are the key drivers for change?
2   What approach to change has the organization taken? To what extent has that worked for them?
3   How have employees been impacted by the changes. Why do you think they have reacted to change in the way they have?
4   What are the key challenges the organization faces now?

Below are three other topics from this book that you might explore within this case study.

Leadership and power

1   How would you describe Oliver's leadership of the organization? To what extent does being an entrepreneur influence the way he leads his organization?
2   To what extent do you think that Oliver is following through on his own guiding principles?
3   Oliver clearly has a lot of power in the organization. What are the sources of power that he has?
4   What is the impact of the power dynamics in the organization? As a change maker – for example leading one of the small teams – what power would you have and how could you use it to create change at Wellbeing in Mind?

Creativity

1   Creativity is a key part of the business model at Wellbeing in Mind. How has the expansion of the organization impacted creativity (positively and negatively)?
2   Before Oliver was the sole source of innovation in his work; how might collaboration help to bring about more (or less) collaboration at Wellbeing in Mind?

Inclusivity and voice

1   Oliver has indicated that he wants his workplace to have an inclusive culture. To what extent has he achieved this to date?
2   Employees have suggested that they do not feel that their voice is heard in the organization. What needs to change to improve this?

CASE STUDY C

LEADING A TURNAROUND AND EMPOWERING CREATIVITY IN SOFT SILK

Stefano Cirella

Introduction

Soft Silk[1] is an Italian fashion company with around 120 years of history. It is a family business, designing and producing fabric for silk dresses and accessories, for example scarves and ties. Some of the clients are the most prestigious international fashion *maisons*. Soft Silk targets the market segment of premium silk products, in which creativity is key.

Soft Silk is located in Como, northern Italy, close to the beautiful Lake Como (Lago di Como) and not so far from Switzerland. The Como district is a well-reputed set of small to medium-sized companies operating mostly in the textile, chemical and furniture industries. Soft Silk has a commercial office in Paris as well, along with two offices in North America and Asia.

Soft Silk has always been family owned. Three generations of the family had led the company until 2006. From 2006 to 2011, the CEO was an external employee for the first time ever – he was hired by the family to lead a major turnaround. In this period, the president of the company was still from the family (third generation).

Subsequently, from 2011 to 2021, the leadership reverted to the family, with the CEO coming from the fourth generation. From 2021, the deputy CEOs were nominated as new CEOs; so, for the second time from someone outside the family.

The company is very successful. It has around 500 employees and the revenues are, on average, around 100 million euros per year.

---

[1]Soft Silk is a pseudonym, but the case is based on a real process of change. Some details are modified for didactic reasons. The case is mostly based on the following references: Canterino et al. (2018); Cirella et al. (2012); Cirella (2018, 2021); Cirella and Shani (2012).

The case mostly focuses on the process of change from 2006 to 2011, comprising two key parts. The first part of the process was about managing the financial emergency and building efficiency; the second part focused on a new culture of collaboration and creativity.

The conclusion of the case also offers a follow-up concerning more recent years.

Early 2000s and the Crisis

The early 2000s saw a major decline for Soft Silk. The business context, and in particular globalization and challenges in the business model, in particular in relation to the Chinese operations, contributed to the financial issues of the company. In 2000, the company experienced its first significant net financial loss (about three million euros).

Overall, the losing trend lasted for several years. There were several key attempts to fight against it, but with no major success. For example, the number of employees was reduced and two manufacturing sites (out of six) were closed down. This led to some financial recovery, but it was only temporary. Between 2005 and 2016 the company had lost around 50 per cent of its revenues since 2000.

At the same time, many people in Soft Silk do not seem to realize the seriousness of the situation. The company still had a very strong reputation and overcame other difficulties, so they thought the company would smoothly survive this time as well. Unfortunately, that was not the case. A financial crash was impending as the loss accumulated to 80 million euros in the ten years to 2006, with half of it owed to the banks. The company was very close to the risk of being insolvent, with the consequence of 'bringing the books to the court' (Italian expression for going bankrupt) in a very few months.

The family knew that they needed to act quickly. They thought that the only way to save the company was to make a revolutionary decision. They decided to hire, for the first time ever in the company's life, an external CEO. However, rather than a CEO from the fashion industry, they wanted someone with the right financial skills to fix the emergency. In December 2006, the president of Soft Silk (third generation of the family) offered the job to Massimo.

The Turnaround: A Long, Complex Transformation

Massimo had served as consultant and chief financial officer (CFO) in different companies, for example in the IT and energy industry, but never in fashion. Massimo took time to reflect but, in the end, accepted the job offer as he understood that his mandate was to repair the financial situation and develop a plan to turn the company around.

There were multiple challenges ahead but fixing the financial crisis was the emergency to manage immediately. Only after that could he continue with a longer-term focus on efficiency, and develop a new strategy and organization, while still protecting (and enhancing) the company's creativity.

Thus, the first step was to have immediate discussions with the unions and banks. Massimo told the union leadership that the only way to save the company was to work together as partners. He transparently explained the gravity of the financial situation and the union understood that, even if the recovery plan was painful, it was the only way to avoid worse damage. So, Massimo agreed with the union about a downsize, from about 700 to 500 employees. This was implemented in a few months, with no strike in the period. Similarly, Massimo discussed with the banks, providing all the financial details and asking for a grace period in order to postpone the financial obligations – which was agreed.

This made it possible to start with the emergency actions. As mentioned, a major downsize took place in early 2007. At the same time, the product lines that were losing money were closed off, general and administrative expenses were reduced, non-operating assets were planned to be eliminated and the long-term debt was renegotiated.

The emergency was resolved but it had made clear that a deep turnaround was necessary. In particular, Massimo's key focus for the rest of 2007 and 2008 was to improve efficiency in the longer term. For this part of the process, he needed the joint effort of all the company's managers. The key points were accountability and performance management. The efforts comprised refocusing product development and manufacturing to keep in consideration margins and reduce non-quality costs. In the past, the focus on the product had taken precedence over consideration of profitability.

So, new managerial tools were introduced, such as a monthly reporting process and a divisional accounting procedure, which made managers of the different divisions accountable for the performance of their unit. This direction was reinforced with a clear change of the company mission. The previous Soft Silk mission, talking about 'weaving emotions' was very inspiring, but not focused on the company business. The new mission, although much more practical, reflected the aim of the company to 'grow with profit' thanks to the 'quality of our innovative creations'. Creativity was still there, but oriented to the sustainability of the company business.

Subsequently, in 2008 and 2009, Massimo started to work on the strategy and organization design. Previously, the strategy had mainly focused on the company as a supplier of silk textiles to large fashion companies. The sales unit was central, but often disconnected with the design and manufacturing units, with limited knowledge shared on design and manufacturing capacity and causing uncertainty, non-quality issues and delays.

The new strategy was to extend the customer base of the company, combining high-quality service to old and new clients and profitability. A new organizational structure was designed to be closer to the clients and to enable design to play a central role. The design unit saw the creation of four new divisions; that is, Womenswear, Menswear, Fashion and Licensing & Distribution. They were attributed sales responsibilities and given all the resources to 'own' the primary business process. The manufacturing, reorganized into two units (printing and weaving), plus quality control and logistics, was their internal supplier. So, the relationship between design and manufacturing became transactional, with clear internal costs.

This, again, helped reinforce the new culture of accountability. In the past, from a cultural perspective, losing money over a product was not a major concern, and there was very limited responsibility in managing costs – 'someone else will fix it' was the logic. The shift to the new culture was huge. It was facilitated by all the interventions described earlier but also by Massimo frequently meeting managers and employees to promote the importance of a new culture around accountability and performance. Massimo's determination was to meet, as often as possible, other managers one-to-one, and employees in group meetings. Group meetings were weekly and involved different groups of about 50 employees each time.

Collaborating with Academia

A view shared by all people in the company, Massimo included, was that the creative power of Soft Silk should be protected and even enhanced. It could be very easy to overlook creativity, in consideration with all the ongoing efforts on efficiency, accountability and new organization. Since the crisis, there were almost no new employees joining the company and Massimo felt that an external, fresh view could be a good trigger to bring attention to creativity. Chatting with Paolo, the HR Manager, Massimo learned that, some years earlier, one of the universities in the area had delivered, very successfully, some training courses (executive education). Also, Paolo was still in touch with the academic who had coordinated the portfolio of courses. The academic, an assistant professor, mentioned to Paolo that a new, small research group studying organizational creativity had recently been established. It included the assistant professor along with a highly esteemed professor from California (on a three-year research visit) and a PhD student recruited to undertake research with him.

It was early 2009. The research group was looking to develop empirical cases on creativity and, at the same time, Soft Silk was looking to empower their creativity – almost thanks to a coincidence, an interesting potential match emerged. But, the possible relationship was still to build, and it took some effort. Paolo spoke with the research team first and then facilitated an initial meeting between the research team and Massimo, and subsequently with several other managers.

The first meeting went very well. Massimo had been an adjunct professor in finance at another university, so he was open to academia. The conversation was smooth and constructive. The visiting professor explained his proposal: launching a collaborative management research (CMR) project, intended as a joint effort to scientifically study the phenomenon of collective creativity in Soft Silk. In particular, the visiting professor suggested Massimo identify three employees from Soft Silk (middle managers and designers) who could join the three academics and, together, constitute a joint CMR team to lead, refine and implement the research. This could help guarantee both rigour (mostly thanks to the academics' side) and relevance (mostly thanks to the practitioners' side).

Massimo understood the potential of such a collaborative research project, as the research could mobilize people to reflect on creativity and also provide original results about how to improve creativity.

After several meetings with other managers, and following three employees being identi-fied to represent different roles and perspectives, the joint CMR began to meet multiple times to develop different activities for the project (a qualitative research, in 2009): refine objec-tives, identify methodologies and tools (for example, an interview guide for semi-structured interviews was drafted jointly), identify potential respondents and collect data (for example, some interviews were co-led by an academic and an employee together). The academics analysed the data and reported initial results back to the CMR team for further refinements. Then, the results were shared with Massimo, other managers and, via a large workshop, employees. The results didn't entail specific action points (it wasn't a consultancy project) but did shed light on areas that were relevant to enhance collective creativity.

The project was so successful that all parties agreed to launch a second CMR project in 2010, adopting the same philosophy and modality. On this occasion, the joint CMR team decided to undertake quantitative survey-based research. Again, everything was jointly designed and implemented (an approximate 80 per cent response rate was achieved for the survey). This second project was also considered successful. The academics were able to undertake (and publish) interesting research and Soft Silk attained the momentum for improving their activities related to creativity. The next section will focus on this creativity.

Empowering Creativity

Creativity had always been an essential factor for the company's success over its many years of history. Everyone in the company, even throughout the difficult period, was convinced that creativity was intrinsic to Soft Silk, yet it needed to be re-discovered. Massimo also thought that enhancing creativity was a key element within the company's long transformation.

The creative power resides in the company's product design and development unit, recently reorganized into the four new divisions, described earlier. In this unit, comprising around 100 employees, creative teams are built to work together on developing collections for specific clients. Each team involves a product manager, three to five designers, a salesper-son and other professionals, for example colour experts and technicians.

The results from the first CMR project had facilitated a widespread organizational reflection on creativity from which shared views clearly emerged in the company. The real power of the design unit was creativity in its collective form. The emerging meaning of collective creativity was about combining different ideas and reactions around the initial objective and the brief and inputs from the client. Without any direction, the creative exchange would have been chaotic; consequently, some structure was seen as essential. Actually, the teams could rely on some clarity on the different roles, knowing 'who does what', and on key phases usually followed to develop the project from the client's brief until the definition of the products for the collection. Each team, including various designers with different styles, was quite diverse, yet the collective dimension went beyond the team boundaries as involving the clients in different key steps was seen as crucial. Collective creativity was also seen to benefit from adequate resources available:

adequate time for the teamwork schedule was essential (although some slight time pressure could be beneficial too), along with technology (in particular printers to create samples, and specific software such as Adobe Illustrator). For example, on one occasion, a team developed ideas to 'rejuvenate' some products as a result of the technology that made it possible to introduce a new, lighter 22-ounce silk.

Having focused on the key characteristics of collective creativity, the next step was to implement mechanisms to enhance collective creativity proactively. Here, Massimo and the managers of the design unit could make use of the results of the second CMR project. In particular, the project highlighted that some mechanisms were particularly relevant to enhance collective creativity by design, thus the commitment to introduce or reinforce such mechanisms was high and widely agreed within the design unit.

Important actions were about the use of the Soft Silk archive which is one of the largest fashion archives in Europe, as it includes about 10,000 volumes, 60,000 original scarves, thousands of hand-made designs and fabric prints. The archive always represented a source of inspiration, but innovative mechanisms were purposefully introduced. For example, a new mechanism saw the product managers, on a monthly basis, picking one item from the archive and discussing it with the team. Another example was about implementing a monthly team visit to the archive. As one designer said:

> This thing about the archives is very interesting because you are inspired by many things that others have done over the years. [...] One never knows what will get triggered by whom and when. [...] Just sitting in the library [archive – ed.] with your team and discussing what other ideas were sparked seems to generate a whole new set of ideas. (Quoted in Cirella and Shani, 2012)

Another example of a new mechanism is the introduction of the procedure of post-collection review. This entails a systematic review on each completed project, led by the product manager and involving the entire team, to reflect on the experience, emerging knowledge, lessons learned, strengths and weaknesses, in order to learn how to do better next time. As another designer said:

> We must be creative, and our creativity must be proactive and focused; to achieve this, we must know our clients and their tastes very well. We need to explore and understand the nature of our past experience with them. The greater the knowledge you have, the easier it gets. (Quoted in Cirella and Shani, 2012)

Other mechanisms, already existing, remained key to convey the collective creativity emphasis. For example, the new strategy and the new mission statement reflected the view on creativity as a collective effort 'channelled' towards the client. More in general, the cultural shift embedded the value of world-class creativity to serve the clients. The periodic staff meetings held by Massimo, described earlier, constituted another important platform for organizational dialogue on creativity.

The End of Massimo's Term and the New Leadership

2011 was the last year of Massimo's term. As the end of his term was fast approaching, Massimo intensified the organizational communication with the entire company to share results achieved, reinforce the new identity of Soft Silk and institutionalize the new ways of working. Organizational communication included Massimo's staff meetings, which were actually kept throughout all phases of the change process. Similarly, managers at all levels were invited to hold frequent meetings with their teams to share results, issues, views and insights.

Also, towards the very end of his term, Massimo sent an impassioned letter to all employees to celebrate all the achievements and to encourage continuing along the same trajectory. After all, Soft Silk had many reasons to celebrate. Not only had they survived a major crisis, but they were also back to positive results. From 2009, the company was back to positive net profits – shedding a bright light on the future. The word about Soft Silk's turnaround was passing around the industry, which favoured attracting new clients and new orders. Finally, Soft Silk could consider attracting new talent again.

The family needed to choose Massimo's successor. Consequently, in 2011, they decided to appoint Franco, from the fourth generation of the family, as the new CEO. Lucia, from the same family generation, had already become marketing director in 2010. Their father (third generation) continued to stay in place as president of the company.

What Happened Next: New Projects and New Challenges

Franco had in-depth managerial education and experience, also covering managerial roles in world-class companies before joining Soft Silk. Franco led Soft Silk as CEO from 2011 to 2021. He and Lucia worked closely together and complemented each other. Soft Silk was back into family leadership, but the story was totally different. Soft Silk was, in 2011, a totally new organization, very far from that of the early 2000s, and it was ready for new projects and challenges. In this ten-year period, the company continued to be successful and to deal with new changes and initiatives.

Previously, the company had two different sites, with the design unit on one site and the factory eight kilometres away. All employees have been moved to one location, creating new spaces in the factory area. Apart from efficiency reasons, the new spaces have been designed to facilitate collaboration and collective creativity, with new offices, open spaces and meeting rooms.

On a different level, examples of key technological innovations from this period included the increased automation of processes and introducing ink jet printing, along with keeping the traditional silk printing techniques.

The archive continued to be at the core of Soft Silk. It was made open to clients and often clients choose specific items from the archive and use them as input for new orders, for example in terms of reproduction of an image or source for new ideas.

Subsequently, the archive was further revived. In 2015, a new company brand, 'Fashion', was launched. It was the first brand owned by the company dedicated to silk scarves created every season as a re-interpretation of archive prints. Fashion was a successful way to 'rediscover' the creative power of Soft Silk's traditions using the archive. Since 2018, the line of products under the Fashion brand has also been extended to silk bags, capes, shawls, turbans and vintage clothing.

Examples of two Fashion-branded collections were 'Young' and 'Traditional'. The Young collection was a group of collections designed for young fashion. This project saw the partnership with a celebrated female designer. For each collection, she selected two contrasting motifs from the archive (for example, flowers plus geometrical shapes) to create a new merged motif. The new motif was generated through intersections of stripes of the two motifs, creating something intriguing and unique. For the 'Traditional' collections, a team of Soft Silk designers searched the archive to select traditional motifs. They are further developed and 'modernized' to create collections for more traditional customers.

These examples show how collective creativity and its mechanisms, such as the use of the archive, have continued to be essential to Soft Silk.

In 2021, the time had come for further changes. Franco became the new president and appointed his two former deputies as new CEOs for Soft Silk. This new couple leading Soft Silk represents the second time where someone external to the family is in charge. Again, the company has new challenges ahead. Nevertheless, now change is the normality for Soft Silk.

Discussion Questions

To understand the context and key features of this change, answer the following questions:

1   What are the key drivers for change?
2   What approach to change has the organization taken? To what extent has that worked for them?
3   What are the key phases within the overall process of change?
4   How have employees been impacted by the changes? Why do you think they have reacted to change in the way they have?
5   What are the key challenges the organization faces now?

Below are three other topics from this book that you might explore within this case study.

Creativity and innovation

1   Creativity is key at Soft Silk. What is the role of creativity in the different phases in the life of the organization (crisis, recovery and transformation, post-transformation)? Has it evolved?
2   What are the key features of collective creativity at Soft Silk?

3   What are the key organizational learning mechanisms (OLMs) Soft Silk has used to enhance collective creativity? Identify OLMs using the categories of cognitive, structural and procedural mechanisms.

4   Do you think that the OLMs are working to enhance creativity? What are their strengths and weaknesses in your opinion? How would you improve them?

5   What are the innovative features of the recent new products launched by Soft Silk?

6   What potential challenges would you predict for creativity and its development in the future of Soft Silk from now on?

Learning and collaboration

1   Collaboration with academia was a milestone for Soft Silk to refocus on creativity. What are the pros and cons related to Soft Silk's choice of collaborating with a university?

2   What are the factors that made the collaboration between Soft Silk and the university successful?

3   How do you see the role of the collaboration with the university to develop learning and change?

4   Would you suggest Soft Silk develop other collaborations in the future? If so, what kind and covering what topics/areas?

Leadership and power

1   How would you describe Massimo's leadership of the organization?

2   To what extent do you think that, during the process of change, leadership was plural?

3   Massimo and the family had a lot of power in the organization. What are the possible tensions you would expect?

4   What kind of leadership and what leadership features are needed to develop collective creativity in a context such Soft Silk?

5   How would you identify key challenges for Franco's leadership of the organization when he started his term?

6   And now a couple is leading Soft Silk (plus Franco, a trio). What are the key challenges for their leadership in your opinion?

CASE STUDY D

A GLOBAL DEVELOPMENT 'KNOWLEDGE PLATFORM': WHAT WINS WHEN LONG-TERM CAPACITY BUILDING CLASHES WITH SHORT-TERM RESULTS PRESSURES?

Paul R. Kelly

Introducing the Knowledge Platform

In the 2010s, a large transnational global contractor won funding for an eight-year $500 million development cluster programme in a Pacific Island nation, hereafter referred to as the Sami Islands to preserve anonymity.[1] Included in the wide range of economic, social, gender, governance and business programmes was a knowledge platform (KP) project. Since the early 2000s, knowledge 'platforms', 'hubs' or 'banks' have featured in many aid programmes. The effort and failure to sustain this particular KP are the main issues in this case.

Key Change Stakeholders

Several key stakeholders are central in the case. Firstly, a university department in a neighbouring country had been instrumental in the early designs for the KP. They became the sub-contractor to own and manage the KP and hired a team of five researchers to develop it.

---

[1]Names of places, organizations, projects, etc. have been given pseudonyms to preserve anonymity. The case is not reporting strictly historical events. The case brings together features from several different initiatives, plus creative edits to add value for teaching and learning about organizational change.

Their funding was small compared to other programmes in the cluster, but still substantial, in the low millions of dollars over four years. In the case, we call this group the 'Research Team'.

Secondly, a large global contractor ran the wider parent cluster of programmes. They managed the awarded funds and sub-contracted the KP to the research team. We shall call this organization 'Global Co'. Global Co hired around 300 staff in years one and two.

Thirdly, governments in the neighbouring advanced economies were the primary funders of the cluster. The funding nations were largely represented by one embassy in the Sami capital. We shall refer to this as the 'Embassy Unit' and it had ultimate authority over funding, governance and political concerns.

Fourthly, the local Sami Islands government was formerly active in trying to make sure that funds were used well, to benefit local organizations and people. Important stakeholders also included a Sami government research institution, a Sami university research department, and a local advocacy and communications NGO. We shall refer to these as Local Research Institutes (LRIs). Influential change makers were situated in the research team, the LRIs and Global Co's programmes. Key leaders and decision-makers were in the Global Co executive team and at the Embassy Unit.

KP Project Structure and Stresses

In terms of the KP change project structure, the research team reported to Global Co senior leaders and program directors following a typical development sector project model. Project and compliance tools included logframe work plans, performance indicators, milestones, regular telephone and on-site meetings, monthly status reports and six-monthly KP project reports.

However, given frequent re-structuring and staff turnover in Global Co programmes, this process was often re-designed by new leaders and managers. The 'theory of change', a development planning tool, was never fully approved or engaged with by Global Co leaders.

Furthermore, the Embassy Unit had a rigorous performance regime in place which featured constant deadline pressures, progress indicators and, at times, a strained relationship between Global Co and the Embassy Unit representatives. This was partly due to funder government and Sami government political relations, and the need to demonstrate the success of the cluster program. Predecessor aid programmes had received criticism, and cost less.

These issues led to frequent personnel changes at all stakeholders.

Overall Objectives: Capacities, Relationships and Products

This overarching KP objective focused on increasing capacity for research and aid programme knowledge 'relationships' and 'products'. Original plans aimed to build relationships between experts, institutions, communities and citizens; build partnerships between programmes, researchers and the national government at ministry levels; and target local government district level services. The original vision included engagement with citizen groups to amplify their voices and participation in generating knowledge about economic and social change. Partnerships were to prioritize collaborations with LRIs too, as they had institutional experience of similar kinds of work, and experienced local researchers.

In terms of knowledge products, the kinds of content capacity the KP aimed to improve spanned skills development, training programmes, and channels for storing and sharing knowledge, for example databases, empirical research data, research archives, project and program reports, plans, evaluations, monitoring information, research publications, and other research or programme media (e.g. imagery, charts, tables, video, web content, etc.).

Existing research knowledge in the Islands was understood, partly in error, by programme leaders to be split across many Sami institutes, often error-ridden, incomplete, not digitized, decades old or hidden behind a fear of sharing, organizational silos, or a simple lack of sharing opportunities. Thus, the KP was intended to be a collaborative example for building research knowledge capacity, programme evidence bases, relationships and specific reports, databases and other products within the country.

Given the capacity objectives above, the KP sought to establish a small-scale platform at first, working with LRIs and Global Co programmes. Later, ambitions were to extend this initial KP to support local government operations in several target districts, partner with ministries, bring in NGO and citizen groups and eventually transfer ownership of the KP to a local government partner, to mature the services and secure a sustainable KP future.

Year 0: Original Vision

The original vision and plans, drafted by an international expert with decades of experience and fluent in the host nation's language and cultural norms, were made for the funding application almost two years before Global Co's programmes began. Original plans viewed knowledge not simply as 'products', but as part of 'relationships', events, training, activities, partnerships, trust building, collaborations, brokering and community building in the Islands. The original aims were designed to build the KP in partnership with local institutes and global development organizations from the start, to encourage buy-in, support, collaborations and experimentation between Sami citizen groups, local experts and international advisers.

The initial KP funding period was intended to be for two years, to be used to build the KP systems, source content, establish partnerships, collaborations and future ownership plans with LRIs. Early plans envisaged a two-year period of initial development followed by two years of support during transfer to the local partner. In sum, development and transfer spanned four years within the eight-year parent programme funding period.

Year 1: Knowledge Products Over Knowledge Processes

At the start, early work in year one involved online meetings, document sharing and regular country visits to Sami Islands by the research team. A key focus during this period was relationship building with LRIs to discuss potential collaborations, future ownership options, and a strategy for the long-term 'home' of the KP. The discussions and insights built on similar efforts by LRIs in the past to establish research archives and knowledge sharing services. However, from the start the Global Co leadership and programme directors pressured the research team to produce a stream of desperately needed separate reports and briefs. This conflicted with the original KP capacity building vision and localization focus.

In the first few weeks, Global Co parent programmes commissioned multiple research reports, topic and scoping briefs from the research team, and area profiles incorporating demographic and public service data about specific areas of the country. Research topics ranged across all Global Co programmes, spanning economic planning, political reform and citizen surveys. These reduced time and resources for the KP research team to relationship-build with LRIs. The research team were asked not to engage with local NGOs or organizations beyond Global Co's own programmes. As such, individual short-term 'knowledge products' (e.g. reports, briefs, charts, data sets) were prioritized over engagement with Sami organizations and LRIs. Even relationship building with Global Co's own programme teams was limited to knowledge products rather than capacity building or KP strategy discussions. The research team thus became a service contractor for Global Co, rather than an equal partner setting up an innovative, locally engaged KP.

Nevertheless, in the background the research team slowly began limited relationship building and platform development processes. This involved collating hundreds of Sami development articles, publications, summaries and fact sheets into an offline database. Early KP collaborations with two Global Co programmes began too, collating past reports, plans, evaluations and development data from programme and project teams, organizing this in an online database and building a pilot web interface. Negotiations began with local LRIs and ministry experts, to see who, how and where the KP might best be eventually hosted. This slow-burn collaboration grew over time, with a growing database, the small-scale web platform, and increasing participation between Global Co programme teams, the research team and LRIs. This work followed the original vision to 'cultivate' development (Mosse, 2005) rather than 'impose' an externally designed package of work upon developing nation institutions.

Despite growing relationships and frequent discussions, progress remained tentative, with LRIs wary of partnerships with internationally funded programmes. Reasons for this attitude, considered by some leaders at Global Co and the Embassy as 'resistance', included past experiences with failures, funding streams that suddenly disappeared, and being seen as 'token' local players that global partners use to market themselves as legitimate 'caring' agents to international funders, rather than as serious, long-term collaborators with equal shares in the project controls and successes. There was also severe competition between precariously funded local LRIs and other allied international organizations, as to who would win the long-term funding to host the KP, plus some justified frustration that it had been unfairly awarded to a foreign university research team in the first place.

Year 2: From Capacity Building to Short-Term Results

During the second year of the project, the research team came under severe pressure to show results and demonstrate the impact of the KP. This pressure came from Global Co programmes wanting to show progress, and pressure from the funding countries, via the Embassy Unit, for Global Co's senior leaders to start delivering demonstrable, systemic social and economic change. The research team at the neighbouring country university had their annual funding changed to become dependent on delivering individual pieces of research, measured by the volume of knowledge products, reports, briefs, ten-pagers, five-pagers and so forth. The collaborative, localizing KP vision was shelved. A new focus was brought in to demonstrate progress, engagement and impact, and to alleviate pressure on Global Co's leadership, which had spent significant funds on hiring start-up staff, bringing in consultants and running initial programmes which had not yet delivered demonstrable change. The funders and Embassy team required evidence of change to deploy in government forums. Public facing media was discouraged. The large-scale cluster programme had become politically sensitive with a perception problem around limited impacts and heavy costs – criticisms common to the aid sector.

The research team pivoted and hired a communications specialist to re-design and re-brand all KP communications, knowledge products and the pilot web interface. They brought in a second contractor to develop multiple research report templates, a brand design with logo, and an attractive colour scheme. The pilot KP under development with Global Co programmes and LRIs was mothballed, and the communications specialist set up a new web content management system they preferred. New web sections to promote events in the host country and a portfolio of research products, reports and briefs already completed in year one by the research team, were prominently placed on the new web site to demonstrate 'what we have done already' to Global Co leadership and the Embassy Unit.

A survey was conducted with Global Co programme staff and a KP evaluation report drafted. This showed that staff valued the fledgling KP and recommended continued support from Global Co and funders. This work, to demonstrate the development of the KP, its products and attractive branding, was effectively a marketing pitch to the influential stakeholders, the Embassy Unit and Global Co's leadership. Sub-programme directors and local LRI leaders who had supported the KP work so far, started building relationships, attending workshops, sharing data and research for the KP with the research team, were not invited to pitches or consulted. Neither were local NGOs, citizen groups nor Sami government representatives.

Looking back, the KP was never formally completed or launched. It was never shared with local LRIs institutes or other stakeholders. Effectively, the two-year KP effort ended in with a single decision, and joined a list of previous development sector knowledge sharing efforts which have, over many years, also often failed in similar ways.

Four Challenges: Why Did the KP Fail?

Four key challenges stand out in this case. Firstly, funder, government and programme leadership relationships were challenging. Global Co suffered criticism for failure to deliver results rapidly, and for spending excessively during the set-up phase, hiring lots of new staff and renting expensive CBD office space. This, arguably, started the 'visibility' problems for what was supposed to be a set of needed aid programs. The need to show results impacted programmes and projects. Such short-termism and results pressure are common in aid projects and in change efforts more broadly, and can be disastrous for long-term relationship building processes or sensitive collaboration efforts. In aid programmes with significant financing, political sensitivities and global contractors, these visibility problems needed managing from the beginning. Change makers at the research team, the LRIs and in Global Co's programmes perhaps should have come together earlier to anticipate such problems and devise a common response but unfortunately these relationships were still themselves embryonic, and precarious, given the history of aid and knowledge sharing failures in the Islands. Was there space early on to discuss such precarious issues?

Secondly, unrelated, high-level diplomatic issues were ongoing between the parent program, funder and relevant governments. This meant that despite repeated efforts to get leadership support for a legitimate, albeit not major, component of the original plans, leadership was never fully aware of or on board with the KP component. Key leaders changed since the original planning, and Global Co leadership, under pressure to show results and account for expenditure, began to limit access to funds for the research team. These are typical change problems concerning leadership, sponsorship and cutting costs for all but the most critical programs. What could change makers have done? In retrospect, change makers at the research team should have worked harder to secure senior leadership buy in and support, possibly based on collaborative quick wins negotiated with local LRIs. Given that the web platform established by the research team communications expert and the initial pilot website and archive were low cost, a different option would have been to pitch early on for more technology funding to build more substantial digital infrastructure. Unfortunately, smaller-scale projects can be ignored more easily than larger-scale ones, and the digital transformation aspect of the KP project was arguably underplayed by the research team as they struggled between relationship building and knowledge product demands. A larger digital transformation agenda may have created space for leadership buy-in and demonstrated impacts in year two. How else might change makers have raised the stakes for the KP?

Thirdly, a local Sami partner to host and own the new KP over the long term was never completely secured. Efforts were made in year one to establish relationships with two LRIs, one a government institute, another a local advocacy organization with many government and civil society partners. On a personal level, negotiations with both organizations went well in year one. However, given the background political challenges, past failures with similar research capacity building efforts, and growing rumours about other multi-partner local/international collaborations setting up competing platforms, hubs and so forth, an agreement with an LRI was never signed. This issue involved the reputational and commercial politics of data and knowledge, such as who might 'own' the data, who would 'manage' the knowledge, who is on the board or what guarantees were in place that the international partner would not dominate the KP. Ownership of data brings its own politics and can spark conflicts, as discussed in earlier chapters of this book. Nevertheless, at times, change makers need to act fast, and having a local Sami government-backed agreement with an LRI on the table could have been another way to draw attention, support and funding to the KP. A key problem was that Global Co wanted to limit negotiations with local LRIs and citizens groups as they were concerned about potential negative comments, but change makers at the research team and within Global Co programmes could have worked harder to convince leaders and Embassy officials that this was a key part of a successful KP. This 'local partnership' was, after all, in the original vision.

Fourthly, the shift in year two to a less collaborative but more branded KP, based on attractive communications rather than effective relationship building or co-design, is a common problem in technology projects and digital change efforts. This conflict hinges on a trade-off between 'what looks good' and 'what works well'. Arguably, both are needed in a new platform. A lack of aesthetics can turn off influential leaders. A lack of usefulness can turn off platform users. Within this issue, change makers at the research team should arguably have brought in the communications specialists from the beginning and, at the same time, built the local partner relationships so that the LRIs had input into the communications, web and branding efforts. This would have potentially built trust and capacity at the same time, rather than as a later change of KP strategy from slow-burn co-design, to a rapidly branded KP as a sign of short-term, tangible impact.

Discussion Questions

To understand the context and key features of this change effort, answer the following questions:

1   What are the key drivers for change?
2   What approach to change has been used in this case, and how effective was it?
3   Examine each of the four challenges outlined in the case. How might you have handled these differently?

Below are four other topics from this book that you might explore through this case study.

Learning and knowledge sharing

1   What kind of learning and knowledge sharing was effective in this case?
2   What kind of learning and knowledge sharing was not effective?
3   What learning tactics could change makers have used to generate support for the KP?

Digital transformation

1   The case suggests several digital transformation issues. What are they?
2   How might digital transformation have been viewed by the research team, programme staff, Global Co's leadership, the Embassy Unit or the local LRIs?
3   How might change makers in the research team, LRIs and Global Co programmes have helped generate consensus and support for the KP?

Power and resistance

1   What power relations, politics and resistance issues are evident in the case?
2   Which power models might help change makers navigate these issues?
3   What dimensions of resistance are evident in the case?
4   How might change makers have helped transform resistance to make it beneficial to the KP change efforts?

Leadership

1   Several key organizations were involved in the case. How could consensus and support have been built better?
2   How might change makers have encouraged interest, buy-in and sustained sponsorship from different groups, e.g. the Embassy Unit, Global Co senior leaders, Global Co programme staff and the LRIs?
3   What should the research team's own leadership have done differently?

CASE STUDY E

ZWILLING: MERGING TWO FAMILY FIRMS

Danielle A. Tucker and Stella Lind

Introduction

Zwilling[1] has been in the business of kitchenware for nearly 300 years. Founded in Germany in 1731, the company has grown from strength to strength. Zwilling has grown from being a niche specialist in cutlery products to offering a wider range of cooking and preparation products. In the 1960s Zwilling was bought by the German Werhahn company (one of Germany's biggest family firms). The company is now owned and run by Erich, the great-grandson of the Werhahn founder and one of the various shareholders of the Werhahn family. Through various successions, the guiding principle for each generation of owner-managers has been to leave the business in a better shape than you inherited it – not only for your family, but also for your whole community. Zwilling now operates as an international business but remains proud of its traditional family heritage.

For owner-manager family firms, Erich is aware that as the owner, he is also a figurehead of the company (not simply its largest shareholder). Like most family firms (Gomez-Mejia, 2011), Zwilling is a high-trust work environment, strategic decisions take a long-term orientation and many employees have a long history with the organization, in some cases with several generations of employees who have worked alongside several generations of owners. Just as his great-grandfather did, Erich really cares for his employees; however, continued growth presents challenges.

Zwilling's growth strategy, for many years, has been to expand into new markets by buying other successful local family businesses and merging them into a large international, but still German-based family business. They have already had several successful mergers and acquisitions, with other family firms choosing to merge with Zwilling because they trusted that as a family firm they had similar values and, particularly, that Zwilling is led by a CEO

---

[1]Zwilling is a real company and the case is based on a real process of change at this organization. Some details are modified for didactic reasons.

who upholds these values with integrity. Zwilling is now looking to acquire Company B – an Italian cookware company.

Giuseppe is the current CEO of Company B. He is facing a common challenge for family firms – finding a successor in the next generation. Giuseppe is the sixth generation of owner-manager for Company B; however, in the new generation his only daughter has other plans. So, the only option is to sell the company. After considering many different options, Giuseppe believes that Zwilling is the perfect merger partner for his company. The main reason he has chosen Zwilling – even though they have been direct competitors – is that Werhahn are a Catholic family with similar values.

The Merger

A merger or acquisition requires a change in the identity of a company. Especially in a case where organizational identity is based on strong core values (such as at both Company B and Zwilling), this identity change can be difficult for employees. There is an especially high level of uncertainty for employees, knowing that a lot of decisions will be made about how the two workforces will work together. Before the merger, Company B and Zwilling thought of themselves as competitors. Although the two companies are similar in age and history, Zwilling is the larger company and will take over ownership and leadership of the merged company. Giuseppe will remain on the board of directors for two years, to oversee a smooth transition before retiring and Erich will become the CEO of both organizations.

Announcing the merger

Employees at Company B were aware of the succession challenges that Giuseppe faced and were concerned about their future. There had been rumours for some time that Giuseppe may have to sell the company, so when Erich and Giuseppe called a joint town hall meeting there was little surprise in the announcement that Zwilling would purchase the company. The announcement was important, however, in setting the tone for the partnership. Erich and Giuseppe both stood together on stage in front of the Italian employees to demonstrate their trust in one another. They wanted to reassure employees that Zwilling's strategy was to continue to let Company B run as independently as possible. Giuseppe explained his choice of acquisition partner and the journey to reaching this decision: 'It is emotionally easier to sell to a family firm. We rejected many offers until we found the right one. We just trusted this family firm to have the right value set. I immediately knew that my people are in safe hands here.' During the town hall meeting, Erich communicated to the Italian employees his great appreciation for the products that Company B produced and how this would fit with the Zwilling brand and complement their own products.

Erich also announced the merger to the German employees of Zwilling, explaining to them the importance of Company B's heritage and promising continuity in the way that Zwilling operated.

Over the months that followed, several 'getting to know one another' activities were organized to build trust and relationships. This included a summer party at headquarters and a site visit to Italy by several of the German management team. All employees were offered training in one another's specialisms, as well as language courses to try to ensure that working relations were as positive as possible.

Changes in processes and structure

Zwilling operates as a decentralized organization, especially when it comes to research and development. As has been the case with previous acquisitions, they intend to allow Company B to become an Italian subsidiary of the organization and, with that, maintain quite a lot of its decision-making power. To facilitate this a managing director from within Company B will be appointed to lead them in research and development, allowing them to maintain some of their identity within the overall organizational structure. However, sales and marketing functions will be centrally controlled from Germany and therefore the development of new products and decisions about production volume would need to be taken in conjunction with the Zwilling board of directors.

Giuseppe was a very strong, yet demanding leader of Company B. Being the sole family member involved in the company, the company culture was derived very much from his directive style. Whilst he consulted with other company directors, he ultimately made decisions himself and assumed responsibility for the company and its outputs. Employees viewed him as a father-like figure, strict in giving clear guidance about what was expected of them, but also respected for his rigid adherence to the traditional values on which the organization was based. Leadership at Zwilling was much looser. Although Erich was the CEO, he made decisions through consensus with a broader board of senior managers, including other members of the owning family. At this time Zwilling already had several other subsidiary organizations, the leaders of which were given great autonomy to make decisions. Rather than dictating how each department or subsidiary should work, Erich relied heavily on the trust relationship between himself and the other leaders, which he facilitated by visiting them often and showing a keen interest in the work of all employees. He placed a lot of emphasis on building relationships with various stakeholders and aimed to ensure that they were all working towards the same goals and vision. The leadership team at Zwilling were more dynamic in their ideas, they embraced innovation and had a very future-orientated view of the company.

Resistance to Change

As more detailed plans about the merger emerged, employees from both companies began to show some signs of resistance. Employees from Company B were concerned about becoming part of a larger, more impersonal (as they viewed it) organization. The changes in structure described above would be implemented as part of a larger restructuring programme. The degree to which they felt that job security was compromised varied between groups (those who worked in the pans and cookware product lines where there was considerable overlap between the two companies' product lines felt less secure than those who had product specialisms that were different from what Zwilling currently offered). Employees at Company B reminded themselves that Giuseppe had looked after their best interests for many years and would not have chosen Erich as a partner without having confidence that he would do the same. Resistance would be best described as a passive 'waiting' and 'observing'. Employees were noticeably less enthusiastic about their work and held back on new ideas that they previously would have shared openly, some of the sense of pride that they exhibited in working for Company B dissipated, they continued to do their work conscientiously and competently, but something was missing. Employees paid close attention to the actions and behaviours of Zwilling managers when they came to visit, they scrutinized their behaviours, their explanations for changes, and asked lots of questions to try to understand the motivation and thinking behind any changes in processes.

Being part of a company merger was not a new experience for employees of Zwilling; this was, in fact, the seventh family firm merger that had occurred under Erich's leadership. With each experience, they learned from their previous experiences and mistakes. In particular, they were confident in Zwilling's management having good intuition and sensitivity towards the acquired company. However, in this case, they did have some reservations about the merger. Mirroring the Company B employees' concerns, Zwilling workers in the pans and cookware product division were concerned that the merger would undermine their products in this area. They resisted collaboration with Company B employees and were unhappy about sharing information with employees who worked for a company they were previously in competition with: 'All these years we were the biggest rivals. And all of a sudden, they tell us that we are partners? This is ridiculous' said one German employee.

Discussion Questions

To understand the context and key features of this change, answer the following questions:

1   What are the key drivers for change for (a) Zwilling and (b) Company B? To what extent are they different and how might this impact on the change?
2   What approach to change has the organization taken? To what extent has that worked for them?
3   Imagine you are a change maker working at (a) Zwilling and (b) Company B. What are the key challenges that you face and what would you do to address these?

Below are three other topics from this book that you might explore within this case study.

Resistance to change

1   Consider the change from the perspective of employees at (a) Zwilling and (b) Company B. Why do you think these employees are resisting the merger? Are they right to feel this way?
2   How might issues of power impact on their feelings about the change?
3   What could the organization do to make employees feel that their voice is being heard?

Creativity and innovation

1   How might the dynamics of the merger impact on (a) knowledge sharing, (b) creativity and (c) innovation in the post-merger organization?
2   As a change maker in the merged organization, what could you do to help increase collaboration across two former rival factions of employees?

Leadership

1   How would you describe the leadership at Zwilling?
2   To what extent do you think that leadership in owner-managed family firms might be different from other organizations? How does this impact on change management?
3   Leadership succession is a challenge in all organizations. As a change maker, how might this impact on your role?

REFERENCES

ACAS (n.d.) Improving equality, diversity and inclusion in your workplace. Available at: www.acas.org.uk/improving-equality-diversity-and-inclusion/unconscious-bias (accessed 28 November 2023).

Ackoff, R.L. (1989) 'From data to wisdom', *Journal of Applied Systems Analysis*, 16: 3–9.

Adams, J.S. (1965) 'Inequity in social exchange'. In L. Berkowitz (ed.), *Advances in Experimental Social Psychology*, Vol. 2. New York: Academic Press, pp. 267–299.

Agogué, M., Yström, A. and Le Masson, P. (2013) 'Rethinking the role of intermediaries as an architect of collective exploration and creation of knowledge in open innovation', *International Journal of Innovation Management*, 17(2): 1350007.

Agterberg, M., van den Hooff, B.J., Huysman, M.H. and Soekijad, M. (2010) 'Keeping the wheels turning: The dynamics of managing networks of practice', *Journal of Management Studies*, 47(1): 85–108.

Aguilar, F.J. (1967) *Scanning the Business Environment*. New York, Macmillan.

Alegre, I., Berbegal-Mirabent, J., Guerrero, A. and Mas-Machuca, M. (2018) 'The real mission of the mission statement: A systematic review of the literature', *Journal of Management and Organization*, 24(4): 456–73. DOI:org/10.1017/jmo.2017.82

Alfes, K., Truss, C. and Gill, J. (2010) The HR manager as change agent: Evidence from the public sector. *Journal of Change Management*, 10(1): 109–27.

Allen, D.K., Brown, A., Karanasios, S. and Norman, A. (2013) 'How should technology-mediated organizational change be explained? A comparison of the contributions of critical realism and activity theory', *MIS Quarterly*, 37(3): 835–54.

Alvesson, M. and Sveningsson, S. (2003) 'Managers doing leadership: The extra-ordinarization of the mundane', *Human Relations*, 56(12): 1435–59.

Amabile, T.M. (1983) 'The social psychology of creativity: A componential conceptualization', *Journal of Personality and Social Psychology*, 45(2): 357–376.

Amabile, T.M. (1988) 'A model of creativity and innovation in organizations', *Research in Organizational Behavior*, 10(1): 123–67.

Amabile, T.M. (1998) 'How to kill creativity', *Harvard Business Review*, 76(5): 76–87.

Amabile, T.M. (1996) *Creativity and Innovation in Organizations*, Vol. 50. Boston, MA: Harvard Business School.

Amabile, T.M. and Gryskiewicz, N.D. (1989) 'The creative environment scales: Work environment inventory', *Creativity Research Journal*, 2(4): 231–53.

Amis, J. and Greenwood, R. (2020) 'Organizational change in a (post-) pandemic world: Rediscovering interests and values', *Journal of Management Studies*, 58(2): 582–6.

Anand, S., Hu, J., Liden, R.C. and Vidyarthi, P.R. (2011) 'Leader–member exchange: Recent research findings and prospects for the future'. In A. Bryman, D. Collinson, K. Grint, B. Jackson and M. Uhl-Bien (eds), *The SAGE Handbook of Leadership*. London: Sage, pp. 311–25.

Argyris, C. (1993) *On Organizational Learning*. Cambridge: Blackwell

Argyris, C. and Schön, D.A. (1978) *Organizational Learning: A Theory of Action Perspective*. Reading, MA: Addison-Wesley.

Ashburner, L., Ferlie, E. and FitzGerald, L. (1996) 'Organizational transformation and top-down change: the case of the NHS', *British Journal of Management*, 7(1): 1–16.

Ashford, S.J., Sutcliffe, K.M. and Christianson, M.K. (2009) 'Speaking up and speaking out: The leadership dynamics of voice in organizations'. In J. Greenberg and M.S. Edwards (eds), *Voice and Silence in Organizations*. Bingley: Emerald Group Publishing, pp. 175–201.

Ashkanasy, N.M. and Daus, C.S. (2002) 'Emotion in the workplace: The new challenge for managers', *Academy of Management Perspectives*, 16(1): 76–86.

Aula, P. and Mantere, S. (2013) 'Making and breaking sense: An inquiry into the reputation change', *Journal of Organizational Change Management*, 26(2), 340–52.

Avgerou, C. (2002) *Information Systems and Global Diversity*. Oxford: Oxford University Press.

Avolio, B.J. (1999) *Full Leadership Development: Building the Vital Forces in Organizations*. Thousand Oaks, CA: Sage.

Avolio, B.J. (2010) *Full Range Leadership Development* (2nd edn). Thousand Oaks, CA: Sage.

Avolio, B.J. and Bass, B.M. (1993) *Cross Generations: A Full Range Leadership Development Program*. Binghamton, NY: Center for Leadership Studies, Binghamton University.

Avolio, B.J. and Bass, B.M. (eds) (2002) *Developing Potential Across a Full Range of Leadership: Cases on Transactional and Transformational Leadership*. Mahwah, NJ: Lawrence Erlbaum.

Avolio, B.J. and Gardner, W.L. (2005) 'Authentic leadership development: Getting to the root of positive forms of leadership', *Leadership Quarterly*, 16(3): 315–38.

Avolio, B.J., Gardner, W.L., Walumbwa, F.O., Luthans, F. and May, D.R. (2004) 'Unlocking the mask: A look at the process by which authentic leaders impact follower attitudes and behaviours', *Leadership Quarterly*, 15: 801–23.

Bain, P., Watson, A., Mulvey, G., Taylor, P. and Gall, G. (2002) 'Taylorism, targets and the pursuit of quantity and quality by call centre management', *New Technology, Work and Employment*, 17(3): 170–85.

Balogun, J. (2010) *When Organizations Change: A Middle Management Perspective on Getting It Right*. Los Angeles, CA: AIM Research.

Balogun, J. and Johnson, G. (2004) 'Organizational restructuring and middle manager sensemaking', *Academy of Management Journal*, 47(4): 523–49.

Bartezzaghi E. (2002) 'Dove va il BPR? L'innovazione organizzativa basata sulle ICT', *Mondo Digitale*, 2: June.

Bartezzaghi E. (2010) *L'organizzazione dell'impresa: Processi, progetti, conoscenza, persone*. Milan: Rizzoli Etas.

Bass, B.M. and Steidlmeier, P. (1999) 'Ethics, character and authentic transformational leadership behavior', *Leadership Quarterly*, 10: 181–217.

Bass, B.M. and Stogdill, R.M. (1990) *Bass and Stogdill's Handbook of Leadership: A Survey of Theory and Research*. New York: Free Press.

Bate, S.P. and Robert, G. (2002) 'Knowledge management and communities of practice in the private sector: Lessons for modernising the National Health Service in England and Wales', *Public Administration*, 80(4): 643–63.

Bauer, T.N. and Erdogan, B. (eds) (2016) *The Oxford Handbook of Leader – Member Exchange*. Oxford: Oxford University Press.

Beaty, R.E., Benedek, M., Barry Kaufman, S. and Silvia, P.J. (2015) 'Default and executive network coupling supports creative idea production', *Scientific Reports*, 5(1): 1–14.

Beckhard, R. (1969) *Organization Development: Strategies and Models*. Reading, MA: Addison-Wesley.

Beer, D. (2018) *The Data Gaze: Capitalism, Power and Perception*. London: Sage.

Beer, M. and Nohria, N. (eds) (2000) *Breaking the Code of Change*. Boston, MA: Harvard Business School Press.

Beerel, A. (2009) *Leadership and Change Management*. London: Sage.

Bell, M.P., Özbilgin, M.F., Beauregard, T.A. and Sürgevil, O. (2011) 'Voice, silence, and diversity in 21st century organizations: Strategies for inclusion of gay, lesbian, bisexual, and transgender employees', *Human Resource Management*, 50(1): 131–46.

Benisom, H.F. (1994) 'Crisis and disaster management: Violence in the workplace', *Training and Development*, 48(1): 27–32.

Bennis, W.G. and Nanus, B. (1985) *Leaders: The Strategies for Taking Charge*. New York: Harper & Row.

Bessant, J., Caffyn, S. and Gallagher, M. (2001) 'An evolutionary model of continuous improvement behaviour', *Technovation*, 21(2): 67–77.

Bessant, J. and Rush, H. (1995) 'Building bridges for innovation: The role of consultants in technology transfer, *Research Policy*, 24: 97–114.

Bessant, J., Caffyn, S., Gilbert, J., Harding, R. and Webb, S. (1994) Rediscovering continuous improvement. *Technovation*, 14(1): 17–29.

Beynon-Davies, P. (2009) *Business Information Systems*. London: Bloomsbury.

Bissola, R. and Imperatori, B. (2011) 'Organizing individual and collective creativity: Flying in the face of creativity clichés', *Creativity and Innovation Management*, 20(2): 77–89.

Blackler, F. (1993) 'Knowledge and the theory of organizations: Organizations as activity systems and the reframing of management', *Journal of Management Studies*, 30(6): 863–84.

Blackler, F. (2011) 'Power, politics, and intervention theory: Lessons from organization studies', *Theory and Psychology*, 21: 724–34. DOI:org/10.1177/0959354311418146.

Blackler, F., Crump, N. and McDonald, S. (2000) Organizing processes in complex activity networks. *Organization*, 7(2), 277–300.

Blake, R.R. and Mouton, J.S. (1964) *The Managerial Grid*. Houston, TX: Gulf Publishing Company.

Blake, R.R. and Mouton, J.S. (1985) *The New Managerial Grid*. Houston TX: Gulf Publishing Company.

Blauner, R. (1964) *Alienation and Freedom: The Factory Worker and His Industry*. Chicago: Chicago University Press.

Bordia, P., Hobman, E., Jones, E., Gallois, C. and Callan, V.J. (2004) 'Uncertainty during organizational change: Types, consequences, and management strategies', *Journal of Business and Psychology*, 18(4): 507–32.

Bordia, P., Restubog, S.L.D., Jimmieson, N.L. and Irmer, B.E. (2011) 'Haunted by the past: Effects of poor change management history on employee attitudes and turnover', *Group and Organization Management*, 36(2): 191–222.

Bossen, C., Jensen, L.G. and Udsen, F.W. (2014) 'Boundary-Object Trimming: On the Invisibility of Medical Secretaries' Care of Records in Healthcare Infrastructures', *Computer Supported Cooperative Work (CSCW)*, 23(1): 75–110.

Boston Consulting Group (2020) 'Flipping the Odds of Digital Transformation Success'. Available at: https://www.bcg.com/de-de/publications/2020/increasing-odds-of-success-in-digital-transformation (accessed 28 November 2023).

Boston Consulting Group (2021) 'What works – and what doesn't – in transformation'. 9 December. Boston Consulting Group. Available at: https://www.bcg.com/publications/2021/how-companies-implement-successful-transformation (accessed 28 November 2023)

Bourdieu, P. (1977) *Outline of a Theory of Practice*. Cambridge: Cambridge University Press.

Bracker, J. (1980) 'The historical development of the strategic management concept', *Academy of Management Review*, 5(2): 219–24.

Brannick, T. and Coghlan, D. (2007) 'In defense of being "native": The case for insider academic research', *Organizational Research Methods*, 10(1): 59–74.

Bratton, J. (2020) *Work and Organizational Behaviour*. London: Bloomsbury.

Braverman, H. (1974) *Labour and Monopoly Capital: The Degradation of Work in the Twentieth Century*. New York: Monthly Review Press.

Bridwell-Mitchell, E.N. (2016) 'Collaborative institutional agency: How peer learning in communities of practice enables and inhibits micro-institutional change', *Organization Studies*, 37(2): 161–92.

Brown, S.L. and Eisenhardt, K.M. (1997) 'The art of continuous change: Linking complexity theory and time-paced evolution in relentlessly shifting organizations', *Administrative Science Quarterly*, 42(1): 1–34.

Brynjolfsson, E. and McAfee, A. (2014) *The Second Machine Age: Work, Progress, and Prosperity in a Time of Brilliant Technologies*. New York: W.W. Norton & Company.

Brynjolfsson, E. and Saunders, A. (2009) *Wired for Innovation: How Information Technology Is Reshaping the Economy*. Cambridge, MA: MIT Press.

Buchanan, D. and Badham, R. (2020) *Power, Politics, and Organizational Change*. London: Sage.

Bullock, R.J. and Batten, D. (1985) 'It's just a phase we're going through: A review and synthesis of OD phase analysis', *Group and Organization Studies*, 10(December): 383–12

Burkitt, I., 2002. 'Complex emotions: Relations, feelings and images in emotional experience', *The Sociological Review*, 50(S2): 151–67.

Burnes, B. (1996) 'No such thing as … a "one best way" to manage organizational change? The case of XYZ construction' *Management Decision*, 34(10): 11–18.

Burnes, B. (2004a) 'Emergent change and planned change – competitors or allies?', *International Journal of Operations and Production Management*, 24(9): 886–902.

Burnes, B. (2004b) 'Kurt Lewin and the planned approach to change: A re-appraisal', *Journal of Management Studies*, 41(6): 977–1002.

Burnes, B. (2005) 'Complexity theories and organizational change', *International Journal of Management Reviews*, 7(2): 73–90.

Burnes, B. (2011) 'Introduction: Why does change fail, and what can we do about it?', *Journal of Change Management*, 11(4): 445–50.

Byrnes, J. (2005) Middle Management Excellence. 12 May. Harvard Business School Business Research for Business Leaders website. Available at: https://hbswk.hbs.edu/archive/middle-management-excellence (accessed 28 November 2023).

Callon, M. (1984) 'Some elements of a sociology of translation: Domestication of the scallops and the fishermen of St Brieuc Bay', *The Sociological Review*, 32(1 suppl.): 196–233.

Candel, J.J. and Biesbroek, R. (2016) 'Toward a processual understanding of policy integration', *Policy Sciences*, 49(3): 211–31.

Canterino, F., Cirella, S. and Shani, A.B. (2018). Leading organizational transformation: An action research study. *Journal of Managerial Psychology*, 33(1), 15–28.

Canterino, F., Cirella, S., Piccoli, B. and Shani, A. B. R. (2020). Leadership and change mobilization: The mediating role of distributed leadership. *Journal of Business Research*, 108, 42–51.

Carayannis, E.G., Barth, T.D. and Campbell, D.F. (2012) 'The quintuple Helix innovation model: Global warming as a challenge and driver for innovation', *Journal of Innovation and Entrepreneurship*, 1(1): 1–12.

Carli, L.L. and Eagly, A.H. (2011) 'Gender and leadership'. In A. Bryman, D. Collinson, K. Grint, B. Jackson and M. Uhl-Bien (eds), *The SAGE Handbook of Leadership*. London: Sage, pp. 103–17.

Carlyle, T. (1866) *On Heroes, Hero-Worship and the Heroic in History*. New York: John Wiley.

Castells, M. and Cardoso, G. (1996) *The Network Society*, Vol. 469. Oxford: Blackwell.

Catmull, E. (2008) 'How Pixar Fosters Collective Creativity', *Harvard Business Review*, 86(9): 64–72.

Caza, A. and Jackson, B. (2011) 'Authentic leadership'. In A. Bryman, D. Collinson, K. Grint, B. Jackson and M. Uhl-Bien (eds), *The SAGE Handbook of Leadership*. London: Sage, pp. 353–64.

Chaharbaghi, K. and Cripps, S. (2007) 'Collective creativity: wisdom or oxymoron?', *Journal of European Industrial Training*, 31(8): 626–38.

Chesbrough, H. (2007) 'Business model innovation: It's not just about technology anymore', *Strategy and Leadership*, 35(6): 12–17.

Chesbrough, H.W. and Appleyard, M.M. (2007) 'Open innovation and strategy', *California Management Review*, 50(1): 57–76.

Chesbrough, H., Vanhaverbeke, W. and West, J. (eds) (2006) *Open Innovation: Researching a New Paradigm*. Oxford: Oxford University Press.

Choi, M. and Ruona, W.E. (2011) 'Individual readiness for organizational change and its implications for human resource and organization development', *Human Resource Development Review*, 10(1): 46–73.

Chreim, S., Williams, B.E. and Coller, K.E. (2012) 'Radical change in healthcare organization: Mapping transition between templates, enabling factors, and implementation processes', *Journal of Health Organization and Management*, 26(2): 215–36.

Christensen, C.M. (2013) *The Innovator's Dilemma: When New Technologies Cause Great Firms to Fail*. Boston, MA: Harvard Business Review Press.

Christensen, C.M., Horn, M.B. and Johnson, C.W. (2011) *Disrupting Class: How Disruptive Innovation Will Change the Way the World Learns*, Vol. 1. New York: McGraw-Hill.

Ciborra, C. (2006) 'Imbrication of representations: Risk and digital technologies', *Journal of Management Studies*, 43(6): 1339–56.

CIPD (2015) Landing transformational change: Closing the gap between theory and practice. September. Chartered Institute of Personnel and Development and University of Bath School of Management. Available at: https://www.cipd.co.uk/Images/landing-transformation-change_2015-gap-theory-practice_tcm18-9050.pdf (accessed 28 November 2023).

Cirella S. (2015) *Teoria e pratica del Comportamento Organizzativo*. Rome: Carocci,

Cirella, S. (2016) 'Organizational variables for developing collective creativity in business: A case from an Italian fashion design company', *Creativity and Innovation Management*, 25(3): 331–43.

Cirella, S. (2018) What happened next? A follow-up study of the long-term relevance and impact of a collaborative research project. In Bosio, G., Minola, T., Origo, F., Tomelleri, S. (eds) *Rethinking Entrepreneurial Human Capital: The Role of Innovation and Collaboration*. Heidelberg: Springer, pp. 153–71.

Cirella, S. (2021) 'Managing collective creativity: Organizational variables to support creative teamwork', *European Management Review*, 18(4): 404–17.

Cirella, S., Canterino, F., Guerci, M. and Shani, A.B. (2016) 'Organizational learning mechanisms and creative climate: Insights from an Italian fashion design company', *Creativity and Innovation Management*, 25(2): 211–22.

Cirella, S., Guerci, M. and Shani, A.B. (2012) 'A process model of collaborative management research: The study of collective creativity in the luxury industry', *Systemic Practice and Action Research*, 25: 281–300.

Cirella, S. and Murphy, S. (2022) 'Exploring intermediary practices of collaboration in university–industry innovation: A practice theory approach', *Creativity and Innovation Management*, 31(2): 358–75.

Cirella, S., Radaelli, G. and Shani, A.B.R. (2014) 'Team creativity: A complex adaptive perspective', *Management Research Review*, 37(7): 590–614.

Cirella, S. and Shani, A.B. (2012) 'Collective creativity by design: Learning from an Italian fashion design company', *Irish Journal of Management*, 32(1): 53–75.

Cirella, S. and Yström, A. (2018) 'Creativity and science parks: More than just a physical platform?', *CERN IdeaSquare Journal of Experimental Innovation*, 2(1): 8–13.

Ciulla, J.B. (2009) 'Leadership and the ethics of care', *Journal of Business Ethics*, 88(1): 3–4.

Clarkson, M.B.E. (1995) 'A stakeholder framework for analyzing and evaluating corporate social performance', *Academy of Management Review*, 20: 92–117.

Clegg, S.R. (1989) *Frameworks of Power*. London: Sage.

Clegg, S.R. and Haugaard, M. (eds) (2009) *The SAGE Handbook of Power*. London: Sage.

Clegg, S.R., Lawrence, T.B. and Hardy, C. (2006) *The SAGE Handbook of Organization Studies*. London: Sage.

Clegg, S.R., Pitsis, T.S. and Mount, M. (2022) *Managing and Organizations: An Introduction to Theory and Practice* (6th edn). London: Sage.

CMI (2020) Management transformed: Managing in a marathon crisis. Published by the Chartered Management Institute. Available at: https://www.managers.org.uk/knowledge-and-insights/research-thought-leadership/management-transformed/ (accessed 28 November 2023).

Cobb, A.T., Wooten, K.C. and Folger, R. (1995) 'Justice in the making: Toward understanding the theory and practice of justice in organizational change and development', *Research in Organizational Change and Development*, 8: 243–95.

Coghlan, D. (2001) 'Insider action research projects: Implications for practising managers', *Management Learning*, 32: 49–60.

Coghlan, D. (2007) 'Insider action research doctorates: Generating actionable knowledge', *Higher Education*, 54(2): 293–306.

Coghlan, D. and Brannick, T. (2001) *Doing Action Research in Your Own Organization*. London: Sage.

Coghlan, D. and Casey, M. (2001) 'Action research from the inside: Issues and challenges in doing action research in your own hospital', *Journal of Advanced Nursing*, 35(5): 674–82.

Colquitt, J.A. (2012) 'Organizational justice'. In S.W.J. Kozlowski (ed.), *The Oxford Handbook of Organizational Psychology*, Vol. 1. Oxford: Oxford University Press, pp. 526–47.

Connor, D.R. (1995) *Managing at the Speed of Change: How Resilient Managers Succeed and Prosper Where Others Fail*. New York: Villard Books.

Creed, A., Worley, C.G., Cummings, T.G. and Waddell, D. (2019) *Organisational Change: Development and Transformation*. Melbourne: Cengage Learning Australia.

Cresswell, K.M., Worth, A. and Sheikh, A. (2010). 'Actor-Network Theory and its role in understanding the implementation of information technology developments in healthcare', *BMC Medical Informatics and Decision Making*, 10(67). DOI:10.1186/1472-6947-10-67

Cropanzano, R., Prehar, C.A. and Chen, P.Y. (2002) 'Using social exchange theory to distinguish procedural from interactional justice', *Group and Organization Management*, 27(3): 324–51.

Cross, R., Ernst, C. and Pasmore, B. (2013) 'A bridge too far? How boundary spanning networks drive organizational change and effectiveness', *Organizational Dynamics*, 42(2): 81–91.

Crozier, M. (1973) 'The problem of power', *Social Research*, 40(2): 211–28.

Cummings, S., Bridgman, T. and Brown, K.G. (2016) 'Unfreezing change as three steps: Rethinking Kurt Lewin's legacy for change management', *Human Relations*, 69(1): 33–60.

Cummings, T.J. and Cummings, C. (2014) 'Appreciating organization development: A comparative essay on divergent perspectives', *Human Resource Development Quarterly*, 25(2): 141–54.

Currie, G., Lockett, A. and Suhomlinova, O. (2009) 'Leadership and institutional change in the public sector: The case of secondary schools in England', *Leadership Quarterly*, 20(5): 664–79.

Currie, G. and Procter, S.J. (2005) 'The antecedents of middle managers' strategic contribution: The case of a professional bureaucracy', *Journal of Management Studies*, 42(7): 1325–56.

Currie, G. and Spyridonidis, D. (2019) 'Sharing leadership for diffusion of innovation in professionalized settings', *Human Relations*, 72(7): 1209–33.

Dahl, M. (2011) 'Organizational change and employee stress', *Management Science*, 57(2): 240–56.

Dalkir, K. (2011/2017) *Knowledge Management in Theory and Practice*. Cambridge, MA: MIT Press.

Daniels, R.A., Miller, L.A., Mian, M.Z. and Black, S. (2022) 'One size does NOT fit all: Understanding differences in perceived organizational support during the COVID-19 pandemic', *Business and Society Review*, 127: 193–222.

Davenport, T.H. and Short, J.E. (1990) 'The new industrial engineering: Information technology and business process redesign', *Sloan Management Review*, 31(4): 11–27.

De Bono, E. (1985) *Six Thinking Hats: An Essential Approach to Business Management*. Boston: Little, Brown & Company.

Delbecq, A.L. and Van de Ven, A.H. (1971) 'A group process model for problem identification and program planning', *The Journal of Applied Behavioral Science*, 7(4): 466–92.

DeLone, W.H. and McLean, E.R. (1992) 'Information systems success: The quest for the dependent variable', *Information Systems Research*, 3: 60–95.

DeLone, W.H. and McLean, E.R. (2003) 'The DeLone and McLean model of information systems success: A ten-year update', *Journal of Management Information Systems*, 19: 9–30.

Deming, W.E. (1986) *Out of the crisis*. Cambridge, MA: Massachusetts Institute of Technology, Center for Advanced Engineering Study.

Demos (2003) Inside out: Rethinking inclusive communities. DEMOS Report, Barrow Cadbury Trust, Birmingham. Available at: https://www.demos.co.uk/files/insideout.pdf (accessed 28 November 2023).

Denis, J.-L., Dompierre, G., Langley, A. and Rouleau, L. (2011) 'Escalating indecision: Between reification and strategic ambiguity', *Organization Science*, 22(1): 225–44. DOI:10.1287/orsc.1090.0501.

Dent, E. and Goldberg, S. (1999) 'Challenging "resistance to change"', *Journal of Applied Behavioral Science*, 35: 25–41.

Desplaces, D.E., Congden, S.W. and Boothe, P. (2007) 'The group creativity exercise getting MBAs to work and think effectively in groups', *Organization Management Journal*, 4(1): 69–86.

DeVito, M.A., Birnholtz, J. and Hancock, J.T. (2017) *Platforms, people, and perception: Using affordances to understand self-presentation on social media*. In Proceedings of the 2017 ACM Conference on Computer Supported Cooperative Work and Social Computing (pp. 740–54)

DiMaggio, P. (1988) 'Interest and agency in institutional theory', In L. G. Zucker (Ed.) *Institutional Patterns and Organizations Culture and Environment*. Cambridge: Ballinger Publishing Co., pp. 3–21.

Dirks, K.T., Cummings, L.L. and Pierce, J.L. (1996) 'Psychological ownership in organizations: Conditions under which individuals promote and resist change'. In R.W. Woodman and W.A. Pasmore (eds), *Research in Organizational Change and Development*, Vol. 9. Greenwich, CT: JAI Press, pp. 1–23.

Donaghey, J., Cullinane, N., Dundon, T. and Wilkinson, A. (2011) 'Reconceptualising employee silence: Problems and prognosis', *Work, Employment and Society*, 25(1): 51–67.

Dopson, S. and Fitzgerald, L. (2006) 'The role of the middle manager in the implementation of evidence-based health care', *Journal of Nursing Management*, 14(1): 43–51.

Dopson, S., Fitzgerald, L. and Ferlie, E. (2008) 'Understanding change and innovation in healthcare settings: Reconceptualizing the active role of context', *Journal of Change Management*, 8(3–4): 213–31.

Dopson, S., Fitzgerald, L., Ferlie, E., Gabbay, G. and Locock, L. (2010) 'No magic targets! Changing clinical practice to become more evidence based', *Healthcare Management Review*, 35(1): 2–12.

Dubin, R. (1979) 'Metaphors of leadership: An overview'. In J.G. Hunt and L.L. Larson (eds), *Cross Currents in Leadership*. Carbondale, IL: Southern Illinois University Press, pp. 225–38.

Duck, J.D. (2001) *The Change Monster: The Human Forces That Fuel or Foil Corporate Transformation and Change*. New York: Crown Business.

Dvir, D., Sadeh, A. and Malach-Pines, A. (2006) Projects and project managers: The relationship between project managers' personality, project types, and project success. *Project Management Institute*, 37(5): 36–48.

Dwivedi, Y.K., Wastell, D., Laumer, S., Henriksen, H.Z., Myers, M. and Srivastava, S.C. (2015) 'Research on information systems failures and successes: Status update and future directions', *Information Systems Frontiers*, 17(1): 143–57.

Dybe, T. and Dings Jr, T. (2008) 'Empirical studies of agile software development: A systematic review', *Information and Software Technology*, 50(9): 833–59.

Eagly, A.H. and Carli, L.L. (2003) 'The female leadership advantage: An evaluation of the evidence', *Leadership Quarterly*, 14: 807–34.

Eagly, A.H. and Johnson, B.T. (1990) 'Gender and leadership style: A meta-analysis', *Psychological Bulletin*, 108(2): 233–56.

Eagly, A.H., Makhijani, M.G. and Klonsky, B. (1992) 'Gender and the evaluation of leaders: A meta-analysis', *Psychological Bulletin*, 111: 3–22.

Earl, S., Carden, F. and Smuttylo, T. (2001) *Outcome Mapping: Building Learning and Reflection into Development Programs*. Ottawa: International Development Research Centre (IDRC).

Easterby-Smith, M., Graça, M., Antonacopoulou, E. and Ferdinand, J. (2008) 'Absorptive capacity: A process perspective', *Management Learning*, 39(5): 483–501.

Ekvall, G. (1988) *Förnyelse och friction: Om organization, kreativitet och innovation* (1st edn, second printing, 1991). Borås: Natur och kultur.

Ekvall, G. (1996) 'Organizational climate for creativity and innovation', *European Journal of Work and Organizational Psychology*, 5(1): 105–23.

Engeström, Y. (1987) *Learning by Expanding: An Activity-theoretical Approach to Developmental Research*. Helsinki: Orienta-Konsultit.

Engeström, Y., Miettinen, R. and Punamäki, R. (1999) *Perspectives on Activity Theory*. Cambridge: Cambridge University Press.

Etzioni, A. (1961) *A Comparative Analysis of Complex Organizations*. Glencoe, IL: Free Press.

Etzkowitz, H. and Leydesdorff, L. (2000) 'The dynamics of innovation: From National Systems and "mode 2" to a triple Helix of university–industry–government relations', *Research Policy*, 29: 109–23.

Evans, S. and Scarbrough, H. (2014) 'Supporting knowledge translation through collaborative translational research initiatives: "Bridging" versus "blurring" boundary-spanning approaches in the UK CLAHRC initiative', *Social Science and Medicine*, 106: 119–27.

Feldman, M.S. and Orlikowski, W.J. (2011) 'Theorizing practice and practicing theory', *Organization Science*, 22(5): 1240–53.

Ferlie, E.B. and Shortell, S.M. (2001) 'Improving the quality of health care in the United Kingdom and the United States: A framework for change', *The Milbank Quarterly*, 79(2): 281–315.

Ferry, N. and Guthey, E. (2020) 'Start 'em early: Pastoral power and the confessional culture of leadership development in US universities', *Journal of Business Ethics,* 173, 723–736. DOI: 10.1007/s10551-020-04565-7

Fiedler, F.E. (1964) 'A contingency model of leadership effectiveness'. In L. Berkowitz (ed.), *Advances in Experimental Social Psychology*, Vol. 1. New York: Academic Press, pp. 149–90.

Fiedler, F.E. (1967) *A Theory of Leadership Effectiveness*. New York: McGraw-Hill.

Fiedler, F.E. and Garcia, J.E. (1987) *New Approaches to Leadership: Cognitive Resources and Organizational Performance*. New York: Wiley.

Fisher, C. and Lovell, A. (2009) *Business Ethics and Values: Individual, Corporate and International Perspectives* (3rd edn). Harlow: FT Prentice Hall.

Fleming, P. and Spicer, A. (2008) 'Beyond power and resistance: New approaches to organizational politics', *Management Communication Quarterly*, 21(3): 301–9.

Flocco, N., Canterino, F., Cirella, S., Coget, J.F. and Shani, A.B.R. (2018) 'Exploring integrative creative leadership in the filmmaking industry'. In C. Mainemelis, O. Epitropaki and R. Kark (eds), *Creative Leadership: Contexts and Prospects*. London: Routledge, pp. 244–58.

Florida R. (2019) *The Rise of the Creative Class*. New York: Basic Books.

Floyd, S.W. and Wooldridge, B. (1997) 'Middle management's strategic influence and organizational performance', *Journal of Management Studies*, 34(3): 465–85.

Follett, M.P. (1940) In H.C. Metcalf and L. Urwick (eds), *Dynamic Administration: The Collected Papers of Mary Parker Follett*. New York: Harper & Brothers.

Ford, J. (2010) 'Studying leadership critically: A psychosocial lens on leadership identities', *Leadership*, 6(1): 47–65.

Ford, J.D. and Ford, L.W. (2010) 'Stop blaming resistance to change and start using it', *Organizational Dynamics*, 39(1): 24–36.

Ford, J.D., Ford, L.W. and Amelio, A.D. (2008) 'Resistance to change: The rest of the story', *Academy of Management Review*, 33(2): 362–77.

Fotaki, M. and Hyde, P. (2015) 'Organizational blind spots: Splitting, blame and idealization in the National Health Service', *Human Relations*, 68(3): 441–62.

Foucault, M. (1977) *Discipline and Punish: The Birth of the Prison*, trans. A. Sheridan. New York: Vintage.

Foucault, M. (1981) 'The Order of Discourse'. In R. Young (ed.), *Untying the Text: A Post-Structural Anthology*. Boston, MA: Routledge & Kegan Paul, pp. 48–78.

Foucault, M. (1991) 'Governmentality', trans. R. Braidotti, rev. C. Gordon. In G. Burchell, C. Gordon and P. Miller (eds), *The Foucault Effect: Studies in Governmentality*. Chicago: University of Chicago Press, pp. 87–104.

Fox, K. (2023) Nobel prize winner Giorgio Parisi: 'There's a lack of trust in science – we need to show how it's done'. *The Observer* 25/06/2023. Available at: https://www.theguardian.com/science/2023/jun/25/giorgio-parisi-nobel-prize-physics-spin-glasses-complex-systems-in-a-flight-of-starlings (accessed on 28 November 2023).

Franke, N. and Shah, S. (2003) 'How communities support innovative activities: An exploration of assistance and sharing among end-users', *Research Policy*, 32(1): 157–78.

Frederick, W.C. (1998) 'Creatures, corporations, communities, chaos, complexity: A naturological view of the corporate social role', *Business and Society*, 37(4): 358–89.

Freeman, C. (1974) *The Economics of Industrial Innovation*. Harmondsworth: Penguin Books.

French, J. and Raven, B.H. (1959) 'The bases of social power'. In D. Cartwright (ed.), *Studies of Social Power*. Ann Arbor, MI: Institute for Social Research, 150–67.

French, W.L. and Bell, C. (1995) *Organization Development: Behavioral Science Interventions for Organization Improvement*. Englewood Cliffs, NJ: Prentice Hall.

Fuchs, S. and Prouska, R. (2014) 'Creating positive employee change evaluation: The role of different levels of organizational support and change participation', *Journal of Change Management*, 14(3): 361–83.

Fullan, M. (2007) *Leading in a Culture of Change*. Chichester: John Wiley & Sons.

Furst, S.A. and Cable, D.M. (2008) 'Employee resistance to organizational change: Managerial influence tactics and leader–member exchange', *Journal of Applied Psychology*, 93(2): 453–62.

Gabriel, Y. (2000) *Storytelling in Organizations: Facts, Fictions, and Fantasies: Facts, Fictions, and Fantasies*. Oxford: Oxford University Press.

Gabriel, Y. (2015) 'The caring leader – what followers expect of their leaders and why?', *Leadership*, 11(3): 316–34.

Gardner, W.L., Cogliser, C.C., Davis, K.M. and Dickens, M.P. (2011) 'Authentic leadership: A review of the literature and research agenda', *Leadership Quarterly*, 22(6): 1120–45.

Garvin, D.A. (1993) 'Building a learning organization', *Harvard Business Review*, 71(4): 378–91.

Geoghegan, T. (2005, 26 May) 'A step by step guide to charisma'. *BBC News*. Available at: news.bbc.co.uk/1/hi/magazine/4579681.stm (accessed 28 November 2023).

Giddens, A. (1986) *The Constitution of Society: Outline of the Theory of Structuration*. Cambridge: Polity Press.

Giles, J. (2005) 'Internet encyclopaedias go head to head', *Nature*, 438: 900–901.

Gill, R. (2006) *Theory and Practice of Leadership*. London: Sage.

Gimpel, H., Hosseini, S., Huber, R., Probst, L., Röglinger, M. and Faisst, U. (2018) 'Structuring digital transformation: A framework of action fields and its application at ZEISS', *Journal of Information Technology Theory and Application (JITTA)* 19(1): 31–54.

Gioia, D.A. and Chittipeddi, K. (1991) 'Sensemaking and sensegiving in strategic change initiation', *Strategic Management Journal*, 12(6): 433–48.

Gioia, D.A., Thomas, J.B., Clark, S.M. and Chittipeddi, K. (1994) 'Symbolism and strategic change in academia: The dynamics of sensemaking and influence', *Organization Science*, 5(3): 363–83.

Goffman, E. (1961) *Encounters: Two Studies in the Sociology of Interaction*. Indianapolis, Bobbs-Merrill.

Goffman, E. (1978) *The Presentation of Self in Everyday Life*. Harmondsworth: Penguin.

Goleman, D. and Boyatzis, R. (2008) 'Social intelligence and the biology of leadership', *Harvard Business Review*, 86(9): 74–81.

Gomez-Mejia, L. R., Cruz, C., Berrone, P. and De Castro, J. (2011) 'The bind that ties: Socioemotional wealth preservation in family firms', *The Academy of Management Annals*, 5(1), 653–707.

Gooderham, P., Minbaeva, D.B. and Pedersen, T. (2011) 'Governance mechanisms for the promotion of social capital for knowledge transfer in multinational corporations', *Journal of Management Studies*, 48(1): 123–50.

Gordon, R.D. (2011) 'Leadership and power'. In A. Bryman, D. Collinson, K. Grint, B. Jackson and M. Uhl-Bien (eds), *The SAGE Handbook of Leadership*. London: Sage, pp. 195–202.

Gould, R.V. and Fernandez, R.M. (1989) 'Structures of mediation: A formal approach to brokerage in transaction networks', *Sociological Methodology*, 19: 89–126.

Green, L.R. (2002) *Technoculture: From Alphabet to Cybersex*. Melbourne: Routledge.

Greenhalgh, T., Robert, G., Macfarlane, F., Bate, P. and Kyriakidou, O. (2004) 'Diffusion of innovations in service organizations: Systematic review and recommendations', *The Milbank Quarterly*, 82(4): 581–629.

Greenwood, R. and Hinings, C.R. (1988) 'Organizational design types, tracks and the dynamics of strategic change', *Organization Studies*, 9(3): 293–316.

Greenwood, R. and Hinings, C.R. (1993) 'Understanding strategic change: The contribution of archetypes', *Academy of Management Journal*, 36(5): 1052–81. DOI:10.2307/256645.

Greenwood, D.J. and Levin, M. (1998) 'Action research, science, and the co-optation of social research', *Studies in Cultures, Organizations and Societies*, 4(2): 237–61.

Greenwood, R., Suddaby, R. and Hinings, C.R. (2002) 'Theorizing change: The role of professional associations in the transformation of institutionalized fields', *Academy of Management Journal*, 45(1): 58–80.

Gregory, R.W., Keil, M., Muntermann, J. and Mähring, M. (2015) 'Paradoxes and the nature of ambidexterity in IT transformation programs', *Information Systems Research*, 26(1): 57–80.

Gronn, P. (2008) 'The future of distributed leadership', *Journal of Educational Administration*, 46(2): 141–58.

Grover, V. (1999) 'From business reengineering to business process change management: A longitudinal study of trends and practices', *IEEE Transactions on Engineering Management*, 46(1): 36–46.

Guilford, J.P. (1950) 'Creativity', *American Psychologist*, 5: 444–54.

Gupta, A.K., Smith, K.G. and Shalley, C.E. (2006) 'The interplay between exploration and exploitation', *Academy of Management Journal*, 49(4): 693–706.

Guthey, E., Clark, T. and Jackson, B. (2009) *Demystifying Business Celebrity*. London: Routledge.

Haas, A. (2015) 'Crowding at the frontier: Boundary spanners, gatekeepers and knowledge brokers', *Journal of Knowledge Management*, 19(5): 1029–47.

Hadjimanolis, A. (2011) 'Management fads, communities of practice and innovation'. In E. Bueno and O. Rivera (eds), *Handbook of Research on Communities of Practice for Organizational Management and Networking: Methodologies for Competitive Advantage*. Hershey: IGI Global Publications, pp. 222–44.

Halpern, D. (2015) *Inside the Nudge Unit: How Small Changes Can Make a Big Difference*. London: W.H. Allen.

Hambrick, D.C. (1989) 'Guest Editor's Introduction: Putting top managers back in the strategy picture', *Strategic Management Journal*, 10(1): 5–15.

Hammer, M. (1990) 'Re-engineering work: Don't automate, obliterate', *Harvard Business Review*, July–August: 104–12.

Hancock, P. and Tucker, D.A. (2020) 'Recognition and change: Embracing a mobile policing initiative', *Journal of Organizational Change Management*, 33(5): 965–77.

Hanney, S.R., Gonzalez-Block, M.A., Buxton, M.J. and Kogan, M. (2003) 'The utilisation of health research in policy making: Concepts, examples and methods of assessment', *Health Research Policy and Systems*, 1(2): DOI:10.1186/1478-4505-1-2.

Hargadon, A.B. and Bechky, B.A. (2006) 'When collections of creatives become creative collectives: A field study of problem solving at work', *Organization Science*, 17(4): 484–500.

Hargadon, A.B. and Sutton, R.I. (1997) 'Technology brokering and innovation in a product development firm', *Administrative Science Quarterly*, 42: 716–49.

Haslam, S.A. and Ryan, M. (2008) 'The road to the glass cliff: Differences in the perceived suitability of men and women for leadership positions in succeeding and failing organizations', *Leadership Quarterly*, 19: 530–46.

Hass, K.B. (2007) 'The blending of traditional and agile project management', *PM World Today*, 9(5): 1–8.

Hatchuel, A. (2001) 'The two pillars of new management research', *British Journal of Management*, 12: S33–S39.

Hatfield, E., Cacioppo, J. and Rapson, R. (1994) *Emotional Contagion*. Cambridge: Cambridge University Press.

Hayes, J. (2022) *The Theory and Practice of Change Management*. London: Bloomsbury Academic.

Henderson, E.F. and Burford, J. (2020) '*Thoughtful gatherings: Gendering conferences as spaces of learning, knowledge production and community*', Gender and Education, 32(1): 1–10.

Hendy, J. and Barlow, J. (2012) 'The role of the organizational champion in achieving health system change', *Social Science and Medicine*, 74(3): 348–55.

Hendy, J. and Tucker, D.A. (2021) 'Public sector organizational failure: A study of collective denial in the UK National health service', *Journal of Business Ethics*, 172(4): 691–706.

Herbert, L. (2017) *Digital Transformation: Build Your Organization's Future for the Innovation Age*. London: Bloomsbury Publishing.

Hersey, P. and Blanchard, K. H. (1977) *Management of Organizational Behaviour: Utilizing Human Resources* (3rd ed.) New Jersey/Prentice Hall.

Hersey, P. and Blanchard, K.H. (1988) *Management of Organizational Behaviour* (5th edn). Englewood Cliffs, NJ: Prentice-Hall.

Hersey, P., Blanchard, K.H. and Natemeyer, W.E. (1979) 'Situational leadership, perception, and the impact of power', *Group & Organization Studies*, 4(4), 418–28.

Herstatt, C. and von Hippel, E. (1992) 'From experience: Developing new product concepts via the lead user method: A case study in a 'low tech' field', *Journal of Product Innovation Management*, 9: 213–222.

Hienerth, C. and Lettl, C. (2011) 'Exploring how peer communities enable lead user innovations to become standard equipment in the industry: Community pull effects', *Journal of Product Innovation Management*, 28(s1): 175–195.

Hienerth, C. and Lettl, C. (2017). 'Perspective: Understanding the nature and measurement of the lead user construct', *Journal of Product Innovation Management*, 34(1): 3–12.

Hienerth, C., Lettl, C. and Keinz, P. (2014) 'Synergies among producer firms, lead users, and user communities: The case of the LEGO producer–user ecosystem'. *Journal of Product Innovation Management*, 31(4): 848–866.

Hobbes, T. and Missner, M. (2016) *Thomas Hobbes: Leviathan*. Longman Library of Primary Sources in Philosophy. London: Routledge.

Holtgrewe, U. (2001) 'Recognition, intersubjectivity and service work: Labour conflicts in call centres', *Industrielle Beziehungen*, 8(3): 37–55.

Honneth, A. (1996) *The Struggle for Recognition: The Moral Grammar of Social Conflicts*. Cambridge: Polity.

Howell, J.M. and Shea, C.M. (2001) 'Individual differences, environmental scanning, innovation framing, and champion behavior: Key predictors of project performance', *Journal of Product Innovation Management*, 18(1): 15–27.

Hoyt, C. (2007) 'Women and leadership'. In P.G. Northouse (ed.) *Leadership: Theory and Practice*. Thousand Oaks, CA: Sage, pp. 265–99.

Hughes, M. (2010) *Managing Change: A Critical Perspective*. London: Kogan Page.

Hughes, M. (2011) 'Do 70 per cent of all organizational change initiatives really fail?', *Journal of Change Management*, 11(4): 451–64.

Hurley, R.F., Church, A.H., Burke, W.W. and Van Eynde, D.F. (1992) 'Tension, change and values in OD', *OD Practitioner*, 29(3): 1–5.

Huy, Q.N. (2002) 'Emotional balancing of organizational continuity and radical change: The contribution of middle managers', *Administrative Science Quarterly*, 47(1): 31–69.

Iannacci, F. and Cornford, T. (2018) 'Unravelling causal and temporal influences underpinning monitoring systems success: A typological approach', *Information Systems Journal*, 28(2): 384–407.

IBM (2022) 'What is digital transformation?'. Available at: https://www.ibm.com/topics/digital-transformation (accessed 28 November 2023).

Isaacs, W. (1993) 'Taking flight: Dialogue, collective thinking, and organizational learning', *Organizational Dynamics*, 22(2): 24–39.

Isaksen, S.G., Lauer, K.J., Murdock, M.C., Dorval, K.B. and Puccio, G.J. (1995) 'Situational outlook questionnaire: Understanding the climate for creativity and change (SOQ™)—A technical manual'. Buffalo, NY: Creative Problem Solving Group-Buffalo.

Ishikawa, K. (1976). *Guide to Quality Control*. Tokyo: Asian Productivity Organization.

Islam, G. (2012) 'Recognition, reification and practices of forgetting: Ethical implications of Human Resource Management', *Journal of Business Ethics*, 11(1): 37–48.

Jago, A.G. (1982) 'Leadership: Perspectives in theory and research', *Management Science*, 28(3): 315–36.

Jones, M. (2014) 'A matter of life and death: Exploring conceptualizations of sociomateriality in the context of critical care', *MIS Quarterly*, 38(3): 895–925.

Judge, T.A., Bono, J.E., Ilies, R. and Gerhardt, M.W. (2002) 'Personality and leadership: A qualitative and quantitative review', *Journal of Applied Psychology*, 87: 765–80.

Kalfa, S., Wilkinson, A. and Gollan, P.J. (2017) 'The academic game: Compliance and resistance in universities', *Work, Employment and Society*. DOI:10.1177/0950017017695043

Kane, G.C., Nguyen Phillips, S., Copulsky, J.R. and Andrus, G.R. (2019) *The Technology Fallacy: How People are the Real Key to Digital Transformation*. Cambridge, MA: MIT Press.

Kane, G.C., Palmer, D., Phillips, A.N., Kiron, D. and Buckley, N. (2015) 'Strategy, not technology, drives digital transformation', *MIT Sloan Management Review and Deloitte University Press*, 14: 1–25.

Kanter, R.M. (1984) *Change Masters*. New York: Simon & Schuster.

Kaplan, R. and Norton, D. (1992) 'The Balanced Scorecard—Measures That Drive Performance', *Harvard Business Review*, January–February: 71–79.

Kaptelinen, V. (2011) 'Activity theory'. In M. Soegaard and R.F. Damm (eds), *The Encyclopaedia of Human Computer Interaction* (2nd edn). Interaction Design Foundation. Available at: https://www.interaction-design.org/literature/book/the-encyclopedia-of-human-computer-interaction-2nd-ed/activity-theory (accessed 28 November 2023).

Katz, D. and Kahn, R. (1978) *The Social Psychology of Organizations* (2nd edn). New York: Wiley.

Katz, R. (1955) 'Skills of an effective administrator', *Harvard Business Review*, 33(1): 33–42.

Keen, P.G.W. (1981) 'Information systems and organizational change', *Communications of the ACM*, 24: 24–33.

Kelan, E.K. (2020) 'Why aren't we making more progress towards gender equity', *Harvard Business Review*, December: 2–4.

Kelan, E.K. (2022) 'Men as middle managers doing and undoing gender in organizations', *European Management Review*, 19(2): 236–247.

Kelan, E.K. (2023) *Men Stepping Forward: Leading Your Organisation on the Path to Inclusion*. Bristol: Bristol University Press.

Kellerman, B. (2004) *Bad Leadership: What It Is, How It Happens, Why It Matters*. Boston, MA: Harvard Business School Press.

Kellerman, B. (2008) *How Followers Are Creating Change and Changing Leaders*. Boston, MA: Harvard Business School Press.

Kelly, A. (2008) *Changing Software Development: Learning to Become Agile*. Wiley.

Kelly, A. (2018) Continuous Digital: An agile alternative to projects (#NoProjects). Software Strategy Limited.

Kelly, P.R. (2018) 'An activity theory study of data, knowledge, and power in the design of an international development NGO impact evaluation', *Information Systems Journal*, 28(3): 465–88. DOI:10.1111/isj.12187.

Kelly, P.R. (2019) *Power, Data, and Knowledge in Development Sector Impact Evaluation Activities: Critically Engaging with the Impact Iceberg*. Lancaster University.

Kenefick, D. and Kirrane, M. (2022) 'A little less conversation, a little more action: Participatory insider action research in an executive team', *Systemic Practice and Action Research*, 35(4): 453–69.

Kets de Vries, M. (2003) *Leaders, Fools and Imposters: Essays on the Psychology of Leadership*. Bloomington, IN: Universe.

Khojastehpour, M. and Johns, R. (2014) 'The effect of environmental CSR issues on corporate/brand reputation and corporate profitability', *European Business Review*, 26(4): 330–39.

Kim, C.S. and Peterson, D.K. (2000) 'Developers' perceptions of information systems success factors', *Journal of Computer Information Systems*, 41: 29–35.

Kirkpatick, S.A. and Locke, E.A. (1991) 'Leadership: Do traits matter?', *Academy of Management Perspectives*, 5(2): 48–60.

Klein, D. (1976) 'Some notes on the dynamics of resistance to change: The defender role'. In W.G. Bennis, K.D. Benne, K.D., R. Chin and K.E. Corey (eds), *The Planning of Change* (3rd edn). New York: Holt, Rinehart & Winston, pp. 117–24.

Klein, H.K. and Myers, M.D. (1999) 'A set of principles for conducting and evaluating interpretive field studies in information systems', *MIS Quarterly*, 23: 67–94.

Kling, R. and Scacchi, W. (1982) 'The web of computing: Computer technology as social organization', *Advances in Computers*, 21: 1–90.

Knowles, E.S. and Linn, J.A. (2004) 'The importance of resistance to persuasion'. In E.S. Knowles and J.A. Linn (eds), *Resistance and Persuasion*. Mahwah, NJ: Lawrence Erlbaum Associates, pp. 3–9.

Köhler, W. (2018) *The Mentality of Apes*, trans. E. Winter. London: Routledge.

Kohli, R. and Melville, N.P. (2019) 'Digital innovation: A review and synthesis', *Information Systems Journal*, 29(1): 200–3.

Kolb, D.A. (1984) *Experiential Learning: Experience as the Source of Learning and Development*. Upper Saddle River, NJ: Prentice Hall.

Korpela, M., Mursu, A. and Soriyan, H.A. (2002) 'Information systems development as an activity', *Computer Supported Cooperative Work* (CSCW), 11(1): 111–28.

Kotarba, M. (2017) 'Measuring digitalization: Key metrics', *Foundations of Management*, 9(1): 123–38.

Kotter, J.P. (1990a) *A Force for Change: How Leadership Differs from Management*. New York: Free Press.

Kotter, J. P. (1990b) 'What leaders really do', *Harvard Business Review*, 68, 103–111.

Kotter, J.P. (1995a) *The New Rules: How to Succeed in Today's Post-corporate World*. New York: Free Press.

Kotter J.P. (1995b) 'Leading change: Why transformation efforts fail', *Harvard Business Review*, May–June: 59–67.

Kotter, J.P. (2002) *The Heart of Change*. Boston, MA: Harvard Business School Press.

Kotter, J.P. (2012) *Leading Change*. Boston, MA: Harvard Business Review.

Kotter, J.P. and Schlesinger, L.A. (1979) 'Choosing strategies for change', *Harvard Business Review*, March–April: 106–14.

Krasikova, D.V., Green, S.G. and LeBreton, J.M. (2013) 'Destructive leadership: A theoretical review, integration and future research agenda', *Journal of Management*, 39(5): 1308–38.

Kretschmer, T. and Khashabi, P. (2020) 'Digital transformation and organization design: An integrated approach', *California Management Review*, 62(4): 86–104.

Krijnen, A. (2007) 'The Toyota way: 14 management principles from the world's greatest manufacturer', *Action Learning: Research and Practice*, 4(1): 109–11.

Krippendorff, K. (1989) 'On the essential contexts of artifacts or on the proposition that "design is making sense (of things)"', *Design Issues*, 5(2): 9–39.

Kurtzberg, T.R. and Amabile, T.M. (2001) 'From Guilford to creative synergy: Opening the black box of team-level creativity'. *Creativity Research Journal*, 13(3–4): 285–94.

Kyffin, S. and Gardien, P. (2009) 'Navigating the innovation matrix: An approach to design-led innovation', *International Journal of Design*, 3(1): 57–69.

Langley, A. (1999) 'Strategies for theorizing from process data', *Academy of Management Review*, 24(4): 691–710.

Larsen, T.J., Niederman, F., Limayem, M. and Chan, J. (2009) 'The role of modelling in achieving information systems success: UML to the rescue?', *Information Systems Journal*, 19(1): 83–117.

Latour, B. (1987) *Science in Action: How to Follow Scientists and Engineers through Society*. Cambridge, MA: Harvard University Press.

Latour, B. (2007) *Reassembling the Social: An Introduction to Actor-Network-Theory*. Oxford: Oxford University Press.

Lave, J. and Wenger, E. (1991) *Situated Learning: Legitimate Peripheral Participation*. Cambridge: Cambridge University Press.

Law, J. (1992) 'Notes on the theory of the actor-network: Ordering, strategy, and heterogeneity', *Systems Practice*, 5(4): 379–93.

Leclercq-Vandelannoitte, A. (2021) 'The new paternalism? The workplace as a place to work—and to live', *Organization*, 28(6): 949–75.

Lencioni, P. (2005) *Overcoming the Five Dysfunctions of a Team*. San Francisco, CA: Jossey Bass.

Leonardi, P.M. (2011) 'When flexible routines meet flexible technologies: Affordance, constraint, and the imbrication of human and material agencies', *MIS Quarterly*, 31(1), 147–67.

Lesser, E. and Storck, J. (2001) 'Communities of practice and organizational performance', *IBM Systems Journal*, 40(4): 831–41.

Lettl, C., Herstatt, C. and Gemuenden, H.G. (2006) 'Users' contributions to radical innovation: Evidence from four cases in the field of medical equipment technology', *R and D Management*, 36(3): 251–72.

Lettl, C., Hienerth, C. and Gemuenden, H.G. (2008) 'Exploring how lead users develop radical innovation: opportunity recognition and exploitation in the field of medical equipment technology', *IEEE Transactions on Engineering Management*, 55(2): 219–33.

Levy, A. (1986) 'Second-order planned change: Definition and conceptualization', *Organizational Dynamics*, 15(1): 5–23.

Lewin, K. (1946) 'Action research and minority problems', *Journal of Social Issues*, 2(4): 34–46.

Lewin, K. (1947a) 'Frontiers in group dynamics'. In D. Cartwright (ed.), *Field Theory in Social Science*. London: Social Science Paperbacks.

Lewin, K. (1947b) 'Frontiers in group dynamics', *Human Relations*, 1(2): 143–53. DOI:10.1177/001872674700100201.

Lewin, K. (1952) *Field theory in Social Science: Selected Theoretical Papers*. London: Tavistock.

Liker, J.K. and Morgan, J.M. (2006) 'The Toyota way in services: The case of lean product development', *Academy of Management Perspectives*, 20(20): 5–20.

Lind, E.A. and Van den Bos, K. (2002) 'When fairness works: Toward a general theory of uncertainty management', *Research in Organizational Behavior*, 24, 181–223.

Lines, R. (2005) 'The structure and function of attitudes toward organizational change', *Human Resource Development Review*, 4(1): 8–32.

Lipman-Blumen, J. (2005) *The Allure of Toxic Leaders: Why We Follow Destructive Bosses and Corrupt Politicians – and How We Can Survive Them*. New York: Oxford University Press.

Lissack, M.R. (1999) 'Complexity: The science, its vocabulary, and its relation to organizations', *Emergence*, 1(1): 110–26.

Liu, H., Cutcher, L. and Grant, D. (2016) 'Authentic leadership in context: An analysis of banking CEO narratives during the global financial crisis', *Human Relations, (Epub ahead of print)*, 19 November 2016. DOI:0018726716672920.

Locock, L., Dopson, S., Chambers, D. and Gabbay, J. (2001) 'Understanding the role of opinion leaders in improving clinical effectiveness', *Social Science and Medicine*, 53(6): 745–57.

Lodge, M. and Boin, A. (2020) 'COVID-19 as the ultimate leadership challenge: Making critical decisions without enough data'. *LSE Politics and Policy Blog*. Available at: https://blogs.lse.ac.uk/politicsandpolicy/covid-19-as-the-ultimate-leadership-challenge/ (accessed 28 November 2023).

Lukes, S. (2005) Power: *A Radical View*. New York: Macmillan.

Lumbreras, J. and Campbell, K. (2020) 'Generational changes in personality, values and abilities'. In B.J. Hoffman, L.A. Wegman and M.K. Shoes (eds), *The Cambridge Handbook of the Changing Nature of Work*. Cambridge: Cambridge University Press, pp. 261–73.

Luscher, L.S., Lewis, M. and Ingram, A. (2006) 'The social construction of organizational change paradoxes', *Journal of Organizational Change Management*, 19(4): 491–502.

Lüthje, C. and Herstatt, C. (2004) 'The lead user method: An outline of empirical findings and issues for future research', *R and D Management*, 34(5): 553–68.

Lüthje, C., Herstatt, C. and von Hippel, E. (2005) 'User-innovators and "local" information: The case of mountain biking', *Research Policy*, 34(6): 951–65.

Maak, T. and Pless, N.M. (2006) 'Responsible leadership in a stakeholder society – a relational perspective', *Journal of Business Ethics*, 66: 99–115.

Maben, J., Griffiths, P., Penfold, C., Simon, M., Anderson, J.E., Robert, G., Pizzo, E., Hughes, J., Murrells, T. and Barlow, J. (2015) 'One size fits all? Mixed methods evaluation of the impact of 100% single room accommodation on staff and patient experience, safety and costs', *BMJ Quality & Safety*. DOI:10.1136/bmjqs-2015-004265.

Mainemelis, C., Epitropaki, O. and Kark, R. (eds) (2018) *Creative Leadership: Contexts and Prospects*. London: Routledge.

Mainemelis, C., Kark, R. and Epitropaki, O. (2015) 'Creative leadership: A multi-context conceptualization', *Academy of Management Annals*, 9(1): 393–482.

Maitlis, S. and Christianson, M. (2014) 'Sensemaking in organizations: Taking stock and moving forward', *Academy of Management Annals*, 8(1): 57–125.

Maitlis, S. and Lawrence, T.B. (2007) 'Triggers and enablers of sensegiving in organizations', *Academy of Management Journal*, 50(1): 57–84.

Mann, R.D. (1959) 'A review of the relationships between personality and performance in small groups', *Psychological Bulletin*, 56(4): 241–70.

Mantere, S. (2005) 'Strategic practices as enablers and disablers of championing activity', *Strategic Organization*, 3(2): 157–83.

Mantere, S. (2008) 'Role expectations and middle manager strategic agency', *Journal of Management Studies*, 45(2): 294–316.

Mantere, S., Schildt, H.A. and Sillince, J.A. (2012) 'Reversal of strategic change', *Academy of Management Journal*, 55(1): 172–96. DOI:10.5465/amj.2008.0045

March, J.G. (1991) 'Exploration and exploitation in organizational learning', *Organization Science*, 2(1): 71–87.

Marcelo, G. (2013) 'Recognition and critical theory today: An interview with Axel Honneth', *Philosophy and Social Criticism*, 39(2): 209–21.

Marchington, M. (2007) 'Employee voice systems'. In P. Boxall, J. Purcell and P. Wright (eds), *The Oxford Handbook of Human Resource Management*. Oxford: Oxford University Press, pp. 231–50.

Markham, S.K. (1998) 'A longitudinal examination of how champions influence others to support their projects', *Journal of Product Innovation Management*, 15(6): 490–504.

Marks, M.L. and Mirvis, P.H. (2011) 'A framework for the human resources role in managing culture in mergers and acquisitions', *Human Resource Management*, 50(6): 859–77.

Markus, M.L. (1983) 'Power, politics, and MIS implementation', *Communications of the ACM*, 26(6): 430–44.

Martinelli, D.P. 2001. 'Systems hierarchies and management', *Systems Research and Behavioral Science*, 18(1): 69–82.

Mathers, J., Taylor. R. and Parry, J. (2014) 'The challenge of implementing peer-led interventions in professionalized health service: A case study of the National Health Trainers Service in England', *Milbank Quarterly*, 92(4): 725–53.

Mathias, B.D., Mckenny, A.F. and Crook, T.R. (2018) 'Managing the tensions between exploration and exploitation: The role of time', *Strategic Entrepreneurship Journal*, 12(3): 316–34.

Maurer, I., Bartsch, V. and Ebers, M. (2011) 'The value of intra-organizational social capital: How it fosters knowledge transfer, innovation performance and growth', *Organization Studies*, 32(2): 157–85.

McConnell, A. (2015) 'What is policy failure? A primer to help navigate the maze', *Public Policy and Administration*, 30(3–4): 221–42.

McGinnis Johnson, J. and Ng, E.S. (2016) 'Money talks or millennials walk: The effect of compensation on nonprofit millennial workers sector-switching intentions', *Review of Public Personnel Administration*, 36(3): 283–305.

McGuire, W.J. (1964) 'Inducing resistance to persuasion: Some contemporary approaches'. In L. Berkowitz (ed.), *Advances in Experimental and Social Psychology*, Vol. 1. New York: Academic Press, pp. 191–229.

McKinsey & Company (2014) The secrets of successful organizational redesigns: McKinsey Global Survey results. Available at: https://www.mckinsey.com/capabilities/people-and-organizational-performance/our-insights/the-secrets-of-successful-organizational-redesigns-mckinsey-global-survey-results#/ (accessed 28 November 2023)

McKinsey & Company (2018) 'How the implementation of organizational change is evolving'. Available at: https://www.mckinsey.com/business-functions/implementation/our-insights/how-the-implementation-of-organizational-change-is-evolving (accessed 28 November 2023).

McKinsey & Company (2021) 'Losing from day one: Why even successful transformations fall short'. Available at: https://www.mckinsey.com/business-functions/people-and-organizational-performance/our-insights/successful-transformations (accessed 28 November 2023).

McKinsey & Company (2023) 'What is digital transformation?' Available at: https://www.mckinsey.com/featured-insights/mckinsey-explainers/what-is-digital-transformation (accessed 28 November 2023).

McLoughlin, I. and Harris, M. (eds) (1997) *Innovation, Organizational Change and Technology*. Melbourne: Cengage Learning Business Press.

Melin, L., Whittington, R., Johnson, G. and Langley, A. (2007) *Strategy as Practice: Research Directions and Resources*. Cambridge: Cambridge University Press.

Mendelow, A.L. (1981) 'Environmental scanning – the impact of the stakeholder concept'. In *International Conference on Information Systems 1981 Proceedings*. Available at: https://aisel.aisnet.org/icis1981/20/ (accessed 28 November 2023).

Mendelow, A. (1991) *Stakeholder Mapping: Proceedings of the 2nd International Conference on Information Systems*. Cambridge, MA.

Meshkati, N. (1991) 'Human factors in large-scale technological systems' accidents: Three Mile Island, Bhopal, Chernobyl', *Industrial Crisis Quarterly*, 5(2): 133–54.

Michalski, M.P. (2014) 'Symbolic meanings and e-learning in the workplace: The case of an intranet-based training tool', *Management Learning*, 45(2): 145–66.

Michel, S. (2014) 'Capture more value', *Harvard Business Review*, 92(10): 78–85.

Microsoft (2017) *Creating a Culture of Digital Transformation*. Available at: https://info.microsoft.com/rs/157-GQE-382/images/digital_spreads_00950_MICROSOFT_DT%20Report_A4_COVER.PDF (accessed 28 November 2023).

Miettinen, R., Samra-Fredericks, D. and Yanow, D. (2009) 'Re-turn to practice: An introductory essay', *Organization Studies*, 30(12): 1309–27.

Mihalache, M. and Mihalache, O.R. (2022) 'How workplace support for the COVID-19 pandemic and personality traits affect changes in employees' affective commitment to the organization and job-related well-being', *Human Resource Management*, 61(3): 295–314.

Milliken, F.J., Schipani, C.A., Bishara, N.D. and Prado, A.M. (2015) 'Linking workplace practices to community engagement: The case for encouraging employee voice', *Academy of Management Perspectives*, 29(4): 405–21.

Mintzberg, H. (1973) *The Nature of Managerial Work*. New York: Harper & Row.

Mintzberg, H. (1975) 'The manager's job: Folklore and fact', *Harvard Business Review*, 53(4), 163–76.

Mintzberg, H. (1980) *The Nature of Managerial Work*. Englewood Cliffs, NJ: Prentice-Hall.

Mintzberg, H. (1994) 'Rounding out the managerial job', *Sloan Management Review*, Fall: 11–26.

Mitchell, R.K., Agle, B.R. and Wood, D.J. (1997) 'Toward a theory of stakeholder identification and salience: Defining the principle of who and what really counts', *The Academy of Management Review*, 22(4): 853–86. DOI:10.2307/259247.

Mohrman, S.A. and Cummings, T.G. (1989) *Self-Designing Organizations: Learning How to Create High Performance*. Reading, MA: Addison-Wesley Longman.

Monod, E. and Boland, R.J. (2007) 'Editorial: Special issue on philosophy and epistemology: "a Peter Pan syndrome"?', *Information Systems Journal*, 17: 133–41.

Morrison, E.W. (2014) 'Employee voice and silence', *Annual Review of Organizational Psychology and Organizational Behavior*, 1: 173–97.

Morrison, E.W. and Milliken, F.J. (2000) 'Organizational silence: A barrier to change and development in a pluralistic world', *Academy of Management Review*, 25(4): 706–25.

Mosse, D. (2005) *Cultivating Development: An Ethnography of Aid Policy and Practice*. London: Pluto Press.

Mumford, M.D., Antes, A.L., Caughron, J.J. and Friedrich, T.L. (2008) 'Charismatic, ideological, and pragmatic leadership: Multi-level influences on emergence and performance', *Leadership Quarterly*, 19(2): 144–60.

Murphy, A. (2017) 'You need to know the 7 types of power if you want to succeed', *Forbes*. Available at: https://www.forbes.com/sites/markmurphy/2017/03/19/you-need-to-know-the-7- types-of-power-if-you-want-to-succeed/#18febed2536d (accessed 28 November 2023).

Myers, G.J., Sandler, C. and Badgett, T. (2011) *The Art of Software Testing*. Chichester: John Wiley & Sons.

Nadler, D. and Tushman, M. (1989) 'Organizational frame bending: Principles for managing reorientation', *Academy of Management Executive*, 3(3): 194–204.

Nardi, B.A. (ed.) (1996) *Context and Consciousness: Activity Theory and Human–Computer Interaction*. Cambridge, MA: MIT Press.

Näslund, L. and Pemer, F. (2012) 'The appropriated language: Dominant stories as a source of organizational inertia', *Human Relations*, 65(1): 89–10. DOI: 10.1177/0018726711424322.

Nayak, P.R. and Ketteringham, J.M. (1986) '3M's Little Yellow Note Pads: "Never Mind. I'll Do It Myself"'. In *Breakthroughs!*, Boston, MA: Harvard Business School Press, pp. 50–73.

Nemeth, C.J., Brown, K.S. and Rogers, J.D. (2001) 'Devil's advocate versus authentic dissent: Stimulating quantity and quality', *European Journal of Social Psychology*, 31: 707–20.

Nicolini, D. (2012) *Practice Theory, Work, and Organization: An Introduction*. Oxford: Oxford University Press.

Nohria, N. and Beer, M. (2000) 'Change management: Cracking the code of change', *Harvard Business Review*, May–June: 133–41.

Nonaka, I. (1994) 'A dynamic theory of organizational knowledge creation', *Organization Science*, 5(1): 14–37.

Nonaka, I., Konno, N. and Toyama, R. (2001) 'Emergence of "ba"', *Knowledge Emergence: Social, Technical, and Evolutionary Dimensions of Knowledge Creation*, 1: 13–29.

Northouse, P.G. (2021) *Leadership: Theory and Practice*. Thousand Oaks, CA: Sage Publications.

OECD (1992) *Frascati Manual – 1992*. DSTI/STP(92)16. Paris: OECD Publishing.

Okafor, A., Adeleye, B.N. and Adusei, M. (2021) 'Corporate social responsibility and financial performance: Evidence from US tech firms', *Journal of Cleaner Production*, 292: 126078.

Ollila, S. and Yström, A. (2016) 'Exploring design principles of organizing for collaborative innovation: The case of an open innovation initiative', *Creativity and Innovation Management*, 25: 363–77.

O'Malley, L., O'Dwyer, M., McNally, R.C. and Murphy, S. (2014) 'Identity, collaboration and radical innovation: The role of dual organization identification', *Industrial Marketing Management*, 43: 1335–42.

Oreg, S. (2003) 'Resistance to change: "Developing an individual differences measure"', *Journal of Applied Psychology*, 88(4): 680–93.

Oreg, S., Bartunek, J.M., Lee, G. and Do, B. (2018) 'An affect-based model of recipients' responses to organizational change events', *Academy of Management Review*, 43(1): 65–86.

Orlikowski, W.J. (2001) 'Using technology and constituting structures: A practice lens for studying technology in organizations', *Organization Science*, 11(4): 404–28.

Orlikowski, W.J. (2005) 'Material works: Exploring the situated entanglement of technological performativity and human agency', *Scandinavian Journal of Information Systems*, 17(1): 183–86.

Orlikowski, W.J. (2010) 'The sociomateriality of organizational life: Considering technology in management research', *Cambridge Journal of Economics*, 34: 125–41.

Orlikowski, W.J. and Iacono, C.S. (2001) 'Research commentary: Desperately seeking the "IT" in IT research—A call to theorizing the IT artifact', *Information Systems Research*, 12(2): 121–34.

Orlikowski, W.J. and Scott, S.V. (2014) 'What happens when evaluation goes online? Exploring apparatuses of valuation in the travel sector', *Organization Science*, 25(3): 868–91.

Panagiotou, G. (2003) 'Bringing SWOT into focus', *Business Strategy Review*, 14(2): 8–10.

Pansardi, P. and Bindi, M. (2021) 'The new concepts of power? Power-over, power-to and power-with', *Journal of Political Power*, 14(1): 51–71.

Parisi, G. (2023) In a Flight of Starlings: The Wonders of Complex Systems. Penguin Press: New York

Parry, J. (2003) 'Making sense of executive sensemaking: A phenomenological case study with methodological criticism', *Journal of Health Organization and Management*, 17(4): 240–63.

Pasmore, W.A., Stymne, B., Shani, A.B., Mohrman, S.A. and Adler, N. (2008) 'The promise of collaborative management research'. In A.B. Shani, S. Mohrman, W.A. Pasmore, B. Stymne and N. Adler (eds), *Handbook of Collaborative Management Research*. Thousand Oaks, CA: Sage, pp. 7–31.

Paulus, P.B. and Nijstad, B.A. (eds) (2003) *Group Creativity: Innovation through Collaboration*. Oxford: Oxford University Press.

Pavitt, K. (1984) 'Sectoral patterns of technical change: Towards a taxonomy and a theory', *Research Policy*, 13(6): 343–73.

Pearn, M. and Mulrooney, C. (1998) *Ending the Blame Culture* (1st ed.). London: Routledge.

Pettigrew, A.M. (1992) 'The character and significance of strategy process research', *Strategic Management Journal*, 13(S2): 5–16.

Pettigrew, A., Ferlie, E. and McKee, L. (1992) 'Shaping strategic change: The case of the NHS in the 1980s', *Public Money and Management*, 12(3): 27–31.

Pettigrew, A.M. and Whipp, R. (1991) *Managing Change for Competitive Success*. Oxford: Blackwell.

Pettigrew, A.M., Woodman, R.W. and Cameron, K.S. (2001) 'Studying organizational change and development: Challenges for future research', *Academy of Management Journal*, 44(4): 697–713.

Pfaffenberger, B. (1992) 'Social anthropology of technology', *Annual Review of Anthropology*, 21: 491–516.

Piderit, S.K. (2000) 'Rethinking resistance and recognizing ambivalence: A multidimensional view of attitudes toward an organizational change', *Academy of Management Review*, 25(4): 783–94.

Polanyi, M. (1966) *The Tacit Dimension*. Chicago: University of Chicago Press.

Pollock, N. and D'Adderio, L. (2012) 'Give me a two-by-two matrix and I will create the market: Rankings, graphic visualisations and sociomateriality', *Accounting, Organizations and Society*, 37: 565–86.

Popper, M. and Lipshitz, R. (1998) 'Organizational learning mechanisms: A structural and cultural approach to organizational learning', *The Journal of Applied Behavioral Science*, 34(2): 161–79.

Price, D. and van Dick, R. (2012) 'Identity and change: Recent developments and future directions', *Journal of Change Management*, 12(1): 7–11.

Price, T.L. (2003) 'The ethics of authentic transformational leadership', *Leadership Quarterly*, 14: 67–81.

Quinn, J.B. (1992) *Intelligent Enterprise*. New York: Free Press.

Quinn, R.E. (1996) *Deep Change: Discovering the Leader Within*. Chichester: John Wiley & Sons.

Raffnsøe, S., Mennicken, A. and Miller, P. (2019) 'The Foucault effect in organization studies', *Organization Studies*, 40(2): 155–82.

Ralph, P. and Kelly, P. (2014) 'The dimensions of software engineering success'. *In 36th International Conference on Software Engineering*, 31 May.

Reason, P. and Bradbury, H. (eds) (2012) *The SAGE Handbook of Action Research: Participative Inquiry and Practice* (2nd edn). London: Sage.

Reckwitz, A. (2002) 'Toward a theory of social practices: A development in culturalist theorizing', *European Journal of Social Theory*, 5(2): 243–63.

Remus, U. and Wiener, M. (2010) 'A multi-method, holistic strategy for researching critical success factors in IT projects', *Information Systems Journal*, 20(1): 25–52.

Rhodes, C. and Brown, A.D. (2005) 'Narrative, organizations and research', *International Journal of Management Reviews*, 7(3): 167–88.

Rhodes, M. (1961) 'An analysis of creativity', *Phi Delta Kappa International*, 2: 305–10

Rice, A.K. (1958) *Productivity and Social Organization: The Ahmedabad Experiment*. London: Tavistock.

Richter, A.W., West, M.A., Van Dick, R. and Dawson, J.F. (2006) 'Boundary spanners' identification, intergroup contact, and effective intergroup relations', *Academy of Management Journal*, 49(6): 1252–69.

Roberts, J. (2006) 'Limits to communities of practice', *Journal of Management Studies*, 43 (3, May): 623–39.

Rogers, E.M. (2003) *Diffusion of Innovations* (5th edn). New York: Free Press.

Rohrbach, B. (1969) 'Kreativ nach Regeln – Methode 635, eine neue Technik zum Lösen von Problemen, (Creative by rules – Method 635, a new technique for solving problems)', *Absatzwirtschaft*, 12: 73–5.

Rooney, D., Paulsen, N., Callan, V.J., Brabant, M., Gallois, C. and Jones, E. (2010) 'A new role for place identity in managing organizational change', *Management Communication Quarterly*, 24(1): 44–73.

Rose, D.M. and Gordon, R. (2015) 'Age-related cognitive changes and distributed leadership', *Journal of Management Development*, 34(3): 330–9.

Rouleau, L. (2005) 'Micro-practices of strategic sensemaking and sensegiving: How middle managers interpret and sell change every day', *Journal of Management Studies*, 42(7): 1413–41.

Rouleau, L. and Balogun, J. (2011) 'Middle managers, strategic sensemaking, and discursive competence', *Journal of Management Studies*, 48(5): 953–83.

Rousseau, D.M. (1989) 'Psychological and implied contracts in organizations', *Employee Responsibilities and Rights Journal*, 2: 121–39.

Rousseau, D.M. and Tijoriwala, S.A. (1999) 'What's a good reason to change? Motivated reasoning and social accounts in promoting organizational change', *Journal of Applied Psychology*, 84(4): 514–28.

Rowe, W.G. (2001) 'Creating wealth in organizations: The role of strategic leadership', *Academy of Management Executive*, 15(1): 81–94.

Rowley, J.E. (2007) 'The wisdom hierarchy: representations of the DIKW hierarchy', *Journal of Information Science*, 33(2): 163–80. DOI: 10.1177/0165551506070706.

Russell, B. (1938) *A New Social Analysis*. London: George Allen & Unwin.

Sako, M. (2006) 'Does trust improve business performance'. In R.M. Kramer (ed.), *Organizational Trust: A Reader*. Oxford: Oxford Management Readers.

Salampasis, D.G., Mention, A.L. and Torkkeli, M. (2014) 'Trust embeddedness within an open innovation mindset', *International Journal of Business and Globalisation*, 14: 32–57.

Saldanha, T. (2019) *Why Digital Transformations Fail: The Surprising Disciplines of How to Take Off and Stay Ahead*. Oakland, CA: Berrett-Koehler.

Salesforce (2022) 'What is digital transformation?'. Available at: www.salesforce.com/eu/products/platform/what-is-digital-transformation/ (accessed 28 November 2023).

Sassen, S. (2012) 'Interactions of the technical and the social: Digital formations of the powerful and the powerless', *Information, Communication and Society*, 15(4): 455–78.e

Sawyer, S. and Jarrahi, M.H. (2014) 'Sociotechnical approaches to the study of information systems'. In *Computing Handbook, Third Edition: Information Systems and Information Technology*. Boca Raton: CRC Press, pp. 5-1–5-27.

Scarbrough, H. (1996) Strategic change in financial services: The social construction of strategic IS. In *Information Technology and Changes in Organizational Work*. Boston, MA: Springer, pp. 197–212.

Schatzki, T.R. (2000) 'Introduction'. In K.K. Cetina, T.R. Schatzki and E.E. Von Savigny (eds), *The Practice Turn in Contemporary Theory*. London: Routledge.

Schedlitzki, D. and Edwards, G. (2018) *Studying Leadership: Traditional and Critical Approaches*. London: Sage.

Schein, E.H. (2010) *Organizational Culture and Leadership*, Vol. 2. New York: John Wiley & Sons.

Schenkel, A. and Teigland, R. (2008) 'Improved organizational performance through communities of practice', *Journal of Knowledge Management*, 12(1): 106–18.

Schildt, H., Mantere, S. and Cornelissen, J. (2020) 'Power in sensemaking processes', *Organization Studies*, 41(2): 241–65.

Schmarzo, B. (2017) 'What is Digital Transformation?', 12 June. Available at: www.linkedin.com/pulse/what-digital-transformation-bill-schmarzo (accessed 28 November 2023).

Schmidt, E. and Rosenberg, J. (2014) *How Google Works*. New York: Grand Central Publishing.

Schon, D.A. (1963) 'Champions for radical new inventions', *Harvard Business Review*, 41(2): 77–86.

Schraeder, M. and Self, D.R. (2003) 'Enhancing the success of mergers and acquisitions: An organizational culture perspective', *Management Decision*, 41(5): 511–22.

Schulz-Hardt, S., Jochims, M. and Frey, D. (2002) 'Productive conflict in group decision making: Genuine and contrived dissent as strategies to counteract biased information seeking', *Organizational Behavior and Human Performance*, 88: 563–86.

Schumpeter, J.A. (1934) *The Theory of Economic Development*. Cambridge, MA: Harvard University Press.

Schwab, K., Marcus, A., Oyola, J. and Hoffman, W. (2011) Personal data: The emergence of a new asset class. *World Economic Forum*. Available at: www.weforum.org/reports/personal-data-emergence-new-asset-class#:~:text= (accessed 28 November 2023).

Scott, J.C. (1985) *Weapons of the Weak: Everyday Forms of Resistance*. New Haven, CT: Yale University Press.

Seddon, P.B. (1997) 'A respecification and extension of the DeLone and McLean model of IS success', *Information Systems Research*, 8: 240–53.

Senge, P.M. (1990) *The Fifth Discipline*. London: Century Business.

Senge, P., Kleiner, A., Roberts, C., Ross, R., Roth, G. and Smith, B. (1999) *The Dance of Change: The Challenges to Sustaining Momentum in Learning Organizations*. New York: Doubleday.

Shani, A.B. and Docherty, P. (2003) *Learning by Design: Building Sustainable Organizations*. Malden, MA: Blackwell Publishing.

Shani, A.B. and Docherty, P. (2008) 'Learning by design: Key mechanisms in organization development'. In T. Cummings (ed.), *Handbook of Organizational Change and Development* Thousand Oaks, CA: Sage, pp. 499–518.

Shani, A.B., Guerci, M. and Cirella, S. (2014) *Collaborative Management Research: Teoria, Metodi, Esperienze*. Milan: Raffaello Cortina Editore.

Shani, A.B., Mohrman, S.A., Pasmore, W.A., Stymne, B. and Adler, N. (eds) (2007) *Handbook of Collaborative Management Research*. London: Sage Publications.

Shani, A.B., Chandler, D., Coget, J.F. and Lau, J.B. (2009) *Behavior in organizations: An experiential approach*. 9th edition. New York: McGraw-Hill.

Shaw, B. (1998) 'Innovation and new product development in the UK medical equipment industry', *International Journal of Technology Management*, 15(3–5): 433–45.

Shewhart, W.A. (1986) *Statistical Method from the Viewpoint of Quality Control*. New York: Dover Publications.

Siebel, T.M. (2019) *Digital Transformation: Survive and Thrive in an Era of Mass Extinction*. New York: Rosetta Books.

Smircich, L. and Morgan, G. (1982) 'Leadership: The management of meaning', *Journal of Applied Behavioural Science*, 18: 257–73.

Smith, A. (1776) 'Of the Division of Labour'. In *An Inquiry into the Nature and Causes of the Wealth of Nations*. London: W. Strahan and T. Cadell.

Smith, E.A. (2001) 'The role of tacit and explicit knowledge in the workplace', *Journal of Knowledge Management*, 5(4): 311–321.

Soekijad, M., van den Hoof, B., Agterberg, M. and Huysman, M. (2011) 'Leading to learn in networks of practice: Two leadership strategies', *Organization Studies*, 32(8): 1005–27.

Soumerai, S.B., McLaughlin, T.J., Gurwitz, J.H., Guadagnoli, E., Hauptman, P.J., Borbas, C., Morris, N., McLaughlin, B., Gao, X., Willison, D.J., Asinger, R. and Gobel, F. (1998) 'Effect of local medical opinion leaders on quality of care for acute myocardial infarction: A randomized control trial', *Journal of the American Medical Association*, 279(17): 1358–63.

Spector, B.A. (2016) 'Carlyle, Freud and the Great Man Theory more fully considered', *Leadership*, 12(2): 250–60.

Spyridonidis, D., Hendy, J. and Barlow, J. (2015) 'Understanding hybrid roles: The role of identity processes amongst physicians', *Public Administration*, 93(2): 395–411.

Stacey, R.D. (1996) *Complexity and Creativity in Organizations*. San Francisco: Berrett-Koehler Publishers.

Stacey, R.D., Griffin, D. and Shaw, P. (2002) *Complexity and Management: Fad or Radical Challenge to Systems Thinking?* London: Routledge.

Sternberg, R.J. and Lubart, T.I. (1991) 'An investment theory of creativity and its development', *Human Development*, 34(1): 1–31.

Stogdill, R.M. (1948) 'Personal factors associated with leadership: A survey of the literature', *Journal of Psychology*, 25: 35–71.

Stogdill, R.M. (1972) 'Group productivity, drive, and cohesiveness'. *Organizational Behavior and Human Performance*, 8(1): 26–43.

Storey, J. (2005) 'What next for strategic-level leadership research?', *Leadership*, 1(1): 89–104.

Suchman, L.A. (1987) *Plans and Situated Actions: The Problem of Human–Machine Communication*. Cambridge: Cambridge University Press.

Sveningsson, S., Sörgärde, N. (2019) *Managing Change in Organizations: How, What and Why?* London: Sage Publications.

Swan, J., Scarbrough, H. and Ziebro, M. (2016) 'Liminal roles as a source of creative agency in management: The case of knowledge-sharing communities', *Human Relations*, 69(3): 781–811.

Syed, J. (2020) 'Diversity management and missing voices'. In A. Wilkinson, J. Donaghey, T. Dundon and R.B. Freeman (eds), *Handbook of Research on Employee Voice* (2nd edn). Cheltenham: Edward Elgar Publishing.

Symon, G. (2005) 'Exploring resistance from a rhetorical perspective', *Organization Studies*, 26(11): 1641–63.

Taffel, S. (2021) 'Data and oil: Metaphor, materiality and metabolic rifts', *New Media and Society*, 14614448211017887.

Tarafdar, M., DArcy, J., Turel, O. and Gupta, A. (2016) 'The dark side of information technology', *MIT Sloan Management Review*, 56(2), 61–70.

Tarakci, M., Ateş, N.Y., Floyd, S.W., Ahn, Y. and Wooldridge, B. (2018) 'Performance feedback and middle managers' divergent strategic behavior: The roles of social comparisons and organizational identification', *Strategic Management Journal*, 39(4): 1139–62.

Teece, D.J. (1976) *The Multinational Corporation and the Resource Cost of International Technology Transfer*. Cambridge, MA: Ballinger Publishing.

Teece, D.J. (2017) *Dynamic Capabilities and (Digital) Platform Lifecycles: Entrepreneurship, Innovation, and Platforms*. Bingley: Emerald Publishing.

Teece, D., Pisano, G. and Shuen, A. (1997) 'Dynamic capabilities and strategic management', *Strategic Management Journal*, 18(7): 509–33.

Testing Experts (2020) 'What is User Acceptance Testing (UAT) – A detailed guide', 16 June. Available at: https://www.testingxperts.com/blog/uat-testing (accessed 28 November 2023).

Thaler, R. H. and Sunstein, C. R. (2009) *Nudge: Improving Decisions about Health, Wealth, and Happiness*. New York, NY: Penguin.

Theodossopoulos, D. (2014) 'On de-pathologizing resistance', *History and Anthropology*, 25(4): 415–30.

Thompson, L.F. and Coovert, M.D. (2006) Understanding and developing virtual computer-supported cooperative work teams. In C. Bowers, E. Salas and F. Jentsch (eds), *Creating High-Tech Teams: Practical Guidance on Work Performance and Technology. American Psychological Association*, pp. 213–41. DOI: 10.1037/11263-010.

Tidd, J. and Bessant, J.R. (2014) *Strategic Innovation Management*. Chichester: Wiley.

Tomkins, L. and Simpson, P. (2015) 'Caring leadership: A Heideggerian perspective', *Organization Studies*, 36(8): 1013–31.

Torrance, E.P. (1962) *Guiding Creative Talent*. Englewood Cliffs, NJ: Prentice Hall.

Torrance, E.P. (1974) *The Torrance Tests of Creative Thinking Norms-Technical Manual*. Princeton, NJ: Personal Press.

Tosey, P., Visser, M. and Saunders, M.N. (2012) 'The origins and conceptualizations of "triple-loop" learning: A critical review', *Management Learning*, 43(3): 291–307.

Trabucchi, D. and Buganza, T. (2022) 'Landlords with no lands: A systematic literature review on hybrid multi-sided platforms and platform thinking', *European Journal of Innovation Management*, 25(6): 64–96.

Trist, E.L. and Bamforth, K.W. (1951) 'Some social and psychological consequences of the longwall method of coal-getting: An examination of the psychological situation and defences of a work group in relation to the social structure and technological content of the work system', *Human Relations*, 4(1): 3–38.

Tucker, D.A. and Cirella, S. (2018) 'Agents of change: insights from three case studies of hospital transformations'. In *Research in Organizational Change and Development*. Bingley: Emerald Publishing.

Tucker, D.A., Hendy, J. and Barlow, J. (2014) 'When infrastructure transition and work practice redesign collide', *Journal of Organizational Change Management*, 27(6): 955–72. DOI:10.1108/JOCM-09-2013-0173

Tucker, D.A., Hendy, J. and Barlow, J. (2015) 'The importance of role sending in the sensemaking of change agent Roles', *Journal of Health Organization and Management*, 29(7): 1047–64.

Tucker, D.A., Hendy, J. and Barlow, J. (2016) 'The dynamic nature of social accounts: An examination of how interpretive processes impact on account effectiveness', *Journal of Business Research*, 69(12): 6079–87.

Tucker, D.A., Hendy, J. and Chrysanthaki, T. (2022) 'How does policy alienation develop? Exploring street-level bureaucrats' agency in policy context shift in UK telehealthcare', *Human Relations*, 75(9), 1679–706. DOI:10.1177/00187267211003633.

Tucker, D.A., Yeow, P. and Viki, G.T. (2013) 'Communicating during organizational change using social accounts: The importance of ideological accounts', *Management Communication Quarterly*, 27(2): 184–209.

Tuomi, I. (1999) 'Data is more than knowledge: Implications of the reversed knowledge hierarchy for knowledge management and organizational memory', *Journal of Management Information Systems*, 16: 103–117.

Tushman, M.L. and O'Reilly III, C.A. (1996) 'Ambidextrous organizations: Managing evolutionary and revolutionary change', *California Management Review*, 38(4): 8–29.

Vaara, E., Sonenshein, S. and Boje, D. (2016) 'Narratives as sources of stability and change in organizations: Approaches and directions for future research', *Academy of Management Annals*, 10(1): 495–560.

van Zoonen, W. and ter Hoeven, C.L. (2022) 'Disruptions and general distress for essential and nonessential employees during the COVID-19 Pandemic', *Journal of Business Psychology*, 37: 443–58. DOI:10.1007/s10869-021-09744-5

Venkatesh, V., Morris, M.G., Davis, G.B. and Davis, F.D. (2003) 'User acceptance of information technology: Toward a unified view', *MIS Quarterly*, 27(3): 425–78.

Verganti, R. (2009) *Design Driven Innovation: Changing the Rules of Competition by Radically Innovating What Things Mean*. Boston, MA: Harvard Business Press.

Vial, G. (2019) 'Understanding digital transformation: A review and a research agenda', *Journal of Strategic Information Systems*, 28(2): 118–44.

Visnjic, I., Birkinshaw, J. and Linz, C. (2022) 'When gradual change beats radical transformation', *MIT Sloan Management Review*, 63(3): 74–8.

von Hippel, E. (1976) 'The dominant role of users in the scientific instrument innovation process', *Research Policy*, 5(3): 212–39.

von Hippel, E. (1986) 'Lead users: A source of novel product concepts', *Management Science*, 32(7): 791–805.

von Hippel, E. (1994) '"Sticky information" and the locus of problem solving: implications for innovation', *Management Science*, 40(4): 429–439.

von Hippel, E. (1998) 'Economics of product development by users: The impact of 'sticky' local information', *Management Science*, 44(5): 629–44.

von Hippel, E. (2005) 'Democratizing innovation: The evolving phenomenon of user innovation', *Journal für Betriebswirtschaft*, 55(1): 63–78.

von Hippel, E. (2006) *Democratizing Innovation*. Cambridge, MA: MIT Press.

von Hippel, E. (2007) 'Horizontal innovation networks—by and for users', *Industrial and Corporate Change*, 16(2): 293–315.

Wallace, T., Bornstein, L. and Chapman, J. (2006) *Coercion and Commitment: Development NGOs and the Aid Chain*. Rugby: ITDG Publishing.

Wallas, G. (2014) *The Art of Thought, 1926*. Poole: Solis Press.

Wanberg, C.R. and Banas, J.T. (2000) 'Predictors and outcomes of openness to changes in a reorganizing workplace', *Journal of Applied Psychology*, 85(1): 132–42.

Wang, T. 2004. 'From general system theory to total quality management', *Journal of American Academy of Business*, 4(1/2): 394–400.

Wang, Y.S. (2008) 'Assessing e-commerce systems success: A respecification and validation of the DeLone and McLean model of IS success', *Information Systems Journal*, 18(5): 529–57.

Ward, V., House, A. and Hamer, S. (2009) 'Developing a framework for transferring knowledge into action: A thematic analysis of the literature', *Journal of Health Services Research and Policy*, 14(3): 156–64.

Weber, M. (1947) *The Theory of Social and Economic Organizations*, trans. T. Parsons. New York: Free Press.

Weick, K.E. (1995) *Sensemaking in Organizations*. Vol. 3. London: Sage.

Weick, K.E., Sutcliffe, K.M. and Obstfeld, D. (2005) 'Organizing and the process of sensemaking', *Organization Science*, 16(4): 409–21.

Wenger, E. (1999) *Communities of Practice: Learning, Meaning, and Identity*. Cambridge: Cambridge University Press.

Wenger, E., McDermott, R. and Snyder, W.M. (2002) *A Guide to Managing Knowledge: Cultivating Communities of Practice*. Boston, MA: Harvard Business School Press.

Westerman, G., Bonnet, D. and McAfee, A. (2014) *Leading Digital: Turning Technology into Business Transformation*. Boston, MA: Harvard Business Review Press.

Western, S. (2019) *Leadership: A Critical Text*. London: Sage.

Wilkinson, A., Dundon, T., Donaghey, J. and Freeman, R.B. (2020) 'Employee voice: Bridging new terrains and disciplinary boundaries'. In A. Wilkinson, J. Donaghey, T. Dundon and R.B. Freeman (eds), *Handbook of Research on Employee Voice* (2nd edn). Cheltenham: Edward Elgar Publishing.

Willcocks, L.P. and Lioliou, E. (2011) 'Everything is dangerous: Rethinking Michel Foucault and the social study of ICT'. In R.D. Galliers and W. Currie (eds), *The Oxford Handbook of Management Information Systems: Critical Perspectives and New Directions*. Oxford: Oxford University Press.

Williams, D. (2014) 'Models, metaphors and symbols for information and knowledge systems', *Journal of Entrepreneurship, Management and Innovation*, 10(1): 79–108.

Williams, P. (2002) 'The Competent Boundary Spanner', *Public Administration*, 80(1): 103–24.

Wilson, I. (1992) 'Realizing the power of strategic vision', *Long Range Planning*, 25(5): 18–28.

Wilson, J.P. (ed.) (2005) *Human Resource Development: Learning and Training for Individuals and Organizations*. London: Kogan Page Publishers.

Wilson, J.Q. (2019) *Bureaucracy: What Government Agencies Do and Why They Do It*. New York: Basic Books.

Wimelius, H., Mathiassen, L., Holmström, J. and Keil, M. (2021) 'A paradoxical perspective on technology renewal in digital transformation', *Information Systems Journal*, 31(1): 198–225.

Woodman, R.W., Sawyer, J.E. and Griffin, R.W. (1993) 'Toward a theory of organizational creativity', *Academy of Management Review*, 18(2): 293–321.

Wooldridge, B., Schmid, T. and Floyd, S.W. (2008) 'The middle management perspective on strategy process: Contributions, synthesis, and future research', *Journal of Management*, 34(6): 1190–221.

World Health Organization (WHO) (2023) Coronavirus (COVID-19) Dashboard. Available at: https://covid19.who.int/ (accessed 28 November 2023).

Worley, C. and Feyerherm, A. (2003) 'Reflections on the future of OD', *Journal of Applied Behavioral Science*, 39: 97–115.

Yeow, P.M. and Jackson, P.R. (2006) 'Complexity theory and the management of change', In Shams, M. and Jackson, P. (eds) *Developments in Work and Organizational Psychology: Implications for International Business*. Bingley: Emerald Publishing, pp. 163–84.

Yoon, S. and Kuchinke, K.P. (2005). 'Systems theory and technology: Lenses to analyze an organization', *Performance Improvement*, 44(4): 15–20.

Yström, A., and Agogué, M. (2020) 'Exploring practices in collaborative innovation: Unpacking dynamics, relations, and enactment in in-between spaces', *Creativity and Innovation Management*, 29(1): 141–5.

Yukl, G. (2010) *Leadership in Organizations* (7th edn). Upper Saddle River, NJ: Pearson Education.

Yukl, G. (2011) 'Contingency theories of effective leadership'. In A. Bryman, D. Collinson, K. Grint, B. Jackson and M. Uhl-Bien (eds), *The SAGE Handbook of Leadership*. London: Sage, pp. 286–98.

Zubac, A., Tucker, D., Zwikael, O., Hughes, K. and Kirkpatrick, S. (2022) 'Introduction: Navigating the strategy and change interface successfully'. In *Effective Implementation of Transformation Strategies*. Basingstoke: Palgrave Macmillan, pp. 1–22.

Zuboff, S. (1988) *In the Age of the Smart Machine: The Future of Work and Power*. New York: Basic Books.

Zuboff, S. (2019) *The Age of Surveillance Capitalism: The Fight for a Human Future at the New Frontier of Power*. London: Profile Books.

INDEX

Page numbers in *italics* refer to figures; page numbers in **bold** refer to tables.